THE POLITICAL ECONOMY OF PERU 1956–78

Economic development and the restructuring of capital

THE POLITICAL ECONOMY
OF PERU 1956–78

Economic development and the
restructuring of capital

E. V. K. FITZGERALD

Assistant Director of Development Studies
University of Cambridge

CAMBRIDGE UNIVERSITY PRESS
CAMBRIDGE
LONDON NEW YORK NEW ROCHELLE
MELBOURNE SYDNEY

Published by the Press Syndicate of the University of Cambridge
The Pitt Building, Trumpington Street, Cambridge CB 2 1RP
32 East 57th Street, New York, NY 10022, USA
296 Beaconsfield Parade, Middle Park, Melbourne 3206, Australia

First published 1979

Text set in 11/14 pt Photon Baskerville, printed and bound
in Great Britain at The Pitman Press, Bath

Library of Congress Cataloguing in Publication Data

FitzGerald, Edmund Valpy Knox, 1947–
The political economy of Peru, 1956–78.

Bibliography: p.
Includes index.
1. Peru—Economic conditions 1918–1968.
2. Peru—Economic conditions—1968– 3. Capital—Peru.
I. Title.
HC227.F5   330.9′85′063   78–72086
ISBN 0 521 22289 3

Para Gregorio y Lorenzo

'One nation can and should learn from others. And even when a society has got upon the right track for the discovery of the natural laws of its movement . . . it can neither clear by bold leaps nor remove by legal enactments the obstacles offered by the successive phases of its normal development. But it can shorten and lessen the birthpangs.'

(Preface to the First German Edition of *Capital Vol. I*)

Contents

	Preface	ix
	List of abbreviations	xi
1	Introductory	1
2	The theoretical issues	13
3	The political background	40
4	The structure of the Peruvian economy	66
5	The ownership of capital and the distribution of income	105
6	The accumulation of capital	142
7	The public sector	180
8	Economic policy and planning	217
9	Industrialization	260
10	Conclusions	293
	Statistical appendix	302
	Notes	315
	Bibliography	344
	Index	357

Preface

As the 1970s draw to a close and the prospects for economic and social reform in Latin America are fading, the Peruvian experience in recent years is of more than passing significance. Having experienced *laissez-faire* liberalism, gradualist reformism and state capitalism as the bases for economic strategy within this short span of time, Peru provides a particularly good case study of the efforts of a poor country to overcome the obstacles to development encountered by economies on the periphery of the international capitalist system. In particular, the successes and failures of the *Gobierno Revolucionario de la Fuerza Armada* during the last ten years have considerable implications for our understanding of the role of the state in restructuring capital as part of the economic development process.

In this study I have attempted to make some methodological progress in the handling of the economic statistics which provide the quantitative basis for my analysis of the Peruvian political economy by taking advantage of the excellent national accounts compiled by the *Banco Central de Reserva del Perú.* It has proved possible to integrate estimates of the extent of dualism in each production sector, the ownership of capital and the functional income distribution on the one hand with the patterns of savings, investment, taxation, public expenditure and external transactions on the other into a single numerical framework. This appears to be a helpful way of exploring economic and social change and as far as I am aware, a novel one – whether or not it has been worth while only the reader can judge.

My first acknowledgements must be to the Cambridge University Overseas Studies Committee, the Ministry of Overseas Development and the United Nations Development Programme for supporting my fieldwork between 1974 and 1976. During my visits to Peru, I worked with the National Planning Office and the Ministry of Industry, as well as teaching at the Catholic and San Marcos Universities; I would like to thank the staff of these institutions for their generous help, not only in the provision of data but what was more valuable still, the discussion of the *problemática* of contemporary Peru. At home the list of those who should be acknowledged seems almost endless, for the community of Peruvianists is a large and helpful one; I am particularly indebted to colleagues and reviewers for their constructive comments on the essay (*The State and Economic Development: Peru since 1968* Cambridge University Department of Applied Economics Occasional Paper No. 49, CUP, 1976) which preceded this book. Nonetheless, specific mention must be made of Rosemary Thorp, without whose constant encouragement my research would not have made what little progress it has. I would also like to thank Trevor Downing for patiently checking the final typescript. Last, but far from least, I want to express my deep gratitude to my wife and children for their tolerance of my long absences in Peru and patient support in the months of scribbling consequent upon them. The responsibility for errors and misconceptions is, of course, mine alone.

At the time of writing, elections for an *Asamblea Constituyente* have recently been held and the assembly is presently engaged in the drafting of a new constitution – the first for nearly fifty years – as a prelude to the transfer of power to civilian hands promised by the military government. It seems likely that this transition will take place in 1980, despite the ever-present possibility of another *golpe*, but the economic problems confronted by a democratic government will be no less intractable, nor the options any more attractive, than those experienced by its predecessor. Perhaps a broader base of political support will allow the Peruvians to press forward with social reforms, but the constraints imposed by the need to achieve a coherent model of capital accumulation will continue to dominate the political economy of Peru.

E. V. K. FITZGERALD,
Faculty of Economics and Politics
Cambridge, November 1978

Abbreviations

Listed here are those abbreviations that occur frequently in the text; other abbreviations and acronyms can be found in the Index.

APRA	*Alianza Popular Revolucionaria Americana*
BCR	*Banco Central de Reserva (del Perú)*
CI	*Comunidad Industrial*
COAP	*Comisión Asesora de la República*
EAP	Economically Active Population
ECLA	Economic Commission for Latin America
EPS	*Empresa de Propiedad Social*
GDP	Gross Domestic Product
GFCF	Gross Fixed Capital Formation
GNP	Gross National Product
GRFA	*Gobierno Revolucionario de la Fuerza Armada*
IBRD	International Bank for Reconstruction and Development
IMF	International Monetary Fund
INE	*Instituto Nacional de Estadística*
INP	*Instituto Nacional de Planificación*
MIT	*Ministerio de Industrias y Turismo*
OIP	*Oficina de Investigación para la Planificación*
ONEC	*Oficina Nacional de Estadística y Censo*
OSP	*Oficina Sectorial de Planificación*
SINAMOS	*Sistema Nacional de Apoyo a la Movilización Social*
SITC	Standard International Trade Classification

Symbols

Listed here are the symbols most frequently used in the Tables.

..	no data available
—	no entry by definition or assumption
0.0	smaller than half the minimum entry

1

Introductory

The unbalanced form that economic expansion takes on the periphery of the international market system has recently come to be seen as the core of the analysis of 'underdevelopment': although many of the technical sub-branches of the subject continue to be based on models derived directly from the experience of the 'developed' economies, the last decade has witnessed a sea-change in the basis of development theory. This change is partly the result of dissatisfaction with the logical coherence of the reigning orthodoxy itself and partly the consequence of accumulated case studies, comparative economic data and the findings of scholars in related fields of the social sciences. But political changes on the periphery itself – particularly the experience of successful post-colonial transition to socialism in some countries and authoritarian repression of these trends in others, combined with spreading 'Third World' nationalism – and the growing difficulties of sustaining economic expansion at the centre have also been major contributory factors. These phenomena (which even if they do not presage a fundamental breakdown in the international capitalist system certainly represent serious strains) have been reflected in a 'radicalization' of the social sciences at both centre and periphery which has involved not only an increasing interest in the more creative aspects of Marxist thought but also a reflowering of the classical tradition itself, leading towards what might be termed a 'political economy of development'.

In effect, the mainstream of development studies[1] seems to have passed through three distinct phases over the last three decades. Initially, interest was centred on the growth of the developing economy as a whole, and above all on export-led expansion, the benefits of which could later be used to 'modernize' a society.

Subsequently, the manifest failure of these countries to grow very fast, their exposure to fluctuations in international commodity markets and their growing internal inequalities led to a preoccupation with the need to industrialize so as to reorganize the productive structure of the economy and to achieve both sustained growth and some redistribution of the benefits. Finally, as import substitution, too, failed to resolve these problems, attention turned towards the relationship between underdevelopment and continued economic exploitation, both from abroad and within these economies, thus bringing ownership and economic control into the heart of the debate. This sea-change, although far from merging with the orthodox Marxist current, has meant that the political and economic perspectives on development are being brought together again in a manner reminiscent of the classical political economists. The central theme has become the study of the consequences of the insertion of the 'third world' economies into the international capitalist system and the attempts to achieve development – understood as not only the growth of output[2] but also the integration of the domestic production system, and the equitable distribution of its benefits through the employment pattern – within that system or to escape from it by means of a transition to socialism.

Major advances along this route have come, interestingly enough, from Latin America – particularly in the forms of analysis known as 'structuralist' and 'dependency' writing.[3] The reasons for this intellectual primacy may well be related to the historical experience of a continent that has remained underdeveloped while in possession of abundant natural resources and a relatively well-trained workforce, but without the overt remnants of a recent colonial past that have so preoccupied writers on Africa and Asia. The absence of obvious environmental obstacles upon which to throw the blame for underdevelopment has forced Latin-American social scientists to dwell upon the underlying social forces in greater depth. Moreover, although their critique has often emanated from official institutions, such as the United Nations Economic Commission for Latin America (ECLA), this has not prevented a fruitful dialogue with a more radical tradition of Marxist thought, generating in the process a somewhat heterogeneous but none the less penetrating approach to the interpretation of the historical origins of Latinamerican underdevelopment and the proposal of specific strategies for change. Moreover, in contrast to the tendencies noted in much development writing this tradition has stressed the importance of both 'economics as the study of economies'[4] and the historical origins of individual economic structures.[5]

Peru in the post-war period might well be described as a paradigm of the problems of Latinamerican economic development, but not in the sense of representing the 'average' of the continental economy; rather the analogue would be that of an interesting pathological specimen which exhibits commonly held symptoms in a readily identifiable form so that they may be recognized and inter-related. During the 1956–78 period that we shall be examining in detail, the political economy of Peru passed through three successive stages: the first, from 1956 to 1962, was one of rapid export-led growth based on natural resources, massive penetration by foreign enterprise and the waning of political control by a traditional 'oligarchy'; the second, from 1963 to 1968, saw slower growth and widening inequality, but the failure of civilian government to carry through the ownership reforms necessary to establish a sound basis for sustained industrialization, and a declining rate of investment; and the third, from 1969 to 1978, involved an attempt to achieve a restructuring of capital through state investment, widespread ownership reform and a planned economy, an attempt that appears to have ended in economic disaster and political instability. It is ironic that at times broadly corresponding to the 'phases' in development studies that we have noted the Peruvian experience has been held up to the world in turn as a shining example of *laissez-faire* growth, democratic reformism and radical social change.[6] The comparative failure of each of these attempts to achieve the development of a dependent capitalist economy has significant implications for the future of Latin America as well as for our understanding of the nature of economic development itself.

This book is a case study of the evolution of the Peruvian political economy in recent years, but by implication it is also an exercise in the application of the 'new' political economy to a specific developing country. Such an exercise involves the integration of the analysis of economic structures with that of the control over the means of production in order to show how the different social

classes are affected by the process of production and how their
political strength affects the distribution of the product; it also sees
capital accumulation as the key element of economic change and the
state as central to the political process. It is in this sense that we can
talk of 'political economy'. Broadly, our account hinges on the
political and economic impasse reached in Peru by the mid 1960s,
when a reformist civilian government was attempting unsuccessfully
to come to grips with an unbalanced economy, declining investment, excessive foreign ownership and the disintegration of the
traditional social structure. To explain the origin of these problems
is our first concern, relating them to the logic of dependent capitalist
growth; the second is to examine the efforts to resolve them through
the reform of ownership and the establishment of state control over
the economy by a radical military regime. The Peruvian experience
turns out to have been not just a pathological specimen but also, to
retain the medical analogy, a culture-dish where the pre-conditions
for development stipulated by many Latinamerican social scientists
(such as land reform, nationalization of foreign enterprises and
strong state intervention in the economy) have obtained; the subsequent failure to achieve economic development thereby should
give cause for reflection on the adequacy of the theory that gave rise
to such prescriptions.

This economic development, as distinct from continued expansion of a given production system, involves a process that – in a
mixed economy – may be termed a 'restructuring of capital'. This
restructuring involves a changed output system, one that shifts its
dynamic from the primary to the secondary sector, with consequent
shifts in input use, technology and labour organization. This change
requires a different model of capital accumulation – in terms of
sources and uses of funds – and an altered pattern of ownership; the
combination of these and the new employment pattern will effect
changes in the distribution of income. The new structure of capital
will also require a fresh basis of political support in order to make
the new model of accumulation politically feasible, a coalition of
class forces (including foreign interests) which will depend initially
upon the ownership and distributional implications of the model
itself. Above all, the new model must be consistent in economic and
political terms if it is to be viable and permit industrialization to take

place.

Historically those countries which have achieved sustained industrialization have undergone a restructuring of this kind; moreover, those countries which were 'late starters' required considerable state intervention in order to bring this restructuring about. In other words, this is not a process that occurs naturally. However, for the state to fulfil this 'historic task' it must possess a certain degree of autonomy relative to the dominant elite – particularly the traditional agrarian and financial groups on the one hand and foreign interests on the other – and seek support among other social classes because in restructuring capital it must inevitably prejudice the interests of those fractions of capital that benefit from the existing order of things even though in the long run the effect is to allow capitalism to develop more effectively. The social and political conditions under which the state can achieve this 'relative autonomy' form the most important non-economic component of our analysis; these conditions will necessarily be different from those historically encountered in the metropolitan countries, if only because domestic capital is comparatively weak and foreign capital comparatively strong on the periphery.

There is clearly considerable ground to be made up at the theoretical level if our understanding of industrialization, capital restructuring and state action on the periphery is to reach the level already attained in the analysis of the experience of metropolitan economies. To some extent this awaits deeper study of the world economy as a whole, but there is also a need for a better understanding of the political economy of individual countries such as that which is the object of discussion in this book.

This study centres on the political economy of Peru between 1956 and 1978 and is organized primarily along the lines of the categories that we have mentioned as being central to the concept of the restructuring of capital – the pattern of production, the system of ownership and income distribution, the model of accumulation, the role of the state and the industrialization process – and thus does not follow the chronological pattern characteristic of economic history or treat the major sectors separately.[7] From the discussion of the central themes of development theory in Chapter 2 spring the three 'core' chapters of the book: on the structural changes in the

Peruvian economy, leading to an interpretation of duality (Chapter 4); on the pattern of capital ownership, leading to an interpretation of income distribution and dependence (Chapter 5); and on the process of accumulation (Chapter 6). The main strategic issues then follow within the framework established in the previous chapters: the economic articulation of the state apparatus (Chapter 7); the effects of economic policy and planning (Chapter 8); and the progress towards industrialization (Chapter 9). The concluding observations to each of these chapters on the relation between the Peruvian experience and that of Latin America as a whole are then brought together in Chapter 10 to form the basis of some general conclusions.

Any approach to a problem in the social sciences (some would say in any science) is necessarily ideological in the sense that the choice of material and of analytical tools involves the explicit or implicit choice of a particular view of the world; otherwise the selection of 'facts' would be a purely arbitrary affair. Here we have included a considerable institutional and political element directly related to the functioning of the economy in our analytical framework; in particular, our frame of reference is the development of capitalism on the periphery of the world market. However, this is not a Marxist account, and does not suppose any particular or necessary course for the development of capitalist economies. Rather, we are attempting to make a modest contribution to the 'political economy' approach to the analysis of underdevelopment by steering a somewhat erratic course between economic and political analysis on the supposition that there exists a certain common logic to the process of capitalist growth but that there are also significant national variants which are only revealed by history. The bearings of this course will become clearer in Chapter 2, where the theoretical discussion is continued, but it should be remembered that in the last resort this is a book about the Peruvian political economy written by an economist, and thus it is to this aspect that most attention will be paid. Specifically, this will mean placing an emphasis upon the articulation of capital rather than the labour process – and thus a stress upon production and accumulation rather than upon employment and wages, upon the corporate rather than the household sector, upon the state as entrepreneur or supporter of private enterprise rather than as creator of ideology or controller of popular movements, and upon the relationship between capitals rather than between capital and labour. This is not to deny the importance of these latter considerations, nor will they be ignored in this study, but apart from the limitations of professional competence it can be reasonably argued that the strength of Peruvian social studies (and indeed of Latinamerican studies generally) has been in sociology – particularly social anthropology but increasingly political sociology and social history – and that this strength is matched by a weakness in economic scholarship, indicating a need for some rectification of the imbalance.

The argument presented in this book centres on the problems of economic development and the restructuring of capital, illustrated by the experience of Peru between 1956 and 1978. As we have noted, the experience of development in Latin America generated a body of thought which identified two main contradictions in capitalist growth on the periphery of the world economy. The first was seen as arising from structural distortions created by export-led growth in the past, conveniently summarized in the concept of 'duality' – not that between 'modern industry' and 'traditional agriculture' but rather a division between large monopoly capital and small enterprises, which forms the basis of the unequal income distribution as well as the imbalances in the economy. The second arose from the degree of external control over the economy, a situation commonly known as 'dependency' – the ownership of technology and productive assets by multinational enterprises which was seen as leading not only to the extraction of the surplus as expatriated profit but also to serious distortions in the structure of production. Further to these two 'economic' problems, there was identified the 'political' one of the apparent inability (or unwillingness) of the domestic bourgeoisie to promote national capitalism, and the consequent dilemma of the appropriate role for the state – either in support of independent industrial capital or as controller of the economy – in the resolution of these contradictions.[8]

Peru is a country rich in natural resources (other than land) and the dependent dualism characteristic of its underdevelopment stems from a history of economic growth based on the export of these resources by an alliance of foreign enterprise and domestic finance capital. In the twentieth century, despite the early emergence of a broadly based populist party, the working class did not become organized on a wide enough scale to achieve state power although it was able to seriously weaken bourgeois political hegemony when exercised through civil institutions, thus occasioning frequent military intervention in government. The last government of the 'grand bourgeoisie' under Prado (1956–62) based its economic development strategy on a renewed penetration of the economy by foreign capital, but was forced to ensure succession by a military junta when it appeared that a populist election victory was to take place. This junta did initiate some reforms, but relied for their implementation on a civilian government under Belaunde (1963–68), although this could not cope with the combined opposition of the grand bourgeoisie and populist forces either, while the grip of multinational enterprises on the economy tightened still further. In consequence, the military intervened again in 1968, this time with a view to long-term control of the state and the achievement of a 'revolution from above' based on ownership reforms that would reduce the power of both foreign corporations and the grand bourgeoisie while ensuring popular support for the state, so that public enterprises and nationalist entrepreneurs could organize the independent industrialization of the economy. However, economic instability generated by the state capitalist model itself and increasing pressure exercised by international banks eventually forced the regime, in the absence of mass popular support, to abandon its attempt at accelerated development by 1978.[9]

Much of the explanation for this impasse would seem to lie in the very economic structure of Peru and above all in the nature of the corporate sector which produced most of national output on the basis of foreign technology, relying on natural resource exports to purchase capital goods and lacking integration with the rest of the economy. This model had the characteristics of excluding the bulk of the workforce from productive employment at a reasonable income level, while locking the corporate sector firmly into the international market system. To continue growth on previous lines, even under state control, tended to benefit only a minority of the populace while strengthening the economic links with foreign capital, thus contradicting the strategic aims of greater equity and national autonomy while weakening political support for the regime.[10] This structure corresponded, naturally enough, to the interests of the owners of the means of production. In 1956 these were still dominated by large finance capital groups which coordinated firms in exports, agriculture, industry, commerce, finance and real estate, while wielding determinate power at the government level. In the 1956–68 period, both a renewed penetration of the economy by foreign enterprise and increasing popular pressures on government as industrialization proceeded weakened this system. The military intervention of 1968 was largely a reaction to this ownership pattern; the result of this intervention was to break the power of the grand bourgeoisie and constrain the activities of foreign capital but the reforms did not confer the determinate control enjoyed by the elite over the economy before 1956 to the state, nor did they result in a broad base of political support for the regime, thus making it impossible to attain the necessary restructuring of the economy itself.[11]

But the problems of both structure and ownership derived from that of accumulation, upon which both output growth and asset creation depend. The rate of private investment in Peru declined steadily between 1956 and 1978, and the state expanded its role at an accelerated rate. But the replacement of the 'nexus' of accumulation formed by finance capital by direct state control after 1968 did not involve a restructuring of the system of financing investment even though it raised the investment rate: rather than extract further surplus from the private sector (reducing thereby the consumption of politically important groups) the state turned to external borrowing. These three factors became the underlying economic contradictions of the 'Peruvian Revolution' leading to instability in the new model of accumulation and thus the projected restructuring of capital.[12]

The economic organization of the state is thus central to the analysis of accumulation in Peru. As the Peruvian fiscal and administrative structures were inherited from a period when the public sector was only required to lend background support to private accumulation, they quickly demonstrated an incapacity to achieve the relatively modest reformist ambitions of the Belaunde administration; and even though they were complemented after 1968 by a series of state corporations which, although reasonably effective in attaining specific investment and production targets, did so without regard for social objectives such as employment or economic aims such as technological independence and foreign exchange savings. The combination of low tax levels and costly attempts to recapitalize the export sector resulted in a 'fiscal crisis' of the Peruvian state and the instability of the new accumulation model.[13] Throughout our period, macro-economic policy as employed in Peru to maintain stability in the domestic market and planning to rationalize investment within the public sector, the limits of state control over the economy being defined by the extent of state ownership and constrained by the opposition of foreign capital. But despite the steady extension of state control over the period, the neglect of food agriculture, the incurrence of excessive foreign debt and the need to resort to abrupt deflation in periods of external disequilibrium continued. These weaknesses combined to make the restructuring of capital extremely difficult, if not impossible.[14]

If industrialization is to be taken as the touchstone of development, then it must provide the means of integrating different production branches and generate the capacity for autonomous accumulation, thus establishing an endogenous dynamic for the economy. In the Peruvian experience, as in that of Latin America generally, the problems of manufacturing form a microcosm of those of the economy as a whole: narrow markets, imported technology, little employment and foreign ownership. In the 1955–65 period a typical import-substitution process took place, dominated by foreign enterprise and without the emergence of an independent industrialist group, which while expanding the industrial base locked it firmly into the world economy. The 1966–78 period was, in contrast, one of very little private investment and a brake upon the structural development of the previous decade, despite government incentives. Only the presence of excess capacity prevented a crisis from occurring earlier, but when it did in 1975 the failure to achieve intersectoral integration or an adequate supply of basic wage goods contributed critically to economic disequilibrium, while the opposition of foreign capital prevented extension of worker participation in the form of Industrial Communities and Social Property.[15]

In sum, the theme of the contradictions of capitalism on the periphery penetrated by foreign enterprise and apparently incapable of balanced growth on the one hand, and the attempts to establish a more rational economy through state control on the other, is central to this study. The Peruvian experience can thus be seen both as an example of and as an example for Latin America as a whole. The distortions of export-led growth may have been more acute in Peru than in countries with a broader agrarian base such as Colombia but the dynamic remains largely exogenous, internal dualism is just as marked and the distribution of personal income exhibits very similar characteristics; industrialization may have proceeded further but it betrays the same weaknesses of disarticulation, dependence on foreign technology and reliance on imported inputs. The concentration and alienation of asset ownership in Peru may indeed have been more extreme than elsewhere, but the pattern of land tenure before 1968 was similar to that obtaining in other Andean countries, and although major economies such as Mexico and Argentina had established independent industrial capital at an earlier date, this too had been displaced by the 1960s under the renewed expansion of the multinationals, while the smaller economies such as Ecuador have followed a path similar to that of Peru up to 1968. However, the only other Latin American country to attempt to confront private capital through state power without a social revolution (Chile) was far from successful in the attempt, while the two countries to use large state sectors to successfully restructure capital as a means to industrialization (Brazil and Mexico) did so without confronting private enterprise or attempting income redistribution at the same time.

To the extent that this is a true picture the severe limitations of state capitalism would also obtain elsewhere: the difficulty of establishing a new model of accumulation without taking over the private sector entirely; the impossibility of wresting control from foreign capital while continuing to rely upon foreign technology and funds; and the problems of simultaneously overcoming dualism and reviving economic growth. In other words, there seem to be intrinsic obstacles to the viability of state capitalism as a means of achieving economic development – as defined in terms of equity and independence as well as industrialization – that go beyond the fundamental contradiction of capitalism itself.[16] In the Peruvian case, as we shall see, these obstacles were compounded by unfavourable trade conditions, errors in macroeconomic management and the failure of the military to achieve an effective political base; nonetheless, there does seem to be a generalizable conclusion to be drawn.

2

The theoretical issues

As we have already outlined the overall approach adopted in this study, in this chapter we shall take up three specific topics in more detail: the condition of underdevelopment; the Latinamerican interpretation of that condition; and the role of the state in achieving economic development. These topics have an important part to play in our analysis of the Peruvian experience, but as these are well-known areas of debate we shall not attempt to give a comprehensive bibliographical treatment. Rather we shall set out a particular line of argument on these topics as clearly as possible, paying particular attention to those aspects of the expansion of capitalism on the periphery of the world economy that are characteristic of the 'third world' of which Latin America forms a part and distinguish it from the experience of the 'metropolitan' economies: the economic dualism brought about by the unbalanced growth of modern capitalist corporations within an underdeveloped economy and the close linkage between these and the metropolitan economies that both sustains and is sustained by that dualism while draining profits from production and trade in the periphery. Social scientists in Latin America, especially those associated with the 'ECLA school', have made a considerable original contribution to the development debate while reflecting upon the growth problems of their own continent, particularly in the form of 'structuralist' and 'dependency' approaches to internal and external problems – these, too, deserve some further discussion. Finally, implicitly or explicitly, the state is regarded by all writers on this theme as central to the condition of underdevelopment not only as the point of crystallization of class forces but also as the means by which that condition may be overcome by forcing industrialization and undertaking the so-called 'historic task' of the national bourgeoisie.

The condition of underdevelopment

Definitions of 'underdevelopment' cannot be separated from implied statements or theories as to its cause and possible resolution. At first sight, the features are easily identified: an economy at an early stage of industrialization with low per capita income and widespread poverty on the one hand, and a reliance on raw material exports and foreign investment to promote economic growth on the other. But beyond this it is difficult to go without implying some root cause of the condition; a broad division can be made between those authors who place the emphasis on the first aspect, attributing underdevelopment to internal causes, and those who stress the second, implying that it has mainly external causes. In this discussion we are looking at the problem from the point of view of capitalist growth on the periphery of the world economy, and this immediately imposes certain considerations. In particular, it allows us to combine these factors in a logical manner and by so doing implies that they cannot be considered separately. Both the two 'polar' views imply certain strategic directions for the achievement of economic development by identifying root problems the resolution of which are presumed to allow it to proceed, but, as we shall argue, a broader view that integrates the two implies that the difficulties inherent in achieving development are greater than their sum.

Most underdeveloped countries have the common heritage of a colonial past, of having their economies structured for the benefit of the metropolitan powers, a relationship that in most cases has continued long after the formal political independence of these countries. The 'dependent' relationship of the third world is clearly a matter of degree rather than absolute definition, as to some extent all economies in the world are dependent upon one another. The term[1] refers to a condition where the structure and dynamic of an economy are not mainly determined by internal forces but on the contrary by the indirect influence of international markets or the direct action of foreign corporations; a condition where the pattern of accumulation (in terms of ownership, profitability, rates of investment, choice of technology and sectoral allocation) and thus the structure of capital is adjusted to the needs of capitalist expansion at the centre (in terms of raw material needs, the search for markets and the extraction of profit) rather than capitalist expansion on the periphery as such. The theoretical bases of this point of view are firmly rooted in the classical tradition. Although it is true that Marx along with his predecessors regarded the effect of the expansion of European capitalism through trade and colonialism as being beneficial because it would promote industrialization on the periphery of the world economy, Lenin did, of course, revise this view in the light of the evidence of imperialist powers forming alliances with the dominant classes of the precapitalist system, a position of more relevance to the Latinamerican experience.

Modern interpretations of imperialism in what is claimed to be the same tradition initially concentrated upon circulation rather than production; the analysis of the extraction of surplus from the periphery by unfavourable terms of trade or excessive export of profits took precedence over the examination of production or accumulation. Authors such as Baran[2] and Frank[3] concentrate upon the distribution of the 'surplus'[4] and in particular on the way in which this is extracted from the economy by colonial powers or foreign investors, both of which can resort to institutional force in order to ensure the outflow of surplus – in sharp contrast to the classical emphasis (continued in the contemporary neo-classical tradition) upon the effect of foreign investment in *increasing* local profits – a point of view which has gathered strength with increasing evidence of and concern about the activities of multinational corporations. The condition of underdevelopment is seen, correctly enough, as the result of centuries of colonial exploitation rather than a natural state of poverty, but this exploitation tends to be regarded in almost mercantilist terms as the pillage of resources and the export of profits, with insufficient regard for the structural effects of the insertion of such economies into the world market system on the one hand and for their own internal dynamics on the other: underdevelopment is seen merely as a continuous exploitative chain stretching monotonically from the metropolis through the capital cities of dependent nations out to their hinterlands. Above all, this line of argument tends to lead to 'stagnationism': the suggestion that sustained capitalist industrialization is effectively prevented by the extraction of surplus from these economies and the pressure applied for them to continue as suppliers of raw materials to the metropolis, while what little industrialization that does take place inevitably encounters an 'underconsumption crisis' due to the poverty of the work-force and their inability to purchase the consequent output while industrial exports are blocked by metropolitan protection. This sort of approach has become extremely popular, particularly as the basis for a radical '*tercermundismo*'[5] which is used by nationalists to blame external influences for everything that is wrong with their economies and societies; ironically enough it is also used by local elites at international fora to negotiate for better terms on international trade and finance. It can reasonably be argued that this viewpoint has become a 'pseudo-concept which explains everything in general and hence nothing in particular'.[6]

A more sophisticated form of this type of dependency writing is to be found in the writing on 'unequal exchange'.[7] Here the argument takes on an almost neo-Ricardian form: rather than equilibrium prices on competitive international commodity markets determining income levels in the trading countries, it is suggested that income levels are previously determined and the prices resolved to balance the equation, so to speak. This view does have the advantage of emphasizing the effect of oligopsony on primary commodity markets and a corresponding oligopoly in those for manufactures, and that of suggesting that the prime determinant of low incomes in dependent countries is the high level of both profits and wages in the central economies (maintained by concentrated corporations and trades unions) which also prevents substantial accumulation taking place on the periphery. Further, the international financial and 'aid' flows are seen as ensuring that the little investment that does take place in the dependent economies is geared to the resource requirements of the metropolitan economies or supports the profitability of multinational corporations. This model is distinct from the 'neo-mercantilist' one because it takes institutionally determined income levels at the centre rather than profit maximization by multinationals as its motive force, and it can accommodate the evident (albeit partial and temporary) successes of groups of raw material producers in raising prices without difficulty. However, apart from any ideological revulsion at the idea that the metropolitan proletariat might be exploiting their comrades in the periphery (e.g. through low prices for imported foodstuffs) – which seems all too true in practice[8] – the theory of unequal exchange suffers from a lack of explanatory power as to the dynamics of the process of dependent development.[9] In essence, this stems from its separation of dependency in trade and finance (i.e. in circulation) from that in production and accumulation, a shortcoming which is immediately obvious in the inadequate explanation of productivity differences. In unequal exchange theory these are held to result from the lack of any necessity to raise productivity on the periphery because labour is so cheap, a proposition only rescued from tautology by the supposition of labour immobility. More seriously, the theory leads to the kind of 'stagnationism' that we have mentioned above, as it denies any independent role to the development of productive forces in the peripheral economies.

A major step in the resolution of this problem is undoubtedly the work of Amin, who is concerned with 'accumulation on a world scale';[10] the concept of centre and periphery is a central theme of his analysis of the international division of labour. Technologically advanced industry is held to be concentrated at the centre while the periphery is confined to light and basic manufacturing, to the production of raw materials for the centre and to backward agriculture; although Amin does point out that it is incorrect to identify the underdeveloped countries with exporters of basic commodities – many advanced capitalist countries such as Canada and Australia also export them. Nor, of course, are low income levels a sufficient definition; rather, Amin defines underdevelopment as the blocking of the transition to industrial capitalism in peripheral social formations by the advanced and already industrialized economies. The peripheral nations, integrated into the capitalist world market, are prevented from accumulating indigenously because profits are transmitted to the centre rather than being used for local development; but beyond this model of unequal exchange, Amin does examine the formations of the periphery. Capital from the centre, far from developing the periphery, distorts its economic structure: investment is concentrated in sectors orientated to the needs of an export market, thus forestalling any capitalism based on

an internal market – and what local demand there is is met by externally dominated light industry without supporting producer goods
branches. Other foreign investments go to the tertiary sector, such
as banking, which again does not promote any form of balanced
development.

The concept of a peripheral social formation, which emphasizes
the 'blocking' and distorting effects of imperialism, is clearly a considerable advance on underdevelopment as depression through unequal exchange alone, while this 'dependency' interpretation based
as it is on the mutual determination of riches at the centre and
poverty at the periphery, is in its turn an advance on the orthodox[11]
view of poor economies proceeding separately on the path to
development, with the central powers extending a helping hand in
the form of trade, aid and investment. But Amin does not allow for
sufficient variation within the concept of the periphery: Western
Europe, North America and Japan clearly constitute the centre[12] and
Asia, Africa and Latin America make up the periphery – but within
the latter category there are equally clear differences between (say)
Brazil and Iran on the one hand and El Salvador and Ethiopia on
the other, while some countries such as Portugal have been both underdeveloped *and* colonizers. Industry in both Africa and Latin
America has been controlled externally but it is important to determine just why the latter continent has achieved a significant, even if
distorted and inegalitarian, form of capitalist industrialization
where the former has not. To do this we must place much more
emphasis upon the internal dynamics of underdeveloped economies
and see dependency as a 'conditioning situation' which constrains
but does not determine entirely the pattern of accumulation, the
form of insertion into the world economy favouring the domestic
elites and thus being supported by them too – although not to the
benefit of the mass of their populations. To the extent that internal
dualism is the result of limited development of capitalism within the
economy, it could even be argued that, contrary to the letter of
Amin's interpretation but perhaps not to its spirit, it is the *incomplete*
integration of the periphery into the world market system that
blocks its capitalist industrialization. As Kay puts it: 'The radical
critics of orthodox development theory were so keen to prove the
ideological point that underdevelopment was the product of

capitalist exploitation, that they let the crucial issue pass them by: capital created underdevelopment not because it exploited the underdeveloped world, but because it did not exploit it enough'.[13]

This unbalanced development of capitalism on the periphery is immediately evident to the observer, resulting in the existence of one sector made up of large capitalist corporations using imported capital-intensive technology and closely linked to the metropolitan economies through both trade and ownership, but which directly employs only a minority of the national workforce at comparatively high wage rates on the one hand; and another sector made up of small enterprises, firms or households using little capital or technology and absorbing the majority of the workforce at low levels of income on the other: a dichotomy which can only be termed 'dualism'.[14] Output in the former sector expands on the basis of raw material exports and import-substituting industrialization but its share of the national workforce grows slowly if at all as capital-intensity is raised; output in the latter sector grows slowly with little investment or technical improvement. Although the drawing of a precise line between the two may be empirically doubtful – there are activities that cannot easily be assigned to one or the other, and there are clearly important functional linkages between the two – this dichotomy obviously exists. Such a dualism was noted by Marx,[15] and is particularly associated with the concentration of capital and exclusion of labour in mature capitalism at the centre, while in the periphery it is associated with the limited scope of capitalist *relations* of production (i.e. wage-labour and private capital) within a capitalist *mode* of production (i.e. a market economy) resulting from the partial insertion of the domestic economy into the world market system. The distinction is related to the classical debate about 'productive' and 'unproductive' labour:[16] forms of labour which produce commodities or services for the capitalist are considered as productive because they produce surplus value (and thus profit) by exchanging labour for wages, in contrast to the labour of the servant, artisan, peasant or small tradesman who exchanges his labour against revenue. This is a crucial historical phenomenon, as Braverman points out: 'The change in the social form of labour from that which is, from the capitalist standpoint, unproductive to that which is productive, means the transformation

from self-employment to capitalist employment, from simple commodity production to capitalist commodity production; from relations between persons to relations between things, from a society of
scattered producers to a society of corporate capitalism'.[17]

This central point is also made by Lewis in his well-known model
of growth with unlimited supplies of labour,[18] where a clear distinction is made between 'capitalist' (i.e. firms using reproducible
capital) and 'subsistence' (i.e. peasant farmer) sectors although trade
and labour supply link the two, a model explicitly intended as an
essay in the classical tradition. However, from this point onwards
the neo-classical development of the dual model[19] seems to be misleading, because it suggests not only that historically the 'modern'
sector was *superimposed* upon an existing 'traditional' sector but also
that it expands independently of it, without adequate consideration
of trade between the sectors or of the direct exploitation of the
former by the latter. Moreover, the neo-classical model generally
identifies the 'modern' sector with manufacturing industry and the
'traditional' with agriculture, while it is quite evident that dualism
exists within industry (e.g. between multinationals and small
semi-artisan firms), agriculture (e.g. between large – albeit
'traditional' – estates and the peasantry) and the services sector. The
market connexion between the two sectors is not only through the
supply of unskilled labour (indeed there is little need for it) and the
maintenance of a reserve army in order to hold down wage rates and
frustrate unionization but also through the exchange of manufactured goods for food supplies and personal services at terms of trade
unfavourable to their producers. Moreover, the operations of large
firms can be much more widespread than their directly employed
workforce, through the 'putting out' of work (such as making up
clothes) to home-workers and the marketing of mass-produced
items such as cigarettes and razor blades through a myriad of small
traders. The emergence of dualism should not be seen, then, as the
result of the superimposition of a 'dynamic' modern sector on a
'backward' traditional economy; rather the depression of peasantry
is the result of past exploitation through unequal terms of trade,
while the vast urban slums are themselves generated by unbalanced
economic growth. In other words, these phenomena are as much a
result of as the cause of dualism. Much of the criticism, especially by

sociologists,[20] of the neo-classical model is justified but does not warrant the abandonment of dualism as an analytical concept, particularly since it underlies the distribution of income, continued external dependency and the difficulties of sustained expansion of domestic capitalism.

This dualism must not be seen as a static concept. As capital accumulation takes place mainly in the corporate sector, and the dynamic effect of foreign trade through export sales and purchase of imported industrial inputs is also felt there, its output grows relatively rapidly. The process of accumulation involves the incorporation of new and more machine-intensive methods of production, and thus the corporate workforce expands at a lower rate than output: as the higher the rate of growth and accumulation the more marked this rise in productivity, employment may well expand at a rate not much greater than that of the economically active population, so that the workforce in the non-corporate sector is not absorbed at any appreciable speed. The resultant increases in value added mostly accrue in the form of profit but can also sustain considerable increases in real wages, particularly in comparison with rural incomes. Meanwhile, output in the 'peasant division' of the non-corporate sector grows very slowly due to the absence of investment or technical improvement and may well rise little faster than the rural workforce.

The consequences of this lack of dynamic in non-corporate agriculture (peasants and traditional pre-capitalist farmers) are many, but probably the most serious economic one is the effect on capital accumulation and thus on the growth of the economy as a whole.[21] Given that food output grows very slowly, then if average real wages in the economy are to be maintained the import of foodstuffs (or a reduction in their export) becomes necessary; but this uses up foreign exchange which would otherwise be used at the margin for the import of capital equipment – or else external debt is built up for repayment out of future foreign exchange earnings – and thus reduces the capacity of the corporate sector to accumulate. Alternatively, domestic food prices can be allowed to rise, but this may well have little effect upon peasant output if there is no new land or inadequate infrastructure, and in any case real wages will fall, as will those of rural wage workers – which latter category includes the poorest in rural areas, those without land or only a sub-subsistence plot. The deterioration in the income distribution also has the effect of narrowing the market for domestic manufactures, and thus places a 'Keynesian' restriction on private investment in the economy. However, one traditional preoccupation of economists over the effect of inadequate food supply does not appear to be a major problem in developing countries today: the supply of labour to manufacturing. An abundant urban food supply has traditionally been seen as a necessary pre-condition for the attraction of sufficient labour to staff the factories; in contrast, underdeveloped countries have urban populations far in excess of the requirements of corporate manufacturing and modern services. But the public expenditure required on urban infrastructure does place a further burden on capital accumulation. Overall, then, quite apart from the undesirable social effects of dualism in general and of stagnating peasant incomes in particular, the effect upon capital accumulation is also a negative one, despite the fact that a deteriorating income distribution means a higher share of profits in national income.

The migratory mechanism is not, then, based on the labour requirements of corporate capitalist enterprises, rather it arises from the expenditure by the corporate sector workforce upon petty services and minor commerce generates a vast number of income opportunities in urban areas, towards which large numbers of rural families will continually migrate. This provides the 'dynamic' element in the employment pattern (although not in the production system) and over time this imbalance appears to get progressively worse in terms of both output and population distribution.[22] Presumably, if those trends are continued – and they are logically inherent to capitalist expansion on the periphery – then the peasantry would be reduced in absolute as well as relative terms, but whether the urban lumpenproletariat would ever be absorbed in the corporate sector would depend upon technological (i.e. labour productivity) trends in relation to output growth on the one hand and population growth on the other.

This perhaps unfashionable insistence on the importance of the phenomenon is supported by one of the most perceptive of recent writers on underdevelopment:

What is emerging in the underdeveloped countries is a form of dualism, not between the subsistence sector of agriculture within a feudal framework and a market industrial sector, but between a high profit/high wage international oligopolistic capitalist sector and a low profit/low wage competitive capitalist sector. Dualism need not mean that there are no ties between the two, nor only the flow of labour from agriculture into industry. Capital may move easily from the local to the international sector but *not* labour. . . . If labour cannot move from one sector to the other, it must be supposed that the subsequent disparities of income will lead, on a Marxist view, to surpluses that cannot be absorbed, or on a Keynesian view, to ineffective demand.[23]

Unless, of course, export-led growth is sustained by factors outside the economy. Barret-Brown goes on to conclude that: 'there is no necessary reason, then, why a dual economy should achieve sustained development unless the state taxes the high profit/high wage sector to finance growth in the low profit/low wage sector'[24] but this is almost impossible in the dependent capitalist economy, by virtue of the political power structure.

Even if we retain this analytical category, as indeed we shall, the problem of nomenclature remains. From the very outset the term 'dualism' has received so much criticism that it seems to act as a red rag to the academic bull, but so far no acceptable substitute has been found – certainly 'unbalanced capitalist growth' is not much help – and because the phenomenon as encountered in developing countries is certainly not the symptom of mature capitalism (although it does reflect its impact from outside) and is probably not that of a temporary transitional phase of early industrialization as experienced in Europe either, we must perforce retain it. The choice of names for the two sectors is an equally difficult task: Lewis' 'capitalist/subsistence' choice seems inapposite, and the neo-classical 'modern/traditional' split is positively misleading; the sociological pairing of 'formal/informal' does at least refer to the organizational structures of the two sectors but is not very illuminating, while the vulgar-Marxist use of 'capitalist/precapitalist' seems very confused – in what sense can the urban slums be described as 'precapitalist'? In this study we use the terminology 'corporate/non-corporate' because this does at least underline two different forms of organization or production within a capitalist economy, with reproducible capital, financial profit and wage relations only existing on any significant scale in the former. For statistical purposes, this can then be translated into a definition of the form of 'enterprises of more than x employees' which can be conveniently fitted into the minimal census definition.

These two phenomena – dependency and dualism – are closely connected and rely upon each other for their origin and their continuing existence. The dualism of capitalist expansion on the periphery implies imported technology embodied in capital equipment in order to expand production without incorporating the local labour force and international export markets to sustain growth in the absence of a domestic market. The multinationals benefit from the demand for sophisticated consumer goods and the local desire to earn foreign exchange from raw material exports. There is no mere coincidence in this, for they are two sides of the same coin – the specie of peripheral capitalism. For one or other of the two to be overcome in order to permit sustained national development, so must the other: an attempt to reduce dependency without reducing dualism would leave the corporate sector without sources of growth or capital inputs while an attempt to overcome dualism while the economy remains export-led and industry controlled by the multinationals would be equally difficult. In conjunctural terms, this combination can be observed in both internal and external economic disequilibria: the internal balance of demand and supply is vitiated by the narrowness of industrial markets (resulting from mal-distribution of income) for the sophisticated goods produced by 'modern' manufacturing on the one hand and the stagnation of food agriculture on the other; while the constraints on export growth imposed by world markets and the constant pressure for higher imports of industrial inputs and even food lead to chronic balance of payments difficulties resolved only by internal wage deflation or foreign borrowing.

This interconnexion is probably the best way of viewing technology in its proper context. Rather than regarding it as a disembodied factor of production, it is better seen as the form in which the capital-intensity of the production systems of the corporate sector is expressed and the activities of foreign enterprise are realized. This is not to go to the extreme of seeing technology as a mystification, as no more than 'commodity fetishism' which disguises social relationships;[25] this would be a gross misrepresentation of reality, particularly on the periphery where new technology is not generated. This new technology brought in is almost invariably labour-saving and intensive in the use of capital (i.e. imported equipment or imported inputs) and thus allows capitalist expansion to proceed within the dual model. Moreover, the multinationals themselves have moved from the exploitation of natural resources, through simple manufacturing and service activities, to the marketing of equipment and techniques for all those sectors – from the ownership of real estate through that of fixed capital to the sale of the technology itself. As Sutcliffe puts it: 'Technology is not disembodied but is embodied in certain capital goods. In a sense, therefore, technology has always been the basis of metropolitan monopoly . . . the basis of [this] monopoly has shifted not to a new category, technology, but to a new more restricted group of capital goods industries.'[26] However, within the general term 'technology' we can distinguish between three distinct categories: 'process' technology, which refers to the techniques of transformation themselves, such as the design of a catalytic cracker; 'skill' technology, which is the training of engineers and managers in the organization of such production; and 'brand' technology, which consists in no more than an expression of the monopoly position built up by product differentiation, often based on advertising alone. Ownership of the first takes the form of patents, which are also taken out on the third – payments for the former being theoretically equivalent to rent and for the latter to monopoly profit – but in neither case (nor, for that matter, in the second) is there a tangible asset to be acquired or transferred. Indeed, while technology might be regarded in theory as the most mobile of factors in the world economy, as far as the developing countries are concerned, if by 'mobility' we are to understand the effective transfer and assimilation of knowledge, then it turns out to be the least mobile – because it is retained by the local subsidiary of the multinational corporation. Unless, of course, it can be acquired through the second form of technology skills, which is the most difficult way. In consequence, as Vaitsos points out: 'Developing countries can nationalize the assets of foreign firms within their own territories (including the foreign registered patents) but cannot "nationalize" the foreign technology used within their economy since it has never been transferred to the domestic technological infrastructure.'[27] In this way the binding economic link between the local and international economy is not under the control of the peripheral nation state.

The Latinamerican interpretation

In contrast to the general tendency for intellectual life on the periphery to be dominated by metropolitan thought – and this applies to both poles of the ideological spectrum – an independent school of social science did emerge in Latin America after the Second World War. What is all the more curious is that it should have emerged within a United Nations institution, the Economic Commission for Latin America.[28] The ECLA school undoubtedly made considerable contributions to economic development theory, contributions which until recently have remained largely unrecognized by the outside world: parallel and in some cases later writings in the theories of dependency and dualism that we have just discussed hardly acknowledge, let alone incorporate, the ECLA work. Doubtless this is partly due to much of the work being in Spanish, but the influential *Economic Survey* and most important studies were issued in English, as is the custom of the United Nations, and many of the major contributions have been published in translation; much of the fault must surely be attributed to the insularity of development economics reared in the aura of the British and French empires on the one hand and within the rigid frameworks of neo-classical and Marxist thought on the other. However, we can hardly embark upon an intellectual history[29] of the ECLA here, so we shall limit ourselves to indicating some of the major points in relation to the theoretical themes we have just outlined.

The 'ECLA school' is usually identified with the Commission and the planning institute (Instituto Latinoamericano de Planificación Económica y Social – ILPES) itself at Santiago de Chile which have counted the foremost Latinamerican social scientists among their staffs, and it is their[30] own work as much as the official reports – although these are important – that makes up the intellectual tradition associated with it. Moreover, as these authors have developed their analyses in divergent directions since the 'heyday' of the ECLA between the late 1940s and early 1960s, it is impossible to present their ideas as a single logical structure. Nonetheless, we can discuss the material in a schematic way without doing too great a disservice to its complexity. Its importance lies not just in its contribution to the analysis of underdevelopment, but also in its influence upon reformist ideology in Latin America – particularly the spreading awareness of the role to be played by national industry in the overcoming of both dependence and dualism.[31]

The original line of ECLA argument may seem almost conventional now, but in the context of the prevailing orthodoxy in the 1950s it was radical enough, especially in contrast to the neo-classical dominance of international trade theory current at the time, which regarded the specialization of production as being based upon resource endowments, the market balancing initial national advantages through prices and subsequently through factor mobility and the transference of technological progress. This essentially Ricardian model implied that all parties would benefit to some extent from this intercourse – a view shared by those[32] on the opposite Marxist pole, who also believed in the positive effect of international trade on the expansion of capitalism to the periphery. Even the emphasis placed by the latter group upon the expansion of multinational capital into the productive systems of the third world as a factor conducive to industrializing development was shared by the former. In opposition to both these sets of ideas, the ECLA school argued[33] that the economic relations between centre and periphery (terms popularized if not introduced by the ECLA) tend to reproduce the conditions of underdevelopment and increase the gap between developed and underdeveloped countries: in particular, that the gains in industrial productivity at the centre are *not* passed on in lower world prices but rather retained by oligopolies and trades unions (through higher profits and wages) in the central economies as a result of the exercise of political and organizational power. The low rates of accumulation on the periphery were attributed to low absolute profit levels and the lack of technological capacity; and low growth to the foreign exchange constraint. Unlike much of the more recent 'unequal exchange' writing, this interpretation was well rooted in the empirical analysis of the Latin-American economies[34] and derived from a coherent historical model of the neo-colonial past of the area under successive British and American domination,[35] but perhaps the major innovation was the analysis of the dynamics of world capitalism from the viewpoint of the periphery.

The logical deduction that industrialization was the way out of this dilemma (in order to acquire productivity gains, reduce the import coefficient of GDP, integrate the economy) led to the second major step in ECLA thought. This step, commonly known as 'structuralism', can be roughly dated from the mid 1950s and is mainly concerned with the barriers to industrialization on the continent, above all with the internal obstacles formed by the traditional primary economy.[36] Underdevelopment of the domestic economy, given the subordinate status of the periphery, was identified with imbalanced factor utilization as opposed to the then-conventional definition in terms of per-capita income:

> Underdevelopment is a state of factor imbalance reflecting a lack of adjustment between the availability of factors and the technology of their use, so that it is impossible to achieve full utilization of both capital and labour simultaneously. [In an underdeveloped structure] full utilization of available capital is not a sufficient condition for complete absorption of the working force at a level of productivity corresponding to the technology prevailing in the dynamic sector of the system.[37]

These obstacles were broadly identified with dualism in the sense we have discussed above, particularly the lack of a large domestic market for manufactures and stagnant food supplies. Their removal was regarded as essential to a successful industrial strategy, even if the means of implementing such a strategy would initially be the replacement of the existing import pattern by domestic supply. Import-substituting industrialization (as it came to be known) was not seen as a self-sustaining process; it was to be supported by complementary measures to increase agricultural productivity – above all land reform, transport infrastructure and rural credit – so as to feed the urban work force, provide a broad market for manufactured products (both consumer goods and farm inputs) and prevent the rapidly growing population from flooding into the towns. It had been recognized at an early stage that industrial output would rise at a rate little above that of externally determined productivity (i.e. technology transfer) change and thus that no great gains in employment could be expected in the short run, particularly since the imports to be substituted were generally of a 'luxury' nature, responding directly or indirectly (i.e. as inputs) to the demand generated by the top strata of the personal income distribution where the bulk of expenditure was concentrated as the result of historically 'exclusive' growth. Nonetheless, it was anticipated that industry would reduce the strain on the balance of payments by eliminating many import requirements, integrate the agricultural sector to the rest of the economy by supplying cheap inputs and processing outputs, and eventually generate endogenous technological capacity.

It was hoped that even if industrialization itself could not provide the necessary income redistribution, agrarian reform and appropriate fiscal measures – particularly progressive tax reform and welfare expenditures – would be undertaken in order to generate effective domestic demand. Structuralist theory thus provided both a positive critique of the difficulties encountered in establishing sustained industrialization in the region and a normative programme for action, which, when combined with the existing ECLA analysis of international trade, was a valuable contribution to the analysis of underdevelopment that – once again – went largely unrecognized by the orthodoxy current in development economics until the late 1960s.[38] However, reliance was still placed upon the beneficial effect of foreign investment and trade in the transfer of technology, if properly controlled within an industrialization strategy designed to overcome dualism and permit sustained capitalist expansion: 'Foreign trade and investment is the principle transmitter of technological progress to the benefit of the late-developing economies. For an underdeveloped country, its international exchange is, above all, the barter of goods produced at technological levels to which it does have access in return for those produced at levels to which it does not.'[39]

There are two further practical outcomes of the structuralist analysis. First, the emphasis placed on the need to restructure the economy and the incapacity of free-market forces to achieve this implied a need for state intervention (to which we shall return shortly) in general and development planning in particular. Planning rapidly became the watchword of progressive technocrats throughout Latin America, and although the planning offices established did not achieve very much,[40] they contributed considerably to the 'legitimization' of state intervention in the economy – albeit in support of private enterprise. Second, the political implication of the proposed economic strategy was that the 'dynamic' industrialist groups should be favoured in their struggle against the 'backward' landlords and primary exporters, multinationals encouraged to promote industrialization, and land reform undertaken in order to head off rural unrest – all of which fitted in with the proclaimed objectives of the 'Alliance for Progress' promoted by the US State Department during the 1960s.[41]

However, by the mid 1960s a considerable degree of industrialization had meanwhile occurred in Latin America[42] – belying the more extreme forms of the 'stagnationist' argument but without the developmental consequences anticipated by the ECLA. It was rapidly becoming clear that import-substituting industrialization was leading only to capital-intensive and unintegrated manufacturing branches while foreign ownership was reaching unacceptable limits. In consequence the strain on the balance of payments was not reduced – indeed it was often increased by continued purchase of tied inputs at inflated transfer prices, the remittance of profits and royalties, and the service of government borrowing to support this industrialization. Further, the support of foreign capital appeared to have helped local elites to resist agrarian and fiscal reform and other measures to redistribute income. From this disillusion (combined, it should be remembered, with the longstanding ECLA critique of the terms of international trade) sprang the 'dependency' school. This is, perhaps, the best-known aspect of ECLA thought[43] – or more accurately, of those who *had* worked with ECLA – and it tends to both overshadow, and be treated in isolation from, previous work in this tradition. Apart from the collection of extensive data on the problems of ownership and foreign control of the Latinamerican economies, varying from detailed analyses of technological contracts to polemical accounts of the overthrow of governments, a general interpretation of the cause of Latinamerican underdevelopment (and by implication a means of resolution) was built up from the two previous 'building blocks' by adding the analysis of the impact of foreign investment – particularly by the multinationals – to the original ECLA model and attributing many of the structural distortions to this cause. Although it is true that this 'dependency school'[44] did see the key to present-day dependency as being 'the penetration of the underdeveloped countries by the most powerful economic agent in the developed countries – the multinational corporation',[45] it regarded the relation between the centre and periphery as being a conditioning situation, rather than a unilateral phenomenon of the 'development of underdevelopment' in the manner that writers such as Frank appear to do. Neither was underdevelopment seen as a separate stage of development, but rather as a particular function or position within the international system – so that any theory of underdevelopment becomes a theory of dependency.[46] As Dos Santos has put it:

> Dependence is a conditioning situation in which the economies of one group of countries are conditioned by the development and expansion of others. A relationship of interdependence between two or more economies or between such economies and the world trading system becomes a dependent relationship when some countries can expand through self-impulsion while others, being in a dependent position, can only expand as a reflection of the expansion of the dominant countries, which may have positive or negative effects on their immediate development.[47]

This view of dependence was combined with the existing ECLA analysis of the internal development of the Latinamerican economies that stressed deteriorating income distribution, worsening economic and social dualism, and the lopsided expansion of industry. This was seen as interacting with external control of the economy – both sustaining it through a demand for 'modern' goods and being sustained by the introduction of 'modern' technology – to produce a 'perverse style of development'.[48] But development nonetheless, so long as this is understood to mean the expansion of capitalism and not some form of egalitarian economic progress: the ECLA school was never guilty of confusing a critique of the viability of a particular form of capitalism with criticism of capitalism itself. For by the end of the 1960s it became evident that the dire predictions of the structuralists (particularly Furtado) to the effect that underconsumption would bring industrialization to a halt were not being fulfilled. Traditionally, the dynamic element on the periphery is primary exports ('Department One' in the Marxist model) the growth of which depends upon a given natural resource base on the one hand and the expansion of demand in the core economies. Under the development model espoused by ECLA, accumulation was to be on dynamic expansion of industry ('Department Two') but in the absence of manufactured export channels, the realization of profits in these sectors clearly depends upon the existence of a large domestic market. The structuralists argued that in the short run this could be based on import-substitution but that it was incompatible with the repression of real wages in the long run so that income redistribution would be necessary in order to permit capitalist expansion to continue. However, in practice, it turned out (Brazil and Mexico being prominent examples of this) that the expansion of the service sector, while essentially unproductive in itself, did permit circulation (i.e. trade), realization of profits and reproduction (i.e. expansion) to take place on the basis of middle-class consumption. It also transpired that the multinationals were prepared to add a capital-goods sector to the 'primary exports for imported equipment' activity of Department One in the larger economies, albeit under their continued technological control, contrary to the initial expectations of dependency writers. In other words, sustained capitalist expansion was possible on the periphery in close association with foreign capital and in the presence of growing underemployment and continued agricultural stagnation. Above all, this form of 'exclusive' development meant that the urban lumpenproletariat (the *'marginados'*) had become a permanent and integral feature of the model, with no foreseeable possibility of being absorbed into stable wage employment:

> By 'marginados' are meant those groups or persons who, as a consequence of the process of modernization are expelled or left aside although they are both a consequence of and contributory to that process – in other words, modernization cannot be understood without their presence. This concept of 'marginados' must be clearly distinguished from the 'no-incorporados' composed of those groups such as indigenous indians who sustain a subsistence economy which is essentially unaffected by contact with modern society, and thus cannot be considered as 'marginalized' by it.[49]

In addition, it can be argued, that the spread of authoritarian rule over the continent may well be related to the need to maintain social order under these circumstances.

It cannot be denied that a great deal of dependency writing has been oversimplistic, tending to blame all economic ills upon the multinationals and the US State Department and becoming little more than a naive nationalism in the process.[50] Nonetheless, in its original form, it does seem to throw light upon the condition of underdevelopment in its combination of the concepts of imperialism and structuralism, permitting an interaction of the two to allow for varying degrees of national development within a subordinate position in the world capitalist system. The most positive steps forward for this model may well turn out to be the current theoretical concern with the accumulation process, which allows diverse phenomena such as factor income shares, technology transfer, dualism and the expropriation of surplus to be integrated. The key concept then becomes the control over accumulation, which determines consequent production structures and trade patterns, rather than just the distribution of the surplus generated thereby, while foreign control over international finance and the capital goods sector is revealed as being as important, if not more so, than ownership of natural resources or even manufacturing plant.[51] But the residual weakness of the ECLA model even in this evolved form lies not in its economics but rather in its lack of concrete analysis of domestic class structures,[52] and particularly of the role of the national bourgeoisie. In terms of development strategy, this has meant an exaggerated reliance on the capacity of the state both to overcome the structural obstacles to capitalist expansion in the domestic economy and to act as a strong negotiator with foreign corporations. It is to the analysis of the role of the state on the periphery that we must now turn.

The state and underdevelopment

Capitalism is a social formation as well as a system of economic organization; the balance of class forces within it is a crucial factor in determining the nature of underdevelopment. The lack of specification of this aspect of the problem is understandable, if unfortunate, in the official ECLA documentation – but hardly so in the

writings of authors such as Amin and Frank, who reduce their
model to a continuous chain of exploitation extending from the
centre to periphery, mediated only by a local 'comprador'[53] elite.
This ignores the vast variations in the degree to which different
peripheral countries have achieved national industrialization, and in
the extent to which local elites have resisted the penetration of
foreign capital. The structuralist analysis is almost as crude, seeing
the class conflict mainly in terms of the industrial capitalists fighting
off the feudal landlords and foreign corporations and thus ignoring
the extent to which alliances are formed between these three.
However, there are two fairly general characteristics of the class
structure that emerge quite logically from the condition of dependent dualism that constitutes underdevelopment. The first is that the
dependent nature of the economy is associated with economic
weakness in the local bourgeoisie to the extent that they do not control the process of accumulation and multi-national corporations
do: in newly-independent countries the existence of a temporary
elite 'vacuum' after the departure of foreigners is only to be
expected, but in Latin America the positions of domestic agrarian
and financial elites were still maintained as externally controlled
industrialization got under way, the foreign investors often supplanting local mining and manufacturing capital and thereby blocking
the emergence of a 'national' bourgeoisie. The second is that the
nature of investment is such that the mining and factory workforce
expands less rapidly than production and often no faster than population as a whole; in consequence, the proletariat is small and
faced with a large 'reserve army' in the urban slums while the unbalanced growth of agriculture results in a small 'modern' sector of
productive estates which cannot employ the mass of landless
peasants. As a result it is hardly surprising that historically the foundations of modern democratic liberalism have not been very firm in
Latin America and the corresponding political institutions appear
to have been declining in importance too.

We cannot enter into a general discussion of Latinamerican class
structures here, but their crystallization within the state does concern us, particularly as it affects the organization of the economy
and above all, accumulation. Specifically, we are concerned with the
relationship between the state and the domestic bourgeoisie on the

one hand and foreign capital on the other, which are the groups which determine the structure of production, rather than the access of popular forces the state. This relationship is complicated by the fact that ever since the formation of nation states in Latin America[54] the securing of profit within their oligopolized economies has depended upon privileges and concessions obtained by access to government, so that a 'proprietary' rather than an 'entrepreneurial' business ethos obtains based on control over a limited market and exclusive licences instead of mass sales and price competition. This has reduced the ideological antagonism between 'public' and 'private' sectors observed in developed economies. Further, the dominant groups in a dependent economy are those which cluster around the interchanges with the metropolitan countries, and these groups develop an interest in maintaining or only renegotiating these interchanges.[55] In consequence, there is no *prima facie* reason to expect a state dominated by such an elite to attempt to change the external relationship.

It is true that the state is often regarded in Weberian terms as a community that successfully claims the monopoly of the legitimate use of physical force within a given territory, but (as Weber himself recognized) such a stable state is only characteristic of modern industrialized economies in which the national bourgeoisie has fully emerged as dominant.[56] Much the same can be said of the orthodox Marxist theory of 'state monopoly capitalism' where the interests and actions of the state and the large corporations are regarded as fused and as forming an organic whole in the mature capitalist economy.[57] However, in reality even mature states vary greatly in form, their capacity for intervention in the economy and their degree of stability. This variation results from the differences in the class forces which interact within the state, because the state and classes are not 'external' to one another; rather the form and action of state institutions and their personnel are an expression of class interests. Nonetheless, for the state to act effectively in a capitalist economy, it must balance the immediate interests of individual capitals against the preservation of the capitalist mode of production as a whole. In order to do this, a certain independence of the state from domestic capitalist groups is necessary, so that the state may not just guarantee dominant class hegemony (the 'normal' state) but more importantly in view of the recurrent crises of capitalism, in order that it may reorganize the economy itself (the 'exceptional' state).[58] Thus the state may need to have considerable freedom to restructure capital in order to maintain capitalist expansion in the long run, even though this may be against the interests of capitalist groups in the short run. This freedom, or 'relative autonomy' appears to obtain in atypical periods of internal social fragmentation when a near equilibrium of class forces occurs, and these periods occur during economic or political crises – particularly when the two are associated. In addition, an external threat to the nation can produce these conditions for the state to obtain relative autonomy.

On the periphery of the world economy, where capitalism is dependent for its expansion upon forces outside the nation and the internal class structure is relatively underdeveloped – with a weak bourgeoisie and a small proletariat – the concept of relative autonomy is more difficult to apply, but it is clearly a useful one. Here we shall restrict ourselves to two points of direct relevance to our study: the persistence of authoritarianism and the emergence of state capitalism. Authoritarianism, understood in the general sense of the control of society from above through the state apparatus – as distinct from but not excluding direct military intervention or flagrant abrogation of human rights – is a frequent feature of dependent capitalism where bourgeois hegemony is not underpinned by broad middle-class support or the working classes organized in 'democratic' trades unions. The small portion of the surplus available to the state after payments to foreign capital and the acquisition of domestic profit, when balanced against the need for massive infrastructural expenditure in order to sustain the process of industrialization[59] means that little can be spent on welfare services for the workforce in order to 'legitimize' the regime – rather it is spent upon mechanisms of internal security. The large bureaucratic and military establishment generated by authoritarian rule gains its own momentum and autonomy, but without direct access to the production system this may not lead to a restructuring of capital, only repressing the symptoms of the contradictions of dependent capitalism rather than resolving them. A particular characteristic of these authoritarian regimes is the close cooperation between the state and foreign corporations, which while weakening the autonomy of the former in international negotiation does increase its internal scope of action with respect to domestic firms. As authoritarianism is common to countries with very different political institutions (such as Brazil and Mexico) it has also been argued that such regimes are a necessary corollary to the 'perverse style' of development criticized by the ECLA school of thought.[60]

But this same weakness of the domestic class structure and particularly of the national bourgeoisie in the third world, combined with a state apparatus strengthened by the process of industrialization and often supported by a recently professionalized military, can give rise to *state capitalism* as the political and economic project[61] of a 'national state-bureaucratic' class; reformist and anti-imperialist even if integration into the world capitalist economy is not questioned as such. This view contrasts with the rather more optimistic view held by some writers of the long-term potential of state capitalism to develop in non-capitalist directions,[62] but it does see this form of organization as a break with neo-colonialism and the expression of a serious attempt to build a national industrial economy in the absence of a national bourgeoisie capable of carrying out this task and in reaction to the evident incapacity of foreign capital to create the conditions for not only sustained growth but also an integrated and balanced economy. Naturally, this state capitalism is not just equivalent to a large state-enterprise sector, for in many cases this merely assists the penetration of foreign capital. But where the domestic bourgeoisie is particularly weak and an industrial fraction incapable of dominating the state, the state itself can substitute for non-existent capitalists, performing the function of 'collective capitalism'[63] as far as wage relations and rapid accumulation are concerned, with the added advantages of central planning and cohesive negotiation with multinational corporations, and thus promote industrialization.

This social formation has certain similarities to both state monopoly capitalism in mature market economies and degenerate socialism in the soviet bloc. In the former we can observe the phenomenon of state intervention in order to compensate for the weaknesses and inefficiencies of private capitalism by coordinating and accelerating investment, and in the latter the tendency for widespread state ownership to allow the bureaucracy to establish itself as a dominant force. To the extent that this state-capitalist project is to be effective, the state bureaucracy must begin to form a class of its own[64] with interests opposed to or largely incompatible with those of private capital (whether local or foreign) or else establish an independent political base in a populist mass party. But it can be expected that growing state control of the processes of production will tend to 'internalize' social conflict within the public sector – that is, bring the government into direct confrontation with the working class – while the public enterprises' own perceived need for foreign technology and finance will force the state into cooperation with the multinationals. In other words, the economic nature of state capitalism may be logically expected to weaken its independent political base, and thus reduce the relative autonomy required for the restructuring of capital.

Economic strategy and the political economy of development

Our concern in this study is, after all, the development of a particular economy rather than the global politics of the third world. But dualism, dependency and the politics of state intervention are not just a matter of 'background' to economic analysis, for they are the result of and a reaction to economic underdevelopment in the past and place severe limits upon the prospects for such development in the future. There are two specific points that are of practical concern for economic strategy here. The first is that dependency is a 'conditioning situation' and not a determining one: it is development in the *domestic* economy that determines the form that this external relationship takes and the terms upon which it is undertaken. If economic development is understood in terms of integration of the productive structure and industrialization, then the model must presumably involve a reliance on domestic rather than foreign markets, on agriculture rather than mining as the support for industry and the use of labour-intensive rather than capital- or import-intensive technologies. In other words, the reduction of dualism involves a reduction of dependency too – a point that is underlined by the manifest failure of import-substituting industrialization as it has been experienced in the capitalist third world to relieve the foreign exchange constraint or generate employment. But the obverse also holds true – that a reduction in dependency is virtually impossible if dualism is not reduced at the same time so as to diminish the need for imported technology and foreign exchange. The second is that if planners are to be able to implement a strategy of 'integrated' rather than 'isolated' industrialization then the state must possess a considerable degree of relative autonomy from the domestic and foreign interests that gain from a continuance of the traditional growth model. This freedom to reorganize the economy in terms of ownership and sectoral balance is necessary because even if it is in the long-run interest of domestic capitalism it will almost inevitably be resisted in the short run – if this were not so then the market system could achieve economic development unaided. But this relative autonomy, and with it the power to plan in the economic sphere, can only be gained in the political sphere and may well be weakened by the economic measures (such as foreign loans or real wage restrictions) found necessary to restructure capital and establish a new model of accumulation.

3

The political background

Before embarking upon the analysis of the economy between 1956 and 1978, which is the main task of this study, we must examine the political structure of Peruvian society and in particular the class forces operating within what can be described as a dependent capitalist social formation. Although the object of such an exercise is mainly to provide a coherent framework for the economic analysis, it must itself presuppose the structure and dynamics of the economy: the underlying internal dualism and external dependency, the frustrated process of industrialization and the expansion of state intervention in an attempt to resolve the problems of capital accumulation make up a theme running through the whole period. In this chapter we shall consider the class structure mainly in terms of the relations of production, and offer an interpretation of the changing balance of class strength over the period as reflected by the role of the state. We must start, however, with a brief outline[1] of the recent political history of Peru so that the subsequent discussion may be seen in context.

The recent political history of Peru

For two decades after the achievement of independence from Spain,[2] Peru suffered from unstable governments, mostly drawn from the armed forces in the absence of a strong post-colonial elite.[3] By the mid nineteenth century, the development of guano and nitrates for the British market not only set the economy on an export-led course but also led to the establishment of a coastal elite[4] with interests in trade, banking, sugar and cotton as well as mineral exports. The first steps in economic development were abruptly halted, however, by the War of the Pacific (1879–84) which resulted in a humiliating defeat by Chile and annexation of the nitrate deposits. It took another two decades to re-establish the economy on a sound basis, but, after that, the northern coastal elite were able to govern the country either directly or through the military for the next half-century despite recurrent disputes within the alliance they formed with highland landlords, Arequipa traders and emerging urban interests. The only significant political threat to this hegemony consisted in the *Alianza Popular Revolucionaria Americana,* a populist party with strong roots in the rural proletariat, urban *barriada* dwellers and the lower middle class. Continued military suppression had kept the APRA under control even during its apogee in the 1930s, and by the opening of our period it had lost its revolutionary pretensions completely,[5] although it did retain its considerable organizational capacity – based on its discipline, expertise in defending the individual claims of the poor against the authorities (e.g. in land litigation and urban electrification), and penetration of the 'inferior' professional organizations such as schoolteachers, police and bank clerks – and represented a considerable political force right up to 1978. Even in the intermittent periods of 'civilian democracy' between military dictatorships (which had accounted for eighty-five out of the one hundred and thirty-five years of the republic by 1956) the franchise had not been extended to the illiterate Indian peasants who made up half the population, and the communications media remained firmly in the hands of the grand bourgeoisie, while party organization (with the possible exception of the APRA) was limited to electoral machines centred upon the personality of the presidential candidate, so that even by the middle of the twentieth century Peru could hardly be described as a democracy in any meaningful sense of the term. In contrast to the overall weakness of the trades unions (also dominated by the APRA up to the mid 1960s) the pressure groups representing capital – above all the *Sociedad Nacional Agraria* and the *Sociedad Nacional de Industrias* – were extremely powerful, exercising direct control over the respective sectoral policies of government. As might be imagined, Peruvian regimes had enjoyed strong diplomatic and commercial support from successive US governments since the First World War.[6]

The immediate prelude to our period is initiated, interestingly enough, by the brief administration (1945–48) of Bustamante, who was constitutionally elected with APRA support, but who after modest proposals to promote industrialization[7] was ousted by General Odría. As the representative of the traditional export interests, his administration implemented a *laissez-faire* economic policy accompanied by a large and corrupt public works programme; the coincidence of the Korean War commodity boom and consequent rapid growth in Peruvian export earnings had the effect of legitimizing what was in a very real sense a 'reactionary' anti-industrial strategy: 'In a continent that was witnessing ever-increasing state intervention in economic life in country after country, Peru had turned around to begin a march in the other direction that continued for the next eighteen years' (Hunt, 1974, p. 10).

In 1956, after eight years of what can only be described as the last 'caudillo' regime in Peruvian history, elections were held which were won by the financier Manuel Prado with APRA support under an agreement known as the *'convivencia'* by which the APRA would at last be allowed to stand independently, in the next presidential elections due in 1962. More significantly, this move represented an attempt by the traditional ruling class to extend its basis of political support in the face of growing urbanization and unionization. However, despite this political move, the Prado administration maintained a liberal economic policy designed to promote foreign investment and private sector profitability. In a real sense, the Prado regime (which was his second, as he has also been president between 1939 and 1945) was the last of the traditional 'oligarchic' administrations: it was a regime which preserved, in the context of the urbanization and industrialization which had taken place over the previous two decades, a serious divergence between the traditional political and emerging social structures. The professed ideological stance of the Prado administration did not take the form of an explicit programme, but was expressed through leader articles in *La Prensa* (owned and edited by the Prime Minister, Pedro Beltran) and consisted in a commitment to free trade, free enterprise, the suppression of independent labour movements (in the name of 'anti-communism') and the encouragement of modernization through foreign investment. The influence of the financial and exporting interests within the cabinet resulted in the refusal to undertake any sort of real agrarian reform even in order to head off growing peasant discontent, a reluctance to protect domestic industrialists from competitive imports or multinationals, and a neglect of social welfare expenditure. When a downturn in export income brought about a balance of payments crisis in 1958, the government implemented a stabilization policy based on real wage reductions until the new mining and fishing projects rectified the external position.

In consequence, when elections were due once again in 1962, popular pressure for change had grown considerably, and the electoral success of the APRA was widely anticipated. Despite the last-minute agreement to resurrect the *convivencia* in the form of Odría as presidential candidate, the army were not prepared to see their traditional opponents in power, despite the loss of any radical pretensions on the part of the APRA: they mounted a *golpe de estado* and installed a military junta led by General Perez Godoy.[8] Although this junta regarded itself as an interim administration, it was particularly significant as being the first 'institutional' intervention of the military in Peruvian government: the joint services command took power, as opposed to an individual *caudillo*. Reformist elements among the senior army officers pressed for ownership reforms and a more favourable policy towards industry; although a start was made on land reform (in the La Convención valley) and the National Planning Institute established, divisions within the military led to fresh elections in 1963.[9] These the APRA narrowly lost, an outcome possibly related to the close supervision of the voting by the military. This short military intervention foreshadowed in many respects the longer one after 1968, and in fact the military continued both to support and to participate directly in the subsequent civilian government.

The Acción Popular party, headed by Fernando Belaunde (an architect from Arequipa) had failed to gain a majority in the 1956 and 1962 elections, but by including land reform and industrial protection in its programme, had extended its support from the urban middle classes to small farmers and manufacturers[10] by 1963, and with military blessing took over government. The ideology of the Acción Popular was summed up in Belaunde's own book *La Conquista de Perú por los Peruanos* which stressed the communal Incaic past, and adopted a 'developmentalist' approach to economic strategy based on public investment in roads and irrigation designed to generate new income and employment opportunities, while promising 'social justice' in terms not only of political involvement but also of access to health and education services.[11] But once in power, Belaunde could not implement even a minimal reform programme due to the opposition from both APRA and right-wing elements in the Congress, where the Acción Popular did not enjoy an absolute majority. This revival of the *convivencia* was once again a tactical one, with the APRA anticipating election victory in 1969 on the basis of popular frustration at the lack of reform (although the party was happy to vote enormous salary increases to teachers, if not the consequent increases in taxation) and the right still hoping to halt reforms prejudicial to its interests. In consequence, the limited agrarian reform proposed (which would have affected only backward highland estates) could not be implemented, much-needed tax reforms could not be put into effect, and control of foreign investment was made virtually impossible. Meanwhile, police action was insufficient to halt land invasions in the highlands and agrarian unrest exploded in the form of guerilla warfare in 1965; despite the rapid and successful military reaction, support for the government both among the middle classes and the military itself was severely affected. Rising inflation, a deteriorating balance of payments position and the inevitable deflationary measures of 1967, combined with incidental smuggling scandals, further weakened the regime. US support for Belaunde also waned, despite original State Department enthusiasm as he had seemed to typify the industrializing modernization strategy of the Alliance for Progress, as his government failed to deal with internal economic and social problems while increasing rhetorical attacks upon the International Petroleum Company. In contrast, the failure of Belaunde to negotiate firmly enough with the IPC over oil concessions and the growing control of multinationals over the manufacturing sector antagonized nationalist elements in domestic politics. Despite last-ditch attempts to re-establish confidence by appointing a military man (Morales Bermudez, who was to become President himself seven years later) and subsequently a well-known financier (Ulloa) to the treasury as symbols of economic rectitude, the regime had lost all credibility by 1968; in October of that year the military high command staged another *golpe de estado*.

The new military junta was headed by the Chief of Staff, General Juan Velasco; it was again an institutional one in that it represented the high command as a whole, which entered government broadly in order of seniority and represented all three services – despite the fact that active support for the *golpe* itself came from a group of relatively junior army officers.[12] The initial political legitimacy claimed by the *Gobierno Revolucionario de la Fuerza Armada*, as it called itself, was undoubtedly based upon the failure of the previous civilian administration to cope with the 'structural crisis'[13] presented not just by the breakdown of government but by rather deeper problems presented by external dependency, maldistribution of income and economic underdevelopment. A 'strong state' and considerable structural reforms were immediately promised, but only when a document claiming to be the original pre-coup strategy (the 'Plan Inca')[14] was released in 1974 was the regime's programme finally made explicit. The first major action of the military government was to expropriate the Talara oilfields held by IPC; a radical land reform programme was started in 1969, and the following six years saw a wave of ownership reforms affecting mining, fishing, heavy industry, banking and communications – a process culminated by the initiation of a system of worker participation throughout the economy in 1975. The progressive element in the military which had failed to gain power in the 1962–63 junta had clearly succeeded in doing so now, and the new government appeared to meet little or no resistance to its programme. The state emerged as the central element in the economic and political spheres, and ambitious attempts were made to generate working-class and peasant support for the military regime through the *Sistema Nacional de Apoyo a la Movilización Social*[15] – a combination of populist party, education programme and public works schemes.

The ideology of the regime between 1968 and 1975 consisted in the claim to be creating a system that would be '*ni comunista ni capitalista*' and would involve the population in decision making through cooperative enterprise, combined with strident anti-imperialism and attacks on the 'oligarchy'; above all, it was claimed that the class conflict could be overcome by somehow dissolving the difference between capital and labour via worker participation in ownership and by state control over the basis of the production system.[16] In addition, the SNA and SNI were dissolved and an attempt made to 'by-pass' the existing unions by the establishment of the *Confederación Nacional Agraria* and the *Confederación de Trabajadores de la Revolución Peruana*. To the evident surprise of the military – despite the land reform, the prospect of worker participation in industry, the undoubted reduction of foreign influence, the virtual elimination of the old 'oligarchy' as a political force and the revolutionary rhetoric of the government itself – there was very little popular response. This was partly due to refusal to allow decisions to slip from the military grasp, but by 1974 the workers' organizations were facing up to the fact that labour relations in state enterprise were little different from those in the private sector, while the limits on the proportion of the peasantry to be benefited by the land reform became clear and resulted in renewed rural unrest. Meanwhile, the continued pressure from foreign capital and the US State Department – which had been successfully resisted until 1973 – forced a compromise in order to finance the new oil and copper projects and subsequently in order to raise enough funds to cover the growing fiscal and external deficits generated by the massive state investment programmes designed to restore capitalist accumulation.

The deteriorating economic situation in 1975, food riots, worsening labour relations and business resistance to the implications of further ownership reforms gave rise to a split within the military – both within the army and more importantly between the army and the navy – and General Velasco (in deteriorating health) was forced to resign in favour of General Morales Bermudez, the Chief of Staff. Although some attempt was made to continue the rhetoric,[17] it soon became clear that the government was neither prepared nor able to '*profundizar la revolución*', and the 'second phase' was characterized by desperate attempts to stabilize the economy by wage control as the balance of payments deteriorated and inflation rose. Although the ownership reforms were not significantly reversed, a halt was called to further reforms by 1976. In 1977, the *Banco Central de Reserva* (representing financial interests) had regained control of economic policy and introduced a stabilization programme with IMF support based mainly on real wage cuts.

Industrialists were supporting the regime after eight years of vituperation; but the trades unions had organized the first general strike and the leaders of the CNA, CTRP and radical army officers had founded the *Partido Socialista Revolucionario*. By 1978 'ambiguous revolution'[18] had apparently come to a close, and the military permitted the election of an '*asamblea constituyente*' in June of that year in order to draw up a new constitution to replace that of 1933 and provide the basis for a transition to civilian rule by 1980; the date by which the '*Plan Tupac Amaru*' of 1977 had promised that the military would return to the *cuartel*, to be replaced by a '*Democracia Social de Participación Plena*'. The decision to go back to barracks appears to have been the result of the effect of the economic crisis upon the public standing of the armed forces, a debilitation which was reducing cohesion within the military command; given the likelihood of an electoral victory by a reassuringly conservative and disciplined APRA, the traditional antagonism was overcome in favour of maintaining the unity of the *institución castrense*. 'Face' could be saved by drawing up a new constitution which institutionalized the main reforms carried out between 1968 and 1975. The balance of power in the assembly represented just how much, and how little, had changed since 1968: the APRA gained just over a third of the seats (about their support in 1963), various conservative groups such as the Christian Democrats another third, and – most significantly – assorted socialist parties gained just under a third of the total. The rise of the left and the decline of the right during a decade of reforms was evident, but the APRA held the balance of power once again.

The Peruvian class structure

The Peruvian class structure has developed to the extent that capitalism has developed in Peru; it reflects the consequences of the limited scope of capitalist relations of production within a capitalist mode of production in general, and the consequences of the subordination of local to international capital[19] in particular. At this point in our argument we shall examine the modern Peruvian class structure in a more or less static fashion (a 'cross-section', so to speak) and turn to a dynamic analysis of class articulation as a subsequent step. For our purposes, we may distinguish[20] the following three groups as they existed in 1956: the bourgeoisie, differentiating between the traditional grand bourgeoisie and the industrialist fraction; the middle classes, including the military professionals and administrators as well as the 'petty bourgeoisie'; and the working classes, comprising the peasantry, urban and rural proletariat and the 'lumpenproletariat' of the slums.

A central theme in most analyses of Peruvian society is the nature of the *'oligarquía'*, or grand bourgeoisie, that dominated the economy for at least a century after independence. This relatively small group[21] was effectively composed of the owners of capital on any significant scale, and thus dominated domestic private enterprise. This in itself did not confer complete control over the means of production, due to the existence of powerful foreign enterprises on the one hand and petty commodity producers on the other. However, this latter group of artisans and peasants was relatively unimportant in the Peruvian economy,[22] while (until the mid 1950s at least) the grand bourgeoisie dominated the state even though foreign corporations controlled major sections of mining, manufacturing and finance.[23] Although far from being an aristocracy in the sense of hereditary succession, since many of the family fortunes were of comparatively recent origin, the *oligarquía* did form a tightly-knit system: a few family groups each covered many production branches (such as export agriculture, real estate, manufacturing and fishing) and centred on finance – indeed the 'presidential' Prado and Belaunde families formed two such groups.[24] Throughout the history of republican Peru, foreign corporations had enjoyed a close relationship with the grand bourgeoisie, who were admitted as 'junior partners' to new ventures such as mining and from whom existing activities such as banking were purchased; in no sense was there conflict between the two, but rather an accommodation of mutual benefit. However, as the weight of the economy shifted away from mining and agriculture towards mining and manufacturing after the second World War, the balance of power began to shift away from the grand bourgeoisie and towards the multinationals. This subordination has led some writers[25] to suggest that the *oligarquía* did not really form a distinct class at all, but was merely an agent for foreign capital. In addition, the highland landowners and

Arequipa traders still formed separate fractions of the bourgeoisie in conflict with the dominant group at national level; the emergence of separate industrial and real estate interests in the post-war period, further weakening the hegemonic control of the oligarchy.

An independent element in the bourgeoisie had begun to emerge as a distinct fraction of capital by the 1950s. The role of these industrialists as the potentially hegemonic fraction in a national bourgeoisie is central to the analysis of the modernization of capitalism on the periphery, and is recognized as such by a number of writers on Peru,[26] although in sociological analyses there has been a tendency to overestimate the economic strength of this group. Given the dominance of multinationals and the large finance-capital groups,[27] independent industrialists were in a pronounced minority in economic terms in the 1960s. Nonetheless, in combination with management employees and with support from those multinationals located in the manufacturing sector, this group did become a fraction with interests distinct from, and in many cases in conflict with, those of the grand bourgeoisie. In particular, they pressed for protection rather than free-trade policies, agrarian reform in order to open up rural markets, and the reduction of the power of the *oligarquía* over the state so that modern industrial capitalism might become the dominant economic formation.

Nonetheless, there seems to be a strong case for arguing that a *national* bourgeoisie (in the sense of a capitalist class committed to the expansion of domestic capitalism in general and autonomous industrialization in particular) did not exist in Peru before 1968. Indeed, there is no reason why it should have developed, given the advantages to the domestic elite of continuing the export-led model in partnership with foreign capital and its considerable flexibility in penetrating new production branches such as manufacturing and fishing.

The petty bourgeoisie is often considered to be 'transitional' between the capitalist and proletarian classes, merging into one or the other as monopoly capital expands, but under the dualism peculiar to developing economies it seems to have a considerable capacity for survival. This is clearly true in the case of Peru,[28] where a petty bourgeoisie consisting of small farmers, artisans and shopkeepers combined with 'traditional' middle-class elements such

as doctors and lawyers on the one hand and a 'new' group made up
of elements such as managers, bureaucrats, engineers and architects
on the other. Despite the relative unimportance of a small-farmer
stratum (as distinct from the peasantry), the petty bourgeoisie
flourished in the large tertiary sector generated by rapid urbanization without parallel growth of proletarian employment, while the
'new' fraction of the middle class experienced a natural growth with
the modernization of the economy and the professionalization of
both private management and public administration. Some middle-
class elements such as teachers and bank employees did form trades
unions and became in effect proletarians, while others such as the
fishing entrepreneurs became considerable capitalists; as a whole,
however, the middle classes represented an independent group
which, although clearly committed to the continuance of capitalism
as a social formation and opposed to a rise of working-class power,
did have a structural interest distinct from the *oligarquía* to the extent
that it benefited from industrialization more than from the
traditional export-led economy. White-collar employment
expanded from 269,000 in 1950 to 662,000 in 1972;[29] Webb takes
private car ownership as an upper bound of 'middle-class size', estimating this at about 50,000 in 1961, the corresponding figure for
1970 being 150,000.[30] Whatever the relevance of these figures, it is
clear that this class was far from being a large one.

However, the politically most important fraction of the middle
class, and the one which generates considerable analytical problems
as to its place in the relations of capitalist production, is the military.
The Peruvian military[31] had a somewhat undistinguished record of
international warfare, and most of its activity in this century had
been the maintenance of internal security. This control of popular
movements (the APRA before 1956 and highland peasant uprisings
in the subsequent decade) was mainly the concern of the army, the
officer corps of which was predominantly drawn from the rural petty
bourgeoisie in contrast to the navy and airforce, which had virtually
no practical function but in virtue of their superior urban extraction
tended to be more closely allied with the grand bourgeoisie. The
long experience of acting as a police force for the domestic elite,
taking over government from time to time as the agent of the dominant class but only involving senior officers in the presidency and

cabinet of an otherwise civilian administration, appears to have led to an internal reaction within the senior army officer corps at a level just below the top during the 1950s. Three major developments took place at or about this time: first, the eventual *convivencia* between the APRA and the Prado administration finally ended the revolutionary threat of the former but apparently reduced the political standing of the latter in the eyes of the military; second, the failure of the ruling elite to resolve the problems of land tenure and foreign penetration that were leading to popular discontent reduced the standing of its social strategy in the military mind;[32] and third, the establishment of the *Centro de Altos Estudios Militares* in 1951[33] as a centre for the training of senior military officers in the theory and practice of 'total security' (covering economics, sociology and politics as well as security as such) gave the military confidence in their own capacity to analyse the Peruvian *problematica*, and a strong belief in the need for central planning and industrialization. These attitudes were strengthened by the brief experience of military government in 1962–63 and the failures of the Belaunde regime which the military had supported. However, these factors do not explain the ease with which the military *as an institution* took over the state in 1968, or the nature of the reforms that they enacted after that date, above all in view of the similar problems faced and training received by the military in other countries (such as Brazil and Ecuador) which resulted in quite different regimes. To answer this question we must turn to an analysis of the changes in Peruvian society as a whole during our period.

The working classes make up well over three quarters of the workforce in Peru. Here we shall consider the rural and urban fractions separately, although the internal migration process connects them closely and effectively converts the former into the latter. The rural workforce (almost entirely of Indian origin) accounted for about sixty per cent of the economically active population in 1950, and still for forty-five per cent in 1972; this in turn was divided between the rural proletariat employed permanently on the large estates on the one hand and the peasantry working their own land but often engaging in seasonal wage employment on the other.[34] There still existed elements of feudal production relationships on the highland estates (such as payment in kind and labour services in return for cultivation rights) before the agrarian reform, and some peasants are still engaged in isolated subsistence production in the remote Andes or depths of the Amazon jungle, but by our period most of the rural population was encompassed within the market system as wage workers or petty commodity producers – often combining the two. The difference between permanent estate workers, who sold their labour directly for wages, and the peasants who sold it indirectly by marketing their output, lay in the integration of the former into capitalist *relations* of production and the inclusion of the latter in *circulation* alone. As we shall see, the former group, which included about a quarter of the rural workforce, experienced a radical change in their status and production relations as a result of the agrarian reform, while the latter continued in conditions of extreme poverty and exploitation through 'unequal exchange' throughout our period. The position of the rural workforce is the result of the 'dualism' discussed in Chapter 2, where the incomplete extension of capitalist production relations (i.e. proletarianization) within a market economy creates a severe structural imbalance. Indeed, although proletarianization of the coastal peasantry was far advanced by 1960, the process had suffered considerable reverses in the sierra; in fact the highland hacienda system was in decline, crumbling under the combination of poor prices and peasant invasions and exacerbated by consequent decapitalization by the landlords.[35] Nonetheless, rural society and politics (i.e. almost the whole of Peru outside Lima) was still dominated by the large landowners (known as *gamonales*) in the 1950s; they ruthlessly suppressed attempts at peasant organization, while the stranglehold of the APRA effectively depoliticized estate workers' unions under the *convivencia*.

The urban working classes are often regarded as being centred upon the industrial proletariat, but in Peru as in so many other Latinamerican countries the capital-intensive nature of industrialization and the importance of mining mean that this group is relatively small. If we take employment in an enterprise of more than five workers as a minimal definition of proletarian status,[36] then although all mining labour was proletarianized by 1960, only about a third of those in the manufacturing sector, and possibly as little as a quarter of the urban working classes as a whole enjoyed this status – the rest falling into the residual category of 'lumpen-proletariat'. Thus, even though the absolute size of the proletariat has risen, as has its share of the national workforce, internal migration limited its share of the urban workforce. The trades union movement has a long history in Peru, with a flourishing anarchist element at the turn of the century and important nuclei in mining and the textile industry, but these were absorbed and effectively neutralized by the APRA in the period between 1919 and 1933.[37] Once the APRA had failed to take power directly after several attempts between 1933 and 1948, its power base in the unions weakened steadily, to be effectively eliminated as a dynamic force by the compromises for the 1956 election, although its influence in organizational terms was to continue for a further decade. Meanwhile, the communist party, despite its illustrious ante-cendents[38] did not manage to gain much influence in the labour movement until in the 1960s class-based organizations reappeared after an interval of forty years. However, the limited extent of the proletariat, the existence of a vast reserve army in the urban slums, antiquated labour legislation, official suppression of communists and the deadening influence of the APRA combined to deprive the trades unions of any political influence until well into the 1970s. Their activity was effectively confined to wage claims and, in the case of the primary sector, to pressure for the nationalization of their respective enterprises.

The process of unbalanced economic growth over the previous century, which had been concentrated on export sectors and urban activities which provided relatively few stable jobs, combined with a high population growth rate and stagnating peasant agriculture, naturally led to a massive population inflow to the towns.[39] Most of these people ended up in small-scale activities such as artisans, clothing, shops, household service, petty street trading, minor construction projects and so on. These are clearly part of the market system, but the workers do not really experience capitalist relations of production – indeed in many cases these are family enterprises, very similar to peasant organization – and are included only through relations of exchange. Such workers do drift in and out of employment in capitalist enterprise (particularly since these often operate a deliberate policy of rapid labour turnover) so that an individual possibly cannot be classified as *either* proletarian *or* as a member of the lumpen[40] even though the two classes are perfectly distinguishable in principle. The consequence in terms of political activity is that there is considerable difficulty in mobilizing such a 'lumpenproletarian' group, atomized and shifting as their labour process is. In fact only the APRA had any political success in the Lima *barriadas* before 1968, on the basis of response to specific local grievances such as demands for urban infrastructure, a channel which SINAMOS used with some effect under the Velasco administration.

In sum, the class structure of Peru reflected the particular pattern of capitalist expansion on the periphery of the world economy: a dependent bourgeoisie relying on foreign capital to provide the dynamic of accumulation; a proletariat limited in size and power by the capital-intensive nature of corporate production; and a large residual workforce integrated to the mode but not the relations of capitalist production. The class structure was, then 'under-developed' in much the same way that the economy itself was. In contrast, the Peruvian class structure of fifty years ago might well be described as relatively advanced by the Latinamerican standards of the time, because the financial and mining fractions of the bourgeoisie had already overcome the landlord elements and a strong populist movement was beginning to emerge.[41] But in the interim the power of the grand bourgeoisie had been weakened by the effects of their partnership with foreign capital while neither an independent and powerful industrial group nor a strong labour movement had emerged – in contrast to the cases of say, Brazil or Mexico.[42]

The changing political balance 1956–78

The underlying problem in Peruvian political development between 1956 and 1978 was the establishment of a strong government capable of restructuring capital so that Peru could make the transition from a traditional primary export economy to a modern industrial one. This problem was related to the class struggle in its widest sense, for the need to control labour is fundamental to the nature of a capitalist state, but in immediate political terms it was related more closely to the difficulty of establishing a state both powerful enough and with sufficient relative autonomy from the different fractions of capital to carry through the necessary reforms and establish a new model of accumulation. In other words, a state with not only the freedom provided by a balance of class forces but also the internal cohesion to press forward with its own project was needed. The political changes during our period clearly reflect this problem; the failure to restructure capital in a new and efficient pattern was derived in part from the failure to construct a new political order while the stresses placed by economic disequilibria upon successive governments – disequilibria that would have been removed by a more successful restructuring of capital – contributed to their political weakness.

The political decline of the traditional 'oligarchy' was signalled by the need to form an alliance with the APRA for the 1956 elections. To rely upon the *convivencia* instead of the military as the instrument for ensuring hegemony was not a decision based upon any inherent belief in democracy as such (although this was certainly an important factor in the legitimization of the Prado regime) and still less on any increased support for the APRA, rather it was the result of the declining commitment of the APRA leadership to economic and social reform (and a willingness to reduce this still further in exchange for access to power) and more significantly still, of the split that had occurred between the army and the civilian elite. The previous 'instrumental' intervention of the armed forces on behalf of the oligarchy had been the overthrow of Bustamante as recently as 1948, but the subsequent Odría administration had alienated civilian support by demonstrating the capacity of the military to act alone as a government – although they evidently did not at this stage possess a specific project to be carried through. The 1956 elections did, however, see the emergence of a 'middle class party', Belaunde's *Acción Popular*, with a reform project but an insufficiently wide political base to achieve power. The project, which involved extensive state expenditure on welfare, tariff protection for industry and the conversion of 'feudal' agriculture to modern farming, represented the interests of the emerging urban middle class in Lima and Arequipa but this was a class without either the direct involvement in the relations of production or the mass voting strength necessary to dominate the state. At the outset of our period, then, we already see the balance of class forces that was to underlie the political scene for the next two decades: no one group in civil society – whether oligarchy, APRA, middle class or popular forces – was able to dominate the political system while the army had no political base outside its own ranks, but seemed unwilling to explicitly ally itself with any one political group.

In the event, the *convivencia* did not provide the political base that Prado had anticipated because the APRA regarded the alliance as merely a tactical one in preparation for the 1962 elections and the economic policies pursued – particularly the open welcome to foreign investors and the repression of real wages during the 1958–59 stabilization programme – strengthened the nationalist and reformist position of the *Acción Popular*. In other words, the proposed restructuring of capital on the basis of low wages, foreign ownership of mining and industry and traditional land ownership was inconsistent with the balance of political power. The army was now unwilling to support this project, but it was not prepared to see the APRA win the 1962 elections either, for despite the growing conservatism of the APRA and the increasingly progressive position of the army they were still historical opponents. Unlike 1948, the 1962 intervention, although supported by the oligarchy, was the action of the military as an independent group – equipped with their own project which, while not fully formed as yet, contained elements of land reform, nationalism and central planning as aspects of the concept of 'national security' developed at the CAEM and clearly inconsistent with the Prado project. However, the military junta still reflected the class struggle within its ranks in the form of a rift between conservative and radical elements; the over-riding need to maintain institutional cohesion of the armed forces meant – as it would again in 1978 – that the officers had to return to their *cuarteles*.

There seems to have been no question of attempting to restore a traditional elite government. The oligarchy had lost its hold over the political system – due more, as we have argued, to its own economic decline and capitulation to foreign capital than to any real threat from popular forces; if there was any political threat from below it was from the middle classes, rather than from organized labour or domestic industrialists. The lack of cohesion within the armed forces, not a lack of relative autonomy, had prevented the military from moving in with a new project in 1962–63; but by preventing APRA from winning the 1963 elections the junta effectively installed the civilian Belaunde administration[43] in order that it could undertake the reforms necessary to remove the obstacles to industrialization posed by traditional forms of land tenure, foreign control of natural resources and inadequate manufacturing infrastructure. This political arrangement was quickly revealed as unviable because the residual forces of populism and conservatism in combination were sufficient to block the reform programme in Congress; but meanwhile the military had gained a new confidence from both their own observation of this 'incapacity of civil society' and their own increased professionalism. The 1963–68 period also saw significant changes in the attitudes of civilian professional groups: a growing ideological commitment to *desarrollismo* ('developmentalism') and thus to planning; an eventual recognition of the need for land reform after the highland guerrilla campaign of 1965–66; and the strengthening of opposition to foreign control over sectors of the economy. All three of these were closely related to the rise of manufacturing industry, which generated a greater awareness not only of the potential of industrialization but also of the implications for the middle class of the obstacles to its continued expansion.

By 1968 the political position of the oligarchy had declined still further than in 1962 and nationalism had emerged as a significant force, but popular elements were still no stronger and the middle class party had proved its inability to govern; the military, in contrast, had now formulated a coherent and specific project. Ironically, as Jaguaribe points out,[44] the historical roles of the APRA and the military had been effectively reversed by 1968, the former becoming the force for modernization, nationalization and land reform and the latter the agent of conservatism. The combination of a political vacuum (which Poulantzas would term a 'crisis of hegemony') and a specific project made military intervention on a sustained and autonomous basis almost inevitable:

Their way was relatively unimpeded from the start. Peru's still relatively low level of prior social mobilization and participation, the weak and dependent nature of Lima's industrial bourgeoisie, the dwindling economic base of Peru's rural elite, and especially the general disrepute which civilian politicans had achieved: all left Peru's officers virtually unchallenged as they took over. The army was vociferously opposed only by the APRA, its traditional antagonist, and APRA – by 1968 mainly a party of old men and their memories – could easily be out-flanked, especially by the immediate nationalization of IPC, so long an issue in Peruvian politics, and then by the agrarian reform.[45]

The project effectively involved the emergence of the state itself as the centre of a new model of accumulation, burdened with all the tasks of economic and political organization concomitant upon such a role. 1968 appeared to the doyen of Peruvian political sociologists to be a crucial turning point in the development of Peru, the transition to modern industrial capitalism which the domestic bourgeoisie had not been able to effect in 1956:

> The Revolutionary Government of the Armed Forces, which came to power on October 3rd, 1968, has unquestionably closed one chapter of Peru's history and opened another. It has brought profound transformations in the economic, political and social life of Peru. Perhaps the central feature of these transformations has been the elimination of what had been in the twentieth century the most important centre of economic and political power in Peruvian society – the export oligarchy and the foreign economic interests with which this sector of the oligarchy had been closely associated. In place of this dependent-oligarchic mode of economic organization, the military government is moving toward the full development of modern capitalism in Peru in the form of a type of state capitalism which is closely linked to the multinational firms. . . . The elimination of the oligarchic-dependent structure goes hand in hand with expanding and strengthening the state, which, as a result of expropriations of national and foreign capital, has assumed a central role as an entrepreneur and promoter of economic activity. Peru's government has thus acquired an unprecedented capacity to accumulate capital and reach new agreements with international capitalism (in the form of multinational corporations), agreements which form the basis for the joint economic exploitation of the country. The attempt to homogenize Peruvian society likewise plays a central role in the government's attempt to form a modern, integrated nation-state. . . . The state, led by the military and by *tecnicos*, is thus carrying out the developmental tasks which in many early-developing countries of Latin America and Europe were performed by the bourgeoisie. In Peru, the bourgeoisie was, by contrast, too weak to carry out these tasks. Among the most important of the reasons for this weakness was the

preponderant role of foreign capital in Peruvian economic growth, which severely limited the development of the national bourgeoisie.[46]

The state was to be the centre of accumulation in the economy, constructing a new state enterprise sector on the basis of the nationalized export sector, heavy industry, banking, transportation networks and infrastructure coordinated through a national planning system. The new cooperative sector, based on the land reform (which would turn all but the smallest private farms into worker-managed enterprises) and the establishment of new *propiedad social* ('social property') firms in the light manufacturing and service sectors, would be coordinated through central state-controlled boards responsible for finance and marketing. The manufacturing sector was to be the spearhead of the industrialization drive, but it was nonetheless to be left to the private domestic industrialists who would be supported by guaranteed markets, import protection, subsidized inputs, cheap credit and fiscal incentives but subjected to worker participation in management and profits. This model emerged gradually over the 1969–75 period although the main outlines were clear as early as 1970. It amounted to state capitalism as a distinct variant on the capitalist mode of production: the coordination of state enterprise, cooperatives and large private firms from the centre, maintaining wage relations at the enterprise level but centralizing the accumulation of capital and production decisions – an image of socio-economic organization naturally preferred by the military.[47] This was to be complemented at the political level by SINAMOS, as a surrogate for a party system, taking advantage of the gratitude anticipated from the beneficiaries of the reforms. In this way, a new model of accumulation would be established: investment would be returned to high levels and shifted towards industry while income was redistributed towards labour in a planned economy.

In fact, most of these elements had been created and put into place between 1968 and 1975, but from the outset these were areas of considerable ambiguity that might be characterized as essential inconsistencies in the model even if there had been time to implement it fully. First, the reorganization of ownership and production affected only the corporate sector of the economy, and although this involved two thirds of production it left two thirds of the workforce outside the new system. In other words, the state capitalist model would maintain the dual structure of the economy and thus the impact of the reforms in terms of income redistribution was bound to be limited, while the long-run problem of wage goods supply (i.e. the peasantry) would remain unresolved. Second, although worker participation in the management of the private sector and *a fortiori* in the cooperatives was initiated, the relations with labour in the public enterprises would continue to be of a traditional kind. As the parastatal sector expanded, the class struggle would inevitably be 'internalized' within the state as workers came into direct conflict with the government; the political consequences of which were unlikely to be avoided by the efforts of SINAMOS to weaken the class-based unions. Third, the role assigned to domestic industrialists by the military was ambiguous in two crucial ways. On the one hand, it was supposed that the domestic industrialists were a dynamic group held back only by the enervating influence of the oligarchy and foreign firms.[48] However, most of manufacturing was directly controlled by the two latter groups, neither of which was likely to react positively to the new arrangements. On the other hand, the attempt to co-opt organized labour through worker participation via the *comunidad industrial* would inevitably weaken capitalists' support for the regime, as would the revolutionary rhetoric. Fourth, the centring of accumulation on the state sector would require not only a massive increase in public investment but also a concomitant mobilization of financial resources either by fiscal reform or by generating large enterprise surpluses, and would mean reducing the share of either profits or wages in national income, which would further antagonize capital or labour. Fifth, it was difficult to see how the strategic 'political' desire to reduce external dependence could be reconciled with the practical 'economic' need for foreign technology if rapid industrialization and renewal of the natural resource export base were to be achieved.

In the event, these inconsistencies emerged as crucial contradictions in the state capitalist model. First, the relatively limited scope of the reform in terms of income redistribution outside the corporate sector soon became apparent, and made the task of SINAMOS in mobilizing popular support almost impossible.[49] At the same time, the continued deprivation of resources from the peasantry led to a crisis in food supplies which in turn contributed to the decline in both working- *and* middle-class support after 1973. The initial popular support for the government[50] waned rapidly thereafter, partly because of the wage restraint that formed a central element in the economic stabilization policy of 1976–78 and partly because of the unrealized expectations generated by previous revolutionary rhetoric. In addition, the contrast between those in the new agrarian cooperatives and the seasonal labourers and between those in the industrial communities and the urban un-employed became a topic of public debate and criticism of the reforms; while the middle classes were alienated[51] by the expropria-tion of the national newspapers in 1974, the nationalist educational reforms in 1972 and the new benefits enjoyed by military personnel generally after 1968. Second, after an initial period of consternation at the rapid succession of reforms and the disorientation resulting from the radical rhetoric of SINAMOS, the trades unions began to regroup, particularly under the influence of the communist CGTP. More importantly, the workers in nationalized industries such as mining came to realize that state management would be little different from private management – a specific manifestation of the internalization of the class conflict within the state itself: the annual average of days lost through strike action rose from about one million in 1969–73 to over three million in 1974 and 1975.[52] General strikes followed in both 1976 and 1977. Third, private capital reacted against the new regime as soon as it became clear that the promised reforms would actually be implemented. In particular, the rate of manufacturing investment fell sharply to a level little above that needed for replacement, even though profitability rose steadily.[53] This reaction was exacerbated by the first steps to in-troduce worker participation in management and profits, and fear of the eventual implications of the growth of the social property sec-tor. However, foreign capital in other sectors adopted a more flexi-ble attitude, coming to terms with the military regime over the mineral projects and the financing of the public debt even before the economic crises allowed it to impose a policy more to its advantage in 1976. Fourth, the accumulation model established by the state was itself unstable, because no fiscal reform was carried out in order to finance the enormous increase in investment – the result being excessive borrowing abroad and inflationary budget deficits at home. Fifth, the major state projects themselves involved considerable multinational involvement in technology and finance and a commitment to a strategy based on mineral exports and equipment imports which in effect locked the Peruvian economy even more firmly into the world market system (albeit on better terms than previously) despite the strongly nationalist position taken by government representatives in international gatherings.

In sum, the inherent contradictions in the Peruvian state capitalist model, depending as it did for its eventual success on the cooperation both of private enterprise and of popular forces, became apparent as soon as its object (increased accumulation) as opposed to the prior arrangements (the ownership reforms) had to be implemented.

Among both Peruvian and foreign Marxists,[54] there has been a tendency to regard the Velasco regime as no more than the outward sign of a realignment of the power structure within the bourgeoisie; the arrangement of a new alliance between the industrialists and multinationals in place of the traditional one between the 'oligarchy' and the multinationals. Although it is true that this might turn out to be the long-run consequence, it grossly underestimates the initial autonomy of the state in the 1968–75 period, almost totally ignores the evident conflict between domestic capital and the state, and plays down the weakening hold of foreign enterprise. Although multinationals did not 'lose out' completely in the end, they certainly would have preferred Belaunde or Prado to Velasco and when the condition of the manufacturing multinationals (as opposed to those in mining or oil) is taken into account the benefits are even less clear. More importantly, this line of argument seems to exaggerate the strength of the industrialist group and by applying a crude model of the modernization process underestimates both the general consequences for the national bourgeoisie of the penetration of foreign capital and the specific circumstances of Peruvian industrial ownership that we have already noted. This argument is partly based, moreover, upon a misinterpretation of the implication of the Agrarian Reform Law and the Industrial Law: Quijano,[55] for example, argues that the provision for the use of landowner compensation bonds as collateral for industrial development loans is evidence that the agrarian reform was merely a scheme to allow landowners to turn themselves into in- dustrialists at the expense of the peasantry. The fact that the major landlords had moved much of their funds into urban real estate before 1968 (which is one of the reasons why land reform went so smoothly) and that only an insignificant proportion of the bonds were used as collateral after 1968 is ignored. On the contrary, the conversion of rural estates into cooperatives and the abolition of all private farming on any substantial scale clearly worked against agri- business interests. This is not to deny that the long-run consequence of land reform may well be to modernize the agricultural sector on an essentially capitalist basis, albeit a collectivized form of capitalism, but rather to assert that it required autonomous state in- tervention to bring this about.

Similarly, the generous provisons for private investors in the General Industrial Law of 1970 were combined with state control of heavy industry and finance, severe limits on foreign investments and provisions for worker participation in management – all of which were anathema to the private sector.[56] Indeed, private investment in manufacturing fell sharply and stayed at a minimum level from 1969 to 1976, hardly the response of an industrialist group behind a military government, and indeed very different from the reaction expected by the regime itself. A more subtle variation on a similar theme[57] is to suggest that, in a 'Bismarckian' fashion, the military were attempting by these provisions to *create* an industrialist class, but there is no direct evidence for this; the implication of govern- ment pronouncements was rather that they believed the group to exist already and that they were expecting it to come forward and in- vest. Although the view that the 'Peruvian Revolution' was essential- ly about the restructuring of capital and the acceleration of in- dustrialization is undoubtedly valid, to deduce from this that 'the coup was engineered by the nationalist industrial bourgeoisie and the multinational corporations'[58] is to grossly misinterpret Peruvian history.

The assumption of power by General Morales Bermudez in 1975 was made possible partly by the circumstances of Velasco's illness and Morales' legitimate position in the military hierarchy, but was mainly the result of political problems. Although the signs of economic crisis were already present, and were to require drastic action in 1976, they do not appear to have been the main reason for the change, which presaged the removal of key 'progressive' generals from power and a halt to any further '*profundización de la revolución peruana*'. This political shift reflected both the increasing strain within the military[59] – particularly between the army and the navy – over the response to be adopted to the pressing claims of organized labour on the one hand and the foreign bankers on the other, and the realization that the resolution of the inconsistencies in the state capitalist model would require further reforms beyond those already carried out on the basis of a consensus with the army. In the absence of widespread support in Peruvian society at large, and despite belated attempts to found an official party to replace the SINAMOS, the progressives proved powerless to resist the pressure of more conservative officers, who could now count upon the backing of foreign bankers in the 'second phase' of the revolution, which would involve no further reforms but rather the consolidation of the existing ones and the strengthening of the economy. The ease with which this change of direction was effected is attributed by Stepan[60] to the failure to 'institutionalize' the regime and establish the political hegemony which would have permitted not only its continuation but also the resolution of at least some of the inconsistencies of the new model.

The second phase was supposed to involve the consolidation of the first (i.e. 1968–75) phase, but the pressing need to cut domestic demand pressure in order to reduce the import bill, and the impossibility of doing this on the basis of reduced profit income under the new political circumstances, meant that large cuts in real wages were imposed in 1976 and 1977. These resulted in widespread labour mobilization, and revealed how much progress had been made by the left between 1968 and 1975, unobstructed either by restrictions on union activities or by the activities of an official party. Economic policy initiatives[61] between 1976 and 1978 dominated the political process, initiatives that were framed in reference to the requirements of the International Monetary Fund and the US banks. However, the Peruvian government refused to implement some measures (such as cuts in military expenditures), a reduction of the size of the bureaucracy proved politically impossible, and although worker participation arrangements were watered down, no major reforms were reversed. It became evident that the military could no longer govern: the conservatives (particularly the navy) did not have enough support either within the military or in civil society to impose a 'Chilean' solution, the progressives had lost their hold over the government but retained considerable support in the bureaucracy, and the existing coalition could not implement the stabilization programme. The resulting stress was threatening the institutional unity of the Peruvian armed forces and little was to be gained by staying in government, so that the best solution was to hand over to the civilians – with the added attraction that the promise of democracy would secure further refinancing of the external debt. Although it had been envisaged in 1977 by the *Plan Tupac Amaru* that such a transition would take place in 1982, when the reforms were to have introduced full worker participation and established a *'democracia social de participación plena'* based on corporativist rather than party principles, elections for the Constituent Assembly on the basis of the traditional parties – plus a new range of popular organizations on the left – were arranged in June 1978.

The result of these elections, with roughly a third of the votes going to the APRA, the middle-class parties and the left-wing respectively, demonstrated how far Peru had advanced politically since 1956. No one group had established hegemony – even the foreign bankers could not impose their policies; despite the fact that the traditional right seemed to have disappeared from the political scene and the left appeared as a major element, the 'power vacuum' which had existed since 1956, and into which the military had moved so confidently ten years before, was still there. In other words, the central political problem which Prado had tried to tackle with the *convivencia* – that of establishing political hegemony in order to underpin a new model of accumulation – remained unresolved. Nonetheless, the balance had shifted considerably, marking the emergence of the working class as a political force in its own right; the historical irony may turn out to be that the Peruvian army was midwife to this birth as well as undertaker to the oligarchy.

4

The structure of the Peruvian economy

The purpose of this chapter is to explore the structure of the Peruvian economy in sufficient detail to provide an adequate background to the analyses of ownership and accumulation that follow, and incidentally to illustrate the analytical model of the Latin-American economies that can be broadly defined as 'structuralist'.[1]

Our analysis starts with a discussion of the production process itself, based on the composition and growth of the gross domestic product. A picture common to the underdeveloped world emerges: declining agriculture, expanding but isolated industry and continued reliance for stimulus upon primary exports, while demand moves in cycles of rapid growth and sudden checks in response to conditions on international markets. The employment pattern, in contrast, shows little substantial change except for the internal migration of surplus labour from the countryside to the towns as it shifts from marginal agricultural activity to similarly unproductive urban services. An examination of external trade patterns reveals the problems of continued integration into the world capitalist system: exposure to fluctuating international prices for primary exports, mainly produced by multinational firms, was not reduced by the process of import-substituting industrialization – indeed the trend towards mono-production (copper) on the one hand, and reliance on imported industrial inputs on the other, led to a rigidity in the balance of payments that proved difficult to resolve (despite direct state control of external trade and finance after 1968) and made stabilization through demand restraint progressively more difficult. These characteristics of output, employment and external trade lead us naturally into an examination of the dual structure of the economy as a whole; here we shall estimate the size of the modern corporate sector in terms of both output and employment and attempt to adduce their trends over time.

The argument of this chapter is that the structure of production, employment and trade is both dual and dependent, as the result of a long historical process[2] which has established a system which in any one period sustains a particular structure of poverty and accumulation – even though it is the result of their cumulative effect in the past – and places limits upon the potential of changes in ownership and investment to overcome dependent dualism in the short run.

The pattern of output

The central feature of the Peruvian output pattern is its dualism. The export sectors (mining, fishmeal and industrial crops) provide the underlying dynamic of the corporate economy[3] in terms both of demand factors at an aggregate level and of the surplus generated for reinvestment in other sectors; these effects are subsumed in the key role of supplying foreign exchange to what is by any standards an extremely 'open' economy. Within the economy itself the main sectors of manufacturing, construction and government make up the dynamic elements, with the support of branches such as finance and commerce. Most of this activity is organized in large production units[4] of considerable capital intensity, low labour requirements and high technology input which make up the corporate sector. In contrast, food agriculture, artisan industry, small commerce and petty services are to a substantial extent separate from this dynamic core in terms of production relationships, although not, of course, in those of exchange. In the case of food agriculture, an independent albeit weak dynamic does exist, but the other components of the non-corporate sector react mainly to the expenditure on personal services by the workforce in the corporate sector.

A parallel feature of the output pattern, and itself part of the same dependent dualism, is the pattern of demand – a central element in a market economy. First, international markets for export products are dominated by the input requirements of the metropolitan economies, which means that expansion of mining production has

always been easier than attempts to export manufactures, particularly if foreign investors are involved. Second, internal consumption demand is highly concentrated in a double sense, both
'vertically' in terms of the concentration of expenditure in the
highest income strata, and 'horizontally' in terms of its concentration on the coast and on Lima in particular.[5] The consequences of
this concentration of demand, itself a result of the effect of the concentration of production in generating a limited wage bill but a
large amount of consumption out of profits and centring of well-
paid employment on the capital, are multiple; the location of
manufacturing plant and the spatial allocation of the workforce are
immediate consequences, but in the present context the most important effect is to sustain a particular style of consumption which
relies for its satisfaction upon the use of foreign technology,
'modern' goods (such as cars and televisions) and imported brand
names.[6] This in its turn has generated, particularly since the Second
World War, a certain justification for the presence of multinational
corporations as a supplier of these products, just as traditionally it
has been considered necessary for foreign companies to exploit
natural resources as a means by which Peru could gain access to
production technology, overseas markets and advanced finance.

Within this model of economic growth, Peru has experienced
considerable change in the pattern of output over the past quarter-
century. Perhaps the most striking of these has been the secular
decline in agricultural activities in relation to the rest of the
economy and the rising share of manufacturing. On a less dramatic
scale, we can observe the rise and fall of the relative importance of
mining, with a similar pattern at a slightly later date for
fishing – both of which phenomena are of central significance for
the export pattern. Moreover, if we take the period 1950–75 as a
whole, and aggregate the branches into the conventional three,[7] we
find that an interesting complementarity emerges: the primary sector declined steadily from 28 per cent of GDP in 1950 to 19 per cent
in 1975, while the secondary sector rose from 24 per cent to 33 per
cent between the same two years, so that the tertiary sector remained
at more or less the same share. In some crude sense (which we shall
refine further on) this can be seen as a 'development' in the pattern
of output, with the replacement of agriculture by manufacturing as

the largest single productive sector being of some moment.

These changes in the output pattern reflect a period of unbalanced growth that has itself experienced three important cycles in the period under consideration:[8] a rapid expansion during 1950–57, followed by a balance of payments crisis and deflation in 1958–59; a similar pattern of rapid growth in 1960–65, with the crisis in 1966–67; and finally renewed expansion in 1968–75 with disequilibrium again in 1976–78. Each of these cycles is characterized

Table 4.1. *Composition and growth of gross domestic product in Peru 1950–75*

Sectoral composition	1950	1955	1960	1965	1970	1975
Agriculture	20.4	19.3	18.5	15.3	15.1	12.7
Fishing	0.4	0.6	1.4	2.1	2.7	0.7
Mining	6.8	7.5	10.4	8.5	8.2	6.0
Manufacturing	16.7	18.0	20.0	22.2	23.8	26.2
Construction	6.3	7.5	5.0	5.2	4.2	6.1
Utilities	0.6	0.6	0.8	1.0	1.1	1.1
Government	9.1	8.2	8.0	8.3	8.0	7.7
Finance	2.3	2.6	2.8	3.0	3.2	5.5
Transport	3.9	4.6	4.3	4.5	6.0	3.5
Commerce	11.4	11.1	12.1	15.1	13.2	15.0
Services	22.1	20.0	16.7	14.8	14.5	15.5
Total GDP	100.0	100.0	100.0	100.0	100.0	100.0

Sectoral growth rates	1955–60	1960–65	1965–70	1970–75	1975–78
Agriculture	3.6	2.7	4.0	1.8	1.2
Fishing	25.5	15.9	10.4	−18.8	5.7
Mining	11.4	2.4	3.8	−1.1	17.8
Primary	6.6	3.4	4.5	−0.6	6.9
Manufacturing	6.7	8.9	5.9	7.1	−2.3
Construction	−3.7	7.7	−0.3	13.7	−5.5
Utilities	13.8	9.7	6.7	6.6	3.5
Secondary	4.3	8.7	4.8	8.4	−2.6
Tertiary	3.3	7.6	4.0	6.3	2.4
Total GDP	4.5	6.7	4.4	5.5	−0.1

Sources: BCR *Cuentas* Table 8 (various years). 1950, 1955 figures at 1963 prices, 'finance, transport, commerce' being pro-rata from Table 4 *op. cit.* and 'services' the remainder; 1960–75 figures at 1970 prices, from BCR *Memoria 1975*; 1975–78 figures from BCR directly, also at 1970 prices.

by the interplay of the dynamic of the export sector against the internal expansion of the economy: as Table 4.1 indicates, the upswing in secondary activities (particularly manufacturing and construction) lagged behind the expansion of primary activities (and thus exports) in response to the increased demand and availability of investment funds from the latter and supported by public expenditure; in each case this happened just as primary output was decelerating, creating thereby massive disequilibria throughout the economy. It should also be noted that the three points of major economic disequilibrium were also those of political crisis as well (the collapse of oligarchic hegemony at the end of the 1950s, the fall of Belaunde in 1968 and the 'realignment' of the Revolution in 1976–77), although we should not infer a simple causality in these events, because they had as much to do with world market conditions as internal ones, these crises certainly did influence political events by heightening class conflict.

We may now turn to the major production sectors in somewhat more detail, although we shall restrict our treatment of them to the minimum required to sustain the main arguments of this study.[9]

The fertile land endowment of Peru is poor despite its vast area – an arid coast (Costa), infertile highlands (Sierra) and tropical jungle (Selva). The area of arable land has been extended during the past century by extremely costly irrigation works on the coast and by improved trans-Andean roads, but the marginal cost of such increases had become extremely high by our period;[10] the considerable increase between 1950 and 1975 still only represents a third of the arable land that might be created if adequate infrastructure works were provided. Although only a third of the arable land was on the coast, this was mainly devoted to industrial crops such as sugar and cotton, which provided roughly a half of agricultural output during our period, despite the fact that most of the increase in total arable land was allocated to foodcrops under successive government attempts to resolve the perennial shortages of food supply to Lima. Moreover, the extension of arable land only just kept pace with the population, maintaining a ratio of one fifth of a hectare (one tenth under foodcrops) per head of population: this did little to promote national self-sufficiency in food or resolve the root cause of rural poverty.

Agriculture in Peru[11] can be conveniently divided into two parts: irrigated coastal production of industrial and commercial food crops on the one hand, and highland production of livestock and subsistence foodstuffs on the other. Most coastal production was organized in large units which had been steadily mechanized and become almost 'industrial' enterprises, while the Sierra farms were mainly either large estates dedicated to livestock at a relatively low

Table 4.2. *Land use in Peru (million hectares)*

	Potential arable	Pasture etc.	Forest etc.	Unusable	Total land
All land:					
Costa	3.6	2.1	0.8	7.2	13.6
Sierra	1.9	8.6	4.0	23.5	38.0
Selva	5.5	22.1	30.9	17.9	76.0
	11.0	32.8	35.7	48.6	128.0
	1951–55	1960–64	1970	1975	
Actual arable:					
Costa	0.47	0.65	0.79	0.93	
Sierra	0.98	1.07	1.19	1.26	
Selva	0.16	0.34	0.42	0.52	
	1.60	2.06	2.40	2.71	
Foodcrops	1.04	1.22	1.44	1.61	
Industrial	0.25	0.34	0.35	0.38	
Other	0.31	0.51	0.61	0.72	

Source: Ministerio de Agricultura–OSPA, as reported in ILO (1976)

technological level, or small-scale peasant farmers producing food-crops – much of which were retained for their own consumption. While a steadily higher proportion of industrial crop output was absorbed into domestic industry, thereby reducing its export potential, the slow growth in food output (about 2 per cent per annum against the inexorable expansion of basic demand at between 4 and 5 per cent per annum generated by population and income growth[12] over the past quarter-century) led to an increasing shortfall, to be met from imports and only countered by constraining the standard of living of the poorer strata of the urban population. The stagnation of Peruvian agriculture, itself the consequence of unbalanced capitalist expansion concentrating on mining and manufacturing, was a major source of rural poverty, inadequate urban nutrition levels and balance of payments disequilibrium. The rapid expansion of export crops in 1950 was based on sugar and cotton irrigation on the coast, but this was not sustained in subsequent years; indeed much of the increased output of foodcrops in the mid 1960s was based on the shift of cotton land on the coast to food for Lima as international prices declined – a 'once and for all' phenomenon. Moreover, the growth in livestock output was in fact mostly the result of establishing intensive chicken rearing units on the outskirts of Lima in later years – 'fowls' having risen from a quarter of livestock production in 1963 to two thirds in 1975. In other words, even the modest agricultural growth record was a highly localized phenomenon.

The major problem in Peruvian agriculture has always been held to be the system of land tenure – a topic which we shall return to in the next chapter – but also implicit in the capitalist growth path has been the concentration of interest on coastal industrial crops and a consequent dearth of irrigation, transport, marketing infrastructure, credit, seeds and technical assistance in the Sierra, especially for the peasant enterprise. This, combined with the scarcity of arable land, the high population pressure and the unfavourable internal terms of trade, left little or no room for accumulation or even the use of modern inputs in the peasant sectors which were mainly responsible for food production. Indeed, the FAO estimates that a third of Peruvian food needs were imported by the 1970s.[13] On the consumption side, the stagnation in food output (meat output was localized and purchases confined to upper income groups) implies not only a lack of growth in peasant incomes but also in the real income levels of the urban poor, for without a deteriorating income distribution the growth of 'basic demand' we have calculated would have led to far greater food shortages than did in fact occur. The land reform of 1969, because it did not involve the breaking up of these large units or special support for small farmers, did not depress agricultural output – but nor did it accelerate it either.

Mining has always been an important element in the Peruvian economy, although more as a supplier of foreign exchange than as an employer or creator of value added; despite the presence of small and medium operators, the sector is dominated by the large enterprises known as the '*gran mineria*'. One of these four large mines (Cerro de Pasco) had been in operation with a wide range of metals (including copper, lead and silver) since the early part of the century, but the other three were of relatively recent creation. Two of them were opened in the 1950s – the iron ore operation at Nazca (initially for export but increasingly absorbed by national steel production) and the major open cast copper deposits at Toquepala – and the third, opencast copper mine at Cuajone, only entered production in

Table 4.3. *Agricultural production 1950–75*

	1950	1960	1967	1970	1975
Output (bn soles at 1963 prices)					
Export/industrial crops	1.48	5.64	5.05	5.06	5.42
Foodcrops	3.82	3.81	5.87	6.31	5.90
Livestock	0.93	1.78	2.25	2.42	4.50
Total	6.72	12.56	13.17	13.78	15.81
	1951–55	1955–60	1961–65	1966–70	1971–75
Output/head of popu-lation (1946–50 = 100)					
Foodcrops	108	87	99	102	97
Livestock	149	168	192	208	262
Both	115	101	115	120	125

Source: Ministry of Agriculture (Sectoral Planning Office).

1976. Between them, the first three mines accounted for approximately three quarters of mining output by value in our period; we shall return to them in the context of trade, ownership and accumulation in subsequent chapters. However, it is worth pointing out that while the net composition of mining production had been remarkably diversified in the past, over the last two decades it became increasingly concentrated on one product – copper – with attendant problems in terms of exposure to international market instability. Moreover, the difficulty of identifying new mineral deposits with locations and grades suitable for economic operation (that at Cerro Verde which started production under Mineroperu in 1977 being the last of a list already known for half a century) makes the long-term future of mining in Peru very uncertain. Oil from the fields on the northern coast had been an important branch of the export economy in the first third of the present century, but had declined in relative importance until by our period supply was just about enough for domestic requirements, and almost entirely controlled by one foreign corporation, the International Petroleum Company. After 1968, vast exploration efforts were made at great cost in the Amazon basin, but (as we shall see) did little more than secure domestic supply for the future – although given the subsequent increase in international oil prices this was in itself a considerable achievement in terms of import saving if not in export generation.

Fishing for domestic consumption purposes had been an artisan activity in Peru since time immemorial, but the expansion of intensive livestock rearing in Europe after the Second World War led to a sudden boom in the exploitation of Pacific anchovy for processing to fishmeal and fish oil, based on an industry already expanding to meet the US demand for tinned fish – especially tunny. The extremely rapid growth of the sector[14] – Peru accounted for 40 per cent of world production and 54 per cent of world exports by 1967 – led to the establishment of industrial centres on the coast and even to an incipient shipbuilding industry as well as a massive increase in export income in the early 1960s. However, the sector remained unregulated by any serious conservation measures or control over productive capacity so that by the end of that decade, barely ten years after the boom had got under way, it was already almost over and the industry in a state of crisis. The constant commercial pressures to exceed the ecologically tolerable offtake of around eight million tons of anchovy a year (catches reached 7 million tons in 1965 and almost 12 million tons in 1970) had depleted the resource base to near the non-reproductive point and available fleet and processing capacity was double this level at the end of the decade. In addition, there appears to have occurred an ecological change in the Pacific ocean currents off the coast of Peru in the early 1970s, which resulted in the accessible anchovy shoals being sharply reduced. Despite the reorganization of the sector after 1973, when the entire industry was taken over by the state and a start was made on scaling down the whole sector to a small and efficient operation processing around five million tons a year, the resource problem could not be

Table 4.4. *Mining and fishing production 1950–77*

	1955	1960	1965	1970	1975	1977
Copper ('000 tons)	43	184	175	218	171	344
Iron (m. tons)	2.91	5.23	7.11	9.71	7.75	7.00
Silver ('000 tons)	0.62	1.02	1.13	1.22	1.17	1.21
Zinc ('000 tons)	153	157	254	360	385	468
Oil (m. barrels)	18.4	19.3	23.1	26.3	26.4	43.6
Fishmeal ('000 tons)	20	530	1282	2253	706	987

Sources: BCR *Anuario Estadístico*, ONEC *Anuario Estadístico* (various years), INP.

overcome and it seemed unlikely that fishmeal would regain its dynamic role in the Peruvian economy.

Manufacturing industry is the sector of most rapid and sustained output growth in the Peruvian economy and because of its central importance to economic development as we have defined it is treated separately in Chapter 9. Here it is sufficient to point out that during our period roughly one quarter of manufacturing output was in fact the processing of primary exports as part of their own extraction as natural resources – sugar refining, fishmeal processing and mineral concentration – and that the rest of the manufacturing sector was dominated by two traditional consumer goods lines (food and clothing); and even though a small but rapidly growing consumer durables branch and the elements of heavy industrial inputs were established a true 'capital goods' branch had still not been set up by 1978. In fact, most of the significant structural changes in the manufacturing sector took place between 1955 and 1965 as part of the process of 'import-substituting industrialization' and much of the growth in the subsequent decade was a matter of filling excess capacity established during that phase. Moreover, the particular manner of industrializing involved a dominant role for foreign firms and foreign technology, with capital-intensive output geared to the needs of a relatively narrow market. In consequence, even though manufacturing emerged as the largest single production sector in the economy it remained concentrated on Lima, producing relatively sophisticated goods for a minority of the population without being integrated into the rest of the economic structure and heavily reliant on imports for its input requirements, while providing little employment. In contrast, construction was probably a more integrative force in economic expansion, particularly after 1963 when the combination of vastly expanded public works programmes and real estate development in Lima generated substantial linkages into manufacturing industry and considerable fortunes for those involved. This sector provided an important source of employment, especially for recent immigrants to urban areas, but as urbanization is essentially 'unproductive', it provided no lasting impulse. The private sector contracted for between two thirds and three quarters of annual construction in the 1960–75 period; the direct activity of the public sector in housing was insignificant.[15]

The tertiary sector grew at more or less the same rate as total output and although this may be partly due to national accounting conventions, its size relative to the economy as a whole – equivalent to nearly half of gross domestic product throughout our period – reflected two different phenomena. The first was the support services required by the corporate sector, particularly finance and government. The financial sector was particularly well developed in Peru as the result of the historical tradition of diversified export branches, and expanded more rapidly than the economy as a whole – although probably at much the same rate as the corporate sector. In contrast, 'government' – that is, administration as opposed to state enterprises – grew relatively slowly in the absence of widespread welfare expenditure on activities such as health and education. The second was the expansion of commerce and services based on the activities of urban migrants responding to the consumption expenditure of those employed in corporate enterprise. Overall, the prominence of the tertiary sector in a poor economy such as Peru can only be interpreted as a symptom of unbalanced growth, in contrast to the case of mature capitalist economies where it can be argued with some justification that the dynamic of the services sector is a genuine manifestation of a 'post-industrial era'.

The output structure as a whole, then, was still dominated by the export sector in our period but steadily less so, although the internal dynamic of manufacturing was still insufficient to replace that of agriculture and was itself contributory to the fragility of the external payments position. The only reliable estimate of the input–output pattern for Peru is that for 1969, but this year is probably not untypical for the period as a whole. In Table 4.5 below, the original forty-two-sector table has been reclassified to show the main features we have mentioned above. As can be seen, the 'primex' sector (that is, agro-exports, fishmeal, and mineral production and processing) accounted for a sixth of value added but had little integration with the other main sectors in terms of either purchases or sales. Similarly, food agriculture was a minor and relatively isolated activity, despite employing nearly half the population, while manufacturing industry sold little on to either foreign markets or to the other major production sectors, although it was responsible for the bulk of the import bill. In a sense, then, we are justified in calling the Peruvian economy 'disarticulated'[16] and argue that despite signs of 'development' that may be deduced from the increased share of the secondary sector in aggregate production, the lack of linkage within the economy and the concomitant integration to the 'overseas' sector is symptomatic of 'structural underdevelopment' as we have seen it defined in Chapter 2.

The pattern of external trade

By any standards Peru is an 'open' economy, with exports and imports each averaging around a fifth of gross domestic product in the 1955–75 period, so it is the external trade position that provides both the dynamic for and the constraint upon economic growth as a whole. Foreign trade was entirely in private hands until 1968 (except in the technical sense that all transactions had to pass through the Central Bank and meet with customs regulations) and was dominated by multinational enterprises; ownership of export sectors gave foreign capital direct control over half of exports and multinational prominence in manufacturing led to control over about the same proportion of imports. After 1968, however, foreign trade came almost completely under state control, and even though in 1976 the public sector itself only produced two fifths of exports and was responsible for half of imports, state enterprises marketed all exports from the primary sector and specific licences were needed for private-sector imports. The level of tariff protection in Peru had been traditionally very low, especially by the standards of Latin-American economies such as Mexico and Argentina, which had passed through an earlier 'national industrialization' phase in their

Table 4.5. *Aggregate input–output table for Peru 1969*

	Primex sector	Food agr.	Mfg. ind.	Other	Inter-sectoral sales	Final domestic sales	Exports	Final output
Primex sector	–	0	28	0	28	14	115	157
Food agriculture	0	–	18	0	18	87	2	107
Manufacturing industry	16	11	–	41	68	273	19	360
Other	16	1	35	—	52	324	0	376
Intersectoral purchases	32	12	81	41	165	698	136	
Imports	14	2	76	8	100			
Value added	111	93	203	327	735			
Total inputs	157	107	360	376				1000

Source: FitzGerald (1976a, Appendix II) standardized by dividing through by total inputs/outputs and eliminating instrasectoral transactions. See also Table 9.3 below.

economic history. After a sustained 'free-trade' policy in the 1956-62 period, even the relatively protectionist policies of the Belaunde administration only raised the *ex post* mean rate of duty collected on imports to about twenty per cent of c.i.f. value (mostly on consumer goods). After 1968 protection and import restraint were achieved by direct import controls rather than price measures.[17]

The pattern of exports is a natural concomitant of the production structure that we have already discussed. The leading element emerging over our period was minerals, and above all copper as iron ore was increasingly absorbed into domestic steel production. The falling off in both relative and absolute terms of exported agricultural products was mainly due to their absorption into the domestic market as local demand grew against a constrained resource base – irrigated coastal land. Fish products (mostly fishmeal) were a leading element in the expansion of exports in the 1960s although the collapse of the industry towards the end of the decade made this a declining element in the 1970s too. As a result, the remarkable diversity of Peruvian exports, which had been of such importance in the past – not only as a means of defence against fluctuations in international markets but also as a source of en-trepreneurial flexibility in the domestic bourgeoisie – was steadily reduced. In effect, with future export potential confined to the low-grade cupiferous deposits, Peru was on the way to becoming a vir-tual mono-exporter. Underlying this problem was the limited scope of the natural resource base; a central element in what Thorp and Bertram describe as an 'emerging crisis' in the mid 1960s:

> In the 1920s . . . copper and oil reserves were still large; huge deposits of lead, zinc and iron were known but underdeveloped; the fisheries along the Coast had hardly been touched; cotton, sugar and wool producers were all hindered more by market problems than by physical constraints on output. During the 1930s and 1940s the groundwork was laid to bring into production this large range of untapped resources, and from the late 1940s to the mid 1960s the economy was swept forward on a wave of expanding export production . . .
>
> [However] the most striking characteristic of the late 1960s was that almost all of the 'untapped resources' noted by observers in the 1920s had been brought into production, while few new export possibilities had come to light [1978, pp. 253–5].

This was paralleled by a lack of success in generating manufactured exports; to a certain extent the two phenomena were inter-related in the sense that the relative ease of primary exporting in the past had reduced the need to find markets for manufactures as a source of foreign exchange, but the dominance of multinational affiliates in manufacturing (which were unwilling to compete with sister-companies in other markets unless selected as an 'export-centre' by the mother company), clauses restricting exports in imported technology contracts, high production costs and the decline in industrial investment after 1965 all precluded an aggressive export drive on to foreign markets. Throughout our period it was an established tenet of economic strategy that increases in export income were to be obtained by increasing primary sector supply – first fishing, then oil and copper.

The structure of Peruvian imports, in common with most economies at a similar stage of development, was made up of four inter-related elements, each of which reflects the vicissitudes of growth at the periphery: first, the virtual elimination of consumer goods (other than food) as the initial stage of import-substituting industrialization was undertaken and concluded; second, and as a direct consequence of the first, the growing importance of the industrial inputs required in order to produce the consumer goods now produced locally; third, the prominence of capital goods as the process of industrialization had not reached the stage of producing heavy machinery; and fourth, the relative neglect of non-export agriculture reflected in the growing deficit of foodstuffs, particularly wheat, vegetable oils, meat, milk, and industrial inputs such as paper pulp. These elements are clearly showed in Table 4.6: the decline of consumer goods as a proportion of total imports from a sixth to less than a twentieth while industrial inputs rose from less than a third to nearly a half, accompanied by the rising imports of foodstuffs– although it should be noted that this last category remained a fairly stable proportion of the total import bill throughout the period, as did the purchase of capital equipment.

Although the changing pattern of exports and imports themselves affect the markets upon which they are sold and bought, ever since the shift in continental hegemony from Britain to the USA, at the turn of the century, Peru's largest client and supplier has been North America; the trends shown in Table 4.6 clearly illustrate the

Table 4.6. *Peruvian external trade*

US $ millions:	1955	1960	1965	1970	1975
Exports (f.o.b.):					
Agriculture products[a]	119	147	162	166	418
Fisheries products[b]	15	50	186	338	221
Mining products[c]	115	209	290	487	573
Other	32	38	47	43	81
Total	281	444	685	1034	1379
Main items:					
Sugar	37	48	37	65	295
Cotton	68	73	87	45	61
Cooper	29	95	121	269	154
Fishmeal and oil	15	50	186	338	221
Imports (f.o.b.):					
Consumer goods[d]	49	54	87	48	94
Food and products	49	57	120	108	306
Industrial inputs[d]	92	125	266	241	1080
Capital goods[e]	106	135	244	224	752
Other	4	2	2	1	9
Total	300	373	719	622	2241
	1950	1960	1965	1970	1975
Percentage of exports to:					
North America	28	37	34	32	20
Latin America	26	8	8	6	18
Europe[f]	15	31	32	32	17
Socialist bloc[g]	0	1	3	7	27
Other	31	23	23	23	18
Percentage of imports from:					
North America	55	47	44	38	36
Latin America	8	8	10	15	14
Europe	9	22	21	21	26
Socialist bloc	0	0	0	1	2
Other	28	23	25	25	22

Source: BCR *Cuentas Nacionales* (Tables 17, 18 – various years), BCR *Boletín* (various issues).
Notes: [a] cotton, sugar, coffee, wool; [b] fishmeal and oil; [c] copper, silver, lead, zinc, iron and petroleum; [d] except foodstuffs; [e] including construction materials and transport equipment; [f] the nine EEC countries; [g] COMECON plus China.

way in which Peru was integrated into the international commercial system. On the export side, the initial move away from Latin-american and towards Northamerican markets reflected the increased importance of mineral exports, and the subsequent shift towards Europe was the result of a quest for fishmeal markets; under the policy of market diversification in both a geographical and a political sense after 1968, the socialist bloc became the most important single purchasing group. Subsequently, however, the political shift within the Peruvian regime itself in 1975, which meant less stress on trade relations with socialist countries after that date, and the new reliance upon copper exports, resulted in an increased importance for Northamerican export markets once more. On the import side, the flexibility was far less, due to the predominance of industrial inputs and the relationship of these to certain technologies already in use – more specifically to sales within multinational corporations. The sources of imports reflect, therefore, the external dependence of Peruvian industry upon the USA but increasingly upon European companies as well.

In the late 1960s, after the lapse of the Latin American Free Trade Association (ALALC), a major attempt was made by the Andean Countries (Bolivia, Chile, Colombia, Ecuador, Peru and Venezuela) to form a customs union – known as the Andean Pact.[18] The initial intentions were not based on trade complementarity (for which there was little potential – in the case of Peru, trade with these countries was little more than five per cent of imports or exports) but rather upon the stimulation of industry. Thus the main provisions were a common external tariff for manufactures, the gradual elimination of internal trade barriers, the imposition of joint restrictions upon the penetration of foreign enterprise and the subsequent repatriation of profits, and the establishment of a system of regional allocation of productive capacity so as to achieve scale economies. However, the changing political complexions of some of the members (particularly Chile, but also Bolivia, Colombia and Ecuador) reduced their commitment to this sort of regional cooperation – which was based in part on a 'dependency' view of the obstacles to industrialization – and the attempts by Venezuela, despite being a late entrant, to occupy a predominant role in automobiles and petrochemicals (which were the two key areas for regional integration) meant that by 1976 it was clear that the Pact had little future.

The dissection of visible trade into volume and price trends reveals a more complex picture. The value of exports and imports we have already noted in Table 4.6 are shown in index form for selected years in Table 4.7. The difficulties in sustaining the growth

Table 4.7. *Visible trade indices 1956–78*

(1963 = 100)	1956	1959	1965	1968	1970	1973	1976	1978
Exports[a] ($ value)	57.7	58.2	118.6	151.4	186.3	200.4	244.9	377.2
Imports[a] ($ value)	66.0	54.2	127.4	129.9	135.1	199.4	405.4	381.1
Export volume[b]	55.6	66.9	108.9	123.7	124.9	105.9	109.9	124.0
Import volume[b]	66.0	56.2	123.2	145.4	149.5	167.5	208.0	149.6
Export unit value[c]	103.8	87.0	91.8	81.7	149.2	189.2	222.8	304.2
Import unit value[d]	100.1	96.4	103.4	89.3	99.8	119.0	194.9	254.5
Purchasing power of exports[e]	57.7	60.3	114.7	169.5	186.7	168.4	125.6	148.2
External terms of trade[f]	103.7	90.2	88.8	91.5	149.5	159.0	114.3	119.5

Notes: [a] exports and imports f.o.b.; [b] constant-price values used in the national accounts estimate of GDP, 1956–68 at 1963 weights and 1970–78 at 1970 weights, linked on a 1963 = 100 basis; [c] 'export value' divided by 'export volume' and thus a 'dollar price' index; [d] 'import value' divided by 'import volume', a dollar price index also; [e] 'export value' divided by 'import unit value'; [f] 'export unit value' divided by 'import unit value'.
Source: BCR *Cuentas Nacionales* (Tables 7, 9, 15, various years) and direct from BCR.

in export quantum underlined by Thorp and Bertram are clear: the volume index nearly doubled between 1956 and 1965 – due to the two new mining projects and the anchovy boom – but rose by barely a quarter between the latter date and 1970, and after that actually declined as fishmeal exports fell off, only rising as the long-overdue mining project (Cuajone) came on stream at the end of the period. Prices for Peruvian exports were determined on world markets; even in the case of fishmeal during the 1960s when Peru was the major world exporter, no attempt seems to have been made to affect the international price deliberately, or to coordinate other exporters in such an exercise. The fluctuations in unit values had a crucial part to play in the weakening of income growth in 1958 and 1967, and thus the balance of payments crises of those years; after 1968 the improvement in unit values resulting from the world commodity price boom sustained that income growth despite falling output, so that only when unit values stabilized (copper prices had risen from 64 US cents per pound on London in 1970 to 93 in 1974, but were back down to 62 in 1976, for example) did the extent of the export crisis really become apparent. In terms of 1963 prices, Peruvian exports in 1978 had only regained the real volume of ten years before.

Import volume, despite the progress in import-substitution during our period – or perhaps because of it – closely reflected the pressure of domestic demand: the decline in volume in 1959 as a result of the stabilization policy after the balance of payments crisis of the previous year; the rapid rise as the economy expanded in the wake of an export boom in the mid 1960s, a rise that continued even as exports slackened off, only to be cut back once again after the stabilization programme of 1968; the increase after 1972 as the new investment projects got under way, and the reduction to a level almost equal to that obtaining ten years before by 1978 as the result of yet another stabilization policy.[19] Here too, Peru was largely subject to externally determined prices; these appear to have remained more or less stable between 1956 and 1970 (the apparent declines are probably due to the shifting composition) but after 1973, in particular, they rose extremely rapidly, at a rate far exceeding world prices and almost certainly reflecting large-scale over-invoicing by importing firms as a means of transferring funds out of the country.[20]

The 'purchasing power of exports' (that is, the 'real' value of exports expressed in terms of the imports that they can purchase) became the central problem in Peruvian growth during our period, as the primary export sector shifted from being the prime 'motor' of the economy towards the constraint on further expansion caused by the manufacturing sector. This index almost tripled between 1956 and 1968, but stabilized and then fell after that; in 1976 the purchasing power of exports was down to the level of ten years before, despite the fact that the economy had expanded to a level about one half greater. This failure to sustain real foreign earnings was a major problem for the 'Peruvian Revolution'. However, a considerable part of this problem lay in the external terms of trade, which deteriorated between 1956 and 1965, contributing to the balance of payments crises of 1958 and 1967; but their improvement just after both these dates was a key factor (as important as cutbacks in import volume) in subsequent recovery. As we have already indicated, the improvement between 1968 and 1973 was due to export prices, and the deterioration thereafter to import prices, the final result being to leave Peru in 1978 in only a slightly better position than in 1956. Although it is not possible to argue, therefore, that Peru has suffered a long-run deterioration in the terms of trade of the type originally considered by the ECLA school to be one of the main barriers to Latinamerican economic development, the evidence on export purchasing power does underline the problems encountered by economies relying on primary exports produced at increasing marginal cost to pay for imported industrial inputs upon which continued growth depends.[21]

Putting the pieces of the external trade structure together reveals the trends and the recurrent imbalances. There was a tendency for the proportion of exports in the total product to decline over time,[22] which, when combined with the expansion of an import-intensive industrial sector, led to chronic structural difficulties in the balance of trade: in particular, imports were liable to run up over exports at the end of each balance of payments cycle as it worked through the economy – a cycle examined in more detail in Chapter 8. These difficulties were exacerbated by the considerable outflow of foreign exchange on invisible account, partly from the steadily increasing overseas expenditure on services such as insurance and air transport

Table 4.8. *The Peruvian balance of payments 1956–78*

(US $ millions)	1956–58	1959–64	1965–67	1968–73	1974–76	1977–78
Exports (f.o.b.)	+315	+512	+739	+950	+1384	+1930
Imports (f.o.b.)	−363	−427	−760	−768	−2133	−2035
Trade balance	−48	+86	−22	+182	−749	−105
Private profit and interest payments	−30	−56	−97	−104	−48	..
Public interest payments	−6	−8	−22	−45	−181	−252
Other services (net)	−38	−46	−75	−49	−202	..
Services balance	−73	−109	−194	−198	−431	−511
Balance on current account	−122	−23	−216	−16	−1180	−616
Long-term capital (net):						
Public	+8	+20	+112	+129	+655	+483
Private	+79	+19	+28	−17	+247	+66
Short-term capital Movements[a]	+14	−11	+52	−53	−298	−92
	+101	+27	+193	+60	+604	+457
Reserves and related Items[b]	+21	−5	+23	−44	+376	+159

Notes: [a] including 'errors and omissions'; [b] includes all compensatory movements, minus indicates increase; the annual averages are 'row' means and thus may not total exactly.
Source: BCR *Cuentas Nacionales* (Table 15, various years) ONEC Anuario Estadistico 1966, BCR *Memoria 1976* and direct from BCR.

which was not balanced by incoming tourism, but more importantly as a result of profit and interest payments. Whereas the repatriation of profits by foreign companies made up most of this latter item until the mid 1960s, these were overshadowed by interest payments after 1968 as a result of both the massive increase in public overseas indebtedness and the restrictions on profit remittances. Overall, the current account of the balance of payments was in approximate balance between 1959 and 1964 and between 1968 and 1973, but in substantial deficit in the other years of our period, requiring massive capital inflows to cover the shortfall. Further, when we look at long-term private capital inflows (net of repayments), which mainly take the form of direct investment, we see that these were surprisingly small (apart from the funds required for the enormous mineral projects in the mid 1950s and the mid 1970s), due to the habit of multinational companies of obtaining finance from local borrowing and retained profits. Public sector borrowing gradually became the major means of covering the deficit on current account, a deficit which exceeded the financial needs of the public sector alone by a considerable margin. Reported short movements were mostly made up of private transactions, while unreported movements ('errors and omissions') can also be taken as attributable to the private sector; fully *half* of public sector borrowing in 1959–64 and 1968–76 was required in order to balance these private short capital movements.

In sum, the balance of payments is a reflection of the structure of production itself on current account and of the pattern of accumulation on capital account, a pattern we shall discuss in Chapter 6.

Table 4.9. *Sectoral allocation of the labour force (per cent of total)*

	1950	1955	1960	1965	1970	1974
Agriculture and fishing	58.9	56.2	52.8	50.4	47.2	44.6
Mining	2.2	2.1	2.2	2.2	2.2	2.3
Manufacturing	13.0	13.2	13.5	13.7	13.9	14.1
Construction	2.7	3.0	3.4	3.7	4.1	4.3
Utilities	0.1	0.2	0.3	0.3	0.4	0.4
Transport, etc.	2.7	2.9	3.1	3.2	3.4	3.5
Commerce	6.6	7.5	8.6	9.4	10.4	11.3
Banking	0.4	0.5	0.6	0.6	0.7	0.7
Government	4.0	4.6	5.5	6.0	7.0	7.5
Services	9.3	9.8	10.1	10.4	10.7	11.1
Totals (millions):						
Labour force	2.55	2.79	3.15	3.61	4.14	4.61
Population	8.07	8.89	10.13	11.75	13.68	15.46

Source: BCR *Cuentas Nacionales* (Tables 1, 11), various years.

The pattern of employment

The first approximation to the analysis of employment must be an examination of the allocation of the economically active population by productive sector, even though this may not correspond to 'full employment' in the normal sense – particularly in the cases of agriculture and services. In the Peruvian experience, and in that of most other underdeveloped countries, the largest single employment sector was agriculture, which accounted for roughly half the labour force; its relative share had been steadily declining, although its absolute numbers rose at nearly the same rate as output (about two per cent per annum during the two decades) indicating a roughly constant productivity. The labour absorption by fishing and mining had always been small, while the proportion of the workforce employed in manufacturing remained almost constant – the numbers employed growing only marginally faster than the labour force as a whole – and in fact it formed a declining share of non-agricultural employment. In consequence, it was the tertiary branches, and above all government and commerce that increased their shares of employment significantly over the period, balancing the fall in that of agriculture; at an aggregate level, in contrast to the shift in output shares from the primary to the secondary sector with the tertiary sector share stable that we have already observed, the shift in employment shares was from the primary to the tertiary sector, leaving the secondary sector share stable. The first fell from 61 per cent of the labour force in 1950 to 47 per cent in 1974, and the third rose from 23 per cent to 34 per cent; the secondary sector raised its share from 16 per cent to only 19 per cent over the entire period.

In fact, this shift in 'employment' had taken place mostly *outside* the corporate sector, consisting of a net movement from peasant agriculture to small-scale urban service activities and resulting in a marked decline in 'independent' workers in the economy (from 55 per cent of the economically active population in 1950 to 44 per cent in 1974) as many immigrants to urban areas entered wage employment, albeit of a casual nature and often in very small enterprises; nevertheless, the proportion of *'agricultores independientes'* (i.e. peasants) remained considerable, even though it fell from 40 per cent of the workforce in 1950 to 29 per cent in 1974.[23] The pattern of regional population shares reflects this movement of the labour force extremely well, as Table 4.10 shows. The regions with proportional population loss (although none had absolute losses) were 'Centro' and 'Sur', and above all the highland areas within them; their decline of fifteen percentage points between 1940 and 1972 was almost balanced by the expansion of Lima. The process of internal migration was more complex than this might imply, however:[24] in the first place, there was a 'stepping stone' process in which peasants

Table 4.10. *Regional population distribution*
(per cent)

	1940	1961	1972
Norte	27.7	28.8	28.8
Centro	32.9	28.9	26.9
Sur	27.8	21.9	19.4
Oriente	1.7	2.0	2.0
Lima Metropolitana	9.9	18.4	22.9
Urbanized[a]	35	47	52

[a] living in towns of more than 2000 inhabitants.
Source: INP (1974).

moved to rural towns and then they (or the original townspeople) moved to the capital; in the second, the initial employment of recent arrivals in the city was often in secondary sector activities such as construction, with the move to petty commerce only taking place once some funds had been accumulated. Nonetheless, the *net* population movement conformed to the model discussed in Chapter 2.

The data we have examined on the sectoral allocation of the workforce should not be taken to imply 'employment' in the full sense of the word as used in a mature capitalist economy. There are three problems here: first, in agriculture the seasonal nature of production means that although the available labour may be fully used at harvest time, it is surplus to technical requirements at other times of the year. A crude calculation of the number of man-days per year required to produce a certain crop may well indicate an erroneously large excess of labour time, therefore.[25] Moreover, in the Andean case at least, peasant families tend to operate a number of separate plots at the same time, as well as engage in commerce, as a form of insurance against crop failure.[26] Second, in a society where comprehensive social security is only available to a minority (roughly those in the corporate sector) there is little possibility of surviving 'open' unemployment anyway, and even if a recent immigrant is living off his relatives in the city this would normally take a form such as that of working in his cousin's shop. Third, the nature of enterprise organization in the non-corporate sector is such that labour is constantly shifting between jobs, or working in more than one activity (e.g. construction during the day and restaurants at night), or moving in and out of formal employment several times during the year.[27]

It is only comparatively recently that underemployment estimates have been made for Peru, and even then only on the basis of sample surveys of urban areas. The figures for the 1970–75 period show no significant trend, but do indicate open unemployment of about five per cent and underemployment of about forty per cent, indicating that only just over half the urban workforce is adequately employed.[28] Much of the underemployment is not, however, accounted for by the definition 'less than whole week worked' but rather by that of 'earnings of less than a third of the minimum wage' and thus reflects the distribution of income rather than inactivity as such.[29]

The problem of unemployment in Peru, as elsewhere in the underdeveloped world, merges therefore into that of dualism and income distribution. The low requirements of the corporate sector for unskilled labour and the relative attraction of urban areas (in terms both of income opportunities and of access to services such as health

Table 4.11. *Relative productivity by main production sector*

| | Per cent of gross domestic product | | Per cent of economically active population | | 'Relative productivity' | | |
	1955	1975	1955	1975	1955[a]	1975[a]	1975/55[b]
Primary sector	27	19	58	47	0.47	0.40	1.32
Secondary sector	26	34	17	19	1.52	1.79	1.83
Tertiary sector	47	47	25	34	1.88	1.34	1.10
Total	100	100	100	100	1.00	1.00	1.55

Source: Appendix and BCR *Cuentas Nacionales*.
Notes: [a] ratio of sectoral share of GDP to share of EAP; [b] ratio of sectoral output per head in 1975 to that in 1955, at constant prices.

and education – with which rural Peru is very poorly endowed) combine to bring about a translation of disguised unemployment from rural to urban areas without much effect on the structure of production. As Table 4.11 shows, while productivity rose rapidly in the secondary sector, it grew very slowly in the primary and tertiary sectors. This would tend to support the view that the latter two acted as 'sponges' for the labour the secondary sector did not absorb; had industrial productivity been held constant at its 1950 level, the secondary sector could have expanded its proportion of the labour force in line with its share of GDP to 29 per cent by 1975. The employment position in Peru was severely imbalanced during our period in a double sense, therefore: first, nearly a half of the workforce was not being fully utilized and insofar as labour power is the ultimate basis of production output was not as large as it might have been; second, in not being adequately employed this part of the workforce was not receiving an adequate earnings either, giving rise to an extremely unequal distribution of the national income.

Dualism in the Peruvian economy

Underlying the structural problems of the unbalanced production and employment patterns on the one hand and the reliance on external trade as both motor of and brake upon growth on the other is the dual nature of the Peruvian economy. This is not a dichotomy between industry and agriculture, as the original neo-classical and ECLA models suggested, but rather dualism associated with the organization of production within each sector – as we have seen in Chapter 2. Broadly, the corporate sector in Peru during our period grouped estate agriculture, mining, anchovy fishing, factory industry, finance, government and substantial service enterprises in one complex which, although not functionally integrated in terms of production, had exhibited a high degree of joint ownership in the past – as we shall see in Chapter 5. The external relationships of the corporate sector were a key element in this dualism because they both sustained its dynamic and made it possible to achieve growth without development of the rest of the economy, specifically by providing an external market through which primary exports could be converted to industrial inputs, while multinational enterprise supplied the technology required to modernize the production process. The corporate sector generated all the exports from and absorbed virtually all the imports to the Peruvian economy, and thus was itself directly integrated into the world economy, in contrast to the non-corporate sector which had no such direct link. The use of modern imported technology in the corporate sector was both a link with the world economy and a distinction from the non-corporate sector, whether the field of activity was agriculture, manufacturing or services; although such technology could only be made profitable by paying wages well below those in the advanced economies, these were still much higher than earnings in the non-corporate sector.[30] Moreover, virtually all investment went into the corporate sector (almost by definition, if we exclude activities such as the small irrigation works by peasants and self-help housing in the slums) and this only served to strengthen the duality of the economy. Meanwhile, peasant agriculture continued with its own weak dynamic, responding to food prices and possibly to population pressure on the land but without significant amounts of modern production inputs such as fertilizers or machinery – leading to the chronic shortfalls in the national supply of foodstuffs. In the urban petty tertiary sector the available income from consumers' expenditure was in effect shared out between the swelling lumpen-proletariat as they compete for the limited market in personal services and small-scale trade.[31] The employment structure formed the other side of the same coin: the highly productive corporate sector required relatively little labour (above all of the unskilled type) and as the opportunities for full employment in the non-corporate sector were steadily reduced by population pressure, 'structural underemployment' reflected in low-income service activities became endemic.

This picture should not be allowed, however, to give a false image of a hermetic separation between the corporate and household sectors in the Peruvian case. While it is certainly true that there was a more tangible 'gap' than obtains in more predominantly agrarian economies, there was also a clear inter-dependence between the two sectors in the case of Peru: for example, the corporate sector 'put out' a great deal of work to artisan workshops (the shoe manufacturing process is a case in point), export agriculture employed landless labour on a seasonal basis, and large distributors depended upon petty commerce as the last link in the marketing chain. Peasant agriculture, of course, sold most of its marketable produce to the towns and thus in part to the corporate workforce. Beyond this, the 'reserve army' of recent immigrants to urban areas had the effect of holding down corporate labour costs, mainly by allowing a rapid turnover of the workforce and weakening unionization. Finally, the expansion of employment in the tertiary sector relied upon the expenditure by those employed in corporate enterprise of some part of their income on such services – as the sector is not potentially self-sustaining in the way that, say, peasant agriculture is. We would expect then, that this dual structure would have generated an income distribution concentrated in the corporate sector (and within that on the owners of capital), with urban non-corporate incomes somewhat higher than those of peasants, although the lower end of the former should have approximated to the latter as the internal

Table 4.12. *Dualism in the Peruvian economy 1968*

	Output (% GDP)			Employment (% EAP)		
	Corp-orate	Non-corp.	Total economy	Corp-orate	Non-corp.	Total economy
Primary sector	18	8	26	14	37	51
Secondary sector	24	5	29	7	11	18
Tertiary sector	25	20	45	14	17	31
Total	67	33	100	35	65	100
Lima–Callao	38	19	57	14	10	24
Rest of Peru	29	14	43	21	55	76

Source: Appendix, Table A.5.

migration flows responded to the urban–rural income differential and by so doing reduced it.

In order to make a quantitative estimate of the scale of the phenomenon, a somewhat arbitrary division must be made between the corporate and non-corporate sectors, and a distinction in terms of enterprise size would seem most appropriate. In particular, some minimum of numbers employed per firm could be held to correspond to a reasonable definition of capitalist (as opposed to artisan) enterprise in terms of the organization of labour and the use of reproducible capital. In the Peruvian case, a division on the basis of 'five or more workers' happens to coincide with various censal definitions, and would seem to correspond with a reasonable concept of the size of 'artisan' enterprise. Further, this could be held to be a minimum definition, and thus our estimate will tend to be a maximum one for the size of the corporate sector. Working along these lines it is possible to allocate both employment and output in each production branch between the two categories of enterprise, and thus gauge the scale of the duality in the economy. The aggregate results are given in Table 4.12, which is itself based on the complete breakdown of the eleven output and employment branches shown in Tables 4.1 and 4.9 above,[32] the central estimate being that for 1968, a year not only important as a turning point in our historical analysis but also one for which most data is available. In that year, as the table shows, roughly one third of the workforce was employed in the corporate enterprises which accounted for two thirds of national output; the complete sectoral breakdown is given in the Appendix. As can be seen, the dualism was not the result of a dichotomy between primary and secondary sectors; rather the pattern of the minority of the workforce accounting for the greater part of production is repeated in most branches. The effect was most marked in the secondary sector, as might be expected, with a 'disparity ratio' (i.e. the ratio of value added per head in the corporate sector to that in the non-corporate) of six, as opposed to five in the primary sector. Specifically, agriculture and manufacturing express this division well: our estimates indicate that in 1968 estate agriculture accounted for 54 per cent of production but only 22 per cent of employment in the sector, giving rise to a disparity ratio of over four; in the case of manufacturing, factories were responsible for 83 per cent of output but only 35 per cent of the workforce in the sector, corresponding to a disparity ratio of nine. These ratios are at market prices, and thus reflect the internal terms of trade between the two sectors and factor remuneration within them as well as physical levels of productivity, but given their relative endowments of resources and capital the ratios do seem to reflect reality.

Much of the corporate sector, moreover, was concentrated on the Lima–Callao area (particularly industry, construction, utilities, finance and government) so we would expect the spatial distribution of production and labour to reflect a dual structure as well, even though the pattern was modified by the existence of considerable corporate enterprise on the northern coast (sugar) and in the central and southern highlands (mining), as well as the large non-corporate sector in Lima. The only reliable estimate of spatial income distribution is that in the national accounts for 1961,[33] but even the

Lima–Callao area, with only a fifth of the population (as against a quarter in 1972) enjoyed 43 per cent of national income, and a level of income per head double that of the national average – that is, three times that in the rest of the country. If we take our estimates of duality for 1968, with some reasonable assumptions as to the location of production we find just this: that duality was experienced in both the metropolis *and* the hinterland, and thus was not just a simple matter of *urbs contra rurem*.[34]

There exist two other estimates of dualism in the Peruvian economy which, although they differ from each other and from our estimate, do confirm the overall pattern outlined above. The more substantial of the two is that prepared by Webb,[35] who estimates dualism in the course of compiling the personal income distribution tables that we shall examine in the next chapter. His division between the two sectors (which he calls 'modern' and 'traditional') in the primary and secondary sectors is similar to ours (although his 'modern agriculture' sector only covers sugar production), but his definition of the 'modern' tertiary sector is confined to government, banking and professionals, thus giving a narrower, and less satisfactory, definition of the 'modern/corporate' sector which naturally involves a lower estimate than ours of the absorption of labour by the corporate sector and a smaller output share as well. The second is that by Sciari[36] who, working for the ILO on the basis of unpublished results from the 1972 population census, comes up with a figure of 35 per cent of the workforce in the modern sector – strikingly similar to ours, albeit for a slightly later date; unfortunately he does not calculate production shares. Overall, the three estimates in Table 4.13 would appear to coincide in implying that the corporate sector contained no more than a third of the workforce and accounted for roughly two thirds of production. Presumably the proportions of total capital stock and appropriated surplus in the Peruvian corporate sector would be even higher, possibly approaching unity in both cases. In addition, this sector was responsible for the totality of export production and nearly all imports, as well as the bulk of direct and indirect taxation and most of the benefits of government expenditure – as we shall see in Chapter 7.

As significant as the absolute estimate of duality at any one date is its trend over time, because eventually the success or failure of capitalist growth in a peripheral economy depends upon the capacity of the system to absorb the greater part of the labour force into the corporate sector – in other words, to extend capitalist relations of production through the whole economy. In terms of output, this is not particularly difficult; it is the requirement that corporate employment grow substantially faster than the labour force that is crucial. In the Peruvian case, it is clear that the original ECLA anticipation that this could be achieved through the employment-generating power of factory industry was misplaced – although manufacturing output grew rapidly over a long period, it failed to raise its share of the national labour force above five per cent, due to increasing capital intensity as new imported technologies were introduced.

Both Webb and Sciari provide estimates of dualism in the Peruvian economy for the beginning and end of the 1960s, a period which one might expect to have seen some reduction of disparities in view of the changes in the production structure. Webb works from his central estimates based on the 1961 census of population and production, extrapolating both forwards and backwards on the basis of the sectoral employment and output figures given in the national accounts in order to come up with an estimate for the share of the 'modern sector' workforce (as he calls it) in the national total of 19 per cent in 1950, 21 per cent in 1961 and 22 per cent in 1970. This implies that the rate of labour absorption by the corporate sector was very little higher than that of population growth and thus that the extension of capitalist relations of production to the whole population was proceeding very slowly indeed. Sciari, in contrast, while working from the 1961 census on apparently more or less the same definitions as Webb obtains a similar result for 1961 (22 per cent of the workforce in the modern sector), but used unpublished results of the 1972 population census to obtain a much higher one for the later date, as we have seen, an estimate which corresponds much more nearly to our own. Assuming that his results are reliable (unfortunately he gives little indication of his methodology) and not just the result of interpolating between Webb's 1961 estimate and our 1968 estimate in FitzGerald (1976a), this gives a much higher rate of absorption and one which, given the direct evidence on the growth of employment in factory industry in Chapter 9 would appear to be far too optimistic. We have based our estimate of employment trends on Webb, therefore, calculating a figure *pro rata* with his for 1950 and 1960, maintaining the same proportion as that between our 1970 figure and his. Webb's estimate of the changing share of value added generated in the 'modern' sector over time is a stable figure and one which, given the rapid growth of dynamic sectors such as fishmeal and manufacturing on the one hand and the slow growth of food agriculture on the other, would seem somewhat conservative. Our own estimates of the trend in the corporate share of output are based on the increase in the share of fishing, mining, manufacturing, government and finance in GDP (which rose from 35 per cent in 1950 to 46 per cent in 1970) applied to our 'central' estimate for the corporate sector share of output in 1968. Allowing for the difference between Webb's rather narrow definition of the 'modern' sector and our wider concept of the 'corporate' sector, the resulting trends are broadly consistent.

The overall conclusion seems inescapable: that while the corporate sector output was growing much faster than output in the non-corporate sector, its employment was expanding quite slowly. According to our estimates, labour productivity in the corporate sector rose at 3.2 per cent per annum between 1950 and 1970 while it rose at only 1.1 per cent in the non-corporate sector, due to the allocation of capital almost exclusively to the former. If the observed trends were to be continued, we would expect around 85 per cent of output to be in the corporate sector but still less than half the total workforce would have a permanent and reasonably paid job at the end of the century.

This expansion, expressed as it is in terms of a bipolar model, must not let us overlook the fact that the growth of corporate employment may often be at the expense of small-scale enterprise providing stable employment. Clearly in mining, or (in the Peruvian case) agriculture this was not important, but it certainly was a significant factor in industrial expansion as the growth of firms involved the control of markets through new product lines and the elimination of small 'traditional' producers. Similarly, the reorganization and modernization of commerce and transport so as to gain scale economies probably broke down much of the 'natural economy' of the non-corporate sector, with gains to the owners of capital but no great increase in output and substantial losses in employment. As the ILO points out for the case of Colombia, which applies just as well to that of Peru:

> The displacement of a large number and variety of small retail shops by a single supermarket is a case in point in the distribution sector. With population growing at a very high rate in the principal cities, and the number of motor cars increasing, the private profitability of super-markets is bound to rise. It must be remembered, however, that the *social* returns on such investment would be very low, since they would drive out of work a large number of retailers who would not easily find alternative employment opportunities.[37]

Table 4.13. *Estimates of dualism in the Peruvian economy*

Source:	Webb		FitzGerald
Central estimates:			
Date	1961		1968
Workforce:			
Corporate	21%		35%
Non-corporate	79%		65%
Output:			
Corporate	56%		67%
Non-corporate	44%		33%
Corporate labour share:			
1950	19%		30%
1960	21%		33%
1970	22%		35%
Corporate output share:			
1950	..		52%
1960	56%		63%
1970	59%		67%
Combined estimate:			Per cent
	1950	1970	per annum
Output (billion soles at 1963 prices):			
Corporate	20.3	72.8	6.6
Non-corporate	18.7	35.8	3.3
Total	39.0	108.6	5.3
Employment (millions):			
Corporate	0.77	1.44	3.2
Non-corporate	1.78	2.70	2.1
	2.55	4.14	2.4

Sources: Tables 4.1, 4.9, Appendix and Webb (1977, pp. 39, 78).

Direct observation of the process in Peru would tend to suggest that two trends were interacting: on the one hand, the corporate sector was steadily expanding its share of total production because its rate of growth and investment was so much higher, but the employment requirements grew relatively more slowly; on the other, the corporate sector was also expanding by displacing firms in the non-corporate sector (and this held true for medium firms in the corporate sector as well) and only taking up part of their labour force. In the process, both a proletariat and a 'lumpen' class were formed. The spatial aspect of this process was reinforced by the effect of improved transport facilities upon the economic structure of rural areas; as Roberts[38] has shown in the case of Andean towns such as Huancayo, the cheaper freight costs brought about by improved roads meant that local markets were integrated into the national one and as a result local producers of products such as textiles, beer and tiles could no longer compete effectively with large firms from Lima, so that over time the rural economy actually 'underdeveloped' and reverted to agricultural stagnation.

In this way, it was quite possible to have underdevelopment – in terms of structural imbalance, disarticulated production and inadequate employment for the bulk of the workforce – accompanied by relatively rapid economic growth.

Concluding remarks

The major features to emerge from this analysis of the economic structure of Peru are its duality and external dependence. In relation to the first, we have seen the importance for output of mining, export agriculture and industry in contrast to their restricted employment potential on the one hand and the poor performance of food agriculture which still occupied nearly half the population on the other. In relation to the second, the importance of external trade to the functioning of exchange relations and of foreign technology to production have also been noted. Underlying both phenomena and linking them together is the fact that the dynamic of the economy continued to rely upon the growth of export income, although the working of this mechanism did change early on in our period; as the corporate sector began to become industrialized, the key role of exports changed from being the direct generator of demand and investible funds for the domestic economy to that of providing foreign exchange for industrial inputs, acting as an indirect constraint on growth generated within the economy, only the relaxation of which allowed further expansion to take place. The dominance of the capital-intensive and externally linked corporate sector remained.

Table 4.14 below indicates the main characteristics of the output structure of the seven major Latin-American economies.[39] The relative decline of agriculture is evident throughout the area, and although the performance on food production in Peru is the worst of the seven, it is not much worse than that for Chile or even Argentina and is arguably part of a more widespread pattern of neglect of the non-export sector of agriculture. This in turn contributed to the continuation of widespread poverty in view of the continuing high proportion of the population in rural areas; well over half the workforce was producing and receiving one sixth of the national income in Latin America. This underlies the duality of the economic structure, which is repeated within industry and the tertiary sector as well. According to an aggregate estimate of dualism prepared by the ECLA[40] for the whole of Latin America 'towards the end of the 1960s', 18 per cent of the workforce could be classified in the 'modern' sector (mainly mining, factory manufacturing, government and banking) which accounted for 62 per cent of production – a figure strikingly similar to Webb's for Peru. If we include the 'intermediate' portions of manufacturing and utilities, this gives us 35 per cent of employment and 69 per cent of output. These figures are necessarily very approximate, but do serve to indicate that our estimates for Peru are not that extraordinary. Although we have argued that the dualism in Peru is to a great extent the result of the dichotomy between mining expansion and agricultural stagnation, even a country with a much stronger and dynamic agricultural sector such as Colombia appears to exhibit similar imbalance. In 1964, two thirds of the Colombian workforce could be classified in the 'traditional' sector as being peasants, non-factory artisans, small traders and service workers not included in the social security system – a category similar to our 'non-corporate' sector. Within agriculture this employment dualism was mirrored by the unequal

Table 4.14. *Comparative production structure.*

Sectoral composition of GDP (per cent)

	1955				1965				1973			
	Agricult.	Mining	Industry[a]	Services	Agricult.	Mining	Industry	Services	Agricult.	Mining	Industry	Services
Argentina	19.6	0.8	43.3	36.3	16.2	1.7	46.1	36.0	12.1	1.0	49.2	37.7
Brazil	31.0	0.3	27.5	41.2	31.0	0.6	33.8	34.6	12.3	0.5	39.8	47.4
Colombia	35.2	3.5	27.5	33.8	32.2	4.0	28.5	35.4	27.1	1.6	33.2	38.1
Chile	12.8	6.9	30.6	49.7	10.9	6.8	31.3	51.0	6.1	11.7	40.6	41.6
Mexico	20.2	4.4	31.9	43.5	15.7	3.9	32.9	47.5	10.2	3.8	34.2	51.8
Peru	23.8	6.4	25.4	44.4	22.5	7.6	28.7	41.2	16.3	7.8	31.9	44.0
Venezuela	7.3	27.0	20.4	45.3	7.7	25.2	23.2	43.9	7.2	16.7	32.5	43.6

	GDP growth p.a.[b]		Food output growth p.a.	GDP/head (1965 US$)		Trade[c] coefficient		Urban[d] population	
	1955–64	1965–71	1964–70	1960	1971	1960	1971	1960	1970
Argentina	3.0	4.0	0.8	792	1043	10.8	10.1	57	67
Brazil	5.8	7.5	3.8	268	392	6.8	6.8	29	39
Colombia	4.6	5.8	4.4	311	377	15.6	13.3	30	43
Chile	3.7	3.7	1.7	498	644	15.3	14.6	50	57
Mexico	6.1	7.1	2.8	486	683	11.7	10.1	32	41
Peru	4.9	3.3	0.5	313	383	22.4	21.5	26	33
Venezuela	7.7	3.9	5.0	669	844	26.1	18.1	42	56

Sources: ECLA (1973), ECLA (1975), Furtado (1970).

[a] manufacturing, construction and utilities; [b] at 1960 prices; [c] average ratio of imports and exports to GDP; [d] percentage of population in towns of twenty thousand or more.

division of production, with two thirds of the workforce receiving only 37 per cent of income in 1960.[41] The implications for employment were drawn out by the ILO in the first of their well-known studies:[42] they are very similar to ours for Peru and stress the influence of the lack of access to land in rural areas and inappropriate choice of technology in urban areas. However, the ILO policy suggestion for the former problem (land reform) was unacceptable to the Colombian government and as we shall see, did not in fact increase rural employment in Peru. The suggestion that the latter problem could be resolved by lowering wage rates in the modern sector was apparently more acceptable to the Colombian government but less so to the unions, and more seriously was logically at fault in supposing that more labour-intensive techniques would be

Table 4.15. *Employment dualism in Peru and Colombia (per cent of EAP)*

	Colombia (1964)			Peru (1968)		
	'Modern'	'Traditional'	Total	Corporate	Non-corporate	Total
Agriculture etc.	16	31	47	12	37	49
Mining, manufacturing, construction and utilities	7	12	19	9	11	20
Commerce and transport	6	7	13	5	8	13
Services, etc.	8	13	21	9	9	18
Total	37	63	100	35	65	100

Source: Appendix Table A.5 and Urrutia and Villalba (1969).

adopted in consequence – for these were imported technologies and related to the primary-export and import-substituting industrialization pattern itself.

The parallel that springs to mind in relation to the importance of the mining industry in Peru is the case of Chile; here too mining was relatively unimportant in terms of contribution to GDP and accounted for only 5 per cent of employment in the late 1960s, yet it provide by far the greater part of exports – in 1968–70 minerals made up five sixths of export income and copper for three quarters. Peru did, of course, have a wider 'basket' of export commodities than its southern neighbour, but as it moved towards the status of mono-exporter with the decline of fishmeal and the domestic absorption of export crops the fluctuations of international copper prices and the need to get new projects under way became as important as they had been in Chile for decades.[43] Chilean mining was the main source of investible surplus and tax revenue as well as of foreign exchange; despite the fact that efforts since the 1930s to transfer these resources through agencies such as CORFO into industry had brought the import-substitution process to its later stages much earlier in Chile than in Peru, mining remained the motor of growth, if only through the provision of the capacity to import industrial inputs.[44] In addition, Chile also suffered from the problems of inadequate food supply, which placed considerable strain on the balance of payments – a strain that was enormously increased by the downward income redistribution between 1970 and 1973. Industry (including in this definition manufacturing, construction and utilities) was evidently growing rapidly throughout Latin America between 1955 and 1973, but while Peru gained ground relative to its neighbours in the first decade, it appears to have lost it in the second; we shall return to this topic in Chapter 9. Moreover, the much greater absolute size of industry in the larger economies (the Brazilian industrial sector was about eight times larger than that of Peru in 1973 although it was not that much greater as a share of GDP) allowed for more economies of scale and sophistication in production methods. The extremely high share of service activities in GDP in all cases should be noted.

The relatively high level of the trade coefficient for Peru is remarkable, and underlines the vulnerability of the economy to fluctuations in international markets, as compared to both the average and even to that paradigm of an export-led economy, Venezuela. The importance of external trade to the seven economies varies considerably, but there appears to have been only a slight tendency to decline in all of them during the 1960s, compared to a more rapid fall in the previous decade.[45] This decline should reflect the progress of import-substitution, and thus the steady reduction of the foreign exchange constraint on expansion; the relative stability of industry is frequently attributed to the use of extremely import-intensive techniques of production, which contribute to continued external dependency.[46] To the extent that the bulk of imports in all these countries are industrial inputs, the ratio of imports to industrial output (i.e. the ratio of the shares of imports and industry in GDP as in Table 4.14) reflects the relative 'import-intensity' of the seven economies, and thus the effectiveness with which foreign exchange is used. This derived ratio has a value of over a half for Peru, Venezuela and Colombia in the 1960s, compared to between a third and a quarter in the other four, more advanced economies. But apart from this constraint, which may well only reflect the length of time for which the industrialization process has been under way, more fundamental factors such as resource endowment are also important. In the absence of the sort of natural resource base which gave agricultural strength to Argentina, Brazil, Mexico and Colombia or tremendous mineral output to Chile and Venezuela, Peru had neither the surplus funds nor the internal market for sustained industrialization based on commercial criteria.

Nonetheless, none of the seven economies, with the obvious although probably temporary exception of Venezuela, has managed to overcome the foreign exchange constraint on development, and this, along with a stagnant agriculture holding much of the population, forms the basis of the 'structuralist' interpretation of persistent underdevelopment in Latin America, an interpretation which had considerable influence on Peruvian policy makers. The structure of ownership in general, and the systems of land tenure and foreign control over industry in particular, were held to lie at the heart of this difficulty. As Furtado points out:[47]

> the emphasis [in agriculture] is on the production of a few commodities, mainly those destined for export, enjoying a privileged position and monopolising the available credit facilities and infrastructure ... the population explosion, rapid urbanisation and the rise in purchasing power of a part of the population failed to elicit the required response from the Latinamerican agrarian sector ... taking into account the foreign control of industrial investment, which seems to imply a high content of imported inputs, and the size of the domestic markets concerned, it can be deduced that import-substituting industrialization is relatively ineffective as a factor for bringing about structural change in countries where it has been under way only since the fifties.

5

The ownership of capital and the distribution of income

The purpose of this chapter is to advance our discussion of Peruvian underdevelopment a step further; from the analysis of the structure of the economy in the previous chapter we go on to look at the way in which capital was owned in Peru, on the one hand, and the distribution of income generated by the combination of this ownership pattern and the dual structure of production of the economy on the other. The argument advances from what might be termed the 'structuralist' point of view implicit in the analysis of the last chapter to what might be described as a 'dependency' approach to underdevelopment.

Specifically, we shall concentrate upon the ownership of corporate enterprise in the main productive sectors as it has evolved over the past two decades and then view it as a conglomerate system, taking 1968 as a pivotal year, after which the trends in private ownership were sharply changed by state intervention. Ownership is central to an understanding of economic development, not just because private ownership and wage relations are central characteristics of capitalism, but because those who control productive assets also determine the direction of change in the structure of production. The issue of income distribution also emerges as a logical part of the analysis, founded as it is upon the relationship between labour and capital (exploitation in the sphere of production) on the one hand, and on the dependent dualism of the economy (exploitation in the sphere of exchange) on the other. In particular, the steps towards worker participation in some forms of enterprise and state control of others undertaken in Peru after 1968 had a significant impact on income distribution as well as on ownership, although less than had been anticipated.

Ownership of the main production sectors

Although agriculture directly occupied about half the population during our period, and a considerably greater proportion if related activities in transport and marketing were to be taken into account, this sector was not central to the Peruvian economy either as a dynamic growth factor or as a source of investible surplus. As we have seen, the most important components were the irrigated production of industrial crops on the coast and the rearing of livestock and semi-subsistence foodstuffs in the highlands, the bulk of production being in relatively large units; the size distribution of production units was highly concentrated and remained so throughout our period, although some subdivision did occur in the larger units as a result of the economic decline of highland estates and peasant invasions in the mid 1960s. This distribution did not, however, correspond exactly to ownership, for three reasons: first, many of the largest units were in fact *'comunidades'* – traditional collective forms of ownership with particular importance in the highlands, where large areas of poor grazing land were held in common, and small food plots held individually; second, many small peasants owned or at least had access to a number of small sub-subsistence plots in different ecological zones of the Andes; and third, individual landlords or their families owned considerable numbers of estates before 1969. Nonetheless, the distribution of land was clearly extremely unequal in terms of units, particularly when the varying quality of soils is taken into account: until 1969, about half the farmed area was under large private 'haciendas', mostly producing either industrial crops on the coast or livestock in the highlands.[1] In 1961, there were 1091 holdings of over 2500 hectares; although these accounted for only 0.1 per cent of all holdings they included 61 per cent of the total area. Of the 0.85 million holdings, 67 per cent were worked by their owners, 9 per cent by employees and 24 per cent leased or belonging to *comunidades*. The coastal estates were virtually fully capitalist enterprises using reproducible capital and engaged in wage relations, while those in the highlands retained some 'feudal' practices such as labour payment in kind, rents paid in labour services and labour-intensive production. In both cases most of the land was held by a relatively small number of owners and these formed a key element of the 'oligarchy' which we have discussed in Chapter 3. The conflict between the highland estates and the surrounding *comunidades* had been a permanent feature of rural life for half a millenium,[2] with the former always able to invoke the power of the state to repress the revindications of the latter. On the coast, in contrast, the sugar and cotton estates had been the breeding-ground for the APRA and syndicalism: the great popular uprising of 1936 had been in Trujillo, the capital of the northern coast. Foreign ownership was not,

Table 5.1. *Size distribution of units in Peruvian agriculture*

	Per cent of farm units		Per cent of farmed area	
	1961	1972	1961	1972
Farm size:				
⩽ 1 hectare	35	35	1	1
>1 and ⩽5 hectares	48	43	5	6
>5 and ⩽20 hectares	13	17	5	9
>20 and ⩽100 hectares	3	4	5	9
>100 hectares	1	1	84	75

Source: Agricultural Censuses 1961, 1972: *Oficina Nacional de Estadistica y Censos*, Lima.

however, very important in agriculture by our period (even though European immigrants had been in the early years of the century) except for the Cerro de Pasco estates in the central highlands and the Grace holdings in coastal sugar; both were significant not only because of their intersectoral linkages (to mining and chemicals, respectively) but also because of their prominence as targets of nationalist sentiment.

Draft legislation on land reform had been introduced by the 1962–63 military government and Belaunde had promulgated a law to subdivide highland estates, but internal divisions within the high command and congressional opposition from an Apra–Odría alliance respectively prevented either from coming to fruition.[3] Nonetheless, peasant land invasions culminating in the highland guerrilla activities of 1965–66 weakened the commitment of Peruvian capital to estate agriculture; and, possibly more importantly, the declining relative profitability of estate agriculture as world prices slackened and Lima real estate prices rose reduced bourgeois resistance to the concept of modernizing land reform. Meanwhile, the idea that the transformation of 'feudal' estates into more modest commercial farms could stimulate agricultural growth and widen the domestic market for manufactures was receiving increasing support from technocrats and industrialists, in common with similar groups throughout Latin America.

On coming to power in 1968, one of the first actions of the Revolutionary government was to initiate a comprehensive land reform that would give '*la tierra a quien la trabaja*'. Initially there was apparently some intention to allow preventive subdivision of land by landlords, but peasant union pressure on the government secured the complete transfer of estates to the permanent labour force in the form of production cooperatives, all farms of over 30 hectares in the highlands and 50 on the coast being eventually affected between 1969 and 1977, when the Agrarian Reform was officially declared complete.[4] Some grazing land was transferred to highland *comunidades*, but the most important development was the establishment of production cooperatives – the SAIS (*Sociedades Agricolas de Interés Social*) in the Sierra and the CAPs (*Cooperatives Agrarias de Producción*) on the coast – on the basis of the former private estates as integral enterprises. Compensation was based on the landlords' previous tax returns (ensuring a low valuation!); the total compensation budget for the 9 million hectares affected was only 11 billion soles – of which 8 billions were in the form of long-term government paper[5] – and the new owners were to pay off the debt to the government over about twenty years.

As Caballero[6] points out, the aims of the land reform seem to have been more political than economic, being concerned with reducing the power of the 'oligarchy' and defusing social conflict in rural areas rather than increasing production or mobilizing a surplus for industrial production. The effect was to give small tenant farmers ('*feudatarios*') on the large decentralized estates and the permanently-employed rural proletariat on the more modern ones access to their own means of production, but within the framework of a market economy and under considerable state supervision. The figures for the number of beneficiaries and the land affected are given in Table 5.2 below, but these tend to overstate the impact because generally the allocation of large areas of poor grazing land to highland communities resulted in modest increases in family income; a more realistic estimate would be that about a quarter of rural families benefited substantially from the land reform, while the landless peasants (who were the worst off) received little or

Table 5.2. *Impact of the land reform 1969–77*

	Original status		Achieved mid-1976		Final target	
	Million hectares	Million families	Million hectares	Million families	Million hectares	Million families
Cooperatives (CAP, SAIS)	—	—	6.6	0.3	7.3	0.4
Comunidades campesinas	7.8	0.4	8.8	0.4	9.2	0.4
Independent farmers	21.3	0.2	13.7	0.2	12.6	0.2
	29.1	0.6	29.1	0.9	29.1	1.0
Landless labour	—	0.6	—	0.3	—	0.2
Total	29.1	1.2	29.1	1.2	29.1	1.2

Source: Ministry of Agriculture: *Oficina Sectorial de Planificación*, Lima.

nothing. Caballero estimates that when the land reform was completed in 1977, land equivalent to about half the productive potential of agriculture was transferred to some 80 000 labourers of what was the rural proletariat and another 275 000 families benefited in various ways by having access to estate land, ceasing to pay rent, or having pastures incorporated into their communities. Excluded were most *comunidades* (although some rather unsuccessful attempts at regrouping them with contiguous cooperatives as '*Proyectos Integrados de Asentamiento Rural*' were made between 1973 and 1975) and landless labour – which continued working on a seasonal basis for the large cooperatives or small farmers. Criticism of the limited scope of the Reforma Agraria was only to be expected in view of populist rhetoric with which it was launched, but the limitations arose not from the neglect of 'large' landlords (i.e. farms of over 100 hectares, virtually all of which were affected) but from the dual nature of agriculture which had resulted from centuries of unbalanced agrarian growth and engaged only the minority of the workforce in estates. The reform did eliminate an important land-owning class, and although some of their economic power may have remained in private control over parts of input supplies, transport and food processing, a radical change in the rural class structure undoubtedly took place, the long-run social or political effect of which would be difficult to overestimate.

It is difficult, if not impossible, to arrive at a definite conclusion on the economic effect of the land reform as this depends not only upon the long-run dynamics of agrarian capitalism (for cooperatives in a market economy are essentially joint-stock companies) but also upon the development strategy adopted for the economy as a whole – but we shall return to both these themes later on. At this point it should be noted that if the system of assigning the bulk of resources such as bank credit and technical assistance to the new reform enterprises continues, the gap between them and the rural masses who (with or without land) are at very low levels of productivity and income, will widen and the new enterprises will absorb little labour, thus reinforcing the existing dual structure. Indeed, it appears that the most advantageous economic strategy for Peru in the medium term may well be to concentrate upon large modernized units to produce food and export crops; the needs of the small peasants would only then gain attention when migration and renewed rural tension pose social and political barriers to continued growth once again.

The pattern of ownership in mining is relatively simple to describe, given the degree of oligopoly in the sector. As we have seen, three firms in the '*gran mineria*' category dominated metals production in the 1960s – Cerro de Pasco, Marcona and Southern Peru Copper – while one enterprise, International Petroleum Company, dominated oil production and distribution. All four enterprises were interconnected North American firms and at the centre of the political debate over the extent of foreign ownership; much of government policy in the sector both before and after 1968 was fashioned in relation to their activities. At the outset of our period, the only major firm in mining was the Cerro de Pasco Corporation, owned and controlled from the USA for half a century and operating a complex of mines integrated with smelters and refineries in the central Sierra. In addition, through equity participation and smelting contracts a group of local 'independents' were also con-trolled *de facto* by this firm, so that about half of total mining production was in the hands of one foreign enterprise which was also a substantial landowner in the area. In 1950, after a particularly favourable mining law was passed in order to encourage foreign in-vestment, Southern Peru Copper began to develop the open-cast Toquepala copper deposits, starting production in 1959; in 1954, Marcona Mining started exports from the iron deposits previously owned by the state Santa enterprise, ceded by President Odría. In both cases, foreign capital had put pressure on the Peruvian govern-ment in a situation where there was no interest from domestic private capital in developing the deposits.[7] These new projects provided a substantial part of the 1959–65 export boom, and by 1968 about three quarters of mining output was controlled directly by these three firms and in total some 85 per cent of production was processed and marketed through them.

By 1968, two major problems had come to a head in the metals sector, both of which were of crucial importance to the new military government. First, the extent of foreign ownership of the sector, combined with the massive export of profits, evidence of transfer pricing[8] and continual labour troubles, led to strong political pressure for nationalization of the three mines. Second, the copper deposits at Cuajone and Cerro Verde, conceded to SPC and Anaconda respectively ten years before, had still not been developed – apparently because this did not fit into the worldwide 'sourcing' strategies of these multinationals.[9] The resulting govern-ment strategy was to reclaim Cerro Verde in 1972 (forming a state company, Mineroperu, to exploit it), nationalize Cerro de Pasco in 1973 (which became Centromin) and Marcona in 1975 (becoming Hierroperu) so as to give direct state control over about 60 per cent of mining production. In addition, all refining and export marketing was placed in the hands of Mineroperu in order to give indirect state control over the remaining private sector. Negoti-ations with SPC over the development of Cuajone were started in 1970, but the pressure from international capital was such that 'finance could not be secured' by SPC until compensation on the other nationalizations was paid and the marketing operations of Mineroperu reduced to those of a commission agent.[10] Thus it was only in 1974 that work on the opencast copper mine at Cuajone got under way and at the end of 1976 that production started, seventeen years after the previous major increment to mining output.

In sum, until the 1950s about half the mining sector was controlled by a single foreign firm; two other foreign enterprises brought about a significant expansion of the sector, admittedly by opening new deposits rather than by taking over existing operations as Cerro did, but they still relied upon state concessions to do so. Eventually, this was bound to generate political stress, exacerbated by the foreign companies' unwillingness to embark on new ventures, and state intervention was almost inevitable. Meanwhile, state control of mining production had become widespread in the third world, and it had become apparent that this was not necessarily contrary to the interests of foreign capital as long as a reliable supply of metal was secured and the price could be controlled on metropolitan markets.

Perhaps the most immediate causal circumstance of the fall of Belaunde in 1968 was neither land reform nor mining policy but the scandal over oil concessions.[11] At the centre of the stage was the International Petroleum Company (controlled by what is now Exxon), which operated the oilfields on the northern coast; in the past these had made Peru a significant exporter, but by the 1950s the fields just about supplied local needs with the imminent prospect of having to import to cover the expected deficit. Given that IPC was making no new exploration efforts and that the existing state enterprise (Empresa Petrolera Fiscal) seemed quite capable of carrying on the refining and distribution operations, the enormous profits of the foreign firm did appear unjustified. However, Belaunde (admittedly under heavy pressure from the US government) could not achieve a satisfactory settlement and one of the first symbolic acts of the military regime was to occupy the oilfields by force. Negotiations for compensation[12] were protracted, but the combination of IPC and EPF immediately became a major state enterprise (Petroperu) with exclusive responsibility for exploration, production, refining and distribution of petroleum and products. Over the next five years, Petroperu absorbed Conchan, Lobitos and Gulf operations in Peru. The pressing need for more production, made more urgent by the growing oil deficit and the rise in world prices that began in 1970 made rapid exploration of the Amazon basin (south of the proven Ecuadorean fields) necessary. It was considered that Petroperu was not technically or financially equipped for the entire operation, so about two thirds of the area actually explored was sub-contracted to foreign companies – of which Occidental became the most prominent. The royalty payments were to be in oil, giving Petroperu direct ownership of about two thirds of production, but the cost of the trans-Andean pipeline (financed by a consortium of Japanese banks with a loan repayable in oil) was such that, given that proven reserves were much less than had been hoped for, this asset turned out to be only adequate for domestic self-sufficiency and not for substantial export. In mining and oil then, state dominance had been established in place of virtually exclusive foreign control, but the cost of recapitalizing such assets turned out to be extremely high.

Table 5.3 *Ownership in the metal mining sector*

	1965		1975	
	Sales	Employment	Sales	Employment
Cerro de Pasco/Centromin	30%	36%	36%	33%
Marcona/Hierroperu	14%	9%	8%	9%
Southern Peru Copper	28%	6%	25%	6%
Total *'gran mineria'*	72%	50%	69%	49%
'Independent' mines	28%	50%	31%	51%

Source: Ministry of Energy and Mines, *Oficina Sectorial de Planificación*, Lima.

The evolution of ownership in the fishing sector illustrates almost the entire range of organizational possibilities over a space of two decades.[13] During the initial expansion of the sector between 1957 and 1962 fishing was almost entirely controlled by domestic capital largely independent of the grand bourgeoisie and there was considerable competition between the various concerns. However, when the industry entered its first major crisis in 1963–65, largely as the result of overfishing brought about by this very competition, three events concurred: first, production became concentrated in the hands of fewer owners; second, large domestic capital penetrated the sector as supplier of bank finance; and third, foreign firms were able to gain improved positions from greater survival capacity and control over marketing channels abroad. Although production revived during the 1966–69 period, these tendencies continued so that by the latter date about half of production was in the hands of five large enterprises and about a third under foreign control – a major part of the 'national' part being dominated by the Banchero group in connexion with the Prado financial empire. Consolidation was the inevitable result of excess capacity and dwindling resources, and apparently welcomed by national capital in times of economic difficulties, but full rationalization on a private basis could not be achieved, and when the second major crisis occurred in 1973, the state took over the whole sector – forming Pescaperu for production and Epchap for sales. In less than twenty years, then, the sector had gone from artisan production through competitive capitalism to oligopoly, foreign penetration and finally state capitalism. However, Pescaperu continued with the same problems of overcapacity in terms of fleet, plant and labour, the resolution of which were made all the more difficult by the excessive compensation paid to the previous owners and the natural resistance of the fishermen's union to the massive redundancies and fleet sales necessary to make it a viable enterprise at lower levels of production. Three significant points can be made about this experience. First, although the initial expansion of the sector was undertaken by local and independent entrepreneurs, it was in response to the input requirements of agriculture in the metro-politan countries; after 1968 the state sales corporation (Epchap) continued to export fishmeal mainly through a Panamanian-based American corporation (Purina) at prices determined on inter-national markets. The initial technology was imported in the form of complete fishing boats, though local shipbuilding capacity was subsequently developed. Second, the first crisis revealed the weakness of this independent capital and its need to turn to the grand bourgeoisie for financial help, but this latter was incapable of reorganizing the sector and thus state monopolization was the only alternative – nationalization by default. Third, and as a consequence of the first two, the sector never fully developed backward linkages (e.g. marine engines) with Peruvian manufacturing or developed the domestic market for fish protein, while the depradatory attitudes of capitalist enterprise – unfortunately continued by Pescaperu, initially at least – to the exploitation of an ecological resource prevented either conservation of this valuable source of foreign exchange or the formation of an effective international exporters' cartel.

The manufacturing sector[14] enjoyed rapid expansion in the 1955–65 period on the basis of a typical process of import-substitution. Despite the fact that an industrial base producing foodstuffs, textiles and construction materials already existed in the hands of domestic capital – largely those of the grand bourgeoisie – at the beginning of our period, the main phase of import-substitution was carried out by foreign enterprise. However, this latter operated in close conjunction with domestic capital (which often provided finance and management) when it did not replace or take over existing firms. In this way a number of multinational firms penetrated already highly oligopolized branches such as processed foodstuffs, shoes, household equipment, pharmaceuticals and transport equipment. By 1968 some two hundred firms (about five per cent of those in the 'factory' sector) accounted for 80 per cent of assets and 65 per cent of sales, and well over half of these were controlled by foreign capital; the domestic portion was dominated by a handful of ownership groups closely involved in other sectors, although a small number of substantial independents did exist, particularly in engineering branches. A similar pattern was experienced in the utilities sector where in particular the electrical generation system was still largely in private (and predominantly foreign) hands in 1968.

The reforms after that date were, as we have seen, conditioned by the military's belief that private industrialists, once freed from the shackles of the 'oligarchy', would generate their own dynamic.[15] In consequence, the ownership changes were initially confined to those resulting from other reforms (such as agro-industry), from the state takeover of utilities (electricity and water) in order to rationalize and recapitalize them, and from the strategic requirement expressed in the 1970 Industries Law that heavy industry – particularly steel, cement, paper, petro-chemicals and fertilizers – should all be state owned. In some cases (such as steel and fertilizers) state enterprises already existed, while in others (such as cement and electricity) the firms acquired were close to bankruptcy, so this did not present much difficulty. As a result, the state controlled by 1975 about a quarter of output by manufacturing and all that of utilities, with the remainder more or less evenly divided between foreign and domestic firms. However, the public enterprises acted mainly in support of final manufacturing, which remained predominantly under private control and either directly or indirectly (i.e. through technology or subcontracting) integrated to the activities of multinational enterprises.

The Peruvian banking system was, by Latinamerican standards at least, highly developed and had acted before 1968 as the 'nerve centre' of large domestic capital. In the 1950s, the sector had been concentrated on a small number of financial groups, with 'satellite' operations in insurance and investment companies; there also existed a series of local branches of foreign banks (such as the Banco de Londres y America del Sud) and relatively small state development banks such as the Banco Central Hipotecario. During the 1960s two trends combined to reduce the importance of local banking, both of which were related to the withdrawal of the grand bourgeoisie from the process of accumulation. First, the state banks expanded their operations as part of their 'infrastructural' role of supporting private investment with long loans on soft terms in fields such as agriculture, industry and construction, increasing thereby their share of total bank credit to the private sector from about a fifth to nearly a half between 1960 and 1970. Second, controlling interests in a number of major private banks were sold to foreign concerns, such as the Banco Continental to Chase Manhattan and the Banco Internacional to the Chemical Bank, so that between 1960 and 1968 foreign control of commercial bank assets rose from 36 per cent to 62 per cent of the total.[16] The military government reversed this situation by taking over a number of substantial foreign banks (Continental, Internacional and Progreso), restricting the operations of direct affiliates, nationalizing a major domestic bank (Popular) and forcing the Italian owners of the remaining major private bank (Credito) to sell to local capital. This resulted in about 85 per cent of bank credit to the private sector coming under state control, although that part corresponding to the 'Banca Asociada' (i.e. the former private banks) was integrated into the public sector on the basis of equity ownership rather than as part of the planning process.

Construction and real estate activities became increasingly important due to the massive urbanization of Lima during our period, and all the local capitalist groups were active in the field. In particular, it would appear that traditional landowning groups (such as the de La Piedra family) became prominent once again as speculators in urban land,[17] and that the ownership of both building sites and construction companies became concentrated in a few local hands, although major state construction projects continued to be undertaken by foreign contractors with the requisite experience. The reforms after 1968 did not really affect the sector significantly, possibly because it also provided considerable income for petty capital (including many military officers) in the form of rents; the attempts to curb urbanization of arable land round Lima served only to increase the monopoly profits available to those owning such land already. There was no significant state activity in either housing or urbanization, except for the provision of basic infrastructure to the *pueblos jovenes.*

Finally, foreign capital had penetrated a number of key points in the tertiary sector by 1968, mainly as the result of superior technological expertise in modern services, although the British ownership of the central railway system had resulted from 'foreclosure on government debt in the last century. Apart from the nationalization of the Peruvian Corporation, the IT & T affiliate (on the fall of Allende), the telephone and cables systems (both foreign owned) and a number of commercial operations (such as cotton marketing) were taken over by the Peruvian state between 1970 and 1975. In addition, the mass media – national daily newspapers, radio and television – which had been in the hands of the grand bourgeoisie and served as a medium of opposition to reform even after 1968, were nationalized in 1974. In principle, the newspapers were to be assigned to popular groups representing different sectors (such as the peasantry and schoolteachers) but in fact they were retained under the control of the Ministry of the Interior as organs of official propaganda, although weekly magazines were allowed considerable freedom of criticism.

The changing pattern of ownership

There existed, then, a model of ownership in Peru before 1968 common to almost all production branches: a highly oligopolized corporate sector dominating production, owned and controlled by a small group of national finance-capitalists in increasingly close alliance with foreign enterprise. The intrusion of the state after 1968 changed this pattern both by effectively replacing large domestic capital and by altering the relationship with the multinationals. Here we shall attempt to put this pattern together at an aggregate level and assess the scale of the ownership changes over the period.

What does not emerge clearly from the branch-by-branch analysis of corporate ownership is the fact that until 1968 it was organized in intersectoral groups linked by finance capital. These groups combined interests in exports (such as mining, sugar or fishmeal), landowning (both rural and urban), manufacturing, commerce and construction – knitting the operation together with banks and finance houses.[18] Thus there was no automatic conflict between, say, agrarian and industrial capital of the type often assumed to be common in the Latinamerican experience,[19] and indeed one of the more efficient aspects of these groups was the way in which funds could be moved rapidly from one activity to another in order to take advantage of changing profit opportunities. This particular pattern had its historical roots in the diverse nature of the Peruvian natural resource endowment, which required the early development of finance capital to coordinate the various export activities. These groups, moreover, had every reason to welcome foreign enterprise and even to finance it (as happened in the case of manufacturing multinationals) as well as guaranteeing state support, because multinational firms could supply technology which would have been costly to develop locally.

Two examples of such intersectoral groups are of particular interest because they not only represent cases of 'large' and 'medium' groups respectively, but also correspond to direct leadership of the state during the two civilian regimes of our period – Prado and Belaunde.[20] Manuel Prado (president for the second time between 1956 and 1962) headed a financial group around the Banco Popular which included cement, textiles, real estate, construction, mining (minority partnership in Marcona), fishing (in association with Banchero), newspapers, radio and commerce. The family of Fernando Belaunde (president between 1963 and 1968) formed a somewhat more diffuse grouping with interests in real estate (Belaunde himself having been an architect), agricultural supplies, metal engineering industry, banking (Banco de Credito) and commerce – as well as joint shareholdings with the Prado group. In both these cases, then, the distinction between the public and the private sector became blurred in an extreme fashion; in any case most major Peruvian families had always had members in the cabinet – whether civil or military.

There was not, of course, the same relationship between foreign firms, although their predominantly US origin and joint ethos did tend to produce a certain solidarity, particularly when putting pressure on the government of the day. However, the degree of foreign ownership in almost every sector had clearly reached politically unacceptable limits by 1968 – three quarters of mining, a third of fishing, half of manufacturing industry and two thirds of banking were under direct external control.[21] This had come about not by victorious competition with domestic capital but rather from a close alliance with it, resulting in an expansion from a limited base in mining established in the first quarter of the century, to almost complete control of about half of material production in the third.

The abrupt change in these trends in the pattern of ownership was brought about precisely because of the extremely high degree of monopolization and dependency that had occurred. Before 1968, and confining ourselves to relations within the capitalist class, the close alliance between the grand bourgeoisie and foreign enterprise had had a double consequence. On the one hand, the domestic elite had effectively handed over much of the 'entrepreneurial' task of modernizing the economy to foreign capital by the end of the 1950s, while retaining the role of 'financier' and supplier of government support and appropriating a substantial share of the profits generated thereby. On the other, this alliance prevented the development of the small but independent industrial capital fraction, initially by occupying the available terrain and then by controlling access to markets, credit and government facilities. Indeed, looking at historical trends, Thorp and Bertram (1978) argue that this very flexibility of the traditional elite prevented further progress towards the formation of a truly *national* bourgeoisie with an autonomous industrialization project.

After 1968, the picture is quite different. In a somewhat irregular but cumulative fashion, the *Gobierno Revolucionario* nationalized large sections of mining, fishing, industry, banking, transport, communications and commerce, as well as virtually eliminating private capital in agriculture. In consequence, the state effectively took over the economic role of the domestic grand bourgeoisie – with the political consequences that we have seen in Chapter 3. The former system of large intersectoral groups had clearly been broken up, with the 'base' (exports and heavy industry) and the 'articulation' (banking) removed so as to leave only light industry, real estate and commerce in private hands as isolated activities. The state did not, however, take over the complete network so as to restore the articulation of the previous system – nor was it adequately replaced by the central planning system. Moreover, much of the foreign connexion remained – either in the form of direct ownership (manufacturing) or in that of technical relationships (mining) – even if in a far less important and dominant role. The divergence between the aims of foreign capital and those of the new military regime generated a series of conflicts which had not existed under the hegemony of the grand bourgeoisie, as we shall see in Chapter 8.

We must now attempt to put together the available statistical information so as to draw some overall conclusions as to the scale of the ownership changes over the period. The object of this exercise is to assess the economic and social scope of the various forms of ownership in the corporate sector as expressed by the proportions of gross domestic product produced and labour employed by domestic, foreign and state enterprises respectively. The distinction between the corporate and non-corporate sector is drawn from the analysis of duality in the previous chapter and the ownership categories from the sectoral discussions in this. The pivotal point is 1968: from this date we refer to 1975 as a measure of the reforms (once completed) in ownership under the 'Revolution', and back to 1950 (in a much more tentative fashion) as a date before the renewed penetration of foreign capital took place. The complete methodology is given in the statistical appendix, and a summary shown in Table 5.4. The first point of note is the rise and then fall of the importance of foreign enterprise, which rose from 15 per cent of corporate output (i.e. 10 per cent of GDP) in 1950 to 35 per cent in

1968 – mainly as the result of penetration of mining, fishing and manufacturing – and then fell back to 16 per cent by 1975 as a result of the reforms. This refers, of course, to direct control by foreign enterprise through ownership; indirect control through technology and sales contracts with both public and private firms was more widespread than those figures suggest. The expansion of the state continued steadily, rising from 11 per cent of corporate output in 1950 to 16 per cent in 1968 and then doubling to 32 per cent in 1975, while cooperatives – mainly as the result of the land reform – accounted for 15 per cent by 1975. In consequence, private domestic capital – in a sense the passive participant in the process – fell from 74 per cent of corporate output in 1950 to 49 per cent in 1968 and 37 per cent in 1975. When we turn to employment a similar pattern emerges, except that cooperatives are more important than in production and foreign enterprises less so, due to their relative labour intensity.

Overall, the breakdown of output shares by main sector in Table 5.4 indicates that the reforms displaced private capital from the primary sector, but foreign and domestic capital still dominated the vital secondary sector. These estimates are approximate, but the orders of magnitude appear to be approximately correct and reasonable variations in individual items do not alter the overall results significantly. Cabieses and Otero (1978, p. 74) quote a similar breakdown from a study by Brundenius carried out for the Institute Nacional de Planificación – the form of which has a striking resemblance to that in FitzGerald (1976a, Appendix II) although this source is not cited – with more or less the same results for shares of GDP generated in the public and cooperative sectors before and after the reforms. However, they give a rather higher share for foreign enterprise (31 per cent of GDP in 1968 and 21 per cent in 1975) than we have, with correspondingly lower shares for the 'domestic private' sector (56 and 46 per cent, respectively). Unfortunately, the table as quoted by Cabieses and Otero has several arithmetical errors, but the difference appears to arise from a mistaken attribution of agricultural ownership[22] and the neglect of the extent of non-corporate enterprise in the service sector and thus the necessarily limited scope for foreign penetration. In any case, their estimates only serve to reinforce the argument presented here.

Table 5.4. *Shares of corporate output and employment by main ownership categories 1950–75*

Percentage of gross domestic product controlled by:

Production sector:	1968				1975				
	State	Foreign enterprise	Domestic enterprise	Total corporate sector	State	Foreign enterprise	Domestic enterprise	Cooperatives	Total corporate sector
Primary	0	8	9	17	3	2	1	6	12
Secondary	1	10	13	24	6	8	12	1	27
Tertiary	10	4	12	26	12	1	14	1	28
Total	11	22	34	67	21	11	27	8	67

	Percentage of gross domestic product			Percentage of economically active population		
	1950	1968	1975	1950	1968	1975
State	7	11	21	5	7	13
Foreign enterprise	10	22	11	4	10	8
Domestic enterprise	43	34	27	21	19	11
Cooperatives etc.	—	—	8	—	—	9
Total corporate sector	60	67	67	30	35	36

Source: Appendix, Table A.6.

Worker participation

One of the characteristic features of the programme of the military regime between 1968 and 1975, the so-called 'First Phase of the Peruvian Revolution', was the rapid introduction of direct worker participation in the administration, capital and profits of enterprise.[23] The intellectual origins of *'cogestión'* (joint control of an enterprise by entrepreneur and workers) can be traced back to Roman Catholic thought at the end of the last century, while the concept of *'autogestion'* (workers' control of an enterprise) is fundamentally that of the British cooperative movement, but both of these ideas had antecedents in Peruvian politics. In the original Aprista reform programme the economy was to be based on cooperatives, and subsequently both the Acción Popular (Belaunde's party) and Christian Democrats supported limited worker participation in profits[24] – as long as it did not pose a threat to private property, which was held to be inviolable under the Constitution.[25] Indeed, some small advance towards worker participation in the profits of industrial firms had been made under Bustamante, and credit cooperatives, especially for housing, had been promoted under Belaunde. However, for the *Gobierno Revolucionario de la Fuerza Armada* worker participation was ostensibly to be a central element in the organization of the Peruvian economy and the attainment of a 'true' democracy where social groups would be represented within the economic system rather than through political parties. To some extent this represented a continuation of the previous ideological line – the attempt to identify the interests of the worker with those of the enterprise and so eliminate labour conflicts – but it was combined with a hostility to domestic monopoly capital and foreign enterprise and thus became much more than a simple effort to break up trades union solidarity. Worker management was increasingly seen in official documents between 1969 and 1975 as a potential substitute, in conjunction with state enterprise, for private enterprise and as a central element in a possible transition to 'Peruvian socialism'.

The three key elements were to be the rural cooperatives, the industrial communities and 'social property'. As we have already seen, agrarian production cooperatives were established in place of the former haciendas as part of the land reform, principally in the coastal irrigated zones and the highland ranches. The property rights were transferred to the permanent workforce but the titles were still lodged with the state as collateral against the agrarian debt; the technical management structure was maintained and state control exercised either through state purchasing agencies (in the case of CAPs) or by means of SINAMOS as 'organizational assistance' in the highlands. The strength, and also the weakness of the model was that it maintained an existing organizational structure almost intact; in particular, the non-permanent workforce remained largely excluded from the benefits as marginal wage-earners. Apart from the implications for equity, the decision also had the effect of splitting peasant movements politically. In the cases where new large-scale enterprises were created in the highlands out of a number of *comunidades* these were in an even more economically precarious position than the ex-haciendas,[26] due to the paucity of surplus available for redistribution – enough for a single landowner to live in luxury but little enough for a thousand peasant families; on the coast, a similar conflict between wages and profits became one between consumption and reinvestment. At the heart of the matter was the fact that the economic, as opposed to the social, structure of agriculture in Peru had not been changed by the agrarian reform, so that although the relations of production within capitalist enterprises were fundamentally altered, the technical nature of the farm itself and its relations with the rest of the economy through the market were essentially the same as before.

The impact of the '*comunidades laborales*' (labour communities) was less far-reaching but of more central importance to the economy. We can distinguish two types. First there were those in mining, fishing and telecommunications – which were basically concerned with the reallocation of profits income. Although nominal representation on the board of directors of the community (representing all employees of the firm) was included, the main provision was remunerative – between 5 and 10 per cent of the post-tax profits going to the members of the community for distribution in cash, roughly in proportion to their salaries (although this did not amount to much, given the low accounting profitability of these sectors) and from 5 to 15 per cent going to the *comunidad* as a whole in the form of bonds. The second type was of much more importance, being established under the 1970 *Ley de Industrias*[27] and applying to all manufacturing firms of more than five employees. Here the community received 25 per cent of book profits too, but 15 in the form of new share issues and 10 per cent in the form of cash. Again, the effect was not radical – by the end of 1975, only about 17 per cent of share capital in the sector was in the hands of communities, and the very pattern of firm size in manufacturing meant that only about a third of the workforce (roughly five per cent of the national total) was included, even though the bulk of production was covered by these '*empresas privadas reformadas*'. Nonetheless, the indirect effect was considerable, mainly as a result of worker participation in management – or at least the direct access to entrepreneurial decisions: this led, on the one hand, to resistance to further investment on the part of private capital,[28] and, on the other, to greater labour solidarity through the grouping of industrial communities at a national level in CONACI. Further, the provision for bankrupt firms to become cooperatives with state financial support became a significant feature of labour claims in the economic crisis of 1976–77. This same crisis, however, forced the government to raise the lower limit on firm size (to roughly twenty employees) for *comunidades* in new enterprises in 1976, under the '*Ley de Pequeña Industria*', and to limit the upper limit on equity participation to 35 per cent in 1977.

However, apart from the political consequences of the economic crisis, when domestic industrialists and foreign bankers forced the government to play down worker participation a more fundamental problem with industrial communities, as with rural cooperatives, was that these were modifications to the relations of production within the corporate sector alone – and in the former far less than in the latter. They left the economic structure of the sector unchanged, and to a certain extent set up a division within the working class and implied thereby the formation of a 'labour aristocracy' – although this was a problem recognized by the trades unions and even the workers at plant level.[29] In response to these difficulties, the *Gobierno Revolucionario* introduced between 1973 and 1975 a new form of enterprise known as '*Empresas de Propiedad Social*' (EPS, or Social

Property Enterprises) which was to be given priority over all other forms of enterprise organization in terms of government support, and was originally supposed to 'predominate' in the economy over the long term.[30] The concept of social property, when the lyricism of its supporters is discounted, was basically that of production cooperatives set up by the state, but with three novel features: first, all workers were to be members (so that the cooperativists could not exploit temporary wage labour) and there were provisions to limit earnings differentials within the enterprise; second, the state – having provided the initial capital through the FONAPS (*Fondo Nacional de Propiedad Social*) – was to control labour remuneration by requiring the return of any surplus over the equivalent of twice the Lima minimum wage per worker plus authorized investment projects and certain social expenditures to the central Fund for reinvestment in new EPS; third, the EPS would depend for their initial survival upon embargoes on competitive imports and priority for state contracts, both of which would allow the CONAPS (*Comisión Nacional de Propiedad Social*) to plan the emergent sector in a rational manner. Great hopes were placed in the future of this type of cooperative which, along with large state enterprises, would form the economic basis of 'Peruvian socialism'.[31]

In the event, the very structure of the economy – particularly in manufacturing where most of the potential EPS were to be – posed the main problem. By mid-1976 six EPS were in operation[32] and another sixty or so were in an advanced stage of preparation, representing a total investment of some US $300 million and providing up to 40 000 jobs. They were mostly urban and almost all in manufacturing, with a relatively high 'cost per workplace' (about US $8000) and dependent on foreign technology – although this was balanced between capitalist and socialist sources. Manufacturing industry was chosen because of the low level of private investment in that sector and the desire to develop the economy at 'high linkage' points such as metal engineering, but branch concentration was so high (with the largest two or three firms at the three-digit ISIC level accounting for the bulk of production) that there was little or no room for new firms large enough to compete effectively with those already in existence, even if capacity expansion were denied to these latter. The logical alternatives appeared to be either that EPS should remain a marginal feature confined to unprofitable branches and rural areas, or that existing large firms should be taken over so as to achieve the required 'predominance' for the sector. Growing pressure arose, therefore, in 1975 among both the Industrial Communities and the progressive elements of the bureaucracy for the conversion of the 'top two hundred' manufacturing firms to EPS and the formation of an integrated and planned system. But this proposal was effectively blocked by opposition from foreign capital, which by 1976 was in a strong position to impose its demands, and the government was unable to raise the initial budget of US $150 millions in the 1975–76 Plan significantly.

A central question that does not appear to have been faced in the context of workers' control in general, and of a wide-spread cooperative movement in particular, was that of the implications for the Peruvian political economy as a whole, above all in relation to a transition from capitalism to socialism. Ambitious claims were made for 'autogestion', but usually on the grounds of either microeconomic analysis within the firm or by using abstract equilibrium models of an atomized competitive economy.[33] If we define capitalism only in terms of wage relations in a particular firm, then clearly a cooperative (and more so an EPS) cannot be capitalist – and so it must be socialist. But this is the same sort of fallacy as that which classifies hacienda agriculture as 'feudal' because payments to the workers are made in kind or the rent paid in labour-time.[34] Similarly, the definition of capitalism at an enterprise level as individual bourgeois ownership of the assets leads to the inescapable conclusion that both cooperatives and state corporations are socialist. The error lies, of course, in considering capitalism only in terms of the relations of production within the firm and not as a mode of production related, in particular, to a market economy. In the case of cooperatives working within a market context (in competition with 'pure' private capital, with other cooperatives or with state corporations) they are essentially equivalent to private partnerships and as far as the rest of the community is concerned they have the same attitude towards trade, accumulation and maintenance of their own socioeconomic position as private capitalists. It is in this sense that cooperatives in a market economy become part of a capitalist mode of production, as do the state corporations even though the same institutions could equally well form part of a socialist mode of production. In the Peruvian context, even if economic difficulties and external pressure had not halted the planned progress towards worker participation after 1975, it was far more likely that a dominant class of bureaucrats (or 'state bourgeoisie') and a group of relatively high-earning cooperatives (or 'labour aristocracy') would have emerged and prevented further reallocation of resources towards the poor in order to preserve their own position. Thus the feasible transition was towards state capitalism – with tightly controlled cooperatives surrounding a core of large state enterprises in a sea of petty commodity producers – rather than towards socialism.

The distribution of income

The distribution of income emerges, in both its functional and personal forms – that is, in terms of the remuneration of the factors of production on the one hand, and in those of the earnings of individuals on the other – from the dual structure of production and employment discussed in the previous chapter and the pattern of ownership explored in this. In very crude terms, therefore, we would expect the income distribution to be made up as follows: first, a great divide between those in the corporate sector and those excluded from it, with the lower 'tail' of the latter made up of landless peasants and, second, a considerable division between remuneration to labour and capital within the upper tercile, with activities such as the professions and administration in between.

Unfortunately, there exists no thorough study of the functional distribution of income in Peru, and we must rely upon the data given in the national accounts (from which Table 5.5 is calculated), bearing in mind two important shortcomings: first, the tendency of firms to under-report profits to the Central Bank for the survey upon which this element in the national accounts is based (although the Bank has attempted to correct for this) and the ambiguity of the distinction between profit and salary for owner-managers; second, the difficulty of defining the category 'non-agricultural independents' which ranges from lawyers to street traders. In our estimates, we have also put back expatriated profits (excluded in the enterprise profit figure given in the *Cuentas Nacionales* because the table concerned is for net *national* income) to give a category we have termed 'net *domestic* income' by analogy with the similar distinction between GDP and GNP on the basis of 'net payment to factors from abroad'. If depreciation were also put back (see Table 6.5), this would give us a 'gross income to property' figure of roughly one third of NDI for our period, and on the reasonable assumption that this all occurs in the corporate sector, this figure is roughly

Table 5.5. *Functional distribution of income in Peru 1950–76 (per cent of net domestic income)*

	1950	1955	1960	1965	1970	1973	1976
Earned incomes:							
Empleados	17.1	20.0	22.2	23.8	24.4	24.4	23.9
Obreros	20.9	22.3	22.7	23.4	21.6	23.9	22.1
Independents:							
Agricultores	21.1	18.5	13.3	11.5	11.8	7.9	8.9
Other	14.0	14.8	15.3	15.8	15.1	15.7	15.6
Property:							
Local profits	16.1	13.1	14.9	16.1	19.5	22.0	24.5
Expatriated profits	1.9	2.5	2.8	1.9	1.7	1.3	0.8
Rents and interest	8.8	8.6	8.8	7.5	6.0	4.7	4.2
	100.0	100.0	100.0	100.0	100.0	100.0	100.0

Source: BCR *Cuentas Nacionales* (Tables 3 and 6, various years).

equivalent to a half of all corporate sector income. Some interesting trends can be discerned within the period, moreover, particularly if we combine Table 5.5 with Table 6.11. The decreasing share of 'independent agriculturalists' (i.e. the peasantry) reflects a broadly stagnant real income per head, in contrast with employees' remuneration which rose over the period as a whole. Wages and salaries, however, appear to have moved up broadly in line with one another, although the share of net domestic income received by the latter rose more rapidly due to their faster growth in numbers; as a proportion of the workforce, *'empleados'* (white-collar workers) rose from 11 per cent in 1950 to 16 per cent in 1976 while 'obreros' (blue-collar workers) rose from 35 per cent to 41 per cent – *'agricultores independientes'* fell from 40 to 28 per cent in the same period. Possibly the most significant trends revealed by our calculations are those for property income: the decline in the share of rents and interest was particularly marked after 1970, a change clearly related to the Agrarian Reform; similarly repatriated profits became less important after this date as well – a point we shall take up again shortly. The most striking effect is possibly the rise in the share of 'domestic' profits: in the 1960s, this might be expected in view of the concentration of capital during that decade; but this trend continued in the 1970s despite the reduction in the size of the private corporate sector as a result of nationalization – we shall examine this further in Chapter 6. Partly, this reflects the increasing share of wages, salaries *and* profits in net domestic income and the relative economic decline of the peasantry as part of the worsening dualism of the economy: employee earnings plus profits rose from 58 per cent of net domestic income in 1955 to 65 per cent in 1965 and 71 per cent in 1973. But within this latter category, the share of profits did not rise that rapidly, being 28 per cent in 1955 and 1965 and 32 per cent in 1973 – although it did rise to 35 per cent in 1976 as a result of the wage restraint of that year.

In view of the weight of foreign capital in the economy, a question of considerable interest must be the degree to which this element appropriated the surplus and the extent to which profits were taken out of Peru for accumulation or distribution elsewhere. The 'net payments for factors from abroad' item in the national accounts which differentiates GDP from GNP should be the foreign profit outflow: in the Peruvian case (as Table 6.2 indicates) this outflow averaged a third of distributed profits in 1955–58, rising to 41 per cent in 1959–63 – but in 1969–76 government restrictions under the Andean Pact rules and the nationalization of foreign enterprises cut this back to 15 per cent. These figures, especially for the 1960s, are certainly very large but it should be remembered that they are broadly in proportion to the scale of foreign control over production in the corporate sector. Declared profitability of US firms in Peru during the 1960s appears to have been around 14 per cent per annum, a substantial return by any standards.[35]

However, royalties and management fees, which represent a non-taxable 'cost' for the local affiliate of a multinational firm (as do loans from the mother company) are another means of transferring profits – particularly in the case of royalties for the use of brand names.[36] More difficult still to measure is the phenomenon of 'transfer pricing', where the local affiliate pays more for imports from the parent (i.e. kits for car assembly) or receives less for exports to it – shifting profits without registration of separate payments with the local authorities.[37] All these, of course, are underlaid by the terms of trade upon which international transactions are conducted, which are the prime system of surplus transfer from the periphery to the centre. Taking these three specific components in the Peruvian case, we find that there are considerable differences between the 1960–65 and 1970–75 periods but that the pattern is similar. Royalties were not a large element in either period and did not add substantially to the outflow of declared profits but strict supervision of technology contracts after 1970 (see Chapter 9) cut this substantially. When these two are combined with a conservative estimate for transfer pricing (that is, the difference between the declared export or import prices and those obtaining on world markets – as opposed to the overall effect of the international terms of trade) figures of the order of those shown in Table 5.6 result. These estimates imply that 58 per cent of 'true' distributed company profits (that is, the totals of Table 5.6 plus domestic distribution as in Table 6.2) in

Table 5.6 *Estimated profit outflow 1960–75*[38]
(annual rates as per cent of GDP)

	1960–65	1970–75
Declared profits expatriated	2.2	1.1
Royalties	0.3	0.1
Transfer pricing	1.6	1.3
Total	4.1	2.5

the Peruvian economy were expatriated in 1960–65, a sum far in excess of the inflow of direct foreign investment, but that this ratio fell to 24 per cent in 1970–75. These figures are both disproportionate to the extent of foreign ownership in the corporate sector, and it is reasonable to surmise therefore that although the outflow of profits was sharply reduced after 1968, the profitability of foreign capital in both periods was probably considerably higher than that of domestic capital.

For personal income we do have more reliable data, from which we can derive some rather clearer conclusions as to the structure and trends of per capita income. On the basis of the 1961 Census, Webb[39] compiled the cardinal estimate of personal income distribution in Peru, shown in Table 5.7 below. The differences in income levels implied are astounding, even by Latinamerican standards; in that year the mean income per head was equivalent to US $229 but while the top decile averaged $1136 (and within that the top percentile $5817) the lowest 40 per cent $46 and even the 40 per cent above

Table 5.7 *The size distribution of income in Peru*

Income Class	National income (1961)			Personal income		
	Labour	Property	Total	1961	1971	Growth
Top 10%	32	22	54	49.6	45.1	+1.4%
Next 10%	13	1	14	15.0	17.5	+3.9%
Next 10% ⎫				10.1	11.4	+3.6%
Next 10% ⎬	20	4	24	7.4	8.1	+3.2%
Next 20% ⎭				9.8	10.6	+3.1%
Next 20% ⎫	7	1	8	5.5	5.5	+2.3%
Lowest 20% ⎭				2.6	1.8	−1.4%
	72	28	100	100.0	100.0	+2.3%
Top 1%	10	20	30	25.4	..	..
Top 5%	..	..	..	38.1	31.2	+0.2%

Source: National income calculated from Webb (1977, pp. 9, 78), personal income for 1961 in Webb (1977) and Jain (1975, p. 89), 1971 only in the latter. 'Growth' calculated at constant 1963 prices per annum between 1961 and 1971.

that only $156; as late as 1971, when average income per head had reached $433, the lower 40 per cent of the population still received less than $100 per head. Webb calculates the shares of property and wage income accruing to the various strata as well, also shown in Table 5.7, from which we can distinguish two important characteristics: first, that within the corporate sector (taking the top tercile as proxy) about a third of income arose as income to property, and if we take the salaries of the top percentile as mainly disguised profits accruing to owner-managers, then this proportion rises almost to a half; second, that apart from the wage–profit split the distribution of labour income itself was extremely skewed, with nearly a half of the national total accruing to the top quartile of the workforce. Overall, then personal income does seem to have been distributed along the lines of the model we discussed earlier: an income distribution based on the dual economic structure and the concentration of the ownership of the means of production within the corporate sector.

The trends in income distribution are no less interesting. Webb[40] estimates these for the 1950–70 period, extrapolating backwards and forwards from his 1961 estimate on the basis of national accounts data, but argues that although there is some evidence of widening differentials, there is none of absolute immiseration of significant groups. Specifically, he shows 'modern sector' wages as rising at 5 per cent per annum per capita between 1950 and 1966, slightly faster than modern sector salaries (3 per cent) and rural wages on the coastal estates (4 per cent) while 'urban-traditional' incomes rose at 2 per cent and those of the highland peasantry at only 1 per cent; for the 1961–70 period, he estimates both modern sector wages and salaries as rising at 3 per cent per annum, but rural traditional earnings continuing to grow at only 1 per cent. Nonetheless, evidence of agricultural stagnation would seem to indicate that even these estimates may be optimistic, for despite the reasonably high average per capita income growth between 1950 and 1966 'a large portion of the country and of the population appear to have been left untouched, if not worse off than before'.[41] A separate estimate for 1971 consistent with that for ten years before shows the same sort of pattern of structure and growth being maintained in its broad characteristics but with some interesting changes within this: the bottom quintile continued to lose ground, while the lower half of the distribution received only 12 per cent of personal income in both years; indeed, the Gini coefficient declined from 0.61 to 0.59 between 1961 and 1971. There does appear to have been some redistribution *within* the corporate sector, however, particularly significant gains being made by the second decile and losses (in relative rather than absolute terms) by the top five per cent, which can reasonably be taken as corresponding to gains for corporate labour as the result of unionization and industrialization on the one hand, and to the expansion of the 'new' middle classes at the expense of traditional elites on the other. In contrast, the poorest fifth of the population appears to have suffered a declining share and falling incomes.[42] Whatever the statistical problems, it is clear that two decades of capitalist expansion from 1950 to 1970 neither brought much benefit to the bulk of the population nor widened the relatively narrow high-income market for modern manufactured products – with serious implications for both social tension and sustained industrialization.

One of the express aims of the 'Revolution of 1968' was to improve the distribution of income, particularly for the poorest strata of the population. Admittedly it could be argued that these were long-term aims, to be gained after the accumulation process had been re-established and that the economic crisis of 1976–78 necessarily involved wage restraint; but the redistributive effects of the ownership reforms were rather less than had been anticipated, as we have already implied. There are a number of difficulties in measuring these effects, not least among which is the fact that the group which probably gained most (in terms of power as well as income) after 1968 was the 'bureaucratic' fraction of the middle class and we do not have the data to assess their gains – which were particularly connected to the expansion of the state into areas of economic activity previously controlled by private capital – in the form of the conversion of profit income into the salaries of top civil servants. The gains to enterprise workers from the reforms is somewhat easier to estimate, although we have to assume that profit participation was not replacing wage increases that might otherwise have occurred. Figueroa[43] estimates that the reforms 'transfer some 3 or 4 per cent of GDP to 18 per cent of the workforce', and Webb[44] that 'the gross transfer involved is very large for a few workers but for the modern sector [i.e. 20 per cent of the workforce] as a whole it currently amounts to about 6 per cent of labour income', but there is some reason to believe that this may be an underestimate. Confining the benefits to the top quintile is somewhat conservative, as agrarian beneficiaries stretched down into the third decile and did gain direct control over the 6 per cent of GDP generated by estate agriculture, of which about half was operating surplus. Similarly, the *communidades industriales* probably yielded about 2 per cent of GDP (a quarter of industrial profits – which were about a third of the quarter share of industry in national output), plus another 1 per cent for mining and fishing. In all, then, a transfer of the order of 6 per cent of GDP – or about double the estimate by Figueroa and Webb – probably took place. But both these authors are correct in pointing out that this was only a downward redistribution from roughly the top five per cent to the next twenty-five per cent of the population, so although for those involved the change was quite large and represented a change of about a fifth in the income of these two income groups[45] the key point remains. The vast majority of the population and above all the most disadvantaged groups did not benefit significantly from the two decades of industrialization between 1950 and 1970, nor from the subsequent ownership reforms. This is not surprising, given that throughout our period economic expansion had been on a capitalist basis; even after 1968, when state capitalism began to supplant the traditional model, there was no move towards extensive income redistribution from the corporate to the non-corporate sector. The suggestion that it might have occurred may be based on the false distinction between social classes as income recipients and as participants in the production process. This is not, of course, a new point:

> Marx's emphasis that classes are not income groups is a particular aspect of his general premise, stated in *Capital*, that the distribution of economic goods is not a sphere separate to and independent of production, but is determined by the mode of production. Marx rejects as 'absurd' the contention made by John Stuart Mill and many of the political economists, that while production is governed by definite laws, distribution is controlled by (malleable) human institutions.[46]

But nonetheless, authors such as Webb still insist on criticizing the state capitalist model on grounds of equity:

> Certainly the economic potential already exists to achieve a dramatic improvement in the living standards of the very poor: a selective transfer of 5 per cent of the national income, taken from the richest 1 per cent of the population and given to the poorest quartile, would reduce absolute income at the top by only 16 per cent and would *double* incomes at the bottom.[47]

This is clearly true in an arithmetical sense, but the achievement of such a distribution is not just a problem of 'income transfers' even if that were politically possible; such transfers can only be made effective by giving access to adequate employment opportunities to the majority of the workforce – and that would probably mean the abandonment of the growth model based on mining and manufacturing.

Apart from the equity implications, which are not inconsiderable in political terms, particularly since official rhetoric before 1968 and ownership reforms after that date had initiated a 'revolution of rising expectations', what are the economic implications of the distorted and largely unchanging income distribution? There are two that stand out, and both are indicative of the internal contradictions of the capitalist growth model. The first is that the effective market for manufactures and 'modern' services was confined to a very narrow population group and to specific urban areas: indeed it would not be an exaggeration to postulate a market of some one million families in Peru, and for many luxury goods such as cars it would have been half this. In consequence, the lack of a mass consumption market for wage goods both held back the expansion of industrial branches such as textiles and promoted those producing relatively sophisticated goods for the minority. The second is that the extremes of rural poverty led to massive internal migration, placing an almost unbearable pressure on urban areas and threatening the very social order required to sustain capitalist growth. These are the results of the type of *'desarrollo hacia afuera'* which both the Peruvian bourgeoisie and middle class had found so advantageous in the past and which seemed to be continued in the state capitalist model as well, despite the intention to establish the basis for *'desarrollo hacia adentro'*.

Concluding remarks

We have, then, a pattern of asset ownership in Peru that exhibited two distinct trends: the penetration by foreign enterprise and the retraction of domestic capital up to 1968, and the rapid expansion of the state sector to replace domestic capital after that date. Both these trends entailed severe contradictions as far as the organization of the economy was concerned, and the ownership reforms failed to have a profound effect upon the trends in income distribution, which continued much as before. The concentration in asset ownership did underlie the maldistribution of income, but not just in terms of the wage–profit split and the expatriation of profits in the corporate sector; more importantly, it brought about the dual growth model itself. The reforms after 1968 attempted to deal with the former aspect, with a degree of success that may have been limited in absolute terms but was certainly radical by Latin-american standards. External dependency *was* reduced by the nationalization of foreign assets, the power of domestic capital *was* severely weakened by the expansion of the state, and income *was* redistributed towards the corporate sector workforce after 1968. The problem was that dualism was not reduced by the ownership reforms, and the continuation of the mining–industrial growth model not only made such a reduction very difficult but also severely limited the scope for the reduction of technological dependence.

Turning first to land tenure, the principle comparative study[48] for Latin America indicates that, of the seven countries covered (which include Guatemala and Ecuador as well as those shown in Table 5.8), Peru had by far the most concentrated distribution. Although it

Table 5.8. *Comparative land tenure (per cent of total)*

		Sub-family[a]	Family[b]	Medium[c]	Large[d]	Year
Argentina:	Units	43.2	48.7	7.3	0.8	1960
	Area	3.4	44.7	15.0	36.9	
Brazil:	Units	22.5	39.1	33.7	4.7	1950
	Area	0.5	6.0	34.0	59.5	
Chile:	Units	36.9	40.0	16.2	6.9	1960
	Area	0.2	7.1	11.4	81.3	
Colombia:	Units	64.0	30.2	4.5	1.3	1960
	Area	4.9	22.3	23.3	49.6	
Peru:	Units	88.0	8.5	2.4	1.1	1961
	Area	7.4	4.5	5.7	82.4	

Source: Barraclough (1973, p. 16). Employment of: [a] less than two; [b] two to three; [c] four to twelve; [d] more than twelve.

should be remembered that the extent of large Andean estates with poor pasture in Peru may well distort the picture at the upper end of the size scale, the relatively high proportion of the rural population in 'sub-family' farms was clearly a root cause of rural poverty.

The problems of rural underemployment, low farm productivity and landlord influence over government are all exhibited elsewhere in Latin America, and are adduced as justifications for land reform if successful capitalist growth is to be maintained in the area. Even though the CIDA proposals were framed in terms of the strengthening of commercial farming and a wider market for industrial output, little has in fact been achieved elsewhere on the continent, let alone reform on a Peruvian scale – the Chilean land reform being sadly short-lived. On the contrary, there is evidence that the introduction of new agricultural technology (the so-called 'Green Revolution') elsewhere in Latin America revived estate agriculture, which was further strengthened by a new alliance with 'agribusiness' multinationals in the 1960s and the worldwide boom in agricultural commodities during the 1970s.[49]

Although complete ownership surveys of the type that we have attempted for Peru are not known to exist for other countries, we can examine property patterns in manufacturing sectors elsewhere in Latin America. In the case of Mexico,[50] the top two hundred manufacturing firms accounted for 63 per cent of production in 1967, but only 0.2 per cent of the number of reporting firms and 15 per cent of the sectoral wage bill. Of these firms, the 122 considered to be under foreign control account for 54 per cent of production, the 28 state firms for 30 per cent and the 50 enterprises considered to be wholly domestic for only 16 per cent – so that even if all firms other than the top two hundred were domestic, they would still account for less than half of industrial output. In the case of Brazil, the top 376 companies in 1968 accounted for sixty per cent of manufacturing output, and of this portion those firms under foreign control accounted for 46 per cent of production, private domestic enterprise 42 per cent and state enterprise for 12 per cent.[51] A similar pattern is reported for Colombia.[52] Compared with one another and with the data for Peru in 1968 the similarities are striking – in all four cases roughly half of large manufacturing was controlled by foreign capital. In Brazil, public enterprise appears to have been gradually established by new state investments, while in Mexico a parastatal sector initially based on nationalized oil and railways grew by absorbing bankrupt private firms; both these contrast with the rapidity of the expansion of the Peruvian public sector.

The Peruvian experience in other sectors has been paralleled elsewhere too: US control of copper mining in Chile; British railways in Argentina; multinational bank penetration in Colombia; and foreign-owned utilities almost everywhere. But in most cases the transfer of this type of 'basic sector' to the state had started rather earlier than in Peru so that the extreme position that developed by 1968 appears to have been almost unique. In contrast, the steady squeezing out of medium enterprises and the concentration of output in the hands of larger firms has been noted throughout the continent; this concentration leading in turn to increasing capital-intensity in the corporate sector and reduced employment potential on the one hand, while foreign control over technology results in continued import-intensity on the other.[53]

The only recent case of large-scale ownership changes with which those in Peru might be compared is that of Chile, but the circumstances of this frustrated attempt to achieve a transition to socialism were very different. In addition, the history of attempts to gain national control over the main export sector[54] (copper) was a much longer one; the Frei steps towards 'chileanization' had involved the development of local skills in production and marketing which Peru did not have and there was no immediate need to undertake new projects in Chile. The blockade of Chilean copper sales after nationalization (Chile was imposing much the same system of compensation as Peru, deducting 'excess profits' in the past, but in a more extreme form and with much more political menace) was perhaps a warning to her northern neighbour of the consequences of too independent an economic strategy. Nonetheless, there is a parallel of considerable significance: the ownership reforms under Allende took the form of direct control of capitalist enterprise by the labour force, and thus direct access to the means of production was limited to a minority of the workforce. Of course, the extent of workers' control within a given enterprise was far greater than in Peru, and the non-corporate workers were benefited in other ways – far more than in the Peruvian case. However, even if the full reform plans of the Unidad Popular government had been carried out in agriculture and manufacturing, as little as one fifth of the workforce in each would have benefited directly, as Table 5.9 indicates.[55] In the land reform, only farms of more than eighty 'basic hectares' (equivalent to about 90 hectares of arable land) would have been affected, but these only covered a third of the land area and an

Table 5.9. *Planned ownership reform in Chile 1970–73*

	Agriculture				Manufacturing		
	Land	Labour			Assets	Output	Labour
Small farms[a]	22%	60%	Social area		53%	28%	15%
Medium farms[b]	42%	22%	Mixed area		16%	15%	7%
Reformed sector	36%	18%	Other		31%	57%	78%

Source: De Vylder (1976) pp. 149, 183. [a] up to 20 basic hectares; [b] 20–80 basic hectares.

even smaller proportion of agrarian labour. Similarly, the extension of the 'social area' and 'mixed area' of manufacturing (more than 80 per cent state equity and 50–80 per cent, respectively) was only planned to cover large and medium enterprises – although these accounted for two thirds of fixed assets and nearly half of output, they only included a small part of the workforce. In other words, the dualism of the Chilean economy limited its capacity to reduce external dependency and introduce worker participation, even in the context of a transition to socialism.

As Table 5.10 indicates, Peru had a worse distribution of personal income than the other six economies we are considering (and the rest of Latin America apart from Ecuador for that matter) as defined in terms of a lower share for the bottom forty per cent of the pop-

Table 5.10. *Comparative income distribution*

	Share of personal income (per cent)[a]				Growth (per cent per annum)[b]			
	Top 5%	Top 20%	Mid 40%	Bottom 40%	Top 20%	Mid 40%	Bottom 40%	Period
Argentina	..	47	36	17	—	—	—	1970
Brazil	43	62	28	10	8	5	5	1963–70
Colombia	33	61	30	9	6	7	7	1964–70
Chile	31	57	30	13	—	—	—	1968
Mexico	29	64	25	11	8	7	7	1963–69
Peru	34	60	33	7	5	8	3	1961–71
Venezuela	23	65	27	8	8	4	4	1962–70

Source: Chenery (1974, pp. 8, 42), ECLA (1973, p. 27) [a] in latest year of period, from Chenery for columns 2 to 4; first column from ECLA, apparently for the late 1960s and not exactly comparable to the other figures. [b] from Chenery (*op. cit.*), annual average over the period indicated.

ulation, but a comparatively good one in terms of the share of the top two deciles. The 'drift' towards the middle group that we have noted in the case of Peru does not appear to be present in the other economies; where there is any significant change it is towards the upper quintile. Assuming that the IBRD data really is comparable, the reason for the difference appears to be that other economies have better conditions at the 'tail' due to a relatively more prosperous agriculture, while the lack of employment absorption in the Peruvian corporate sector during the 1960s slowed income growth in the upper quintile; possibly the massive wave of migration towards Lima also led to some spreading of earnings towards the middle. Nonetheless, the underlying structure of income distribution seems to be the same as elsewhere: dualism closely related to export-led growth and capital-intensive import substitution compounded by the wage–profit split within the corporate sector.[56] Differences in the economic structure (e.g. the strength of agriculture) tend to affect the first factor, and differences in political development (e.g. the strength of unions) the second; in Peru the two apparently combined to generate an extremely inequitable distribution of the social product.

In sum, then, the patterns of ownership and income distribution in Peru up to 1968 were not different in kind from those elsewhere in Latin America, even though they may have been more extreme in degree. This common experience gave rise to the shift of the 'dependency debate' from an initial preoccupation with the international terms of trade and duality to a critique of ownership and income distribution. But as we have seen, the implication of that critique– that the reduction of dependency and land reform would increase equality and automatically stimulate development – is hardly borne out by the Peruvian experience. Moreover, although such an analysis may illuminate the allocation of the surplus generated by the production structure at any one point in time, it does not throw much light on how that structure is changed over time, nor on the dynamic articulation of foreign and domestic capital within the corporate sector. For this we must turn to the analysis of accumulation, which is the topic of the next chapter.

6

The accumulation of capital

This chapter forms the pivot of the study, so to speak: it completes the three chapters on the nature of the Peruvian economy, chapters which have also served to illustrate the general arguments presented in Chapter 2 and will serve as a platform from which to view the specific issues to be examined in the next three chapters. Capital accumulation is perhaps the most difficult aspect of the Peruvian economy to analyse, because not only do we depend upon rather slender quantitative data but must also integrate them with more qualitative social aspects – in this case the presentation of factors such as ownership and class conflict within the framework of the statistics on investment, savings and financial intermediation. Nonetheless, the accumulation process is, after all, at the heart of the processes of economic growth and development.

To tackle the subject in as orderly a fashion as possible, we shall first examine the overall process of accumulation in the Peruvian economy between 1956 and 1978, identifying the way in which this process affected the economic structure and the pattern of ownership, defining six component phases in a cycle which moved between two forms of centralized capitalism with widely differing objectives, two models of accumulation that we shall refer to as 'oligarchic' and 'state capitalist'. Next, we shall examine the pattern of capital formation in relation to the accumulation cycle and to the general balance between the various production and ownership sectors, following this with an exploration of the financing of this investment with reference to the contributions of foreign, domestic and state sectors. The analysis of the flows of capital funds as they flowed through the financial system should then allow us to integrate the investment and savings patterns and relate these to the trends in consumption and labour remuneration over the period.

The process of capital accumulation in Peru

In principle, the process of accumulation (once the stage of primitive accumulation has been passed and capitalism established as the dominant mode of production) rests on the extraction of surplus from the economy and its conversion into capital through a series of institutional forms that correspond to that process – above all private ownership of the means of production. The extraction of the surplus can take place in three forms relevant to the case in hand.[1] First, 'rent' on natural resources is generated due to the scarcity of primary products on metropolitan markets, surplus being extracted in the form of taxation and locally spent profits and realized through the use of the foreign exchange acquired thereby to import industrial inputs and capital goods. Second, the exploitation of wage labour within the capitalist (in our case 'corporate') enterprise releases monetary profits, realized in the form of labour time available over and above that required to produce the wage goods for the workforce itself. Third, the exploitation of labour outside the capitalist enterprise (our 'non-corporate' sector) increases profits through the internal terms of trade by supplying foodstuffs at low prices to the corporate sector and cheapening labour, on the one hand, or generating monetary rents on the other. During our period, the second source grew in importance relative to the first in Peru as the corporate sector expanded and industrialized; nonetheless, the first process, that of the extractive economy, predominated in both the 'oligarchic' and 'state capitalist' models. The third category was not of central importance to the Peruvian economy in these years: rather the reverse – the neglect of food agriculture and surplus extraction from that sector in previous centuries had made necessary the expenditure of part of the surplus generated within the corporate sector (i.e. foreign exchange) on the import of food.

In an open economy there is no 'realization problem' in its classical form because in principle almost all goods can be sold on international markets and converted into the required capitalist consumption or investment patterns,[2] so that there is no reason why profits and accumulation rates should not rise almost indefinitely: the problem of the closed economy with no market for the resulting production (as wages are too low) and declining profitability as a result, does not occur. But the problem does occur precisely when the economy 'turns inwards' as part of the industrialization process, abandoning international for internal markets, because the concentration of personal income in a small economy is such as to make domestic markets extremely narrow for all but the most sophisticated industrial goods. This realization problem might be overcome by downward redistribution of income to generate the required markets. The alternative, given the difficulties for peripheric countries of penetrating foreign markets for industrial goods, is a return to primary exports as the basis for growth.

The central theme in Peruvian political economy during our period is not the conflict between labour and capital[3] but rather the struggle for control over the extraction, mobilization and allocation of the surplus between the three 'capitals' involved – domestic, foreign and the state – although at times this struggle does seem to have come under the rules of Venus rather than those of Mars. The main change was the attempt by the state, after the traditional model of accumulation had broken down, to take over the burden of accumulation from the grand bourgeoisie, thereby renegotiating its relationships with foreign capital on the one hand and domestic labour on the other. The failure of the state to acquire the hegemonic control over the economy previously enjoyed by the grand bourgeoisie prevented a complete transition to state capitalism, a failure that was conditioned both by the position of international capital and by forces internal to the economy.

The structure of output at any one point in time is the result of previous cycles of accumulation, which provide the necessary productive capacity. In the Peruvian case, as with that of so many other peripheric economies, the effort – in terms both of entrepreneurship and of funds – was concentrated on export production by the alliance of foreign capital and the domestic bourgeoisie (to the detriment both of food agriculture and of regional development), because this is where the most profitable investment opportunities lay. On the other side of the same coin, the introduction of capital-intensive methods of production requiring imported technology as a means of sustaining profits meant that a relatively small labour force was required in both primary export extraction and the new manufacturing branches based on the substitution of imports previously consumed in the corporate sector. Similarly, the process of capitalist accumulation, which of its nature requires the concentration of production to maintain profits, generated the dual structure of the economy not as an unfortunate accident, or even as the result of faster expansion of the 'modern' than the 'traditional' sector, but rather as an integral part of the model. A structuralist analysis would see external dependence in terms of the reliance on overseas markets to sell output and purchase inputs, the absence of an autonomous capital goods branch, and the lack of integration between the export sector and the rest of the economy; but this situation is not a given one: it comes about as the result of the process of accumulation when domestic capital is integrated into the international capitalist system, and relies not upon the internal logic of the economy but upon that of the world economy.

Nor can we view the pattern of ownership as a given datum, or as no more than the outcome of a chain of isolated entrepreneurial decisions; rather it should be seen as a cumulative process with a coherence of its own. In the Peruvian case we have two major forces: first the withdrawal of large domestic capital from effective control of the economy over the 1955–68 period, the failure to replace this with national industrial capital, and the takeover of the state by the military in an attempt to resolve the problem between 1969 and 1978; second, the shift of interest of foreign capital from raw materials towards industry, and then back to mining again, as part of a worldwide pattern.[4] The increasing monopolization of the economy by foreign capital and declining private accumulation experienced by Peru in the 1960s was radically altered by the state in an effort to reorganize and restore accumulation in the 1970s, but the continuing reliance on foreign technology and finance to achieve it was the central contradiction leading to collapse of the state capitalist model. The income distribution derived from the duality built up by past accumulation and the distribution of income in the corporate sector between labour and capital, but the low level of accumulation in the 1960s meant that workers and employees could make considerable gains without reducing capitalist consumption,[5] which made it all the more difficult to renew accumulation later on. In terms of ownership, external dependence was expressed through the foreign ownership of a large portion of the means of production; decisions as to the pattern of output and the allocation of investment were taken not in relation to the logic of the domestic economy (let alone the interests of the population) but rather to that of accumulation on a world scale as exercised by the multinationals, and through them metropolitan monopoly capital.

In practice, we can only directly observe the accumulation process in quantitative terms through the sums actually realized in investment and the resource flows required to finance this. The Peruvian experience seems to bear out Griffin's view[6] – and more generally a Kaleckian or even a Keynesian one – that it is the volume of investment that determines the rate of savings rather than the other way round. We can see that this was true for all three types of capital in Peru during our period: domestic capitalists controlled a very high proportion of national income, of which comparatively little was invested because either the opportunities did not exist or the traditional system of articulating such decisions had broken down; foreign capital clearly had no local savings constraint with respect to investment projects in Peru, and its decisions were framed in terms of worldwide strategies; and the state invested according to a development programme rather than its own operating surplus. This is not to deny that the pattern of savings was important; indeed it reflected the institutional structure that determined the allocation of the surplus – but rather to point out that the problem of accumulation in the Peruvian economy was not one of an overall 'shortage of savings' that could have been alleviated by further increases in profits or more foreign investment, but rather it was one of the perceived profitability of the investments themselves and the organizational capacity to take advantage of them. This capacity appears to have been possessed by the Peruvian bourgeoisie in the past,[7] and is presumably intrinsic to multinational corporations (even if confined to individual projects), while the role of the 'state as planner' also involves such properties by its very nature. It could be argued, therefore, that the difficulty began with the breakdown of hegemony of the bourgeoisie and ended with the start of an attempt to establish state capitalism as a new model of development. We can identify six distinct phases[8] of accumulation in the period 1956–78, each with its characteristic patterns of investment, ownership and finance. We shall examine these in detail in due course, but an initial summary would probably be helpful.

1955–58: A period of extremely high accumulation rates, with about half of productive investment financed from abroad and the start of a new export boom, despite temporary balance of payments difficulties; these were the 'last high years of the oligarchy' as control of the economy started to pass into the hands of foreign capital.

1959–63: A period of somewhat lower accumulation rates, with less foreign investment and deflation of the economy to combat the external imbalance; the loss of elite hegemony and the threat of populist government required military intervention and some initial attempt to reorganize accumulation – such as the introduction of a planning system and expanding state development banks;

1964–68: The accumulation rate continued to fall off, reaching a point where investment only just covered replacement and much of this went into real estate development; the state started to substitute for private investment, but by support rather than control; despite favourable export prices, the balance of payments again moved into deficit and further deflation was imposed.

1969–73: The military intervened on a permanent basis in order to re-initiate accumulation under state control by restructuring ownership; private investment sank again, and state projects had yet to mature, but favourable export prices sustained economic growth; the basis for state capitalism as a new model was laid.

1974–76: The rate of capital formation rose again, above all in the public sector or foreign investments associated with it, but the state failed to capture sufficient control over the surplus, and relied excessively on foreign finance; consumption out of wages and profits rose rapidly placing further strain on the balance of payments; the failure to restructure the economy led to a foreign exchange crisis when world market conditions deteriorated.

1977–78: A stabilization policy based on lower wages and public investment rates was imposed; the state-capitalist model seemed to have collapsed, but massive foreign borrowing was still required to finance debt repayments and aggregate output actually declined. The military decided to abandon government in favour of civilian rule.

Capital formation

The process of investment, the 'freezing' of current output in the form of productive capacity so as to increase output in the future, also involves the creation of assets. Not all investment increases capacity, as a portion is required in order to replace that installed in the past but now worn out, and some of it may be assigned to housing or public monuments which although possibly desirable in themselves do not really increase output. Productive investment also implies technological change in that new plant and installations contain more advanced methods of work and inputs and probably variations in the product itself. Moreover, in a market economy both assets and technology are also property; as such they make 'capital' a central social force as well as an economic one. Under the capitalist dynamic, capital is not just a means of making money at any one point in time; rather its accumulation is a motive force in itself, which is why an understanding of the restructuring of capital in general and of the pattern of investment and its finance in particular is essential to the comprehension of the political economy of a country.

In the Peruvian case, if we look at the long-run trends[9] two phenomena immediately meet the eye: the downswing of the rate of investment through the 1960s and its recovery towards the end of our period on the one hand; and the tendency for the state share in this to increase steadily, moving from less than a quarter at the outset to a half at the close on the other. Both these trends reflect the fundamental shift in the class structure that we have already identified, and are interconnected in that the second trend is part of an effort to counteract the first – initially by the state lending support to private investment and then by its taking over that role directly. Within the private sector, the trend was for industrial investment rates (which should have been rising as the industrial share in national output rose) to decline as the initial stage of 'easy' substitution for consumer imports was completed, while housing received on average a third of all private investment. Within the expanding public sector, in contrast, the tendency was for the centre of gravity to shift from 'government' (e.g. roads, hospitals) towards 'public enterprise' (e.g. steel, mining) projects as the state moved into productive accumulation. Overall the trend at an aggregate level was for a downswing from very high levels of productive investment in the latter half of the 1950s through extremely low levels in the 1960s, and a recovery under state control in the mid 1970s.

In Table 6.1 below, we have some of the detailed information needed in order to fill in this picture: the balance between private and public investment through the accumulation cycle on the one hand, and the sectoral composition of each on the other. The first phase of the cycle (1955–58) saw extremely high rates of private and public investment, attributable to mining, fishing and the start of import-substituting industrialization in the former and the construction of roads and harbours in the latter. Accumulation of capital was still predominantly private, moved by the export sector and supported by public infrastructure – this was the Indian Summer of the traditional model of Peruvian accumulation. In the second phase (1959–63), electoral uncertainty and military intervention served to cut back investment rates in the private sector, although accumulation was sustained by continued capacity expansion in manufacturing led by the multinationals as they consolidated their monopoly positions in key branches. It was in the third phase (1964–68), however, that the real collapse in investment came about, with productive private investment falling to half the rate in the previous period despite government efforts to encourage both domestic and foreign investors as the economy entered serious disequilibrium and ownership positions were consolidated by acquisition rather than by creation of assets. It was to this crisis in accumulation – above all in the control of the industrial and export sectors – that the military intervention of 1968 was to respond. The fourth phase (1969–73) was one of reorganization in preparation for the fifth: private investment stayed low, but with excess industrial capacity the reluctance of private firms to expand under the 'new rules' was not critical, while the renewal of mining and oil investment was carried out by foreign firms in direct association with the state itself. Public investment, meanwhile, was shifted from infrastructure to exports and heavy industry, and although the largest projects did not work through during this phase, the rate of public productive investment did rise to meet the falling private rate. It was in the penultimate phase (1974–76) that the state-controlled renewal

Table 6.1. *The accumulation cycle – investment*

	1955–58	1959–63	1964–68	1969–73	1974–76	1977–78
(per cent of gross domestic product)						
1 Private gross fixed capital formation	19.4	15.3	10.8	7.9	8.1	7.7
2 Public GFCF	2.9	3.3	4.6	4.8	8.4	6.6
3 Total GFCF	22.3	18.6	15.4	12.7	16.5	14.3
4 Stock building	3.1	2.5	2.8	1.5	2.3	0.5
6 Gross capital formation	25.4	21.1	18.2	14.2	18.8	14.8
7 Gross fixed capital formation	22.3	18.6	15.4	12.7	16.5	14.3
8 Depreciation	4.9	5.6	6.0	6.3	6.5	..
9 Net fixed capital formation	17.4	13.0	9.4	6.4	10.0	..
Private GFCF:						
10 Agriculture	..	0.5	0.4	0.2	0.2	..
11 Mining, oil	..	0.5	0.1	1.0	2.0	..
12 Fishing	..	1.5	0.5	0.0	0.0	..
13 Manufacturing	..	4.9	2.4	1.8	2.4	..
14 Housing	..	2.4	4.9	3.1	2.5	..
15 Transport	..	2.4	1.9	0.5	0.2	..
16 Other	..	3.1	0.6	1.3	0.8	..
Public GFCF:						
17 Government	2.5	1.8	2.6	2.4	2.8	3.5
18 Enterprises	0.4	1.5	2.0	2.4	5.6	3.1
Productive GFCF:						
19 Private	12.8	10.1	4.6	3.9	5.1	4.8
20 Public	1.5	1.7	2.4	3.1	7.2	5.7
	14.3	12.1	8.0	7.0	12.3	10.5
(billion soles at 1970 prices) GFCF:						
21 Private	18.5	18.0	20.3	19.9	26.7	21.6
22 Public	2.9	3.9	8.5	12.5	26.8	18.5
23 Total	21.4	21.9	28.8	32.4	53.5	40.1

Sources: Rows 1 to 6, 17 and 18 from Appendix; Row 8 from *Cuentas Nacionales;* Row 10 from import statistics (BCR *Cuentas Nacionales* and supporting appendices) of agricultural machinery, and probably an underestimate – it includes cooperatives after 1969; Row 11 from INP *La Evolución de la Economía en el Periodo 1950–64* (1966, p. IV-6) and INP *Plan Bienal 1976–77* (1976); Row 12 from Roemer (1970, Chapter 7) and INP (*op. cit.*, 1976); Row 13 from Table 9.7; Row 14 directly from *Camera Peruana de Constructores* files; Row 15 from import statistics of 'transport equipment', which excludes vehicles for personal use but with import-substitution this is probably an underestimate – here we have allocated three quarters of the total to the private sector before 1968 and one half thereafter; Row 16 is the residual; Row 19 is an approximate estimate derived by aggregating Rows 10 to 13 and half of 15 and 16 for 1959–76, and by applying the proportion of productive in total investment in 1959–63 to the totals of 1955–58, and of 1974–76 to 1977–78; Row 20 is similarly calculated from the first five rows of Table 8.4; Rows 21 to 23 from the *Cuentas Nacionales* – these are annual averages, originally at 1963 prices for 1955–59 but 'spliced' onto the 1970-price values for 1970–78 – see also Figure 1.

of accumulation at last took place – with about three quarters of total investment undertaken by public enterprises or foreign firms and the state itself accounting for two fifths of all productive investment. The stabilization programme implemented in the last phase (1977–78) over-rode the needs of capital accumulation, depressing both public and private investment to rates as low as those experienced ten years before – the former by budget cuts and the latter by depressed demand and the completion of the mining projects.

Looking at the cycle as a whole, it is clear that the bulk of productive investment in the private sector went into mining, oil, manufacturing and fishing – indeed between them these four sectors probably accounted for over half of private productive investment. Agriculture certainly received a very small proportion, and most of this in the form of irrigation works and machinery for the large sugar and cotton estates on the coast. The pattern of capital formation was also centred on Lima, with most of the industrial, commercial and luxury housing investments concentrated there – possibly as much as two thirds of the total. Similarly, the pattern of public investment[10] was weighted in favour of the coast in general and Lima in particular; and even the major mining and oil projects were virtually 'enclaves' in the hinterland. In this manner the pattern of accumulation served to accentuate the imbalance between sectors: the cumulative process resulting in the dual structure of the economy we have already noted. If the labour absorption of mining and industry are anything to go by this productive investment was highly capital-intensive, accentuating this duality in terms of the exclusion of the bulk of the workforce from adequate modern employment. Finally, as accumulation took place in those sectors where foreign firms predominated, and indeed they organized much of this investment, it is hardly surprising that up to 1968 the grip of foreign capital over the Peruvian economy increased steadily. But as that date approached it increasingly took the form of acquisition of existing assets rather than creation of new ones, and after 1968 that of control over technology rather than assets – a control not necessarily weakened by nationalization. At a conservative estimate[11] foreign companies accounted for a third of private productive investment in the 1960–68 period and possibly as much as two thirds in 1969–76 when private domestic investment fell off and foreign investment in oil and mining rose.

The trends in fixed capital formation at constant prices and the figures for net fixed capital formation given in Table 6.1 underline the weakness in private investment, a weakness against which increased public investment was to a great extent a reaction. Because public investment was in projects where the private sector was unwilling to invest (e.g. mining) or those traditionally in state hands (e.g. roads) there was no tendency to 'squeeze out' private investment, but rather to support it. Moreover, the extent of private funds available (which we shall discuss shortly) precluded any danger of 'crowding out' on the financial markets.

Taking individual sectors separately, the slackening of private productive investment in the 1960s might seem logical; uncertainty about land reform in agriculture, overcapacity in fishing, alternative multinational strategies in mining and overcapacity in industry, combined with the high returns to real estate speculation are all adequate explanatory factors. After 1968, to those factors were added the land reform itself in agriculture, ecological problems in fishing and uncertainty about ownership in industry, counteracted only by renewed multinational interest in minerals and the continued profitability of private industry. But taken as a whole, it can equally well be argued that those very same obstacles to the expansion of capital at a sectoral level are evidence of the incapacity of the

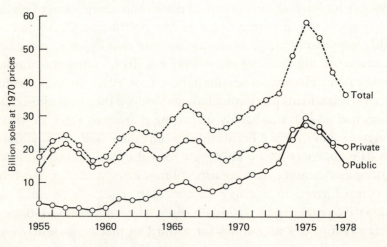

Figure 1 Gross fixed capital formation

domestic elite to organize the economy in a manner consistent with continued capitalist expansion in general and industrialization in particular.

The end result of accumulation is the creation of capital stock, the only known estimates for which, for Peru, are shown in Table 6.2 below. These figures are based on the conventional 'perpetual inventory' method of summing gross fixed investment flows (less depreciation) over time,[12] and have obvious statistical weaknesses in

Table 6.2. *Estimates of the capital stock 1960–75*

	1960	1965	1970	1975
Capital stock (billion soles at 1963 prices)	312	395	490	640
Stock per head (thousand soles at 1963 prices)	99	109	120	133
Capital output ratio (stock÷ GDP at 1963 prices)	4.9	4.5	4.5	5.6

Source: Capital stock from INP (1973), updated by INP–OIP; workforce and GDP from chapter 4.

terms of coverage and even meaning even though the theoretical 'Cambridge' problem of measuring capital is not relevant here, of course, because we have a set of exogenous (i.e. import) prices for capital goods independent of the domestic rate of profit. The figures seem to suggest that capital intensity, in the sense of stock per worker, increased comparatively slowly although the absolute level (about US $3500 in 1963) which must roughly be doubled for the corporate sector where capital is concentrated, seems quite high. Insofar as foreign enterprises operated in capital-intensive branches, we should expect their share of the stock to be higher than their share of production as calculated in Chapter 5; on reasonable assumptions[13] it would appear that foreign enterprises may well have controlled as much as 40 per cent of productive capital in the Peruvian economy by 1968. The trends reflected by the table are two, both of which we have already discussed: first the very slow growth in capital stock per head of population, which rose at only 2 per cent per annum between 1960 and 1975; and second, the decline in the capital–output ratio as the rate of investment fell in the 1960s and its rise as the rate recovered with state intervention in the 1970s.

Unfortunately, there is no information on the breakdown of the capital stock by productive sector. This is a particularly serious lacuna as far as we are concerned, because apart from the changes in ownership and the allocation of the surplus the restructuring of capital also involves its assignment to different productive sectors – indeed it might be argued that this is the object of the first two changes. Without an initial estimate for such a breakdown we cannot even apply the figures from Table 6.1 to gauge the extent of the change. Nonetheless, we can draw some general conclusions as to directions of change from a broad comparison between investment patterns in 1960–68 and 1969–76. As Table 6.3 indicates, the alloca-

Table 6.3. *Composition of GFCF 1960–76*

| | 1960–68 | | | | 1969–76 | | | |
| | Per cent of GDP: | | | Sectoral | Per cent of GDP: | | | Sectoral |
	Private	Public	Total	share	Private	Public	Total	share
Agriculture	0.4	0.3	0.7	4%	0.2	0.6	0.8	6%
Mining	0.3	0.0	0.3	2%	1.5	1.1	2.6	18%
Fishing	1.0	0.0	1.0	6%	0.0	0.0	0.0	· 0%
Industry	3.6	0.5	4.1	24%	2.1	1.6	3.7	25%
	5.3	0.8	6.1	36%	3.8	3.3	7.1	49%
Housing	3.7	0.1	3.8	22%	2.8	0.1	2.9	20%
Transport	2.1	1.2	3.3	20%	0.4	0.9	1.3	9%
Other	1.9	1.8	3.7	22%	1.1	2.2	3.3	22%
Total	13.0	3.9	16.9	100%	8.1	6.5	14.6	100%

Source: Tables 6.1 and 8.4.

tion to agriculture was extremely low in both periods even in view of this sector's share of GDP, let alone its real needs.[14] The rate of investment in industry actually fell between the two periods, and was only prevented from more drastic decline by the increasing outlays by the state. The major shift was towards mining as the state and foreign enterprise attempted to recapitalize the export sector. What, then, can we say about the restructuring of capital? From what we know about the 1950s we can suppose that it was then that the shift from agriculture towards manufacturing and mining took place, but that these rates of investment were not maintained in the 1960s. The 1970s saw the continued shift of the structure towards mining, and to some extent towards industry, leaving agriculture in an increasingly weak position. More it is difficult to gauge.

The sources of finance

For a given pattern of capital formation, the financing of that investment requires that disposable surplus be diverted from consumption – and thus the current consumption of some social group reduced. In the context of the concentration of personal income in Peru this meant an effective reduction in consumption out of profits as much as a reduction in the wage bill – either at present or in the future in repayment of foreign loans – so that the point at issue became the assignment of the surplus between and within the grand and petty bourgeoisie.

If we look at the long-run trends in Peruvian savings,[15] three major characteristics meet the eye. First, there appears to have been a long-run tendency for 'personal' savings to decline as a proportion of gross domestic product, while 'company' savings rose. This trend may well reflect the concentration of capital in the hands of a few firms, but it should be borne in mind that the major personal savers were themselves capitalists for whom retaining profits in the enterprise was more or less equivalent to holding them in a personal bank account,[16] a phenomenon reinforced in the 1960s by the replacement of partnerships by joint-stock companies (*'sociedades anónimas'*) and made more advantageous by the imposition of a tax on distributed profits. That part of savings that was truly 'personal' – pertaining to the middle class in the main – was mostly channelled through the mortgage institutions (*'instituciones de vivienda'*) and did not enter the process of productive accumulation at all. Second, the chronic weakness in government savings (the excess of current income over current expenditure) meant that throughout our period the state could never fund its own investment requirements[17] and relied heavily on borrowing. Third, that while of the average rate of savings over the entire period about four fifths came from internal private sources (fundamentally capitalist profits) this represented less than half of income arising from property[18] and private investment itself was increasingly supplemented by state finance supported by taxation. These three characteristics made for a system of capital finance more than usually reliant upon the 'confidence' of private capital – large domestic firms before 1968 and international banks after that – for its successful operation.

Turning to the details of the various phases of the cycle, we find that as in the case of capital formation, the sources of finance were conditioned by, and in their turn conditioned the institutional and political framework. In the first phase (1955–58), when the level of capital formation was extremely high and foreign enterprise active in mining, Peru received an enormous inflow of foreign funds to complement the already high level of internal private savings, while much of the investment in public works was financed under US aid programmes. The second phase (1959–63), being one of relative retrenchment, required less foreign funding as the manufacturing multinationals sought local finance and public expenditure was restricted, so the level of internal savings rose as a proportion of output and public external debt could even be reduced. But in the third phase (1964–68), the serious decline in capital formation was accompanied by a decline in the proportion of company profits saved and a negligible net inflow of foreign private funds, although the government's attempts to bolster private investment with large infrastructure projects led to substantial official borrowing abroad. The failure to raise tax levels above the increased current expenditure created a deficit on government current account, making the savings position even worse just when the public sector investment rate was rising rapidly, obliging the state to borrow heavily abroad.

After the military intervention of 1968, the lower rate of private capital formation was accompanied by a net outflow of foreign funds[19] covered by – in other words coming out of – private company savings. Meanwhile, the public sector managed to raise its own savings rate by tighter tax administration and the reorganization of investment programmes, and the lack of access to international finance brought about by international reaction to the reform measures was not a serious constraint. Indeed, to a certain extent the low public sector borrowing requirement made the reforms easier to carry through at the time. In the penultimate phase (1974–76) the fundamental instability in state accumulation came to the fore again: private internal savings fell back still further even

Table 6.4. *The accumulation cycle – saving*
(percentage of gross domestic product)

	1955–58	1959–63	1964–68	1969–73	1974–76	1977–78[a]
1 Personal savings	8.9	8.0	3.0	2.6 ⎱	11.2	14.1
2 Company savings	8.8	10.3	13.4	11.9 ⎰		
3 Government current surplus	1.3	1.7	−0.5	0.9	0.5	−1.6
Total internal savings	18.9	20.0	15.9	15.4	11.7	12.5
4 External foreign finance	6.5	1.1	2.3	−1.2	7.1	2.3
Total savings	25.4	21.1	18.2	14.2	18.8	14.8
5 Private funds: Internal	17.6	18.3	16.3	13.6	11.5	12.5
6 External	5.3	1.2	0.4	−3.6	1.5	−1.4
	22.9	19.5	16.7	10.0	13.1	11.1
7 Public funds: Internal	1.3	1.7	−0.4	1.8	0.2	0.0
8 External	1.2	−0.1	1.9	2.4	5.5	3.7
	2.5	1.6	1.5	4.2	5.7	3.7

Source: Appendix; Row 5 = Rows 1 plus 2 *less* public enterprise saving; Row 7 = Row 3 *plus* public enterprise saving; [a] author's estimate.

though the multinationals did bring in funds for their own extractive ventures; and the state enterprises engaged in the recapitalization of what had been (and would be in the future) surplus-generating branches generated financial requirements far in excess of the public sector's own resources, weakened by public enterprise losses. Thus, either determined acquisition of private profits or large-scale foreign borrowing was required, and the latter course was chosen – with predictable results: in the last phase of the cycle (1977–78) the current account deficit on the balance of payments was reduced sharply as a proportion of GDP but the depression in the economy required to bring this about did little to improve public sector savings, while private funds continued to flow out of the country and the state continued to rely upon foreign finance not only for its own investment but also for balance of payments support. The problem that applied implicitly to the reformist attempts of Belaunde became an explicit contradiction within the state capitalist strategy of Velasco: the state can only take on the burden of capital accumulation as well as implement reforms that prejudice the interests of domestic and international capital if it can count upon its own sources of finance.

Table 6.5. *Private company profits in Peru 1955–76*
(*per cent of GDP*)

	1955–58	1958–63	1964–68	1969–73	1974–76
Company savings:					
Depreciation funds	4.9	5.6	6.0	5.0	5.0
Retained profits	3.9	4.8	7.3	6.3	6.5
	8.8	10.4	13.3	11.3	11.5
Distributed profits:					
Domestic	3.9	3.3	2.8	6.1	8.1
Abroad	1.9	2.3	2.1	1.3	0.9
Profit taxation	3.6	3.9	3.1	3.7	3.9
Gross company profits	18.2	19.9	21.3	22.4	24.4

Source: Calculated from BCR *Cuentas Nacionales* Tables 3, 5, 6 (various years), and the BCR *Informe* for 1976; see also note 20. Note that 'company' savings in Table 6.4 includes public enterprises as well, but these are netted out here.

The main source of domestic savings in Peru was private company profits, and Table 6.5 shows how these were used. In looking at this Table we should bear in mind that it is based on the company survey carried out by the Central Bank, and, although adjusted for under-reporting,[20] is not entirely reliable; nonetheless, the main trends seem convincing. Gross profits as a proportion of GDP clearly rose steadily throughout the period, which contrasts sharply with the declining rates of private investment: the latter as a proportion of the former declined from three quarters in 1959–63 to one third in 1974–76. The rising and then falling rate of company savings was based on retained profits, which seem to have strengthened initially as foreign finance to the private sector was replaced by internally generated funds but then weakened as the rate of private capital formation declined. With a declining rate of profit expatriation after

1968 as the result of government restrictions and the stable share of GDP going in profit taxation, the rate of distribution of profits to domestic shareholders rose dramatically; domestic capitalists were consuming rather than reinvesting their profits as their active role was taken over by the state, a reinvestment rate that is even lower than the figures suggest because private mining investment after

Table 6.6. *Patterns of credit allocation (percentage of total outstanding)*

	1960–64	1965–70	1971–75		
Banco de la Nación	25	22	21		
Banca de Fomento	17	21	28		
Banca Comercial	46	26	21		
Instituciones de Vivienda	12	32	30		
	1955	1960	1965	1970	1975
Commercial banks:					
Agriculture	17	15	11	6	3
Industry	26	26	26	35	38
Commerce	43	41	39	28	25
Construction	5	4	4	10	13
Other	9	14	20	21	21
Development banks:					
Agriculture	80	70	66	60	45
Industry	10	22	24	31	47
Mining	10	8	10	9	8

Source: BCR *Anuario Estadístico* and *Memoria*, various years. This Table excludes the operations of the Banco Central de Reserva, which undertook inter-bank transactions in the main.

1968 was financed from abroad. Thus despite the increased public sector borrowing on domestic money markets (see Chapter 7) and the redistribution of profits to the *Comunidad Industrial* (not more than 2 per cent of GDP at most in 1974–76 – see Chapter 9) a large slice of private sector profits was clearly being used for elite consumption and capital flight after 1968. This, and the rising rate of profit in the 1960s cannot but support our argument that the declining rate of private investment was not a problem of current profitability or lack of 'own' funds.

The banking system was the main means of mobilizing funds through the Peruvian economy, and by our period had reached a relatively high degree of development in terms of financial intermediation,[21] although mainly as a means of allocating funds within the corporate sector. Table 6.6 above shows the relative shares of four types of institution in the overall credit outstanding ('*colocaciones*') during the period. As can be seen, the importance of the state bank for government operations (Banco de la Nación) was fairly stable, in line with the treasury's current account activities in the economy. The main increase was on the part of the state development banks ('Banca de Fomento'), which were concerned mainly with the provision of long-term credit for private productive investment. As the commercial banks ('Banca Comercial') were restricted in their use of long-term credit, they turned during the period to the establishment of '*financieras*',[22] which were responsible for about a fifth of commercial credit in 1965–70. These private 'clearing' and 'merchant' banks were of most use to large private enterprises, as the chequeing habit was not widespread, and appear to have financed most of the working capital in the private enterprise sector. The most significant expansion, however, was that of the separate 'housing institutions' ('Instituciones de Vivienda'), which included the state mortgage bank (Banco Central Hipotecario) and savings cooperatives ('Mutuales') – these formed a parallel credit market which eventually absorbed almost all housing finance. In this way, the banking system provided an institutional parallel to the changes in the economic flows making up the accumulation process: the state banking sector reflected fairly stable government current transactions needs and rapid expansion of the investment finance function; the response to the middle-class housing boom was seen in terms of the emergence of specific institutions to handle its finance; and finally the decline in the relative weight of the large commercial banks (centres of the ownership groups discussed in the previous chapter) as the grand bourgeoisie withdrew from the process of accumulation. The expansion of state banks and the nationalization of some of the commercial banks in 1970 led to state control of credit rising from about a third of the total outstanding in 1970 to about two thirds in 1975.

Despite the increase in the importance of state banks over the period there occurred a steady downward trend in the proportion of credit allocated to agriculture; the disproportionate flow of credit to commerce was, however, reversed after 1968, although commercial banks increased their allocations to the construction sector. '*Gran mineria*' generally received funds directly, either from abroad or from public investment, so the share of mining refers mainly to small operators; the substantive change over the two decades shown in the table was the increase in the proportion allocated to industry, which rose from less than a fifth to nearly a half over the period.[23] Nonetheless, the commercial banks were extending the bulk of their credit to commerce and construction throughout the period. The credit system, then, sustained the developing investment pattern of the corporate sector as well as providing working capital, but little or no credit reached the non-corporate sector.[24]

The models of accumulation

We have seen how the process of accumulation in Peru involved a series of phases within a cycle, each phase corresponding to developments on the economic and the political planes and underlaid by a trend towards the replacement of domestic capital by the state. We have also seen how capital formation declined dramatically during the 1960s, only to recover in the mid 1970s under state control, but as the decline in private savings that also took place was not replaced by greater state acquisition of surplus, the resulting accumulation system was unstable and overly dependent on foreign finance. Above all, the capacity of foreign capital to block reforms prejudicial to their perceived interests not only weakened the reformist pretensions of Belaunde beyond the limited strength of this government's fragile popular legitimacy, but also compromised the state-capitalist model of his successors which, although based on far more secure foundations of political power, had far greater nationalist claims as a central aim in its populist ideology. The changing 'nexus' of the model of accumulation moved, as we have seen in Chapter 4, from the large finance-capital groups of the 1950s towards the state in the 1970s. The former was based on multi-sectoral private ownership grouped around large commercial banks, while the second was based on public enterprises in export and basic production branches, with a series of associated cooperatives and a battery of administrative controls over the private sector, organized around a national planning system.[25] Both

Table 6.7. Accumulation – net savings and investment flows (per cent of gross domestic product)

	1955–58 Private	1955–58 Public	1959–63 Private	1959–63 Public	1964–68 Private	1964–68 Public	1969–73 Private	1969–73 Public	1974–76 Private	1974–76 Public	1977–78 Private	1977–78 Public
Own savings	17.6	1.3	18.3	1.7	16.3	-0.4	18.6	1.8	11.5	0.2	12.5	0.0
Foreign finance	5.3	1.2	1.2	-0.1	0.4	1.9	-8.6	2.4	1.6	5.5	-1.4	3.7
	22.9	2.5	19.5	1.6	16.7	1.5	10.0	4.2	13.1	5.7	11.1	3.7
Transfer	-0.8	+0.8	-2.0	+2.0	-3.5	+3.5	-1.0	+1.0	-3.5	+3.5	-3.0	+3.0
Capital formation	22.1	3.3	17.5	3.6	13.2	5.0	9.0	5.2	9.6	9.2	8.1	6.7

Source: 'Transfer' is the item required to make the matrix balance – it is thus equivalent to private finance to the state sector less public finance to the private sector; other rows from Tables 6.1 and 6.4; stockbuilding is allocated between the public and private sectors in proportion to the share of state enterprises in corporate-sector output.

models were concerned with raising the rate of accumulation: the difference between the two being that the former 'nexus' saw this in terms of a means to increased profit, while the latter saw it in terms of the achievement of economic development as such.

The first task is to fit together the major investment and savings flows. Table 6.7 illustrates an overall picture of net inflows of foreign funds over the period, and shows the net effect of the imbalances between saving and investment in the private and public sectors – the 'transfer' item corresponding to the excess of public investment over its 'own' sources (current public sector surplus and official foreign borrowing) that had to be made up from domestic sources. The relative shift in the private and public share of the accumulation burden and the withdrawal of the former from productive capital formation we have already noted. The Table reveals the reliance of the public sector upon transfers of one form or another from the private sector; the growing extent of these transfers between 1955 and 1968 is now clear, and as the improvement in central government finance in 1969–73 proved temporary (the *outflow* of funds abroad from the private sector should be noted – more than countering official borrowing overseas), it returned to the destabilizing level of 1964–68 in 1974–76, to which was added the vastly increased rate of public borrowing abroad. The stabilization policy of 1977–78 only managed to reduce the rate of internal transfer slightly, partly because much of the reduced rate of public foreign borrowing was being used to finance continued flight of private capital. These are, of course, *net* flows – gross flows are shown for two representative years in Table 6.8.

Under those circumstances, with private investment responding to problems of individual sectors or the organizational difficulties of Peruvian capitalism as a whole and private capital flows across the exchanges responding to the requirements of individual mining projects and local confidence in the political actions of the government, it is virtually impossible to view the imbalances in accumulation account as simply a matter of sectoral demand disequilibria. We have already argued that there is no evidence of 'crowding out' in the sense that increased net domestic borrowing by the public sector (the 'transfer' item in Table 6.7) did not reduce investment by excluding business from the credit market, and the figures do not in

Table 6.8. Sources and uses of capital funds in the Peruvian economy
(percentage of gross domestic product)

	1963				1974			
	Public	Private	Foreign	Total	Public	Private	Foreign	Total
Sources:								
1 Own funds	1.5	15.4	0.8	17.7	0.9	12.0	0.6	13.5
2 Local borrowing	2.4	1.1	1.1	4.6	3.4	2.7	—	6.1
3 Foreign finance	1.2	—	1.5	2.7	6.7	-2.7	1.4	5.4
4 Total sources and uses	5.1	16.5	3.4	25.0	11.0	12.0	2.0	25.0
Uses:								
5 Capital formation	4.0	13.0	3.4	20.4	9.3	7.6	2.0	18.9
6 Local loans	1.1	3.5	—	4.6	2.7	3.4	—	6.1

Source: 'Public' is the whole state sector (*Sector Público Nacional*); 'private' is firms controlled by domestic capital; 'foreign' those controlled by foreign capital.

Row 1: 'public' is government current account surplus (as in Table 6.7), plus state enterprise profits and depreciation allowances (Appendix Table A.2); 'foreign' is remainder required to balance that column; 'private' is remainder required to balance the row; 'total' as in Table 6.7.

Row 2: 'public' is 'internal finance' as in Appendix Table A.2; 'private' is total lending by state (row 6); 'foreign' is assumed to be a third of capital formation by foreign firms in 1963 and zero in 1974 by law; 'total' is sum of row.

Row 3: as in Table 6.7 except that it is assumed that all foreign finance is either for the state or for foreign enterprise.

Row 4: column totals.

Row 5: 'public' as in Table 6.1; 'foreign' estimated as discussed in note 11; 'private' as the remainder; 'total' as in Table 6.1.

Row 6: 'public' is the increment in credit from the development banks (Table 7.5); 'private' is sum of borrowing by 'public' and 'foreign' in row 2; 'foreign' assumed zero; 'total' is sum of row.

fact show any marked degree of correlation; private investment rates were declining for different reasons. An alternative view, and one espoused by the IMF in its dealings with the Peruvian authorities, is that of the 'monetary approach to the balance of payments'.[26] It is argued that the private sector accumulation balance (i.e. the balance of private savings and investment) is more or less exogenous, and thus that increases in the public sector deficit are reflected in the external payments deficit ('external savings') either because the government borrows directly abroad or because by borrowing locally it forces the private sector to borrow abroad in order to restore its own accumulation balance to equilibrium. Peru's balance of payments problems could then be attributed to increases in (and by implication resolved by reductions in) the public sector resource deficit. In terms of Table 6.7, this would imply that foreign finance to the private sector would be positively correlated with the extent of the 'transfer' item, but clearly there was no such association; indeed if the figures are taken literally, there might even be a case for arguing that increases in the 'transfer' were associated with decreases in foreign finance to the private sector. Similarly, official borrowing abroad was linked not to the public sector resource deficit as such, but rather to the import content of state investment and (after 1968) to the need to counterbalance the outflow of private capital consequent upon the 'political' effect of the ownership reforms.

The disequilibria in the accumulation balance were fundamental: a stable model of accumulation logically requires either low investment by the state against its narrow resource base and continued high self-financed private accumulation or a high rate of state investment matched by state access to the surplus, if a collapse in the national rate of capital formation is to be avoided. The first solution corresponded to the model of accumulation established at the end of the last century, which worked fairly well up to 1960: ownership groups based on finance capital could move funds from one export branch to another, into industry, or (as increasingly happened) into real estate or luxury consumption. In terms of capitalist efficiency, this system was flexible and well-run, generating the finance required for any particular investment scheme by slightly reducing the very high levels of elite consumption implicit in the income distribution.[27] The second solution would have corresponded to a state capitalist model[28] with a high rate of income from property tax and public enterprise profits used to finance investment, and the reduction in luxury imports (or the inputs used to produce them) to provide the exchange for capital goods – thus financing accumulation in a similar fashion to the first solution but through a different organizational structure (the national planning system) and returning the resulting surplus to the state for further industrial accumulation or possibly downward distribution in the long run. However, neither of these two internally coherent economic solutions was fully consistent with the prevailing balance of political power during our period. The withdrawal of private domestic capital from the accumulation process eventually made the first solution impossible, but its remaining role impeded the second; while foreign enterprise contributed to the weakening of the first system and prevented the full implantation of the second.

The 1960s can now be seen to have been not only an intermediate phase in the cycle but also an indeterminate one: the extremely low levels of investment, the failed attempt at land reform, the ineffectiveness of efforts to promote integrated industrialization by market incentives, and the increasing control by foreign capital of the economy, all served to convince the military that the only feasible alternative was massive state intervention in the accumulation process. The 1969–73 period, although still one of comparatively low rates of capital formation, did see a determined effort to reorganize the ownership structure of the economy along state-capitalist lines in order to allow a consistent accumulation model to operate on the basis of renewed exports and rapid industrialization. The partial nature of state ownership that resulted, however, made it difficult to operate the new model effectively,[29] because the wholesale trade network and final manufacturing, as well as much of food agriculture, were outside state control – denying to the state both the determination of the final output pattern (and thus the most efficient deployment of state capital in intermediate production) and the resources needed to finance the large and slow-maturing export projects. The reliance on foreign cooperation was perhaps inevitable: although the role of foreign capital in the new model was different from that in the traditional one to the extent that finance rather than ownership was involved, the one-sided technological and market relationship was common to them both.

Finally, in an attempt to gauge more exactly how the two models differed from one another in terms of capital flows, estimates of the 'flow-of-funds'[30] under the two systems in representative years are shown in Table 6.8. As can be seen, the total value of capital flows through the system in relation to national output was virtually the same in both years,[31] but their distribution was very different. The expansion of the state sector was dramatic, its participation rising from less than one fifth to over two fifths of the total flows, but as this was on the basis of a slender savings base on both occasions, the local borrowing and foreign finance required more than doubled in size relative to that of the economy in order to accommodate the massive increase in the investment rate. Foreign financing appears to have expanded in both private and public sectors, but in fact almost all of that coming *into* the 'foreign' sector in 1974 was for projects directly associated with the state in oil and copper ventures – which did not use the local finance captured by the industrial affiliates of the multinationals reflected in the 1963 figures. The major concomitant shift is the displacement of domestic capital: its rate of fixed investment fell by over a third between the two years, and if private housing is separated out (3.5 per cent of GDP in both cases) then the fall was of over one half. In addition, domestic private capital appears to have been flowing *out* of Peru in 1974 – mostly as a result of the 'errors and omissions' item in the balance of payments but also amortization on loans raised abroad. Meanwhile, private sector lending to the state expanded sharply, from a sixth to a third of its funds, and at the same time state loans to the private sector for investment purposes, as a proportion of private capital formation, rose from 9 to 36 per cent. The trend away from private capital towards the state as central investor, financier and negotiator with foreign capital, is thus clearly illustrated in the flow-of-funds format.

Consumption and wages

So far we have examined the accumulation process in terms of investment and savings alone; but these are the complement of consumption – and above all of labour remuneration. For accumulation to take place, consumption must be restrained; even though in the short run this can be ameliorated by use of foreign finance, this too must eventually be repaid from reduced consumption. Insofar as wage and salary expenditures make up the greater part of current consumption, their control becomes a major element in economic policy designed to support the accumulation process, although such control will also generate considerable political problems, in which the state will also be involved.

Turning to the major components of gross domestic product in Peru during our period, we see that government consumption experienced its main increase in the 1960s with the larger administrative and welfare responsibilities of the state; after 1968 state expansion was reflected in investment. The crucial variations are, however, in the level of private consumption, which the authorities had great difficulty in restraining throughout our period. Between 1950 and 1954, private consumption accounted for only 70 per cent of GDP, but by 1955–58 this proportion had risen to 73 per cent and, despite the large inflow of external funds to finance foreign mining investments, was clearly incompatible with such a high level of capital accumulation. However, stabilization in 1959–63 was achieved not only by consumption restraint but also by the fall in the rate of private investment (due to the conclusion of mining projects and business uncertainty, as we have already argued) – indeed almost the entire burden of adjustment appears to have been borne by the private sector. However, as the economy recovered it seems that private consumption rather than investment demand (which was falling in relative terms) drove the trade balance into deficit in the mid 1960s despite the process of import substitution which had brought about a decline in the import coefficient. This level of private consumption was maintained in the early years of the Velasco regime but did not have similar disequilibrating effects because the rate of aggregate investment had declined and imports were tightly controlled. However, in 1974–76, when investment demand moved sharply upward again under the pressure of state projects and the export position deteriorated, instead of a cutback we see an unprecedentedly high level of private consumption – which was undoubtedly as important a destabilizing factor as the increased investment rate and one which did not bring its 'own' foreign finance as capital investment did. The expansion of domestic demand was, as Table 6.9 indicates, almost exactly balanced between the public and private sectors; the stabilization programme was based on cuts in public investment and private consumption, but in fact government consumption as a proportion of GDP rose[32] and private investment fell back too, so that the main brunt of the

Table 6.9. *The composition of aggregate demand 1955–78 (per cent of GDP)*

	1955–58	1959–63	1964–68	1969–73	1974–76	1977–78
Private consumption	72.6	70.9	73.5	74.1	77.2	75.2
Government consumption	8.5	9.1	10.6	10.5	11.1	12.3
	81.1	80.0	84.1	84.6	88.3	87.5
Gross capital formation	25.4	21.1	18.2	14.2	18.8	14.8
Domestic demand	106.5	101.1	102.3	98.8	107.1	102.3
Exports of goods and services	20.4	23.2	19.3	18.2	13.8	19.9
Imports of goods and services	26.9	24.3	21.6	17.0	20.9	22.2
External demand[a]	−6.5	−1.1	−2.3	+1.2	+1.2	−2.3
Total demand	100.0	100.0	100.0	100.0	100.0	100.0
Domestic demand						
public sector[b]	11.8	12.7	15.6	15.7	20.3	19.0
private sector[c]	94.7	88.4	86.7	83.1	86.8	83.3
	106.5	101.1	102.3	98.8	107.1	102.3

Source: BCR *Cuentas Nacionales* and BCR (direct).
Notes: [a] shown as 'external foreign finance' in Table 6.4; [b] government consumption plus public capital formation (from Table 6.7); [c] private consumption plus private capital formation (also from Table 6.8).

adjustment was taken by capital accumulation, which proved easier to depress in the short run – thus bringing the new model to a halt.

In the classical model of economic development, it is the restraint of wages that allows savings to be generated through greater profits. However, in Peru – as in other developing countries – there are two major qualifications to be made. First, that there is 'rental' income from natural resource exports, from which funds can be derived directly; and second that given the high level of profits in the economy, it is the allocation of these between capitalist consumption and investment that is as important as the level of wages as such. In consequence, there is no direct and necessary relation between the level of wages and the rate of savings. Nonetheless, in a capitalist economy the natural reaction to an excess of demand in the economy is to cut consumption by means of wage reductions.

We have already noted that the share of private profits in national income was increasing steadily during our period, but despite this the rate of private investment also declined, so that there was an increasing excess to be distributed. In part this was lent to the public sector through the banking system, of course, and particularly after 1968 a considerable portion was exported as flight capital; we have already discussed these phenomena too. Nonetheless, there is every reason to believe that capitalist consumption out of profits, as a proportion of national income, was rising steadily throughout our period, although the exact extent is impossible to gauge without more information on household budgets, which we do not have. To the extent that the rate of capitalist consumption out of profits did rise, unchecked by tax reform (see Chapter 7), then it was this as much as higher real wages that tended to generate excessive demand and destabilize the economy.

However, despite the relative stability of the non-profit share of national income (see Table 5.5) some labour incomes did increase significantly. Between 1950 and 1973, the real earnings of 'white-collar' employees (*empleados*) and 'blue-collar' workers (*obreros*), both almost doubled; but at the same time, the earnings of peasants (*agricultores independientes*) were little better than stable in the long run, so that while on average blue-collar workers and peasants had roughly the same income per head as in 1950, the former received nearly twice as much as the latter by the end of the period. What appears to have happened is this: as the corporate sector expanded more rapidly than the rest of the economy, a relatively stable profit share and wage–salary split in that sector's value added led to higher shares for all three categories in national income and a corresponding lower share for the non-corporate sector. In other words, it was increasing dualism rather than increased exploitation within capitalist enterprise that changed the functional income distribution.[33]

Even if the nature of these trends was basically 'structural', fluctuations around them had a marked impact on the macroeconomic equilibrium.[34] Unfortunately, we have no reliable source of wage and salary statistics for the period as a whole, and once again we must rely on the national accounts estimates, which do not distinguish between workers in different sectors or areas of the country. The Central Bank estimates (used in order to calculate the functional composition of national income) are based upon the 1961 and 1971 censuses for wages and salary structures by sector to which trends derived from reported government and surveyed business labour payments are applied. The only other sources are the Lima minimum wage figures which are of limited (and varying) representativeness, and the manufacturing wages series – upon which see Chapter 9. Nonetheless, the variations exhibited in the Central Bank figures (shown in Table 6.10) do seem significant, and are closely related to the problems of controlling consumption. The 1950s saw labour incomes rising somewhat more rapidly than national income per head, but, significantly enough, *empleados*' incomes rose more rapidly than those of *obreros*, reflecting the growing importance and power of the middle classes. Meanwhile, peasant income stagnated and declined in relation to the national average. These trends were continued into the 1960s, although the devaluation of 1967 and the subsequent deflationary policy successfully restrained wage consumption while a series of good harvests led to a considerable increase in peasant income. Nonetheless, relative to average national income, no labour group had made substantive gains between 1950 and 1970; *empleados* had done better than *obreros* until the mid 1960s, but they too had suffered relative to the national average (and this, by implication to property income) in the subsequent deflation. By 1973 the price controls on foodstuffs had restrained this peasant income (these small farmers did not benefit from land reform) but successful wage claims and redistributive reforms did raise *obrero* real income to twenty per cent above its 1970 level although *empleados* did not do quite so well. By 1976, however, the combination of rapid inflation and wage and salary restraint (all corporate sectors' wage rates were now under direct control of the government) resulted in declining real earnings, and brought the ratio of wages to average income back down to the 1970 level as part of the first attempt at stabilization in that year; nonetheless, the deliberate shift of the internal terms of trade in favour of agriculture did restore

Table 6.10. *Real earnings in Peru 1950–76 ('000 soles per head at 1963 prices)*

	1950	1955	1960	1965	1970	1973	1976	1978
1 Workers ('obreros')	8.1	9.8	10.8	13.0	13.2	16.1	15.2	10.5
2 Employees ('empleados')	22.2	27.5	30.9	38.9	39.9	43.0	42.1	..
3 Peasants ('agricultores independientes')	6.9	7.7	6.6	7.2	9.3	7.4	8.9	8.8
4 Net national income	13.2	15.5	17.2	20.7	23.8	26.8	27.9	25.7
Ratio of (1) to (4):	0.61	0.63	0.63	0.63	0.55	0.60	0.54	0.41
(2) to (4):	1.68	1.77	1.80	1.88	1.68	1.60	1.51	..
(3) to (4):	0.52	0.50	0.38	0.34	0.39	0.28	0.32	0.34

Source: Table 5.5 deflated by the GDP deflator for private consumption, from BCR *Cuentas Nacionales* (Table 9, various years) for 1950–73; BCR *Memoria 1976* for 1976; *Trimestre Económico* (Lima, October 1978) for 1978 estimate of wages; 1978 estimate of peasant incomes based on output trends since 1976.

peasant incomes to near their 1970 level. Despite the fact that the ratio of labour incomes per head to the national average was by now well below the levels obtaining in the previous twenty-five years, *obrero* incomes were dramatically reduced by official freezing of wages while prices continued to rise in 1977–78, thereby producing the real decline in consumption required for stabilization.

From these figures we can draw three general conclusions. First, that wages never rose so fast in relation to national income to be a serious threat to the profit share, supporting the arguments given above; second, that excess demand pressure in the late 1960s and mid 1970s must have been due to other components of demand as much as wages and salaries; and third, that while the relatively rapid rise in white-collar incomes in the 1960s is clearly related to middle-class support for the two civilian regimes, the comparatively slow rise of wages and salaries in real terms after 1970 helps to explain why the 'revolutionary' military regime failed to gain large-scale popular support in the towns up to 1975, let alone after 1976; while the stagnation in peasant incomes despite land reform throws light upon the similar experience in rural areas.

Concluding remarks

Early on in the period under consideration, the Peruvian economy experienced a breakdown in the traditional model of accumulation that had sustained the ruling elite for nearly a century. The search for an alternative model established the basis for state capitalism, but this itself contained crucial internal contradictions which appear to have led, if not to its collapse, to its being brought to a halt. Although this experience was not closely paralleled elsewhere in Latin America, there did occur a general change in the model of accumulation as the main economies of the area made the shift from primary exporting towards industrialization, and it is useful to view the Peruvian experience in this wider context.

The ECLA[35] suggests that Latin America has experienced an important change in its model of accumulation since the last war. When the economies of the continent were dominated by primary exports and estate agriculture, investment was financed directly from the profits of these sectors without complex intermediation or state intervention. Where industrialization did start comparatively early, as in Argentina, it mainly financed itself internally, being on a small scale and retaining the high profits from protection as it was still controlled by local industrialists. As the import substitution process got under way, accompanied by rapid urbanization, the need for intersectoral transfer of funds became more pressing and the increasing scale of production required greater concentration of capital and massive infrastructure provision; although the multinationals gradually took over key production branches, finance was still provided by local partners. From this shift came the growth of investment banking and the expansion of state development funds, accompanied by an increasing penetration of international banks into the traditional financial structure. In addition, the need to sustain demand both for consumer durables and for new housing required that financial facilities be extended to the middle classes, resulting in a further expansion of financial networks.

From these elements a new model of accumulation in Latin-America is held to have emerged based on an alliance between foreign capital as producer, domestic capital as financier and the state in support of the whole, a model which has achieved a certain stability:

> in a number of Latinamerican countries a more or less rapid transition to a new stage and style of development, founded upon the amplification of the consumption of the urban middle classes, and the advance of the state not only as leader of the process and promoter of a series of private activities, but as an independent investor. In this process of transition the new forms of public and private finance linked to the international financial organizations played a central role. They permitted a widening of the markets for consumer durables and achieved a greater complementarity between internal and external resources, with relative independence from the problems of financing the balance of payments.[36]

However, this sort of model does seem to have been more appropriate to larger economies such as Brazil or Mexico where a moderate redistribution of income – or extension of consumer credit – towards white-collar employees and corporate labour created a vast market for manufactures and maintained the industrialization process beyond the first stages of import-substitution on market criteria. These countries have also had much stronger agricultural sectors than Peru, which have provided an autonomous export base as well as a guaranteed source of wage goods and large markets in the hinterland. This option was not really open to a small economy like that of Peru, for to create such an internal market would have required greater (and politically less feasible) redistribution of income downwards. Considerable state intervention in order to promote the establishment of heavy industry has certainly been a major feature of Mexico and Brazil too,[37] but the private sector appears to have been strong enough to get on with the expansion of capacity in consumer goods lines on purely commercial criteria and create the sort of accumulation model emulated by the Belaunde administration. The attempt to establish a 'new Peruvian' model after 1968 was as much a reaction to the failure to implement the 'new Latinamerican' model as to the concept of that form of capital accumulation.

A better basis for comparison might be a smaller mining economy such as Chile. In the 1960s it faced much the same economic problems as Peru[38] even if it had progressed considerably more in the industrialization process: economic growth was constrained by limited copper exports, private investment rates were declining, foreign companies had gained extensive control over industry and the wage share of national income was declining. Between 1964 and 1970, the government of Frei and the Christian Democrats put forward a project which Fortin[39] describes as a 'reformist model of accumulation', based on further import-substitution financed by surplus transfer from agriculture, the attraction of foreign business and increased public investment to support the private sector, the expansion of export capacity (particularly in copper), the modernization of the agrarian structure, the redistribution of income and the mobilization of popular forces such as peasants and slum-dwellers in support of the government. As a result, this model – like that of Belaunde – was a showpiece for the Alliance for Progress.[40] The role of the state was 'interventionist' in support of industrial capital, whether national or foreign, with a considerable component of state accumulation, mostly in the form of infrastructure and joint ventures with state enterprise – particularly copper mining and petro-chemicals. However, the economic contradictions of this Chilean model soon began to be expressed not only in a deceleration of output growth but also in a decline in the rate of private investment, due to the lack of investment opportunities in an agriculture threatened by land reform, in an industry already suffering from excess capacity and a saturated home market, and in an export sector dominated by foreign enterprises. The populist and redistributive elements of the model prevented an increase in the share of the surplus going to private capital:[41] the share of payments to labour in national income, which had declined from 51 per cent in 1960 to 45 per cent in 1963 under the conservative government of Alessandri, rose to 52 per cent in 1970 while private investment sank from 9 to 7 per cent. To fill the gap, public investment rose from 40 per cent of fixed investment in 1961 to 49 per cent in 1969; while the state banks financed 13 per cent of private investment in 1961, they funded 50 per cent in 1969; but still the aggregate rate of investment declined. This combination of the 'failure to generate and sustain an adequate rate of capital accumulation and the process of rapid mobilization of popular sectors created contradictions that the model was not capable of sustaining'.[42] However, the different balance of class forces – particularly the strength of the labour movement – meant that the Frei regime, despite its own similarities to that of the Belaunde, was replaced by one far more radical than that of Velasco.

The degree of economic success of Allende's socialist model of accumulation is hard to judge, given its short life, but it is surely relevant that in this case too the state had considerable difficulty in acquiring sufficient control over the surplus – which went to wages rather than profits– and that the proposed restructuring of capital was confined to ownership and distribution rather than a fundamental change in the export-led growth model itself. The basic feature of the project of the *Unidad Popular* that came into power in November 1970 was the establishment of a vastly expanded sector of state ownership that would control the rest of the economy. Some member parties of the Popular Unity coalition saw this as part of a transition to socialism, but in the medium term it was essentially a state capitalist model: the prime motor of capital accumulation was the state, wage relations were preserved and some sectors were excluded from the nationalization process, to be encouraged by the increase in aggregate demand consequent upon the downward

Table 6.11. Comparative patterns of accumulation (percentages)

| | Investment/GDP | | | Savings/GDP: | | | | Public/total investment | |
| | | | | Internal | | External | | | |
	1960	1965	1971	1960–61	1970–71	1960–61	1970–71	1960–61	1970–71
Argentina	21.6	19.5	24.3	19.8	22.0	2.1	1.0	25	41
Brazil	18.4	18.1	19.3	16.6	16.7	1.7	2.1	39	52
Colombia	20.5	17.8	18.9	19.0	16.5	2.1	3.1	17	34
Chile	17.4	16.4	15.2	12.4	12.9	5.7	2.2	38	56
Mexico	20.1	19.8	20.6	17.9	18.6	1.5	1.4	34	35
Venezuela	17.6	17.5	16.4	26.0	17.5	−9.1	−0.3	39	35
All Latin America	19.2	18.6	20.1	17.9	17.7	1.2	2.0	29	36

Source: ECLA (1973) p. 100.

redistribution of income. The key reforms were in fact the collec-
tivization of agriculture, the nationalization of the copper mines,
and the takeover of two thirds of the private banks and a third of industry by the state. Leaving aside the political resistance to this
project, the economic conditions for accumulation were far from
sound: the labour share of national income rose to 63 per cent in
1972 which certainly stimulated aggregate demand and led to fuller
use of idle capacity in the private sector but also led to massive food
imports and depressed profits; public sector surpluses were further
weakened by the blocking of tax reform in Congress and the freezing
of state enterprise prices.[43] Thus, like Peru but on a larger scale and
against a much more unstable political background, private investment declined while aggregate consumption rose (on the basis of
higher wages rather than the consumption of profits, however) and
the public investment that was to be the centre of a new model of accumulation was inadequately financed; a recipe for internal inflation and external payments problems – without the possibility of
recourse to foreign loans.

Again, the military coup of 1973 in Chile was a very different
affair to the 1975 changeover in Peru, and involved far more
extreme measures to stabilize the economy (the labour share of
national income had fallen to 40 per cent by 1976); but the political
and economic changes also appear to have involved a complete
restructuring of capital on the basis of low wages, weakening of
trade unions, a completely open economy, a reliance on mining and
export agriculture as the engines of growth and the dominance of
finance capital – a reversion to the 'oligarchic' model that Peru had
abandoned ten years before.

In sum, by the 1960s the Peruvian rate of investment had fallen
well below the average of the other main economies of the region,
although its reliance on foreign finance was not perhaps as great and
the general continental trend towards greater state participation in
investment was likewise a widespread response to declining rates of
private investment. Unlike Brazil or Mexico, however, Peru could
not adopt the 'new Latinamerican' model of accumulation for
economic reasons; nor was it about to adopt the extreme solutions
of Allende or Pinochet to restore investment on a socialist or
traditional basis, for political reasons. The solution adopted after

1968 appeared to be potentially more stable both economically and politically but it depended upon the socialization of profits as well as investment. The difficulty of mobilizing sufficient resources to support increased state intervention is the topic to which we must now turn.

7

The public sector

The expanding role of the public sector in Peru, as it emerged from an essentially social function in a free-market economy towards an *economic* one as the basis of state capitalism, is a central theme of our period. We have already noted the increasingly important part played by the state in the ownership of productive assets and the accumulation of capital;[1] in this chapter we shall examine the organization of the public sector itself and the evolution of the fiscal system as a means of resource mobilization in more detail. We have argued that the growth in the state sector over the period was a direct response to the failure of domestic capital to sustain industrialization or negotiate effectively with foreign enterprise, and here we shall examine the economic effectiveness of the public sector as a replacement.

The organization of the state sector in Peru was centralized in a 'unitary' structure; in other words local government was relatively unimportant and the constitution was not a federal one. Local administration was under the control of 'prefects' appointed by the central government, itself organized under a presidency elected directly under the constitution with a concurrently elected legislature except in periods of military rule, when the legislature was suspended. The central administration was almost entirely based on Lima, and although decentralization was an ostensible policy objective of all governments in our period, little was achieved in this direction. In terms of the administration of the economy, it was difficult to see how decisions on the key sectors of mining, industry and finance could have been taken anywhere but in Lima; welfare functions such as health and education were concentrated on Lima too because this is where most of their activity took place.

In other words, the centralization of government was a reflection of the capital concentration of the economy itself. In the other sense of 'centralization', that of decision making, the tendency observed[2] in other Latinamerican nations of establishing autonomous agencies to administer certain regions or economic complexes has not occurred to any great extent in Peru, although there were signs that the Belaunde administration was moving towards this system as a possible solution to the frustrations of congressional control over central government activities.[3] Nonetheless, the sheer size of certain state corporations after 1968 made them difficult for the central government to control in detail.

Within this fairly stable administrative framework, a major change[4] in the social function of the Peruvian state took place as the economic role of the public sector moved from being merely supportive to the private sector under Prado, to a more 'developmental' role under Belaunde, and finally towards state capitalism under Velasco. In terms of administrative power, this also meant the emergence of the state bureaucracy as a significant political force and thus an increase in the capacity of the public sector agencies to act independently of both capital and labour. It is within this frame of reference, and not just in terms of a 'professionalization' of the bureaucracy that we must consider administrative change, although naturally the latter phenomenon did contribute to this new political role.

By 1956 the public sector as a whole was still mainly concerned with 'holding the ring' in terms of security, foreign affairs, justice, commercial regulation and the negotiation of mineral rights with foreign investors. Public health and education services were still in a very rudimentary state, and the extent of economic intervention beyond roadbuilding was extremely limited. Under the military intervention of 1962–63 and the subsequent Belaunde administration it was decided[5] to expand welfare services and the scope of intervention in the economy; the administrative structure was extensively overhauled and expanded in consequence. A system of program budgeting was introduced in 1963, to complement the previous system[6] under which the *Controlaría General* (Comptroller's Office) prepared a *Cuenta General de la República Peruana* some two years after the financial year concerned, and the government budgets extended to cover capital as well as current expenditure. At the same time a new breed of professional civil servants trained as engineers and economists began to replace lawyers in the public administration, the '*tecnicos*' supplanting the '*chupatintas*';[7] but these new and younger men experienced a growing sense of frustration as the difficulties of implementing the modest plans for reform put forward by Belaunde foundered on congressional opposition. In contrast, under the Velasco administration the absence of 'democratic' control and the hierarchical military structure made it much simpler to implement policies once decided upon; indeed the bureaucrats themselves became in effect the only members of civil society with continuous influence upon the military government. The budgetary system was overhauled again in 1971 so as to bring public expenditure under a single budgetary system,[8] and the central planning system established in 1962 was finally made effective by granting control over the whole public sector capital budget to the National Planning Ministry in 1970.[9]

The Prado administration had not found it necessary to specify the role of the state in the Peruvian economy, although by implication it was to be an extremely limited one.[10] When government intervention was extended under Belaunde, no explicit statement of the role of the state was made either,[11] although it was made clear that the public sector was meant to be supportive to the private sector (e.g. by breaking 'bottlenecks') and not intended as a replacement for it.[12] In contrast, the *Gobierno Revolucionario de la Fuerza Armada* was extremely specific:

> The overcoming [*superación*] of the dependent capitalist model and underdevelopment requires the state to undertake a role of active participation as promoter and leader of national development, through its direct and indirect intervention in economic, socio-cultural and political activity ... A philosophy is proposed which attributes to the state the full capacity for directing action [*acción directriz*], as the total expression and representative of society, and which corresponds to the power that the nation requires in order to promote change and redistribute resources and social roles which were the product of the predominance previously exercised by the dominant class.[13]

This necessarily involved the state acting as 'national entrepreneur', and thus the public enterprises rather than ministries became the key element in the state apparatus. The public sector was intended to mobilize investible resources on a large scale:

> The responsibility assumed by the Public Sector requires that it continues to strengthen its financing capacity, establishing a solid structure of resource acquisition which will be obtained through tax reform, appropriate programming of internal debt and recurrence to external debt in a rational manner, so as not to aggravate the problems of external debt service. In addition, emphasis will be given to the greater acquisition of resources by the entrepreneurial activity of the State and the increased efficiency of the state enterprises so that these can generate profits as a contribution to their own finance.[14]

These two themes – the economic activity of the state and the financing of such activity – form the topic of this chapter. As the role of the state expanded so rapidly after 1968, it is upon the latter half of our period that we will concentrate; as a comment upon the 'style' of state intervention in the Peruvian economy under Velasco, the following extract from the 1974 decree nationalizing cotton marketing is illuminating:

> Considering: That it is the duty of the state to channel the resources of the country to the benefit of the national economy, taking into account the interests of the majority; That cotton is held to be basic to the economy of the nation; That it is necessary to effect measures which permit a rationalization of the present methods of commercializing cotton seed and fibre, in order to guarantee the producers a just return, secure an adequate supply for the national textile industry and obtain the best prices on international markets. Article 1: The state assumes exclusively the internal and external commercialization of cotton seed and fibre . . .[15]

Table 7.1 below shows various measures of the 'size of the state'. We have already foreshadowed these in our estimate that the state share of gross domestic product rose from 7 per cent in 1950 to 11 per cent in 1968 and to 21 per cent in 1975, while public sector employment rose from 5 to 7 per cent and finally to 13 per cent of the economically active population,[16] equivalent to about a third of corporate-sector output and employment. Over the period 1955–75, value added in the state sector expanded eightfold, while public employment rose nearly ninefold, the share of investment increased to half the national total, and the proportion of private investment financed by the state banks rose from 5 to 30 per cent. In addition, the state share of exports had increased from nil to almost nine tenths by 1975, and the share of imports from less than a tenth to over a half. In other words, the state had become a predominant force in the economy. It should be noted, however, that this expansion did not take place exclusively after 1968; much of the growth in central government took place under Belaunde, and it was the increase in state enterprise activity under Velasco that mainly accounted for the larger public sector after that date.

Table 7.1 *Estimates of the size of the Peruvian state*

	1955	1960	1967	1970	1975
Value added (% of GDP):					
Government	7.3	8.0	8.9	8.1	11.5
Other public sector	0.5	0.8	1.7	3.3	9.9
Public sector	7.8	8.8	10.6	11.4	21.4
(Soles billion at 1970 prices)	8.2	11.4	23.1	27.4	67.5
Fixed investment (% GDP):					
Government	3.4	1.2	2.4	2.6	2.8
Other public sector	0.5	1.1	1.6	1.9	6.0
Public sector	3.9	2.3	4.0	4.5	8.8
(Share of total GFCF)	21%	14%	27%	36%	51%
Employment ('ooo):					
Government	140	168	251	289	354
Other public sector	8	11	19	43	265
Public sector	148	179	270	332	619
(Share of non-agricultural employment)	10%	9%	14%	15%	24%

Source: BCR *Cuentas Nacionales* (Table 10, various years), INP.

The central government

The core of central government was made up of the presidency, defence, justice, foreign affairs and '*gobernación*' – this last being responsible for police and provincial administration. These activities were performed for the maintenance of the state itself in particular and of the capitalist mode of production in general, the two becoming more closely identified as the bases of state capitalism were laid. Naturally enough, the frequent intervention of the military in the administration of the state led to an expansion of the defence portfolio and the constituent branches of the armed forces. Nonetheless, the defence and security departments absorbed a third of current government expenditure at the outset of our period and nearly a half by the end, as opposed to less than ten per cent on the other 'core' activities. The direct importance of these to the Peruvian economy was not that great, although indirectly they were a fundamental condition for the maintenance of the market system – guaranteeing law, the enforcement of contracts, the maintenance of international commercial relations and the discipline of labour – and in constitutional terms at least, the integrity of the nation itself.

Unfortunately, we only have reliable figures on a comparative basis for 1967–76, but these indicate that although the personnel in the armed forces and the burden of military expenditure in relation to national income and the budget did not rise very much between 1956 and 1973, there was a sharp rise after 1974 in response to the perceived threat from Chile after the military coup in that country:[17] between 1973 and 1976 Chile stepped up its armed forces from 7 to 10 per thousand head of population and its military expenditure from 2 to 5 per cent of GDP. The use of Russian arms (see Table 7.12) is also of some significance; although US equipment remained central to the navy and telecommunications systems, planes and tanks were purchased from the USSR after 1968 in response to the refusal of the US to supply advanced equipment. A similar incident had occurred under the Belaunde administration, but then the refusal of US jets had led to the purchase of French Mirages; the recourse to Russian arms after 1968 does not appear to have had any but technical implications. The burden of arms purchases on the balance of payments, although substantial in absolute terms (see Table 7.12) was hardly large in relation to total imports or total indebtedness. The economic cost of security may be indirect: the decision made in 1974 to build a pipeline over the Andes at great expense in order to take out the Amazon oil was based on the fact that the two alternatives – to ship it down the Amazon through Brazil or construct a spur to the existing Ecuadorian line to the north – were both considered (reasonably enough) to involve excessive strategic exposure, despite the large cost savings.

The 'economic' ministries in Peru are of relatively recent formation; in 1956 the limited scope of state intervention was reflected

Table 7.2. *Military expenditure in Peru 1956–76*

	1956–61	1962–66	1967–73	1974–76
Arms imports: million $ US per annum	..	..	48	122
per cent of imports	..	..	4.8	5.0
Military expenditure:				
per cent of GDP	3.1	2.7	3.1	4.4
per cent of central				
govt. expenditure	21.2	17.1	16.7	21.5
Armed forces per thousand head of				
population	..	..	5.63	6.14

Source: ONEC *Anuario Estadístico 1966* and González (1978) – on this latter see note to Table 7.12.

in the existence of no more than a Ministerio de Hacienda (treasury) and a Ministerio de Fomento (development) charged with fiscal affairs and public works respectively. The first significant step in the articulation of the economic functions of central government was the establishment of a planning commission (the Institute Nacional de Planificación) by the military junta in 1962[18] as part of the presidency; under the subsequent Belaunde administration separate ministries of agriculture and transport were founded. These corresponded to the stress placed by the respective governments on new functions for the state – the coordination of public investment in the first case and the new programmes of irrigation and roads in the second. It was only after 1968, however, that the full range of ministries proper to the modern state finally emerged. The ministry of agriculture developed important land reform agencies and in 1975 with growing difficulties over food supply a separate Ministerio de Alimentación was established. The treasury was reorganized as a Ministerio de Economía y Finanzas and charged with responsibility for the conduct of fiscal and short-term economic policy in 1969, and the planning commission strengthened by being given control over all public sector investment and responsibility for long-term economic policy. A ministry of industry and commerce was also established in 1969 on the basis of some of the former activities of the development portfolio; this was strengthened by the functions conferred by the Industries Law of 1970,[19] and in 1975 a separate ministry of commerce was set up to handle the cumulative statutory powers to regulate domestic prices and external trade previously held by the ministries of finance, agriculture and industry. Finally, the new state interest in energy and mining was entrusted to a ministry of that name in 1970. All these ministries had major state enterprises under their responsibility which carried out public sector activities in their respective branches, so that the ministries themselves were mainly concerned with the regulation of the private sector. It is difficult to assess the adequacy or efficiency of their administration in any objective sense, or indeed to conceive of any way in which such an assessment might be carried out. In our case, we are interested in the effect that the increasing intervention of these ministries in the market had upon private sector accumulation, but as the major reason for this intervention was the lack of private investment and its failure to recover as a result of the ownership reforms after 1968, it is not likely that increased market controls suffocated private initiative. Policy on pricing and investment incentives was certainly mishandled[20] but the generally young, technocratic and enthusiastic staff of the relevant agencies appear to have been relatively efficient in putting them into practice. Bureaucratic procedures, although less labyrinthine and tortoise-like than before 1968, were still far from brisk, and in 1975 a special office to speed authorization for private sector investment in major productive projects had to be established with presidential authority.

The 'social' ministries of education, health and housing had a less dramatic history. Education and health were major policy goals of the Belaunde administration, partly as a means of gaining political support from the urban masses and partly in an attempt to improve the productivity of labour in anticipation of the needs of the manufacturing sector. Public education had been growing as an element of government expenditure since the 1930s,[21] particularly under the first Prado administration (1939–45) which had stressed 'practical' basic education for the children of the workers. By 1960 about 70 per cent of the population between seven and thirteen years old were nominally enrolled in primary education, but only 16 per cent of the 14–19 age group were in secondary education and 4 per cent of the 20–24 age group enjoyed tertiary training.[22] Under the Belaunde administration a renewed effort was made to extend secondary education, particularly in the metropolitan area, so that the relevant 'matriculation rate' had reached 33 per cent by 1971 while that for primary education rose to 85 per cent. The massive university expansion consequent upon the opening of the ancient University of San Marcos to almost all comers after 1968, the founding of two major universities (the National Engineering University and the Catholic University) in the mid 1960s and the creation of a flotilla of smaller private centres (the Universities of the Pacific and of Lima, for example) doubled the tertiary matriculation rate to 8 per cent by 1971. However, the Velasco administration did not devote a significantly larger proportion of its resources to education, but rather concentrated upon the reorganization of existing schools on the basis of local centres and the introduction of a new curriculum – the object of which was to integrate the peasantry to a 'national culture' and to purge this latter from external 'cultural dependency'.[23] An attempt to rationalize the university structure, partly in order to raise standards but also with the aim of reducing militant student opposition to the regime, was abandoned in 1975 as the result of opposition from both staff and students. Despite these efforts, the level of real education received, particularly in rural areas, remained very low; the aim of providing an adequate supply of skilled workers such as mechanics was far from achieved, and those professionals that were trained (e.g. doctors) preferred to stay in Lima rather than practise in the countryside.

Public health services suffered to some extent from the expansion of education within a limited budget allocation to welfare over the whole period. The main chain of hospitals in provincial centres had been established under the Odría administration[24] (1948–56), and these were complemented by local medical posts under the subsequent Prado government. Under Belaunde the emphasis switched to training more doctors, but the declining proportion of the central government budget allocated to health meant that standards of medical assistance actually fell in the 1960s.[25] Although the rate of infant mortality was reduced from 15 per thousand in the 1–4 age group in 1960 to 8 by 1971, mainly as the cumulative result of anti-epidemic campaigns initiated by the Bustamante administration

(1945–48), this reflected only the most basic sanitation and the degree of real access to health services is indicated by the fact that in 1960 only 23 per cent of the workforce was included in social security schemes which covered the principal risks, and by 1971 this had only risen to 28 per cent.[26] Nor was housing a central concern of the Peruvian state; some effort in this field was made by Belaunde, himself an architect, but the major investment was in middle-class housing in Lima, and despite the establishment of a separate Ministry of Housing in 1969 the Velasco policy was to concentrate on the provision of basic services to housing plots in the '*pueblos jóvenes*' around Lima.[27] Potable water was supplied to 58 per cent of urban houses in 1961 and 65 per cent in 1971, but to only 10 and 13 per cent of rural homes respectively, while the proportion of urban houses enjoying access to sewerage actually fell from 63 per cent to 55 per cent (due to the rapid expansion of squatter settlements) and in rural areas remained at 2 per cent.[28] Unfortunately, the urban reform promised by the Velasco regime to parallel the agrarian reform (which had in fact prevented the conversion of agricultural land around cities into building plots and thus forced up urban real estate prices) was not implemented,[29] with deleterious consequences not only for house prices and town planning but also for fiscal income to the state itself.

Overall, then, the pattern of government activity was one of restricted central services with steadily expanding military and security functions, limited economic activities until 1968, and an expansion of welfare functions in the 1960s that was not sustained into the subsequent decade. Indeed, it would not be an exaggeration to characterize central government in Peru as 'underdeveloped' as compared to economies such as Mexico and Brazil, let alone the metropolitan countries. This arose both from the fact that capital had no need of extensive state support in Peru until comparatively late while organized labour did not have enough political power to insist upon extensive social services, and from the decision of the Velasco government to confine the welfare expansion initiated by Belaunde in favour of the more directly productive activities of state enterprise.

The state enterprises

In contrast to the experience of central government, the state enterprise sector was relatively small before 1968, but after that date it took on a predominant role as the expression of government economic strategy in the restructuring of capital and the establishment of a new accumulation model. Indeed, by 1974–76 the state enterprises were accounting for more productive capital formation than the private investors and were responsible for most of the exports.[30] This reliance upon state enterprise as the means of state expansion and of renewed investment in the economy as a whole distinguished Peruvian experience after 1968 both from its own past and the experience of capitalist growth elsewhere in Latin America, and permits a tentative characterization as 'state capitalism'.[31]

The public enterprise sector in Peru has a long if dormant tradition. The state had been involved in the exploitation of guano since the nineteenth century[32] and the *estancos* had monopolized the sales of salt and *coca* since colonial times, but these activities had declined to negligible economic importance by the outset of our period, as had the municipal *beneficencias* which had been established at the turn of the century to cater for artisan funerals and cemeteries. The previous Prado administration had established the first steelworks in Peru, at Cañon del Pato under the Corporación Peruana del Santa, which was also responsible for the large hydroelectric works there in the foothills of the Andes and the port at Chimbote, making this complex the largest industrial installation in Peru. The subsequent Bustamante government founded the Empresa Petrolera Fiscal which began somewhat desultory exploration as a potential rival to the IPC, which it was eventually destined to take over forty years later to form Petroperu. The airport authority (CORPAC) and a small merchant shipping fleet (Companía Peruana de Vapores), mainly used for cabotage service, were also set up during this period. Three state banks (the Banco Central de Reserva,[33] the Banco Hipotecario and the Banco de Crédito Agricola) had been established as early as the Leguia *oncenio* (1919–30), to be supplemented by the Banco Minero and the Banco Industrial in 1932. This structure was not significantly altered either by the second Prado administration or by Belaunde, and although the scale of operations was increased the parastatal sector did not become significant in terms of the economy as a whole. Under Belaunde, investment in the steelworks and hydroelectric system was stepped up and the activities of the state banks expanded: the rate of state enterprise capital formation rose from under 1 to over 2 per cent of GDP, the development banks raised their lending by about a half in relation to national output[34] and state banks came to account for about a third of credit in the Peruvian banking system[35] by the mid 1960s. Finally the Banco de la Nación was founded in 1964 to take over tax receipts and current government payments from the private banking consortium[36] which had previously handled such transactions.

In no sense was the Peruvian public enterprise sector before 1968 a dynamic one, let alone a central element in the economy. The public enterprises had been established to support the private sector by providing the cheap inputs (steel, power and finance) that capitalists, and above all the industrializing multinationals, required. The pattern of production was determined by these needs – the output of concrete reinforcing rods for the construction industry by the steelworks, or the allocation of the bulk of agricultural credit to the export estates, for example – and not by any centrally-determined strategy. In consequence, these enterprises were in no position to revive the accumulation process as this flagged in the 1960s. In addition, these enterprises were noted at the time for their incompetence and tendency to generate considerable losses, although this latter aspect was as much a result of government pricing policy (e.g. subsidized tariffs for power supplies to the private distribution companies or low rates for industrial loans) as of their undoubted inefficiency.[37]

In contrast, the main thrust of the economic strategy of the Velasco regime was based upon the expansion in breadth and depth of public enterprise activity so as to take up the task in which the domestic capitalists were held to have failed. Although it was not intended to *estatizar* the whole of the corporate sector – considerable areas (particularly light manufacturing) were to be left to the 'reformed' private sector and at least potentially to the various forms of worker-managed enterprises[38] – the regime did aim at the establishment of direct control over the underlying 'motor' elements of the Peruvian economy which, with a strong planning system, would allow the accumulation process to be restarted along new lines. 'The position of the state as leader ['*conductor*'] of the economic process will be consolidated, particularly in the context of petroleum exploitation, mining, fishing, basic industry, electricity, communications, transportation, domestic marketing of essential products, external trade and the financial system.'[39]

The establishment of public enterprises after 1968 took place mainly through the acquisition of existing assets, in their most part foreign, and as the result of policies to reform specific sectors rather than an overall expansion programme; that is, they represented the outcome of separate actions taken to achieve other targets such as the reduction of external dependence or the rationalization of a particular branch of production. This led to a somewhat heterogeneous state enterprise sector, with consequent difficulties of articulation and control, as we shall see. We can consider these corporations[40] as being divided into three groups: those taken over from foreign capital; those previously owned domestically; and those originally established as public enterprises. In the first group we find the massive state oil company Petroperu (formed from expropriated IPC and the government-owned EPF in 1969), Centromin (the former Cerro de Pasco mining complex in the central Sierra, nationalized in 1973), Hierroperu (the former Marcona iron ore operation taken over in 1975), Entelperu (based on ITT and Swedish cable and telephone firms in 1973) and Enafer (the railway system previously belonging to the Peruvian Corporation), all of which were key companies in their sectors.[41] In addition, there were a number of enterprises which were foreign-owned and where the state became the only shareholder but which remained subject to private company law – as opposed to being absorbed into the state enterprise sector as such. These included the results of the bank expropriations under the 1970 Bank Reform Law (Continental, Internacional and Progreso), the non-agricultural interests of the Grace Corporation acquired under the agrarian reform and the non-mining interests of the Cerro de Pasco Corporation.

In the second group, we find formerly domestically owned companies. Apart from the agrarian reform, there appears to have been no intention to nationalize domestic capital as such, and most of this group derived from the consequences of the collapse of the fishing industry. This arose[42] from the combination of excess capacity, overfishing and ecological changes; in 1971, one state corporation (Epchap) was set up to market all fishmeal, and another (Epsep) to centralize the supply of services. Subsequently, in 1973, the main consortia (including considerable foreign interests) were taken over, the fleets and factories rationalized and the whole reconstituted as Pescaperu. Partly as a result of this sectoral collapse, the so-called 'Prado Empire' became bankrupt, and a series of key enterprises passed into state hands – adding a major commercial bank (Popular) to the public sector and granting almost total control over cement, paper and fertilizers, as well as an important part of the textiles industry. In the third group we find those corporations originally established as state enterprises, building from the somewhat insubstantial basis already discussed. In heavy industry, there were: the greatly expanded[43] steel corporation (Siderperu); the new organization for the refining of copper and zinc, the exploitation of the Cerro Verde project (formerly Anaconda) and the export of all metals (Mineroperu); the electric power enterprise (Electroperu) which from its original hydroelectric basis absorbed the main distribution companies (some of which were foreign owned) and local generation capacity in 1972; and the fertilizer corporation (Fertiperu) which also undertook the vast Bayovar complex for mineral phosphates. In the transport sector there were the flag airline Aeroperu (formed in 1972), the existing shipping line (CPV), the airport authority (Corpac) and Enatruperu, which took over the main municipal bus companies. In the service sector there were Emadi, which supplied basic housing infrastructure, and Enturperu, which ran the state-owned hotels. Control over trade was seen as particularly important, and the main enterprises here were EPSA (responsible for wholesaling basic foodstuffs and the state supermarket chain), Cecooap (sugar sales and exports) and Enci (commercialization of some strategic imported industrial inputs). Lastly there was the state holding company for new industrial projects (Induperu) and a flotilla of smaller enterprises such as Simaperu (naval dockyards, also building fishing craft and small cargo vessels), Indumilperu (military supplies), and the old *estancos* – Emsal (salt), Emcoca (cocaine), Enai (industrial alcohol) and Enata (tobacco).

Finally, the state development banks (for agricultural, mining, industrial and housing credit) expanded their operations considerably, the Banco de la Nación was made responsible for all current transactions of the public sector, and a new state merchant bank (Cofide) was set up in 1970 as the exclusive financial intermediary for market finance to public enterprise and subsequently (in 1975) as the financing agency for the Social Property sector.

In all, by 1975 a complex of over fifty state enterprises had been created. In that year, this complex was responsible[44] for over half of mining output, a fifth of industrial output and two thirds of banking on the one hand, and a half of productive investment, almost all of exports and about half of imports on the other. Its primary purpose was to expand production in exports and heavy industry, but an important secondary objective was to generate funds for reinvestment. There is not a great deal of information available on the financial structure of the sector, but for 1968–77 we do have consolidated accounts for the whole sector and these are shown in Table 7.3. Broad-

Table 7.3. *Consolidated state enterprise account (per cent of GDP)*

	1968–70	1971–3	1974–76	1977
Current income[a]	3.2	10.7	18.1	21.0
Current expenditure	2.7	9.7	18.3	19.8
Current surplus/deficit	+0.5	+1.0	−0.2	+0.9
Capital income[b]	0.6	1.3	1.2	0.9
Capital expenditure:				
fixed investment	1.6	1.9	5.2	3.5
financial investment	0.3	0.3	0.4	0.1
Overall surplus/deficit	−0.8	−0.1	−4.6	−1.8

Note: [a] includes subsidies from the central government.
    [b] capital transfers from central government.
Source: Direct from BCR.

ly, these figures indicate three important characteristics of the sector between 1968 and 1977: its extremely rapid expansion relative to the economy as a whole, the small or negative surplus (i.e. savings) on current account, and the growing overall deficit resulting in a growing borrowing requirement. We have already discussed the nature of this rapid expansion; the reasons for the weaknesses in current account savings are multiple. In part, these were undoubtedly the result of inefficient administration, waste and corruption, but in the main they were the result of deliberate government price policies – to subsidize sales of imported wheat through Epsa, and to maintain the price of gasoline distributed by Petroperu long after the prices of these commodities had risen on world markets, for instance. If the savings margin on current income obtained in 1968–70 (some 16 per cent) had been maintained in 1974–76, this would have generated nearly 3 per cent of GDP in investible funds and eliminated the bulk of the borrowing requirement. It was the massive increase in the fixed investment programme, not losses on current account, that drove the sector into imbalance. The stabilization programme initiated in 1976 had a pronounced effect on the state enterprise sector in 1977, as can be seen from the table: the devaluation affected both income and expenditure positively (but the latter less than the former because the sector exported more than it imported), local sales prices were raised and subsidies reduced, and the capital expenditure reduced sharply. However, despite these efforts, state enterprise could still only finance a quarter of its own capital outlays. Between 1967 and 1975, the volume of the public enterprise sector had increased seven-fold[45] and this imbalance (subsidies to and losses by state enterprises reached 3 per cent of GDP in 1975) became a major element in the macroeconomic crisis of 1976–78, one result of which was to curtail further expansion of the sector.[46]

For one year, 1973, we do have a breakdown of this consolidated account for the different classes of enterprises, which allows us to examine the sector in a little more detail, on the basis of the figures shown in Table 7.4 below. The figures do not include either Centromin or Hierroperu as these were nationalized at end-1973 and in 1975 respectively, or the assets resulting from the Petroperu oil exploration programme, but it does represent the main characteristics of the sector. First, it was dominated by relatively few entities: four firms (Petroperu, Siderperu, Mineroperu and EPSA) accounted for 83 per cent of sales by non-financial enterprises, and three (Petroperu, Mineroperu and Electroperu) accounted for 77 per cent of fixed investment, while three of the financial enterprises

Table 7.4. *Economic activity of Peruvian state enterprises (soles billion in 1973)*

	Goods producers	Services producers	Commercialization	Sub-total non-financial	Financial enterprise	Total state enterprises
Current income	8.4	6.8	30.4	45.6	10.0	55.6
Current expenditure	8.2	6.6	30.6	45.5	9.2	54.6
Current operating surplus	0.2	0.1	-0.2	0.1	0.8	1.0
Capital expenditure:						
Fixed	4.4	4.2	1.3	10.0	1.8	11.8
Financial	0.5	1.2	0.1	1.7	20.1	21.8
	4.9	5.4	1.4	11.7	21.8	33.6
Total expenditure	13.1	12.0	32.0	57.2	31.0	88.2
Economic deficit[a]	4.7	5.3	1.6	11.6	21.0	32.6
Net worth	11.4	28.1	2.1	36.6	..	..
Other capital	9.5	14.4	5.1	29.0	..	..
Total capital	20.9	37.5	7.2	65.6	7.5[b]	78.1
'Return on capital'[c]	1.6%	0.5%	-7.1%	0.4%	11.1%	1.4%

Notes: [a] total expenditure less total current income; [b] 'capital and reserves'; [c] 'current operating surplus' divided by 'net worth' or 'capital and reserves' as the case may be.

Source: FitzGerald (1976a) pp. 49–50.

(Cofide, the Banco Industrial and Banco Central Hipotecario) ac-counted for 84 per cent of state bank investment in that year.[47] The total asset figure for non-financial enterprises shown in the table is equivalent to one billion US dollars and of the same order of magnitude as those of the entire manufacturing sector in Peru,[48] but the yield on those assets was extremely low. Admittedly, Epsa operations in particular were designed to subsidize imports of wage goods, but even if these are excluded the overall profitability of non-financial enterprises was little over one per cent, while the return to bank capital was held down by interest rates designed to support the private sector. In addition, many enterprises such as Pescaperu owed their existence as state concerns to bankruptcy while others such as Centromin were seriously undercapitalized; nonetheless, the pricing policies were such as to prevent the sector from generating any significant surpluses[49] and thus contribute to their own enormous investment programmes, let alone to those of central government. If, say, a return on capital of 15 per cent could have been achieved in 1973, then the resulting current surplus would have been sufficient to cover a third of public enterprise investment requirements and almost balance the domestic borrowing requirement of the public sector as a whole in that year.

As Hunt put it in 1975,[50] 'in the next decade the Peruvian economy will prosper or atrophy according to the effectiveness with which the new public enterprises are managed'. Any overall evaluation[51] of such a heterogeneous set of enterprises, many of which had been in operation for a very short period even by 1978 and were still completing periods of essential capitalization in terms of both fixed assets and human skills, is extremely difficult but an attempt must be made precisely because these formed the core of the state capitalist model. The central point is that after 1968 the enterprises (with the exception of those involved in commerce) were charged with meeting certain production targets as their prime objective – targets expressed in terms of extracting oil from the jungle, reviving fishmeal production or maximizing electric power supply and so on. In consequence, the enterprises were not acting as profit-maximizing capitalist firms, nor were they acting as agencies of central government in implementing wider social policies. However, it is in these terms that their contribution must be inevitably judged, even though their success can be measured in more immediate 'production' terms. Broadly, it can be said that the Peruvian state enterprise sector was reasonably efficient: it pressed ahead with oil exploration (although the reserves were not as large as originally anticipated), tripled steel output, revived the mining sector, reorganized fishing and set up several major branches of heavy industry in what was by Latinamerican standards a comparatively short period. There were major problems, such as the gross corruption and inefficiency in farmgate collection experienced by EPSA, but the overall record was not bad. The rapid expansion of the state enterprise sector did lead to severe management problems, above all the shortage of skilled and experienced senior engineers from which the private sector had suffered before 1968, and was to suffer all the more after that date as the state enterprises drained off available managerial talent with offers of higher salaries and the opportunity for rapid promotion. The main problems arose from the terms of reference themselves: the single-minded pursuit of output and the continued policy of price restraint.

This had three important consequences: the difficulties of central control and coordination; the lack of wider social or 'development' criteria; and the tendency to acquire technology from abroad. The first problem arose from the system of making enterprises responsible to sectorial ministries, and in many cases (such as fishing) the enterprise was so large in relation to its parent ministry that little or no effective central control could be exercised. In consequence, there were frequent conflicts between enterprises: for example, in 1974 the Centromin mines were still polluting the river Mantaro with metal wastes which were damaging the hydroelectric turbines of Electroperu downstream, a dispute that had been outstanding for a decade previously was not resolved by nationalization. This was compounded by the difficulty of imposing an effective planning system from the centre.[52] The second problem arose from the essentially 'state capitalist' nature of the enterprises. There was a tendency to ignore the impact of the choice of technology upon employment (such as the use of plastic as opposed to tile drains in irrigation work), and the impact upon local society of activities such as oil exploration, where employment rose and then dropped sharply, leaving many Amazon communities totally disarticulated. The production enteprises treated their workforce in a way similar to private firms, if not with less caution as the *Comunidad Industrial* did not apply to state enterprise (the strikes at Centromin in 1974 and 1975 being a case in point) while the state development banks continued to lend on 'commercial' criteria to manufacturers rather than to artisans, to cooperatives rather than to subsistence farmers, and to middle-class house-buyers rather than to the homeless.

The third problem was perhaps the most serious in view of the attempt to reduce external dependence by establishing strong state enterprises to replace the foreign companies. It consisted of the fact that in order to get production under way as quickly as possible cooperation in the form of technology and finance had to be obtained from multinational corporations, sometimes involving direct foreign participation in the process. In the two key cases (oil and mining) the difficulty appeared to be one of speed and the need to raise foreign loans rather than technical shortcomings. Both oil exploration and opencast mining are well-known techniques, and, if necessary, experts could have been hired directly. The same might be said of the copper refinery at Ilo, which was built by the Japanese on a 'turnkey' basis for Mineroperu. In addition, the state enterprises tended to import equipment even where comparable local products were available[53] on the grounds that the former was better, cheaper and more rapidly available. The net effect was to waste the opportunity to develop indigenous technological capacity by directing the vast purchases of state enterprises towards domestic producers.

In sum, despite some success in achieving their overall production objectives, the enterprises remained financially weak, contributed little to social development and did not reduce reliance on foreign technology.

Public finance

From the point of view of capital accumulation the fiscal structure can be seen as a means of mobilizing resources in order to sustain state activities, above all public investment, and as such is a crucial element in political economy. The central problem in Peruvian public finance, a problem which contributed to the instability of the economy throughout our period, particularly in the later stages of state intervention, was the fact that the expansion of first current and then capital expenditure was not paralleled by adequate increases in tax pressure. The economic deficit steadily expanded and the burden of taxation was placed upon labour rather than capital, and the burden of deficit finance upon foreign rather than domestic borrowing, leading to a 'fiscal crisis of the state'. Here we shall examine in turn the tax structure, the pattern of state expenditure on current and capital account, the resulting economic deficits and finally the means by which these deficits were financed.

Major changes in the Peruvian tax system[54] were not made during our period. The total current income of general government was mostly made up of tax income to the central government; local government was a minor income source and although social security quotas rose from five to fifteen per cent of current income between 1955 and 1975, the small proportion of the workforce in the system (essentially confined to white-collar and factory employees) and the low subscription level constrained the importance of this source also, although the excess of current receipts over current expenditure did generate net savings of the order of one per cent of GDP in the 1970s. Public enterprise profits were not, as we have seen, a significant source of income. Tax pressure itself rose from about 13 per cent of GDP in the 1950s to 15 per cent after the reorganization of the tax system in 1963, mainly as the result of increased import tariffs imposed by the Belaunde administration; it remained at more or less this level thereafter. Turning to the separate tax categories we find that profit taxes (which include taxes on exports under the Peruvian national accounting conventions, on the grounds that they cannot be shifted on to international purchasers and thus impinge on profits) were a modest but stable proportion of GDP: variations reflected the fluctuations in profitability of sectors that did bear substantial corporation tax (such as mining and fishing) and their absorption into the non-taxpaying public sector as opposed to more stable sectors (such as manufacturing and agriculture) which received massive exemptions as investment incentives – incentives which seem to have had singularly little effect. Company income tax in fact declined as a proportion of declared company profits (see

Table 6.2) from about 27 per cent in 1955–63 to 21 per cent in 1964–68 and remained at that level thereafter. Personal taxation was an even more exiguous source of income, and even though the rates were raised in 1963 and 1969, the small size of the tax base (mainly white-collar workers, with civil servants enjoying lower rates) meant that the top decile of the population was paying little more than 5 per cent of its personal income in personal income tax in the 1960s; however, the growth of salaried employment and more effective collection in the 1970s raised this source from about 3 per cent of the tax base (distributed profits plus salaries) in 1955–58 to 4 per cent in 1964–68 and 8 per cent in 1974–76.[55] The main and growing source of fiscal revenue was indirect taxation. This was based upon production and consumption taxes (which account for two thirds of this item) which until 1973 were mostly *'timbres'* (stamp duty on alcohol and tobacco), although the Belaunde administration had introduced some 'luxury' taxes on items such as cars; in the 1973 reorganization of indirect taxes *timbres* were subsumed under a more general sales tax (*'bienes y servicios'*) on retail sales, although overall pressure was not much changed. Import duties paid rose from about 10 per cent of total imports in 1955 and 1960 to 21 per cent in 1965; as the import substitution which these tariffs were designed to promote got under way this ratio fell to 19 per cent in 1970 and 14 per cent in 1975; the contribution of tariffs to fiscal income rose from 20 per cent in 1955 to 25 per cent in 1965 but fell to 12 per cent in 1975.

Tax reform had been a key component of the Belaunde electoral platform in 1962 and 1963, but despite the mounting fiscal deficit in 1966 and 1967 tax reform proposals based on higher income tax rates and the introduction of real estate duties were blocked for three years running in the Congress. The failure to implement this reform, which was calculated to raise current revenue from 17 per cent of GDP in 1967 to 19 per cent in 1968, is seen by Kuczinski[56] as central to the crucial economic and political failure of the Belaunde administration:

> It is interesting to reflect on the reasons for the adamant refusal of the Peruvian Congress to pass the tax measures. After all, it was not the first or last Congress, in Peru or elsewhere, to take such a position. There were, of course, special factors, such as the recent devaluation, an APRA

by-election victory in Lima on a 'no más impuestos platform', and the
doubts, some of them genuine, that existed among businessmen and
some politicians about Belaunde's spending programme. The question
then is whether these factors were insurmountable, or merely meant the
postponement of the approval of a tax package by Congress. The main
reason for the APRA attitude was its electoral strategy for 1969, and the
fact that President Belaunde was not able to use his prestige in order to
combat that strategy. The strategy was simply to use the APRA–UNO
majority to keep the Belaunde government discredited enough so that
an APRA victory would be assured in 1969, but not so much that the
APRA would inherit a shambles. As far as the fiscal situation was concerned, the APRA position was also in part the result of disbelief in Central Bank data that showed that there was indeed a fiscal crisis. Belaunde
could have used another political weapon in addition to his own
prestige: the progressive nature of the measures proposed. The income
and land taxes could clearly have been described as 'soak the rich'
measures, but surprisingly this was not done: the fervor of the 1962 and
1963 election campaigns had been lost, and there were exaggerated fears
of business reaction.

But by the time the APRA agreed to pass the necessary legislation in
mid-1968 it was too late for either Belaunde or the APRA.

The Velasco regime suffered from no such democratic restrictions, and originally made tax reform a central element in its
programme. The 1971–75 Plan[57] states that:

> To a great extent the strategy of state participation in enterprise reflects
> the need to give the Public Sector a solid source of resources with which
> it can contribute to national development, thus the great emphasis
> placed by the government on the generation of economic surplus by
> such participation. These surpluses should acquire an increasing role in
> the financing of the public sector over the quinquennium. However, the
> rectification of the financial deficiencies of the sector will also require
> the establishment of a solid and equitable system of resource acquisition
> through taxation of different economic agents. For this reason an in-
> tegral reform of the tax system will be implemented, not only in order to
> provide resources to the treasury but also to support the redistribution
> of income, reorient economic activity, improve fiscal administration and
> change tax mentality ['*mentalidad tributaria*']. Therefore a new law on the
> taxation of profits and property will be implemented, ensuring their
> progressivity, rural land taxes will be modified and mechanisms
> designed to prevent urban land speculation established.

In addition, indirect taxes were to be shifted towards luxury goods,
'eliminating those which affect essential consumer items'. The com-

bined effect was to be 'reflected in an increase of central government tax pressure from 15 per cent in 1970 to 18 per cent in 1975, and a structural change in which direct tax will have a greater weight' (*op. cit.*, p. 44).

But in the event, tax pressure actually fell between 1970 and 1975, mainly due to the reductions in import duty revenues as consumer goods were cut back. The proposed income and profits tax increases were not imposed. Admittedly, the combination of three factors did confine the scope for tax reform after 1968: the weak state of major export branches, which became net users of fiscal resources rather than contributors; the strategic decision to maintain and even extend tax concessions to private industry in an (unsuccessful) attempt to stimulate investment; and the difficulty of raising personal income tax when white-collar and professional groups provided a major source of political support for the regime. Nonetheless, fiscal reform had been proclaimed as a major objective in the 'Plan Inca', and considerable funds could have been raised from urban real estate or, in the last resort, by increasing sales taxes by a substantial amount. Given that the tax incentives to industry were clearly having little effect, corporation tax could have been applied more heavily – in all it should not have been too difficult to raise (say) an extra 3 or

Table 7.5. *Fiscal income (per cent of GDP)*

	1955	1960	1965	1970	1975
Central government:					
Profit taxes	3.7	4.2	3.0	4.4	4.1
Personal taxes	0.7	0.7	1.0	1.6	2.4
Import duties	2.7	2.8	4.4	3.4	2.3
Indirect tax, etc.	4.7	5.6	6.7	6.8	7.0
	11.8	13.3	15.1	16.2	15.8
Social security receipts	0.7	1.1	2.0	2.0	3.0
Local government taxation	0.7	0.7	0.7	0.7	0.7
Total fiscal income	13.2	15.1	17.8	18.9	19.5

Source: Calculated from BCR *Cuentas Nacionales* Tables 12 to 15, various years) and BCR *Memoria 1976*.

even 5 per cent of GDP from the economy and thereby eliminate the greater part of the financial deficit of the public sector, while the reduction in consumption demand would have released more foreign exchange for state imports. To have baulked at the issue of tax reform (or substantially increased prices for publicly provided goods and services, which comes to much the same thing) was clearly a major strategic error. It is difficult to see why this should have been more difficult than the land reform or the introduction of worker participation, both of which were carried through in the teeth of the sort of 'business reaction' Belaunde had feared though without a Congress to block legislation. The Velasco regime almost certainly had the political 'room' to do this between 1970 and 1974, but from 1975 onwards the Morales administration came under increasing pressure from foreign bankers (particularly the IMF) to balance the budget by cutting expenditure rather than by raising tax pressure.

The first claim on tax revenue is the current expenditure of government. It is difficult to compare the composition of current expenditures over time by activity due to changes in administrative responsibilities,[58] but comparing 1963 with 1973 we find that in both cases about 5 per cent of general government expenditure was assigned to central administration, and just over a third to social outlays – although within this latter education rose from 21 per cent in 1963 to 31 per cent in 1973, mainly at the expense of health. Security expenditure (above all on the army) accounted for another third of current expenditure in the 1960s but, as might have been expected, had risen to 41 per cent by 1973. The category to fall as a proportion of the total, therefore, was economic activities (from 26 per cent in 1963 to 17 per cent in 1973), but this represented no real restriction in this category as the public enterprises were expanding at the same time. The reorganization of the state sector in 1963 represented an expansion of current expenditure as a proportion of GDP, mainly in the 'economic' and 'social' categories. However, the resulting level was not increased thereafter, and in fact declined slightly after 1968, as the subsequent expansion of the state involved direct participation in production rather than support services for the private sector. Turning to the functional breakdown of expenditure, we find a rising rate of 'consumption' outlays (mainly wages and salaries) due to the aforementioned expansion of the economic and social ministries. The rise and then fall of subsidies (mostly to public enterprise) may be somewhat misleading, because their post-subsidy losses became very large in 1974–76. 'Transfers' are social security current outlays, pensions and so on, which reflect an expansion of both the civil service and social security coverage in the 1960s.[59] The growing burden of interest payments was generated by the increasing indebtedness of the Peruvian state, particularly after 1968, itself the consequence of earlier fiscal deficits. Overall we have a current expenditure pattern of the most rudimentary type covering the basic needs of the state up to 1963; between which date and 1968 a more 'developmental' pattern was adopted; after 1968 this was maintained almost unaltered.

Table 7.6. *Functional distribution of general government current expenditure (per cent of GDP)*

	1955	1960	1965	1970	1975
Consumption	7.0	8.2	10.3	9.5	10.0
Subsidies	1.4	1.5	2.2	1.3	1.0
Interest payments: internal	0.3	0.3	0.5	0.4	0.8
external				0.5	0.9
Transfers: Social security	1.5	2.0	4.5	1.4	2.0
Pensions etc.				3.1	3.0
Total central government	10.2	12.0	17.5	16.2	17.7
Local government current exp.	0.6	0.7	0.7	0.8	0.6
Total general govt. current exp.	10.8	12.7	18.2	17.0	18.3

Source: As Table 7.5

The difference between current fiscal income and expenditure is expressed in national accounting terms as 'general government savings', and is the greater part of the public savings discussed in Chapter 6. The main trends in taxation and current outlays are immediately clear from Table 7.7: the expansion relative to the economy of both categories during the mid 1960s and their comparative stability thereafter. Nonetheless, small variations in the two components did cause wide fluctuations in their difference – government savings. The rise in income in the 1963–68 period having been exceeded by the expansion of current expenditure, leading to net dis-savings, a major policy step after 1968 was the restoration of the current surplus[60] and this was just maintained even in the fiscal stress of 1974–76, although the resulting contribution to capital formation was little more than marginal.

Both the composition of public investment and its place in the process of capital formation in the economy as a whole are discussed elsewhere;[61] the pertinent aspects here are the shift during our period away from roads and irrigation towards mining and industry on the one hand, and its growing share of the national total on the other. After the retraction of public investment as a result of the stabilization policy of 1958–59, its growth under the Belaunde administration was concentrated upon transport and agricultural infrastructure, but its massive expansion in 1974–76 involved a shift towards public enterprise as state investment was reallocated towards oil, mining, steel and chemicals. In addition to the gross fixed capital formation undertaken by the public sector, the state banks undertook steadily greater financial investments, effectively funding productive investment in the private sector. This activity involved two main steps: one in the mid 1960s towards housing and agriculture and one in the mid 1970s towards industry. Once these capital outlays are set against the narrow margin of government savings, the extent of the resulting resource deficit of the public sector becomes evident. Taking first the excess of fixed investment over savings, we find that the shortfall in 1955–58 was maintained in 1959–63 despite increased savings and cutbacks in government investment resulting from fiscal adjustments as part of the stabilization programme of 1958, because local public works programmes were actually stepped up as exports began to recover and the election approached.[62] Development bank lending was restrained, however, and the result was to slightly reduce the financial deficit of the state sector as a proportion of GDP. In 1964–68, as we have seen, the Belaunde administration failed to obtain sufficient tax income to cover its current expenditure: the deficit on current account and the rapid expansion of public investment, plus the extension of development bank activities, drove the public sector into financial and economic deficits far greater in relation to GDP than anything experienced in previous years.

The public sector surplus was re-established after 1969, mainly by restraining current government expenditure and tightening up on tax collection, but, although the state enterprises also generated a useful contribution to public savings, the sector as a whole could still only manage to finance a third of its own fixed investment. It was in 1974–76, however, that the fiscal crisis really emerged as a major destabilizing element in the Peruvian economy. At the same time as current government expenditure rose to meet its current income, thus almost eliminating savings, and the public enterprises ran into current account deficit (for the reasons we have discussed above) the massive outlays on public investment programmed since 1971 began to work through, almost doubling the rate of fixed capital formation as a proportion of GDP and almost tripling the economic deficit. Combined with the renewed expansion of state banking activities, this shortfall generated a financial shortfall equivalent to over a tenth of the national product. Clearly this imbalance could not be allowed to continue, and, as the IMF[63] had identified the budget deficit as the main cause of inflation and balance of payments difficulties, drastic adjustments to the fiscal balance were made in 1977–78 by cutting back public sector fixed investment to 6.6 per cent of GDP.[64] However, it would appear that

Table 7.7. *Resource deficit of the Peruvian state 1955–76*

(% of GDP).	1955–58	1959–63	1964–68	1969–73	1974–76
General government income	13.4	15.3	17.7	18.7	18.8
General government expenditure	12.1	13.6	18.2	17.7	18.5
General government savings	1.3	1.7	−0.5	1.0	0.3
Public enterprise surplus	0.0	0.0	0.0	0.6	−0.2
Public sector surplus	1.3	1.7	−0.5	1.6	0.1
GFCF: Central government	2.5	1.6	2.4	2.6	2.8
State enterprise, etc.	0.4	1.7	2.2	2.2	5.6
Public sector	2.9	3.3	4.6	4.8	8.4
Economic deficit	1.6	1.6	5.1	3.2	8.3
Public financial investment	0.8	0.6	1.2	1.3	2.7
Financial deficit	2.4	2.2	6.3	4.5	11.0

Source: Appendix, Table A.2

the devaluations and internal inflation led to large increases in current government expenditure while the depression induced by the stabilization policy reduced tax revenues as a share of GDP, so

that despite the restoration of the state enterprise account to surplus, the economic and financial deficits of the state sector as a
whole remained at extremely high levels. The problem was that in
the short term public expenditure was extremely difficult to cut back
in real terms, because current expenditure mainly reflected the
salaries of soldiers, schoolteachers and bureaucrats (all politically
sensitive groups) while capital expenditure already committed in
dollars increased automatically in sol terms.

These deficits had to be covered by acquiring resources from
elsewhere, the alternative sources being monetary emission,
borrowing on domestic capital markets and raising loans on international financial centres or from official institutions. The implications of the uses made of these sources over our period are of
considerable significance: we have already detected some of the
effects in Chapter 6 and will relate them to economic policy in
Chapter 8. In the 1955–58 period, an almost exact balance was
struck between modest fiduciary emission (equivalent to less than
one per cent of GDP per annum) due to a conservative monetary
policy, borrowing directly from local commercial banks and limited
overseas loans, mostly from the US government. The deflationary
policy pursued in 1959–63 as a response to balance of payments
difficulties slightly reduced the public sector financing requirement
as a proportion of GDP, but the decision to run down the external
debt made an increased rate of domestic borrowing necessary, but
without serious strain. The renewed financial deficit under the
Belaunde administration was financed in a manner to be repeated
on a larger scale a decade later – after saturating the narrow
domestic market for government bonds and apprehensive of
excessive inflationary pressure resulting from further monetary
issue, the government borrowed heavily abroad, well in excess of the
import requirements of its own infrastructure projects. The 1969–73
period saw a reduced financial deficit as a proportion of GDP
despite the expanded activities of development banks, and for
political reasons foreign finance was relatively hard to obtain.
However, the recovery in economic growth permitted greater use of
monetary emission within conservative criteria, and thus direct
borrowing from domestic banks was cut back to a level equivalent to
that obtaining ten years before. The massive expansion of the finan-

cial deficit in 1974–76, however, meant an abandonment of these conservative principles and a large increase in the reliance upon each of these three instruments, particularly foreign borrowing (as we shall see in Chapter 8) but also monetary emission and continued borrowing from domestic banks, although the decline in private investment meant that bank funds for this purpose were quite readily available. As we have seen in Chapter 6 the stabilization policy of 1977–78 substantially reduced the rate of borrowing on domestic and foreign markets, but still not to anything like the levels of 1969–73, and thus the fiscal crisis of the Peruvian state was far from over.

Table 7.8. *Financing the resource deficit (per cent of GDP)*

	1955–58	1959–63	1964–68	1969–73	1974–76
Public sector financing requirement	2.4	2.2	6.3	4.5	11.0
Finance: Internal*	0.8	2.9	4.0	2.7	5.4
External	1.6	−0.7	2.3	1.8	5.6
(* of which, monetary emission)	(0.7)	(1.2)	(1.0)	(1.6)	(2.4)

Source: Appendix; monetary emission as in BCR *Memoria 1976*, defined as notes, coins and 'depositos y otras obligaciones en moneda nacional en el BCR'.

Fiscal incidence

The tax system was not an adequate means of mobilizing the resources required by the Peruvian state. Nor was it a very effective means of 'reorienting economic activity': the high tariff barriers undoubtedly promoted import-substituting industrialization in the 1960s but embargoes were found necessary in order to sustain the process after 1968; the generous tax incentives to mining and industrial investment seem to have had little effect in our period either. However, a fiscal system can be used as a way of redistributing income and thus possibly as a means of ameliorating the regressive impact of capitalist growth upon personal income distribution – certainly this was the declared intention of both Belaunde and Velasco.[65]

The first examination of tax incidence in Peru was carried out under the Joint Tax Program in 1958, and is discussed by Hunt, who deduces from this that 'the tax system shows no progression, but rather exhibits what is best described as a wandering proportionality'.[66] He correctly points out that expenditure incidence should also be taken into account in order to calculate the net budget transfer, but can only identify the recipients of social expenditure (health and education) and development investment (mainly transport) separately and although these grew steadily as a proportion of total government expenditure from 31 per cent in 1940 they still only represented 52 per cent in 1965. These recipients he finds mainly to be the third quartile – in other words the modern sector workforce – but suggests that much of the benefit of security expenditure might be attributed to the elite itself. Webb takes up this argument[67] on the basis of much firmer empirical evidence integrated to his pioneering study of personal income distribution: his main results are shown and developed in Table 7.9 below. From

Table 7.9. *The incidence of taxation in Peru*

	% of personal income	1961 % tax incidence	Share of tax yield	% of personal income	1969 % tax incidence	Share of the yield
Highest						
percentile	25.4	23.5	43%	58.1	26.2	63%
90–99	24.2	14.0	25%		22.4	
75–100	20.4	12.0	18%	23.5	17.5	19%
Quartile IV	70.5	17.5	86%	71.6	23.0	82%
III	17.4	8.3	9%	16.6	15.6	13%
II	8.9	5.8	4%	9.0	9.2	4%
I	3.5	3.9	1%	2.8	5.2	1%
Total	100.0	14.5	100%	100.0	20.0	100%

Source: Calculated from the tax incidence figures given in Webb (1977, Table 7) and personal income distribution in Table 5.7.

these estimates, three major conclusions can be drawn. First, despite the widespread opinion to the contrary,[68] the tax system was progressive in spite of its reliance upon indirect taxation. This was because the taxed commodities had an income elasticity greater than unity, and although this only introduced a slight degree of progressivity, the addition of income tax made this effect substantial; indeed, given the extraordinary concentration of personal income in Peru, a regressive tax system would have raised scarcely any fiscal revenue at all! Second, the bulk of tax revenue came from the fourth quartile (and two thirds from the top decile), which means that the tax system was not acting as a means of further exploiting the poor but rather of centralizing capitalist income extracted by other mechanisms. Third, the changes in tax incidence between 1961 and 1969, the period within which some tax reform did take place, was not large and the increased burden was distributed more or less in proportion to the existing one. The absence of tax reform after 1968 meant, moreover, that this incidence pattern (with possibly some modest increase in the top decile) was maintained until the end of our period.

No comprehensive estimate of net fiscal incidence has been made for Peru, possibly because of the difficulties of assigning major items of the budget to particular income groups:[69] the 'users' of the facilities provided by the state in the form of health, education and 'localized' infrastructure for transport and agriculture can be identified, but this is less than half of total expenditure and the rest (defence, security, administration and industrial support) cannot be attributed *directly* to any one population group. The first problem is that if the cost of supplying (say) health to peasants is exceeded by the benefits to the recipients, as it probably is, then the net distributive effect of such expenditure is greater than it appears. The second is that although expenditure on (say) education is undoubtedly received by the working class, its effect (and indeed its purpose) may well be to improve labour productivity and thus raise profits. Nonetheless, it does seem feasible to allocate these outlays to their direct recipients. In contrast, the allocation of expenditure on central administration, security and defence depends upon an interpretation of the role of the state. These are the costs of guaranteeing the maintenance of the prevailing social system, and may be regarded as of equal benefit to all the members of the nation, or in a less naive way as benefiting groups in proportion to their income (i.e. in proportion to what they get out of the economic system) or more dogmatically as of benefit to the dominant elite alone. This last appears to fit the Peruvian case best, until 1968 at least, and if we allow for a redefinition of the capitalist elite to include the bureaucrats of state capitalism, then subsequently as well.

Webb[70] gives a rough estimate of net fiscal incidence, confining himself to the tax incidence statistics and the 'identifiable' expenditure in education, health and infrastructure. We have already examined his estimate of incidence; he allocates education according to school enrolments, and health on the basis of health ministry records, and infrastructure as follows – housing to the modern sector, irrigation to the rural sector, and the roads in proportion to income. Unfortunately he does this by sector[71] rather than by income group, but still the results indicate that even without allowance for any allocation of the 'difficult' categories of state expenditure, there was a modestly redistributive pattern of fiscal incidence in Peru (in that four fifths of the population receive more than they pay for in tax) and that this grew during the 1960s as welfare expenditure expanded. However, the bulk of fiscal income and expenditure was within the 'modern' sector (the top quintile of the population in Webb's definition), and families there received in identifiable benefits considerably less than they paid in tax. It would appear that the Peruvian fiscal system as a whole was mildly progressive even if all 'unidentifiable' benefits such as security were to be allocated to the topmost percentile.

In this context, we should also remember that the post-1968 ownership reforms had a redistributive effect only within the corporate sector, so that the restraints on the trend towards wider availability of education and health services (above all in urban slums and the Andes) and the absence of fiscal reform meant that those in the non-corporate sector received little benefit from state expansion. This effect also means, however, that in terms of resource mobilization, extra funds for capital formation and the repayment of foreign loans were drawn from wages and profits in the corporate sector, and above all from the savings of domestic firms – although it could of course be argued that these were in turn derived from exploitation of labour.

Concluding remarks

The major change in the economic structure of central government occurred under the Belaunde regime, when the tax structure was modernized and a start made on the expansion of welfare services: even though these latter were only extended to the modern sector workforce, the result was to eliminate any surplus on government account. In view of this financial fragility, the increase in public investment over our period resulting from attempts to restructure Peruvian capital could receive little support from the fiscal structure.

Table 7.10. *Net fiscal incidence in Peru*

| | (US $ per head at 1970 prices) | | | | | |
| | 1961 | | | | 1970 | |
	Modern sector	Urban tradi-tional	Rural tradi-tional	Modern sector	Urban tradi-tional	Rural tradi-tional
Education	60	50	20	100	100	50
Health	100	50	10	100	50	10
Infrastructure	70	30	20	60	20	20
	230	130	50	260	170	80
Taxation	530	70	30	800	160	50
Budget transfer	−300	+60	+20	−540	+10	+30

Source: Webb (1977) p. 78.

The unprofitability of state enterprises, due in the main to their strategic tasks of recapitalizing export branches and providing cheap inputs to the private sector, contributed to this imbalance. This difficulty in raising resources formed a crucial contradiction in public sector accumulation and thus in state capitalism as a new development model for Peru.

Although the failure to raise tax revenue, particularly as a means of bringing private profits under state control, was clearly a weakness of the model it cannot be said that the Peruvian tax burden (that is, the ratio of tax income to GDP) was excessively low by international standards. The comparison carried out by Chelliah[72] on a world-wide basis, comparing tax burdens in developing countries in terms of per capita income, on the one hand and the shares of exports, industry and agriculture in GDP on the other, indicates that for the 1966–68 period the tax burden in Peru was very close to the international norm in view of taxation possibilities such as income per head, mineral exports and so on. However, it was necessary to raise tax income beyond the international norm if a successful nationalist state capitalist project was to be implemented – and this was not done when the Velasco regime

Table 7.11. *Comparative fiscal structures*

	General government tax income				(% of GDP) General government current expenditure			
	1950	1960	1970	1975	1950	1960	1970	1975
Argentina	17.0	14.2	15.0	12.8	14.7	16.1	17.3	28.7
Brazil	16.0	20.1	27.0	30.7	13.3	18.6	24.3	23.0
Chile	16.7	16.5	21.8	22.7	13.7	22.5	25.6	24.8
Colombia	12.0	10.4	13.4	13.4	11.5	7.8	10.6	11.0
Mexico	7.5	7.1	7.9	10.5	6.5	5.1	6.0	9.5
Peru	14.0	14.9	18.9	17.6	12.1	12.3	17.0	17.4
Latin America[a]	..	14.4	17.8	..	..	15.1	18.4	..

	Public sector gross fixed capital formation				Public sector economic surplus			
	1950	1960	1970	1975	1950	1960	1970	1975
Argentina	7.8	5.3	7.9	7.0	−5.5	−7.2	−10.2	−22.9
Brazil	4.2	6.7	9.0	9.5	−1.5	−5.2	−6.3	−1.8
Chile	3.3	6.8	9.0	5.0	−0.3	−12.8	−12.8	−7.1
Colombia	1.9	3.4	6.7	7.0	−1.4	−0.8	−4.3	−4.7
Mexico	6.1	5.6	7.5	10.5	−5.1	−3.6	−5.6	−9.5
Peru	1.8	2.3	4.5	8.5	+0.1	−0.3	−2.6	−8.3
Latin America[a]	..	5.6	7.3	..	..	−6.3	−8.5	..

Note: 'Public sector economic surplus' is defined as 'general government tax income' less 'general government current expenditure' less 'public sector GFCF'. [a] weighted by 1960 dollar GDP.

Source: FitzGerald (1978a) based on ECLA and IMF statistics. The definitions for Peru do not correspond exactly to ours, but have been retained in order to preserve international comparability.

had the political power to do so. The macroeconomic imbalance of 1974–76 and subsequent pressure from international bankers to abandon reformist policies in Peru were directly related to this fiscal imbalance through the domestic demand pressure and large-scale foreign borrowing it brought about.

The fiscal consequences of a state sector expanding in order to support post-war industrialization against a constrained tax structure are common to most Latinamerican economies.[73] In particular, it would seem that the hypotheses put forward to explain the 'fiscal crisis of the state' in metropolitan economies[74] might be applicable on the periphery too: to support monopolistic industrialization the state is called upon to provide more and more infrastructural support to and tax incentives for corporations, leading to worsening budget deficits and the imposition of higher tax burdens on labour rather than capital. Low levels of corporation tax, the virtual absence of agricultural and real estate duties, the rise and fall of tariff income as import-substitution proceeds, and the

Table 7.12. *Military Expenditure in Latin America 1967–76*

	Arms imports from (US $ millions):				Military expenditure as:		Armed forces per 'ooo population
	USA	USSR	Other	Total	per cent of GDP	per cent of central govt expenditure	
Argentina	131	—	230	361	1.8	13.4	6.19
Brazil	300	—	390	690	2.0	19.2	4.05
Chile	110	—	245	355	2.9	. .	8.13
Cuba	—	355	—	355	. .	. .	. .
Mexico	21	—	49	70	0.7	6.4	1.57
Peru	105	165	385	655	3.4	18.4	5.78
Other	355	—	609	964	. .	. .	. .
Total Latin America	1022	520	1908	3450	2.0•	15.0•	4.01•

Source: González (1978); these figures are drawn directly from a report by the US Arms Control and Disarmament Agency 'World Military Expenditures and Arms Transfers 1967–76' (Washington, July 1978).
• Excluding Cuba

dominance of consumption taxes experienced by Peru are common to all Latinamerican economies, as is the lack of progressivity in the incidence of taxation upon different income groups, particularly the top percentiles. However, although the increased fiscal deficits are widespread, the means of financing them vary widely: Brazil, for example, made extensive use of social security funds to finance state enterprise and undertook an extensive tax reform based on consumption taxes, while Mexico controlled the capital markets in such a way as to sustain large government bond sales. These economies – including even the fortunate oil exporters such as

Venezuela and Ecuador – have accumulated vast amounts of foreign debt nonetheless, with similar consequences in terms of external leverage over domestic policy as well as the increased burden on the balance of payments of debt service, and have resorted to monetary emission on a grand scale. In sum, the state in Latin America has great difficulty in obtaining the resources necessary to finance its support for industrialization, and in consequence has resorted in recent years to methods which have served to destabilize that process (as in Mexico), or else cut back severely on the economic role of the state – as in Argentina and Chile.

Military outlays in general and arms imports in particular were undoubtedly large in Peru relative to those in other Latinamerican countries. In addition, Peru was the only country other than Cuba to receive arms from Russia, as well as getting one fifth of all US arms supplies to the region at the same time. Throughout our period, the Peruvian military considered that not only Chile but also Brazil and Ecuador posed a geopolitical threat; to the extent that this fear was justified a disproportionate expenditure upon, and the diversification of sources for, mechanized equipment might be considered reasonable – there is no indication that Peru harboured any expansionist ambitions of its own.

8

Economic policy and planning

The exercise of state intervention in an economy beyond the limits of the articulation of the public sector itself involves the formulation and execution of economic policy. In a market economy, the fundamental objective of such intervention is the support of capitalist accumulation. By definition this involves operating on a market system, so the objectives of economic policy are expressed in terms of the maintenance of internal and external equilibria so that private capital can 'get on with the job of providing growth and employment', the main instruments being the budgetary surplus, credit control and adjustment of the parity of the national currency. On the periphery of the world economy, where organized labour cannot impose the same conditions for wages and employment as at the centre, but where there is greater pressure to promote industrialization and foreign investment, the policy objectives are modified to play down the former pair of objectives and stress the latter two. In a centralized economy, the pattern of growth and accumulation is established directly by the state; the role of economic policy is to support these processes by guiding the adjustment of the remaining 'private' sector (including independent cooperatives, peasants, artisans and small traders) to the public sector programmes. In other words, an integrated planning system is introduced and economic policy becomes part of an active 'restructuring' activity rather than a more passive 'stabilizing' one. These two models are distinct in principle; the difficulty lies in defining the roles of policy and planning at an 'intermediate' stage of economic transformation. State control over the economy may not be sufficient to allow a complete planning system, while the impact of the public sector itself on the macroeconomic equilibrium may make a conventional stabilization policy almost impossible to implement.

The problems of managing the Peruvian economy in our period exhibited elements of both continuity and change which merit some general remarks at this stage, before more detailed consideration of short-run problems. Throughout the period between 1956 and 1978, private investment rates declined and were balanced by inadequately financed public investment,[1] leading in 1965–67 and 1974–76 to large budget deficits which made aggregate demand management and equilibration of the balance of payments all the more difficult at times when the external trade account itself was destabilized by declining export purchasing power. In addition, the shift of import composition away from consumer goods towards industrial inputs meant that imports became less flexible and insensitive to depression of domestic demand upon which stabilization policies were based. The conjunction of these trends generated the worsening crises and devaluations of 1958, 1967 and 1976–78.[2]

The other major element of continuity in the economic policy problem – as distinct from the strategic aim of promoting industrialization[3] – was that of securing an adequate urban food supply. As Kalecki points out,[4] the demand for food in a developing country (particularly in the form of wage goods) rises in line with national income adjusted by a suitable income-elasticity factor, while supply growth is structurally constrained by the organizational form of traditional agriculture. If an attempt is made to achieve a rate of growth in national income such as to generate a food demand growth rate greater than supply, then either food prices must rise – depressing the real wage rate – or imports of food must be undertaken to fill the gap and stabilize food prices. The limits on either solution mean that, quite apart from any role that agriculture might play in directly providing an investable surplus to the rest of the economy, food supply can impose an effective brake on growth through income distribution and the balance of payments. Further, in this Kaleckian model, if expanding aggregate demand for necessities is to be kept down in line with growth in supply without worsening the income distribution, then increased taxation must be imposed upon higher income groups – taxation that can be used to finance public sector investment in productive capital or welfare facilities (depending upon the objectives of state intervention) or reduce fiscal imbalances. Under other circumstances, official foreign borrowing to relieve fiscal or import problems may in effect serve to maintain the level of consumption rather than achieve higher rates of accumulation.

The major elements of change in economic policymaking in Peru between 1956 and 1978 occurred after 1968. Firstly, before that date macroeconomic policy decisions had largely been in the hands of the treasury and the Central Bank, where *laissez-faire* principles were paramount, even though these initiatives could be blocked by Congress, as in the case of tax reform. However, the INP and 'economic' ministries such as those of industry and agriculture began to take a certain degree of control over economic policy after 1968 in dissonance with the Central Bank, which attempted to continue pre-1968 policies in terms of monetary and credit control. After 1975 the combination of political changes within the military command, the emergence of macroeconomic disequilibria requiring immediate response in terms of demand management (in which the BCR was experienced, the INP's strength lying in 'structural' policies) and the increasing pressure from foreign creditors in direct professional contact with the Central Bank, served to re-establish the control of the BCR (acting now in open collaboration with the IMF despite the resignation of senior staff in protest[5]) and the treasury over economic policy. However, the implementation of the stabilization policy, a major element of which was public expenditure cuts, was openly and to a considerable extent successfully opposed by the rest of the bureaucracy. Secondly, the official attitude towards foreign enterprise changed radically, so that while before 1968 a reasonable annual inflow of private capital could be counted upon to sustain the balance of payments, after that date such finance was raised only by the state or in direct negotiation with it (as in the case of the mining projects) while on private sector account there was a substantial outflow of funds. Thirdly, as part of the attempt to implement a state capitalist model, a central planning system was set up, which – as we shall see – imposed a certain degree of coherence over the expanded public investment programme and external trade but did not extend to cover food and manufacturing output on the one hand or financial flows on the other. These changes, overlaid upon the elements of continuity and the deeper 'crisis of exports', made economic policymaking – and more specifically the implementation of such policies – steadily more difficult between 1956 and 1978.

In this chapter, we shall consider short-run domestic economic policy in two sub-periods – 1956–68 and 1969–78; we shall then treat negotiation with foreign capital and development planning separately, concentrating upon the period after 1968 when these official activities assumed major importance. Figures 2 to 5 below illustrate some of the major macroeconomic variables over the period as a whole; further details of these and other variables – such as the money supply, reserves and exchange rate – may be found in Appendix Table A.4; the level of investment is depicted in Figure 1 (p. 156).

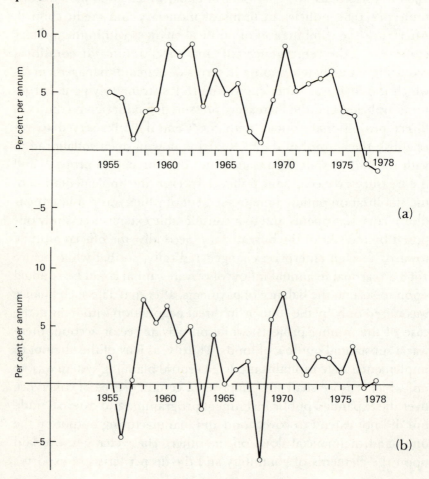

(a)

(b)

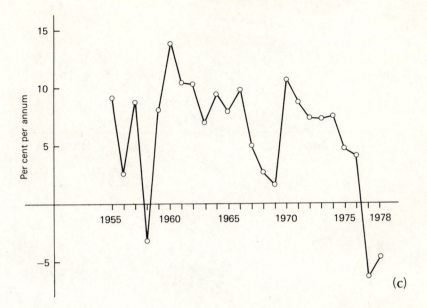

(c)

Figure 2 Growth of GDP, agriculture and manufacturing
(a) Growth of gross domestic product
(b) Growth of agricultural output
(c) Growth of manufacturing output
Source: Appendix Table A.4

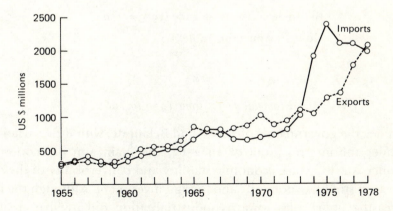

Figure 3 Exports f.o.b. and imports f.o.b.
Source: Appendix Table A.4

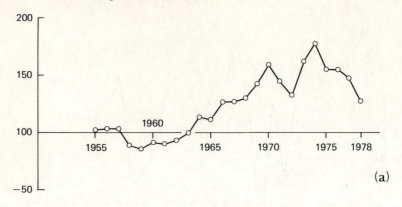

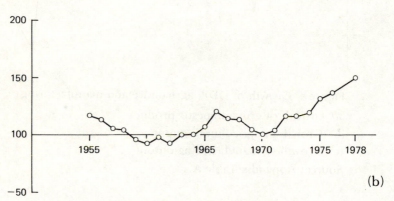

Figure 4 External and internal terms of trade

(a) External terms of trade (1963 = 100)

(b) Internal terms of trade (1963 = 100)

Source: Appendix Table A.4

Economic policy from 1956 to 1968

Under the governments of Prado and Belaunde, with little variation
under the interim junta of 1962–63, the main aim of economic
policy was to assure economic stability and convertibility of the sol
so as to stimulate domestic and foreign investment. Although the increasing policy bias towards industrialization did involve greater
tariff protection[6] the basic aims and methods of policy remained
more or less the same. When exports were growing strongly, as they

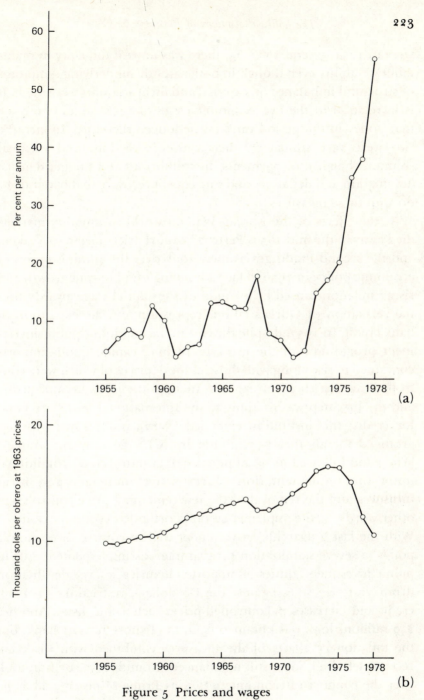

Figure 5 Prices and wages
(a) Changes in GDP deflation
(b) Real wages
Source: Appendix Table A.4

were in 1952–57 and 1960–65, there was no real difficulty in main-taining stability even though in both cases the underlying symptoms of structural imbalance on external and fiscal accounts were there. It is in relation to the two economic crises of 1958–59 and 1967–68 that policy in the period can best be judged therefore. In fact, the two were very similar in their causes,[7] reactions and eventual solution: balance of payments disequilibrium and budget deficits, devaluation and deflation, and subsequent recovery that had little to do with these measures.

As the effects of the Korean War on world commodity markets died away in the mid 1950s Peruvian export prices began to weaken, and the second Prado government took over the administration of economic policy in 1956 to face a levelling off of output growth and rising inflation caused by a round of substantial wage awards after the relaxation of Odría's labour repression and the expansion of bank credit. In 1957, despite the cuts in the ambitious public invest-ment programme of the previous regime, capital goods imports continued to rise along with those of food (prices of which were con-trolled) against stagnant exports. In 1958 the crisis became acute, and the first step was to apply to the International Monetary Fund for credit; this institution extended US $25 million in loans and arranged for another $35 million from US government sources: 'The Fund followed its usual practice of granting credit conditional upon the implementation of restrictive monetary and fiscal measures and the removal of the few remaining price controls – in other words . . . the implementation of orthodox economic policy'.[8] With the last 'oligarchic' government well in control of economic policy, a severe stabilization programme was implemented: cuts in public investment, duties on imported luxuries, a large devaluation (from 19 to 27 soles against the US dollar), restrictions on bank credit and increases in controlled prices such as bus fares. Another $40 millions loan was obtained from the Export-Import Bank, but the inflationary effects of the measures combined with weak tax receipts left the budget still unbalanced. In mid-1959, Beltran took over the conduct of economic policy as Prime Minister, and as he was committed to no tax increases further rounds of expenditure cuts were imposed – affecting above all social services and develop-ment loans.

Meanwhile exports began to recover, due to the entry into production of the Toquepala copper mine and the secular rise of fishing output. As Thorp points out: 'The remarkable recovery in exports in 1959 . . . occurred independently of any immediate policy measures taken. It reflected rather in part the maturity of large investments made years earlier and in part the revival of world demand for Peruvian products at a crucial point in time' (1967, p. 109). This allowed economic growth to resume unchecked by rising imports and success was officially claimed for the stabilization policy, despite the fact that the recovery had been as exogenous as the crisis and the massive deflation probably damaged the industrialization process as well as increasing social tensions. More importantly, it did nothing to resolve the underlying structural problems in the Peruvian economy.

Between 1960 and 1965 economic policy could once again be returned to a passive role as the balance of payments was healthy (due to the fishing boom) and public expenditure could recover within rising tax income from a buoyant economy. It was in this period that some modest improvement in domestic food supplies was achieved;[9] although it is not entirely clear whether this was due to government policy on infrastructure and credit support to commercial cashcrop farmers or the weakening price of cotton relative to domestic food prices, a shift of irrigated coastal cotton land into food production did occur and the immediate problem was staved off. But new import duties were not enough to finance the growing current expenditure on social services and capital spending on transport infrastructure, while the growth of industry placed increasing pressure on imports, so that by 1966 the familiar disequilibrium emerged when export prices weakened and imports continued to rise. Despite Belaunde's explicit intention to break away from orthodox stabilization programmes geared to the balance of payments towards a new policy based on development of the domestic economy, the unwillingness to tackle structural problems and congressional opposition to even those modest reforms that were proposed – such as higher taxation – meant that a new course was not achieved.[10]

By 1967, a disequilibrium similar to that obtaining a decade previously had emerged; although export prices did not weaken, mining production stagnated while imports of industrial inputs were rising rapidly. Foreign investment inflows were insufficient to cover the trade gap, and government income was no longer adequate to cover even current expenditure as the welfare programmes got under way, while the US financial aid that had been used to cover public sector capital imports was frozen against resolution of the IPC dispute.[11] Inflation rose again to what were by Peruvian standards extremely high levels, as a new round of wage pressure backed by strikes broke out and the banking system extended credit for the construction boom. In addition, the government was prevented from further action by its own internal dissension. As in 1958, a 40 per cent devaluation to 42 soles was imposed in 1967, import tariffs were raised and petrol prices increased, the budget cut back and credit restricted – in order to obtain a $43 million credit from the IMF. The internal political difficulties of accepting this course were much greater than in 1958, but, as the alternative of higher taxes and exchange controls were unacceptable not only to the IMF but also to APRA, an orthodox stabilization policy was eventually adopted. This programme did achieve fiscal equilibrium and a reduction in imports, but recovery in 1969 came from the familiar renewal of export income growth – above all from improving world prices – and not as the result of this policy as such. Indeed, once again domestic industry was denied a chance to expand into the established capacity and no alteration of the economic structure was achieved.

Negotiation between the state and foreign investors had not been a major policy issue between 1956 and 1965;[12] as we have argued in Chapter 5, there existed a coincidence of interest between the two parties, underlined by the notoriously generous Mining Code of 1950 and the continual attempts to encourage multinational investment in manufacturing. The IPC issue did become significant in 1967–68, but this was more for political reasons than strictly economic ones, being a test of the government's stamina in relation to assets of comparatively modest value; the aspect of these negotiations that provided the circumstances of military intervention in 1968 was precisely Belaunde's *lack* of effective policy on foreign investors. The 'leverage' effect[13] exercised by the International Monetary Fund (and implicitly by the US government) in insisting upon the burden of deflation programmes being borne by labour rather than capital (and if by capital, by industrialists rather than exporters or financiers) was uncontested in 1958–59; but by 1967–68 it was a major political issue which contributed to the downfall of democratic government.

Economic policy from 1969 to 1978

On taking power in October 1968, the Velasco regime inherited a short-run economic situation of deflation and import restraint as a result of previous cutbacks in public expenditure and devaluation. These measures did not affect exports but prices were beginning to move upwards on international markets so that the trade position was sound as also was the balance of payments, despite the halting of foreign investment. The main policy objective between 1969 and 1975 was to take advantage of this situation in order to carry through the planned ownership reforms with a minimum of economic disturbance: 'The Government . . . has acted in order to achieve a sound financial situation which would permit it to carry out the programmed changes in the economic and social structure.'[14] Thus the economy was to be allowed to expand steadily under the impact of revived export income and increasing state investment, but within the constraints of tight credit, import restrictions and price controls. Despite the lack of private investment and poor agricultural performance, satisfactory results were obtained from this policy until 1974, when the symptoms of the long-run structural faults in the economy appeared once again – balance of payments deficits, food shortages and inflation – to be met by increasingly severe stabilization measures between 1976 and 1978, efforts which turned out to be insufficient and too late. The period as a whole, in terms of the contribution of economic policy to the long-term development strategy, was one of lost opportunity: the decision to leave the '*coyuntura económica*' alone in order to safeguard the reform programme meant that in due course it turned into an effective obstacle to further change.

The impact of the 1967 devaluation was still felt on the import side of the balance of payments well into 1969, and was further strengthened by the imposition of a ten per cent surcharge on all private sector imports. The severe restrictions on bank credit, government current expenditure and public investment were continued, depressing the level of aggregate demand in the economy with indirect effects on industry and a direct effect on the construction sector from the cutback in public works. Agriculture, in contrast, appears to have done quite well, although the buoyant supply of meat was partly due to the slaughter of livestock by ranchers in order to forestall the exiguous compensation for their herds under the Land Reform. The overall result was a healthy balance of payments and a low inflation rate, but also a very small expansion in national income, despite the good agricultural out-turn. No specific action was taken to revive the economy, however, and the reflation in 1970 was mainly caused by further improvement in world prices and a short-lived renewal of anchovy fishing, while in the two succeeding years the motive force to sustain growth came mostly from internal demand generated by public works and the relaxation of constraints on bank credit to industry and construction. Despite a decline in agricultural output (due to bad weather rather than the Land Reform – the affected cooperatives performed much better than the unaffected peasant food producers) and the difficulties with overfishing and mining strikes, aggregate output growth averaged 6 per cent a year and inflation was kept down to 5 per cent over the 1969–72 period as a whole. The balance of payments was still in surplus on current account, and although outflows of private capital were considerable, modest official borrowing abroad covered this without difficulty. Indeed, the Central Bank was able to build up a defensive position in foreign exchange reserves equivalent to over six months' imports in order to better weather any temporary borrowing difficulties that might occur for 'political' reasons. At this point despite the lack of private investment (which had reached an all-time low, averaging only 9 per cent of GDP in the 1969–72 period), the prospect of insufficient food supplies and the evident problem of future exports, the policy of controlled reflation did seem to have been effective. In addition, the establishment of controls over external trade and internal credit consequent upon nationalization made policy implementation that bit less difficult, while the policy of imports and state subsidies prevented the food shortage from hurting the urban poor excessively.

In 1973, although the steady expansion established in the previous three years appeared to be continuing, the signs of strain were beginning to show. Fishmeal exports fell heavily for the second year running, mining had another bad year, and agricultural output growth fell below that for population once again – but these were considered to be temporary factors, and policy remained unchanged. Private investment was still at extremely low levels, imports were rising to meet exports even though the terms of trade turned in Peru's favour, and prices began to rise again more rapidly – 15 per cent in that year. In 1973 government savings were negative for the first time since 1968.[15] What should have been apparent was that the familiar cycle in the Peruvian economy was emerging: a deteriorating balance of payments position exacerbated by fiscal deficits. In short, the economy was 'running too fast' for the unmodified productive structure. By the next year the position was worse; a substantial deficit on the current account of the balance of payments emerged, price inflation continued and the fiscal deficit widened. Above all, the massive public investment programme finally entered the spending stage, putting pressure on foreign exchange resources, drawing heavily on domestic sources of finance (which were replenished by further state bank credit) and sustaining the level of aggregate demand. Still nothing drastic was done: exports had revived a bit, and import controls were imposed, but the shortage of supply both from abroad and from the unexpanded private domestic sector faced rapidly swelling demand sustained by wage rises and public sector purchases. This imbalance continued into 1975, but the policy response was still constrained by the need to keep the public investment programme going and the difficulty of cutting down on imports even further without direct control over private industry. However, agricultural support prices were raised substantially, accompanied by a freeze on wages and salaries only partly balanced by a fixed increment to cover the calculated impact of the new food prices on the average family budget. Direct allocation of foreign exchange was also introduced, and even though this still involved assigning permits to import agencies rather than producers, it did enable competitive imports to be cut back and essential imports to be given priority, successfully restraining import volume – but not prices;[16] in fact, the terms of trade deteriorated sharply as copper prices weakened at the same time. Food imports were growing rapidly, involving not only considerable foreign exchange cost but also a drain on the central government budget to subsidize their local sale. The weight of the new but unbalanced model of accumulation continued to press on the unmodified productive structure.

1976 saw the first efforts by the Morales Bermudez administration to implement a 'new' economic policy in the form of a stabilization programme remarkably similar to those applied in 1958 and 1967 and one directed from the BCR rather than the INP.[17] This programme was started in May of that year, in anticipation of borrowing still further from the US banks, rather than to have recourse to the IMF which was felt to be likely to impose unacceptable conditions. The measures adopted to deflate demand – public investment cuts, devaluation under 'crawling peg' arrangements (the parity of the sol against the US dollar rose from 43 to 65 in July of that year), a wage freeze (albeit with a fixed increment in order to protect the poorer wage-earners) and the reduction of food subsidies – all served to throw the burden of the adjustment upon labour in terms of unemployment and lower real earnings. This was a decision deriving partly from political changes within the armed forces, which involved the abandonment of any attempt at populism, and partly from the need to reduce demand without cutting into profits and thus alienating foreign creditors. By this means some US $500 millions was raised net of debt repayment and the immediate crisis resolved. However, the difficulties experienced by the private banks in monitoring the agreement meant that when a second request was made for further finance in February 1977, they insisted upon the involvement of the IMF,[18] whose terms this time included the suspension of tax incentives, an emergency property tax and the elimination of current and capital transfers from the central government to the state enterprises (all measures which, we have argued, should have been undertaken five years earlier), a cut in public sector expenditure of the order of twenty per cent, further real wage decline and the suspension of job security laws, and the continuation of the crawling peg.

Apart from the continued decline in the living standards of labour implied by these measures, they would have required a severe reduction in military outlays as well as massive redundancies among police and schoolteachers to have any effect, and the tax measures would have cut into private profits, especially of domestic capitalists. In the event, the programme – although officially adopted in October 1977 – did not enjoy the support of the military, domestic capital or the bureaucracy itself, while organized labour initiated a series of general strikes. In consequence the agreement was not kept: although real wages and the parity of the sol continued to decline (passing through 120 at the end of 1977), job security was maintained and the budgetary deficit remained, for, although public investment fell sharply in real terms, current expenditure actually rose as a proportion of GDP while without the proposed tax reforms fiscal income weakened. Aggregate output fell by 1.2 per cent in 1977 and again by 1.8 per cent in the following year, but the best that could be done was to bring the trading account of the balance of payments into equilibrium even with this severe a deflation and a marked increase in exports from copper; domestic prices continued to accelerate and debt servicing alone consumed 44 per cent of export income in 1978. The Peruvian economy was now apparently 'stabilized' and new borrowing only required for refinancing the debt – agreement to do this was based not so much on the long overdue recovery of exports but the elections of July 1978 and the prospect of a return to democracy.

The major concern of policy in 1976–78 was still, as it had been in 1958–59 and 1967–68, the stability of the balance of payments, because the economy continued to be externally oriented. On the export side, long-run strategy was centred on the expansion of oil and mining output (although the former did not come up to initial expectations) but policy in the short run could take export sales as more or less exogenously determined: the one short-run effort to increase receipts led to deliberate overfishing in 1974, with deleterious results on the anchovy stocks. The efforts to increase manufactured exports through subsidies were remarkably ineffective.[19] Nonetheless, a successful policy of diversification of markets was implemented,[20] both in order to spread political dependence (e.g. the reduction of sales to the USA in favour of Comecon) and to save foreign currency, as in the bilateral exchanges of iron ore for wheat with Argentina. Deliberate and quite successful efforts were made to cut down expenditure on invisible account, particularly expatriation of profits and foreign travel, but this merely served to ameliorate the impact of the mounting burden of public debt servicing. The only room for manoeuvre, then, was imports. Again, the initial measures were successful in trimming the surplus, but, unless manufacturing technology was to be altered and the second stage of import-substitution (i.e. for inputs) achieved, little could be done – further restrictions would just stop the factories. Thus, in a sense, it was the lack of a long-run policy to alter the structure of industry – in terms both of production techniques and of ownership – that made imports such a vulnerable factor in the short term. Further, the decision to continue with export-led growth, albeit with higher value-added and greater backward linkages, while perhaps unavoidable did engender both a sense of false security as the purchasing power of exports improved in the 1968–73 period and political weakness as it deteriorated in 1974–76. If the measures of direct exchange allocation imposed in 1975 had been obtained and the temporary decline in export earnings over-to reduce import-intensity in industry and public works could have been obtained and the temporary decline in export earnings, overcome. The massive devaluations of 1976–78 had little impact on export volume (and thus dollar earnings) as output was already at a maximum, while the effect on imports was inevitably less than in 1967 because there were no consumption goods to cut back on: capital goods imports for the public sector were quoted in dollars already, and industrial input costs could be passed on in output prices. The structure of the economy had become more rigid: exports could no longer respond to high world prices and better profit margins (minerals, fish and sugar being resource-constrained) and imports were no longer so price-sensitive either. But in combination with controlled money wages, the domestic inflation engendered by devaluation resulted in a sharp cut in consumption.

The difficulties of securing an adequate urban food supply were central to the policy problem, even though the immediate effects of disequilibrium were not so dramatic. The political importance of a cheap and abundant food supply to Lima was probably more important than its economic significance through wage costs, and was related to the retention of middle-class support for the government as well as to the threat of popular mobilization. The land reform did not, in fact, have much effect as most food supplies came from the smaller 'exempt' farmers, and apart from the premature slaughter of cattle, output from cooperatives was not much disrupted either. Nonetheless, the failure to dedicate funds to improvements in food agriculture and the continued deterioration in the internal terms of trade until about 1972 did little to help supply, which would have had to grow at nearly five per cent a year between 1968 and 1975 to meet demand at constant prices, as opposed to its historical growth rate of less than three. The scope for conversion of irrigated coastal land to foodcrops was limited by the priority claim of continued sugar and cotton production, so that large-scale imports were the only resort if the real wage was to be maintained.[21] Unfortunately, world food prices rose in the international commodity boom too, and soon the Peruvian government was involved in a massive subsidy operation, primarily to keep Lima food prices down. None of this helped the farmers as such, and only when administered food prices were raised sharply in 1975 and subsidies on food imports eliminated in 1976 (the improvement in agricultural prices in 1972 had been due to a bad harvest) did the internal terms of trade move substantially towards food agriculture. Meanwhile, the emphasis of supply policy lay in obtaining marketed output – first through EPSA and then through the Ministerio de Alimentación – rather than increasing production. Agricultural credit and rural infrastructure programmes had been played down in the shift of state investment from public works to public enterprise. A policy, then, of continuing to 'squeeze' agriculture, spending as little as possible on it and importing marginal food requirements was successful in minimizing disturbance during the 'reform period' of 1969–73, but resulted in an unstable situation later on, putting excessive pressure on the budget, the balance of payments and the political credibility of the regime. The underlying policy error was to suppose that a high rate of national income growth could be sustained without a concomitant expansion in food supply, unless it were thought that the production of exports to pay for the imports was a more efficient use of resources at the margin than this investment in food agriculture. There is no evidence of such a calculation having been made, and even if this were to hold in an 'efficiency' sense, the social cost in terms of rural poverty and internal migration was meanwhile steadily increasing. The reduction in food imports experienced in 1977 and 1978, based as it was on falling real wages, was neither a permanent nor a desirable solution.

The control of aggregate demand and inflation was closely linked to the two problems we have just discussed, and also to those of the fiscal balance and industrial supply. A restrictive policy in the 1969–73 period was in concordance with the limited credit requirements of the state sector and the surplus on government current account, while steady expansion could be accommodated within excess industrial capacity and the balance of payments surplus. However, in the 1974–76 period the combination of events made such restriction impossible. As the growing requirement for domestic finance by state enterprise was not being covered by tax or price increases, it was necessarily met by borrowing. Initially, surplus bank funds could be 'mopped up' in this way, but once these had been absorbed increasing bond sales to commercial banks inflated domestic credit; the practice of state bank lending to state enterprises was equivalent to little more than a book-keeping disguise for uncontrolled monetary emission, despite the fact that the Central Bank was still restraining the 'money supply' as formally defined.

The net effect was highly inflationary given the limits on industrial and agricultural supply, and placed further pressure on the balance of payments at a time when the fall in export income and increased investment demand had already placed it in a weak position. This interaction of ineffective supply policy with budget deficits 'overheated' the economy but it was not the only cause of inflation. Rising import prices must have contributed substantially to observed price increases between 1971 and 1975[22] although the evidence for wages would seem to indicate that if anything they lagged prices.[23] To the extent that the reduction of budgetary deficits in 1976 was achieved by cutting subsidies rather than by higher taxes, it could hardly but exacerbate inflation in 1977. Similarly, although the devaluation of that year did restore exporters' profit margins – thus strengthening the state budget through public enterprise profits as well as raising the profitability of Southern Peru Copper at Cuajone – it could only add further to rising industrial prices, while incidentally cancelling out much of the farmers' gain in the internal terms of trade. Substantial tax increases on both profits and salaries could presumably have resolved both the fiscal and demand problems without either inflationary effects or the deterioration in income distribution that undoubtedly resulted from the measures adopted, but as we have seen, this option was not chosen.

There would seem to be two ways of looking at this policy record between 1968 and 1978 as a whole, their respective relevance depending upon the degree of continuity in economic management on the one hand and the degree of independence attributable to the state, on the other. The first approach, which might perhaps be described as a 'conservative' one[24] would hold that the economic structure of Peru was such that neither rapid growth which raised demand beyond the limits of food supply and export income, nor a high rate of public investment which required financing beyond the limits of fiscal revenues and a reasonable debt burden,[25] were feasible. Further, that to attempt such growth was a policy error, compounded by excessive ownership reforms and public sector expansion which frightened off both domestic entrepreneurs and the foreign investment necessary to buy new technology and funds to cover the balance of payments deficit. Moderate growth and moderate reforms were all that should have been aspired to, therefore. The second approach, which could possibly be called a more 'radical' one[26] would call the economic structure itself into question, and hold that a restructuring of industry (or at least import control at an earlier date) would have contained the import bill, massive support to peasant agriculture (in the form of financing inputs and marketing facilities, even if prices were not raised) would have expanded food supply, and a substantial tax reform would have resolved much of the budget, credit and inflationary problems. A high rate of public investment would then have been feasible particularly if it had been based on projects with a high employment and low import content. These two critiques see, then, the relative failure of policy as being due to, respectively, too much and too little state intervention. This is not just a question of the prejudices of the observer, but rather a judgement about the scope open to state action. It seems reasonable to suggest that as far as the control of the domestic economy was concerned, particularly the stimulation of food output and tax policy, much more could have been done with the degree of state power obtaining between 1968 and 1975 – and thus the failure to do so can be judged a 'policy error'. In contrast, in the control of foreign trade, and thus the balance of payments equilibrium, less could have been done. Although it is true that resolution of the 'internal' policy problem would (by reducing food imports and foreign borrowing) have reduced the severity of the 'external' problem, the latter would still have presented a formidable obstacle to further change. Nonetheless, the policy of 'holding the fort' which seemed to work so well in maintaining stability in the 1969–75 period was really putting off and making worse the economic problems which might, in that politically 'easy' period, have been resolved before it became too late.

Negotiating with foreign capital

The extent of foreign ownership in the Peruvian economy had become such a heated political issue by 1968 and because the previous administration had demonstrably failed to deal with the matter satisfactorily, the reduction of this control was bound to become a central policy issue for the military regime after 1968; it was expressed as such in their original programme.[27] The perceived needs for foreign finance and technology in order to recapitalize export production and accelerate industrialization meant that this reduction would have to be negotiated within close constraints and that a complete elimination of foreign involvement in the Peruvian economy was clearly impossible. The progress of negotiations between 1968 and 1976 depended directly upon the balance between these two objectives, but was also greatly influenced by external factors such as the balance of payments and the changing geopolitical structure in South America. Although the government maintained a pragmatically flexible attitude to negotiation, a steady underlying policy line is detectable,[28] but this was eventually blocked by foreign capital the aim of which was to retain control over as much of the productive apparatus of Peru as possible, if not by asset ownership then through marketing channels, finance and technology. In essence, therefore, the conflict was not over whether Peru was to remain an integral part of the world capitalist economy or not, but rather over the terms on which it was to do so.

Table 8.1. *Inflow of long-term foreign finance*

	(US$ millions, annual averages)			
	1956–62	1963–68	1969–73	1974–77
Private: [a] Direct investment	27	3	−7	171
Loans: Utilized	32	35	41	31
Amortized	−11	−23	−41	
	48	15	−7	202
Public: Loans: Utilized	26	138	310	988
Amortized	−23	−56	−176	−328
Other [b]	0	8	0	−3
Total inflow	3 / 51	90 / 105	136 / 128	657 / 859

Source: Appendix, Table A.3.

Notes: [a] Note that the private inflow does not include the outflows under 'short capital' and 'errors and omissions' discussed in Chapters 4 and 6.
[b] Includes changes in the value of official overseas assets and nationalization compensation. The location of the 'Greene' agreement (see page 240) in this is not clear; if the $76 millions involved was paid during 1974–77, then an extra −19 should be entered here, but even this is relatively small.

The key elements of the bargaining process during these years were three; the expropriation by the state of major foreign enterprises and their eventual compensation; the negotiation of new joint ventures in cooperation with the state in mining, oil and industry; and the arrangement of the external financing of the public sector enterprises for their investment programmes. *A priori*, the Peruvian position in relation to foreign capital was strongest in relation to the first element, because the enterprises represented physical assets which could be expropriated unilaterally by decree, although in the case of export activities the marketing channels were not so vulnerable. The second element would naturally involve a balance of bargaining power: the need to acquire new supplies of copper and oil for the US economy on the one hand, against the need to rapidly open up new sources of foreign exchange for the Peruvian economy on the other. The position of foreign capital (coordinated through the multilateral agencies, the US government and the international banking consortia) was clearly to be most powerful in relation to the third element, not only because of the weaknesses in the Peruvian state finance but also because of the discretionary[29] powers of these institutions. Broadly, it was this last that curtailed the scope for Peruvian action on the first and obtained better terms for foreign enterprise in the second, thus demonstrating the role of finance capital in sustaining the profitability of international firms even though the direct return (i.e. the real ratio of interest on foreign debt) may not be particularly high.[30]

The 'bargaining calendar'[31] between 1968 and 1978 can be divided into four distinct stages: the first, 1968–71, was one of considerable expropriation and a 'freeze' on external finance; the second, between 1972 and 1974 involved renewed contact, mineral ventures and negotiation of compensation; the third saw a brief period of renewed confrontation and expropriation in 1975, to be followed by virtual capitulation by Peru in 1976; finally the fourth (1977–78) involved repeated attempts to raise balance of payments loans against promises to stabilize the economy by reducing the size of the public sector. Nonetheless, as we shall see, the trend was not as one-sided as this division might seem to imply; each period saw gains as well as losses to Peru. Practically the first action of the *Gobierno Revolucionario de la Fuerza Armada*, in October 1968, had been to expropriate the IPC installations, and – on the grounds that the original contract for the exploration of the northern oilfield was illegal – to refuse to pay compensation. This was followed by the announcement of the projected agrarian reform, and, although it only affected one major foreign company (Grace) substantially, the exiguous terms of compensation served to convince foreign investors that they were unwelcome in Peru. Despite assurances that investment in non-strategic branches such as tourism and light manufactures would be safe (so long as investors kept to the new Andean Pact rules on profits), the only major new foreign investment in this first stage was the Bayer acrylic fibre plant (planned before 1968 to export to Chile and Bolivia) and even here the state had to take a minority shareholding and subsequently deny equity participation to the *communidad industrial* on the grounds that the firm was '*estratégica para el desarrollo nacional*'. The ITT telephone and telecommunications installations were also taken over in 1969, payment being in blocked soles that were eventually used to build the

Lima Sheraton hotel. Negotiations were opened with Southern Peru Copper in order to develop the Cuajone copper deposits, which became the only major unexplored deposit to remain in private hands after the repossession of all other such concessions to the state in 1970. Peru insisted on control over refining, marketing and foreign exchange receipts and the eventual reversion of the mine to Mineroperu; in response, it was claimed by SPC that difficulties in raising finance on international markets were preventing a start on development of the mine. In the event, the Peruvians were forced to negotiate on the basis of the 1950 Mining Law, with its generous provisions for tax reductions and export of profits, although they did manage to secure exclusive refining and marketing rights on the copper. Also in 1970, the thirteen car assembly firms in Lima were reduced to three and the tenders requested for an exclusive joint venture with the state (eventually taken up by Toyota in 1973) and the Banco Continental was taken over by the government, removing it from the control of the Chase Manhattan group. In 1971, the railway interests of the Peruvian Corporation were taken over and any compensation was cancelled against outstanding tax payments. In consequence, the flow of bilateral and multilateral finance was cut back sharply but this did not have much impact because of the relatively low level of public investment and the strong position on current account of the balance of payments.

In contrast, the subsequent three years were marked by a more common interest between the two sides – the opening up of oil and copper deposits. Foreign interest increased, primarily because of the raising of oil prices and the nationalization of Chilean copper; by now it was also clear that the task would be too much for the new state enterprises (Petroperu and Mineroperu) in the short time-scale available if flagging exports were to be strengthened by copper and the growing oil deficit closed. Negotiations with Petroperu for contracts to explore the Amazon fields were led by Occidental, which had signed the first agreement in late 1971, and some eighteen contracts were eventually agreed with various foreign companies under the 'Peruvian Model' which allowed them to operate on Petroperu's behalf. The terms, which were calculated on the basis of 1971 world oil prices were initially quite favourable to Peru – in that the companies bore all exploring costs and retained only half the crude found – but became less so as world prices rose and the cost of the trans-Andean pipelines (to be repaid in crude to the Japanese financiers) became apparent. Although the subsequent discovery, by 1974, that the resources were less than anticipated meant less profit outflow to foreign enterprise, this was far outweighed by the loss in anticipated income from exports upon which the public debt strategy had been based. Meanwhile, the negotiations for the finance needed to develop Cuajone were concluded by mid-1973, the banking consortia having insisted on two safeguards – that Mineroperu should charge a fixed commission on the refining and sales of copper, and the international diversification of the loan to 'insure' against future nationalization.[32] Fishing itself was nationalized during this period as well, involving several foreign firms, although their near-bankrupt status should not have required the compensation that was eventually gained.

Efforts to encourage foreign investment in sectors other than mining were totally unsuccessful; in fact private capital (other than in oil and copper) flowed out as repatriation of depreciation funds was stepped up, joining the drain of domestic capital. In contrast, the international liquidity surplus generated by the US trade deficit meant that international bank finance had now become much easier to obtain – even for nationalist creditors such as Peru. Whereas under the chairmanship of the IBRD the creditors' Consultative Group meeting in early 1972 agreed to extend up to $780 millions of credit to import capital equipment during 1972–74, this was raised to $1900 millions in mid-1973 to cover the 1973–76 period when the major disbursements in state projects were planned.

The easing of tension in this period was ended by the breakdown of negotiations and the nationalization of Grace's non-agricultural interests and the long-promised acquisition of Cerro de Pasco, both of which were expropriated in early 1974. The US government was forced to send a special negotiator (Greene) in order to formulate a 'package deal' that would consolidate some compensation for these two firms and the fishing companies – the final agreement costing about $150 millions;[33] although this sum exceeded the original Peruvian position, it was balanced by substantial USAID funds and the final 'go-ahead' on Cuajone. The Peruvian government now felt free to proceed to absorb Gulf Oil into Petroperu and cut short the desultory negotiations with Marcona by converting it unilaterally into Hierroperu in mid-1975. No compensation was offered, on the grounds that the company had been undervaluing its exports illegally, but Marcona was able to organize an international embargo on Peruvian ore exports and force both higher compensation and continued use of its fleet. The flow of external finance continued, nonetheless, both because of the change in Presidency and because agreements to consolidate some $3200 million of suppliers' credit for the 1975–78 Development Plan had already been signed by the Consultative Group earlier that year.

In early 1976, however, the deteriorating balance of payments position and the realization that further nationalization or worker participation could affect vital manufacturing investment gave foreign capital both the opportunity and motive for determined action.[34] This time, pressure was exercised by the US not through the IBRD (as in 1968–71, when investment credits were needed) but through the IMF. The Fund, possessing not only its own funds for balance of payments support (i.e. to cover imports of current as well as capital goods) but also the power to assure the international bankers that Peru was 'creditworthy', attempted to impose conditions not only upon the treatment of foreign capital (insisting on unrestricted profit remittance, foreign participation in future mineral ventures and the effective reversion of fishmeal and mineral marketing to foreign interests) but also upon domestic policy – with the consequences we have already noted. These latter conditions eventually drove the Peruvian government into the arms of the US private banks, which between them already held over a half of Peru's official overseas debt. These were prepared to grant further credit at a higher cost in terms of debt service than the IMF but less in terms of control over domestic policy, although the conditions demanded for foreign investors were much the same. Credit for $240 millions was obtained from a group led by Wells Fargo, and another $100 millions from a European consortium, but at international market rates and on short terms, renewable only if Peruvian economic policy was considered 'satisfactory'.[35] This comparative leniency apparently had more to do with concern about the consequences for the asset structure and thus the profitability or even the stability of a number of US 'second line' banks already holding too much Peruvian paper if Peru were to default[36] than with disbelief in the sup-

posed efficacy of the IMF programme as such. However, the Peruvian balance of payments showed few signs of improving in 1977,
the debt service now exceeded a third of exports and in US banking
circles circumstances were changing too: the private banks became
disenchanted with their own somewhat inept attempts to monitor
the Peruvian economy and the Washington authorities had gained
greater control over the foreign activities of US financial in-
termediaries. In consequence, Peru was forced back into the em-
brace of the IMF, and the stabilization programme that had been
put off for two years had to be adopted as a condition for further
short-term support.

What was surprising, perhaps, was not that Peru was eventually
forced into this position – which was mainly the consequence of the
failure to restructure the economy at an earlier stage – but that the
government held out for so long against the prescriptions of the
IMF and US bankers and that it could continue to resist the pressure
to open the economy and abandon its reforms at all. Internally, this
is some evidence of the continuing influence of progressive forces on
the military; externally the fear of the possibility of a third worldwide chain of defaults if Peru were, in desperation, to renege on its
debt was undoubtedly significant; but in the end it was the difficulty
of implementing any stabilization policy with such an intractable
economic and political structure, combined with an almost
desperate hope that a democratic government could somehow
resolve both these problems (just how was never spelled out) that
assured continued foreign support.

There is a certain irony about negotiations between the *Gobierno
Revolucionario* and foreign capital between 1968 and 1978, because
each side was effectively able to block the designs of the other but
unable to impose its own will. The foreign investors were quite
capable of delaying the copper project until their terms had been
met and of preventing further reformist moves – such as the
nationalization of their manufacturing assets – by withholding
funds, but they were unable to reverse the major reforms (except to
dilute the *comunidad industrial*) or to enforce an orthodox stabilization policy. Similarly, the military regime could sustain its reforms,
nationalize Marcona as late as 1975, and resist massive public sector
dismissals in 1976–78, but could not implement the control over

manufacturing required to make the state capitalist model coherent or get its export projects on stream in time to make its 'calculated risk' pay off. What this experience does underline, however, is that beyond the obvious limitations upon a reformist administration

Table 8.2. *Official external debt of Peru 1956–76*

	1956	1960	1963	1968	1972	1976	1978
			(US $ millions)				
Outstanding disbursed debt (end-year):							
Multilateral agencies	21	33	61	134	156	171	..
Official bilateral[a]	19	27	147	148	319	923	..
Suppliers[b]	42	28	76	246	278	352	..
Private banks	9	21	19	126 ⎫	356	2195	..
Other private	63	53	34	90 ⎭			
	154	162	237	744	1109	3641	4617
Disbursements	27	17	83	215	303	846	1016
Amortization	18	41	32	103	159	299	642
Capital inflow	9	−24	51	112	144	547	374
Interest payments	5	8	9	43	54	234	280
Net transfer	4	−32	42	69	90	313	94
Debt service[c]	23	50	41	146	213	533	922
Service ratio[d]	7%	11%	7%	17%	23%	39%	44%

Sources: ONEC, *Anuario 1969* for 1956–63; IBRD, *Debt Tables* (various years) for 1968–72, BCR for 1976–78.

Notes: [a] mostly US before 1968, after that from Japan (pipeline) and Germany.

[b] mostly US before 1968, increase after that from Italy (irrigation).

[c] interest and amortization.

[d] ratio of debt service to exports f.o.b.

attempting to establish a nationalist project financed abroad, the capacity of such a regime to resist external pressures is considerable when the conservative forces within the society or the government itself are relatively weak, a weakness exposed in the Peruvian case by the 1978 election results. In other words, much of the capacity of foreign capital to impose its own project on a dependent economy, as distinct from its capacity to block initiatives, derives from an alliance with domestic groups.

Economic planning

Economic planning as an explicit form of state activity was established in Peru in the early 1960s.[37] Although the first Plan was drawn up in 1961, this was undertaken by the Central Bank and only under the military junta of 1962–63 was a planning office established; its first product, the second Plan (1967–70) was never implemented, so that in effect planning as a serious activity in Peru can be said to date from 1968. After that date, the scope and power of the central planning system increased dramatically and two national development plans (1971–75 and 1975–78) were implemented in our period, forming an integral part of the new model of accumulation as a whole, particularly in relation to state capital formation as this expanded and shifted from infrastructure towards directly productive activities.

The first Plan[38] was drawn up by the Central Bank in 1961 to cover the 1962–71 period, but it consisted in little more than a set of macroeconomic forecasts – without either integration to an aggregate model or relation to specific sectoral structures – and a list of public investment projects. There was no discussion of social problems, nor any provisions for plan implementation, nor any indication of how the Plan was to be financed – although further incentives for private capital were recommended and a large inflow of foreign investment anticipated. As Roel points out:

> The Plan ... had only one objective – so that within the Alliance for Progress, Peru could be considered as one of the countries 'that had plans' [*que contaban con planes*] and thus could solicit the financial services of the Alliance. The country was hardly aware of the Plan, but that was not a matter for concern, for nobody in the Government seriously meant to implement anything resembling integrated planning.[39]

The change of government in 1962 meant that in any case economic strategy objectives would be modified to include both greater state intervention and some ownership reform. In that year, the Instituto Nacional de Planificación was established as a central planning[40] office within the Presidency; although it lacked executive power (above all over the budget and macroeconomic policy) it did start to formulate a coherent critique of the economy and recommended some structural reforms, which were included within the 1967–70 Plan[41] in 1966.

This second Plan was a considerable improvement over the first, above all in diagnosis and internal consistency; duality, underemployment, concentration of ownership, excessive dominance of foreign enterprise and spatial imbalance were all identified as obstacles to Peruvian economic development. The projections themselves were based not on a model reflecting this diagnosis, however, but on much more conventional 'capital–output ratio' and 'two gap' methods for sectoral goals and savings targets. The Plan reflected the growing analytical competence of the INP, which was helping to form a critical consciousness among progressive members of the civilian and military administration, but there was a clear lack of adequate means to implement the Plan. Economic policy variables were not specified, and the public investment programme was no more than a collection of projects proposed by the various ministries, unconnected to the aggregate projections. The government, facing a severe economic disequilibrium in 1967, was in no position to implement the Plan, which was in any event superseded by the military intervention in 1968. This poor record of planning is not surprising, because the economic role of the state at the time was to provide support for private investment – not to control it – while the two major reasons for producing plan documents at all were to meet the administrative requirements of the international aid agencies and to maintain the reformist image of the government.

One of the first acts[42] of the new administration was to extend the scope and power of the national planning system, establishing sectoral offices of the INP in order to assess investment projects at a ministerial level and integrate the capital budget with the Plan. The third Plan,[43] to cover the period 1971–75, was drawn up in 1970, and was mainly concerned with the programme of ownership reforms that we have already discussed in Chapter 5, the economic content being mainly a 'holding operation' while these were carried out; meanwhile the public sector was to prepare the massive projects in exports and heavy industry to come into operation in the second half of the decade. Relatively ambitious targets were set[44] for most sectors, but the unexpectedly low output growth in the primary sector (which led to the plan as a whole not being fulfilled) was virtually impossible to predict. Agriculture and fishing depended upon ecological conditions and world prices; the optimistic forecasts for mining were based on the expectation of oil (an expectation shared by foreign oil companies) and the reasonable hope that Cuajone would come 'on stream' in 1975. Even though the low rate of private investment was foreseen, the substantial outflow of foreign capital was not; indeed there was little consideration of the problem of resource acquisition in the Plan (no savings programme was included) and the subsequent slide into foreign borrowing went unchecked by the planners. Nonetheless, the 1971–75 Plan was successful in providing a detailed framework within which sectorial plans were coordinated and into which investment projects were fitted, an indispensable asset with the state sector expanding so fast.

The 1975–78 Plan[45] was drawn up in 1974 and was based on the completion of the major ownership reforms and the entry into production of the major export projects. It turned, therefore, to the establishment of heavy industry (particularly a capital goods branch) and the consolidation of the new pattern of ownership centring on worker participation. This latter was considered to be essential to the achievement of full development planning because it would allow the INP to redirect the pattern of output and accumulation in the whole corporate sector, not just in the state sector itself:

> In relation to the pluralist organization of the economy, four coexistent property sectors have been defined: the social property sector, which will have most importance and priority; the state sector; the reformed private sector [i.e. with the Industrial Community]; and the small-enterprise sector, made up of the small-scale artisan, commercial and service activity. Within this system a close link will be forged . . . between the social property and state sectors, so that these constitute efficient instruments of development planning.[46]

Although no overall strategy for the reduction of duality in the economy was specified, the planned reduction of salary differentials, positive incentives for employment in the regions, and the priority given to food programmes were aimed at this end. The output forecasts were probably still too optimistic, given the external crisis which the economy was entering, but they were based on firm export projections drawn from the new projects, and did foresee the need to restrict import growth to a minimum. Again, the unanticipated (although perhaps not unforeseeable) change in direction of economic strategy in 1976 meant that the plans for further ownership changes, the expansion of wage goods output in preference to all other branches except heavy industry, and their distribution at controlled or even subsidized prices, could hardly be fulfilled. The revised 1977–78 Plan was a far less ambitious document than its predecessors, limiting itself to 'stabilizing and reactivating the economy, emphasizing the gradual reorientation of the productive structure so as to adjust it to the satisfaction of the basic needs of the population and promote the development of the interior of the country and the internal accumulation of capital'.[47] Although it contained little more than the investment programme, this did include that for the private sector and an integrated plan for the allocation of foreign exchange.

It is, perhaps, invidious to compare these plans with the out-turn, but such an exercise is instructive; Table 8.3 indicates the main

Table 8.3. *Plan targets and results 1971–78*
(average annual growth rates at 1970 prices)

	1971–75		1975–78	
	Planned	Actual	Planned	Actual
Investment: Public	32.0	21.1	7.1	−12.7
Private	9.6	9.5	5.7	−1.8
Consumption: Public	6.2	7.4	4.5	3.0
Private	6.0	6.6	4.7	0.3
Gross domestic product	7.5	5.5	6.5	0.8
Agriculture	4.2	1.9	3.0	1.2
Fishing	4.8	−17.0	10.0	4.8
Mining	5.7	−1.2	23.6	10.6
Manufacturing	12.4	8.0	7.0	−0.5
Other sectors	6.6	6.8	5.7	−1.1

Source: INP (1971, 1975a) BCR *Cuentas Nacionales,* directly from BCR and *Informe Económico Trimestral* (September 1978).

aggregate variables. First, as we have noted before and will examine in more detail in Table 8.4, the rate of public investment growth in real terms was overestimated in the Plans, in the first case because of project delays and difficulties in obtaining finance, and in the

second because of the 1976–78 stabilization policy. Private investment, in contrast, was accurately forecast as growing much less
rapidly. Second, the growth of public consumption exceeded the
forecast in both cases, leading to the weakness in state savings we
have discussed in the previous chapter. Again, private consumption
was quite accurately projected in the 1971–75 Plan, but because the
economy grew a good deal less quickly than had been planned, the
external gap widened much more than anticipated; in the 1975–78
Plan the private consumption out-turn was much lower than
planned, due to the wage restrictions of 1977–78. The difficulty was,
of course, that supply did not reach the Plan targets: agricultural
growth aims were far too optimistic (probably counting on land
reform increasing output in the medium term); fishing did not
recover from overexploitation and indeed the problem was
probably exacerbated by continued overfishing in the Plan period;
mining suffered from crippling strikes in 1975; there were delays in
starting on the Cuajone project and the oil reserves were not nearly
as great as had been hoped; and manufacturing was held back by
the serious decline in private investment, resulting from lack of confidence in the government.

It would seem, then, that the 'calculated risk' taken by the Peruvian planners in 1970 to borrow abroad on the expectation of a substantial rise in exports by the second half of the decade was an un-
wise one. But it did not seem so at the time: the massive outflow of
private capital (which 'used up' a half of all official borrowing in
1970–78, as we have seen) was not foreseen by anyone; the copper
deposits were well known and both sides intended to have them in
production by 1975 at the latest; the foreign oil corporations shared
the expectation that there was oil in the Amazon basin; and finally it
should be remembered that in the early 1970s observers in both the
first and third worlds believed that the shift in the terms of trade
towards the latter (particularly for raw materials such as copper) was
a permanent one. As late as October 1974 (when the 1975–78 Plan
had just been drawn up), the IBRD was of the opinion that 'the level
of non-project borrowing appears justified as a means for bridging
Peru's resource gap until mineral and possibly petroleum exports
expand substantially starting in 1977–78', and although the World
Bank did express a preoccupation that 'external borrowing is being

increasingly used as a substitute for a greater effort at domestic resource mobilization to finance the fiscal deficit' tax reform had been planned, too, only it was opposed by the IMF as damaging to business confidence.[48] By the time it became clear that the calculated risk had not paid off, a drastic reduction in domestic demand was the only policy alternative open – that it should have taken the form

Table 8.4. *Planned and achieved investment rates 1971–78*

	(billion soles at 1970 prices)							
	1971	1972	1973	1974	1975	1976	1977	1978
1971–75 Plan:								
Public	15.9	21.6	28.5	33.8	39.8			
Private	17.8	18.4	20.2	23.4	28.0			
	33.7	39.0	48.7	57.2	67.8			
1975–78 Plan:								
Public					27.1	29.0	31.1	33.3
Private					24.4	26.9	27.3	28.8
					51.5	55.8	58.4	62.1
Actual: Public	12.6	13.7	16.1	25.3	28.4	26.7	21.3	15.6
Private	20.3	21.5	20.9	23.1	28.9	27.2	22.2	21.2
	32.9	35.2	37.0	48.4	57.3	53.9	43.5	36.8

	1960–67[a]	1971–75[b]	1971–75[a]	1975–78[b]	1975–77[a]
Composition of public GFCF:					
Agriculture	8	8	11	11	16
Mining	—	16	19	34	42
Industry	14	25	17	26	14
Transport	30	16	13	12	12
Other	48	35	40	17	16
	100	100	100	100	100

Source: INP (1971, 1975a), BCR *Cuentas Nacionales* (various years), BCR *Memoria 1976*, INP–OIP.
Notes: [a] actual; [b] planned.

of cuts in wages and public investment rather than in profits and private investment was perhaps inevitable in view of the strong position of Peru's external creditors. Thus the most crucial shortcoming turned out to be the delay in getting the copper projects on stream, delays which can be seen as a reflection of the monopoly power of foreign capital or as the consequence of a naive and excessively nationalistic position adopted by the Velasco government; but

however the delay is viewed, had the increment in copper output occurred in 1975 as planned instead of in 1977 the results would certainly have been very different, and might even have permitted a
consolidation of the new Peruvian model. Thorp is of the opinion
that 'compared to this question, the undoubted inefficiencies and
misallocations which occurred appear relatively insignificant – and
also surely the necessary accompaniment of such an extraordinarily
rapid development of the role of the state following on such
underdevelopment'.[49]

However, the main value of the national planning system[50] after
1968 was not as a forecasting mechanism, but rather as a means of
coordinating economic policy and the programming of public investment, acting as the nerve-centre of the new model of accumulation. The INP was granted the status of a ministry, and sectoral
planning offices (*Oficina Sectorial de Planificación*) in each ministry
reported directly to it. At the aggregate level, there were three types
of plan to be drawn up. First, there were the 'development plans'
(*Plan de Desarrollo*) themselves – that is, the 1971–75 and 1975–78
Plans. For these, special commissions were formed in the previous
year to establish sectoral objectives and consider intersectoral issues
such as technology and population, working on the basis of draft
sectoral plans supplied by the OSPs and the draft economic
forecasts produced by the INP. There was no private-sector participation in these plans, representatives of neither labour nor
capital were consulted and the overall guidelines were the strategic
objectives of the military government itself. Second, there were the
two-year plans (*Plan Bienal*) which contained more detailed forecasts
of production, investment, resource requirements and project
progress: it is on these that the public sector investment budgets
were based. These formed the core of the planning system, and
attempted to achieve greater adjustment to circumstances than the
development plans while retaining enough flexibility to alter
programme targets. These two-year plans (the first was for 1969–70)
were drawn up by the INP and the OSPs in a procedure more or less
internal to the state bureaucracy. Third, there were the annual
'economic plans' (*Plan Económico*), which in practice contained little
more than updated macroeconomic forecasts and revisions of the
project lists, but which were essential for the formulation of the

current budget of the central government and the monetary programme – both of which were the responsibility of the Ministry of Finance.

The macroplanning system was based on sectoral estimates of production and investment provided by the OSPs, both their reliability and the power to implement them depending upon the extent of state control over the sector in question. For instance as mining, petroleum and fishing were organized in large units under state control, conditions could be reasonably accurately foreseen in the short if not the long term, while those in food agriculture were very difficult to foresee at all. Integration of the forecasts was then carried out either at a sectoral level – such as the derivation of heavy industry output from the input needs of light manufacturing – or at an aggregate level, to derive the trade element of the balance of payments, for example. The investment estimates were derived from the budget forecasts for the public sector and the application of crude capital–output ratios to the branch production forecasts for the private sector, except where major projects were known in advance (e.g. mining) or in areas of indirect state control such as cooperatives. The resulting estimates of total output were then fed back to the OSPs in order that demand forecasts be brought into line and the data used in project appraisal. This methodology for the construction of a macroeconomic plan suffered from a number of technical shortcomings.[51] First, the output figures were essentially forecasts, that is they did not derive from a final 'bill of goods' framed within a derived consumption pattern at some future date, which could then have been worked back through the intermediate requirements of inputs, investment and imports. Second, there was no exploration of alternative objectives and different paths to them, nor of the effect on the out-turn of the plan of different investment and export levels. Third, there was no treatment of dualism in the programme, which treated each branch as homogeneous and therefore the basis of the future income distribution was not treated either.

The major difficulty with plan formulation was probably that it dealt with production almost to the exclusion of resource considerations. In consequence two crucial aspects were ignored: finance and employment. The problem of how accumulation was to be financed was never really faced by the planners, and it is partly because of this that so much reliance was placed on debt rather than a planned state acquisition of fiscal surpluses and foreign exchange: in other words, tax increases and import control should have been an integral part of the Plan from the start. Employment creation was supposed to be a central objective in both Plans, but this variable was treated as an output of the planning model rather than job targets being an input conditioning the allocation of investment; without specific projections of functional or personal income distribution the equity effect of the ownership reforms tended to be overestimated. Moreover, a major limitation on the implementation of the macro-plan was the continued lack of means of control over crucial elements of production such as final manufacturing and commerce, which remained largely in private hands; a complete production and consumption programme could not have been enforced, even had it been designed. Similarly, without an enforceable incomes policy, a savings plan could not have been implemented even had it existed.

In contrast, the organization of project appraisal in Peru was comparatively advanced by the standards of non-socialist developing countries, and was central to the articulation of the Peruvian public sector. A project concept was conceived by a public agency or state enterprise, and then submitted in outline for approval to the OSP in the corresponding ministry. If approved, it was sent to the INP for inclusion in the list of 'pre-feasibility studies' used in forward planning, and a full feasibility study initiated. On completion, this study was checked by the OSP's own experts for technical feasibility and conformity to sectoral planning objectives,[52] and if accepted was then passed on to the INP, which had meanwhile already evaluated the pre-feasibility report in a wider context. The INP was mainly concerned with the economic value of the project, using techniques of cost–benefit analysis[53] to go beyond the market return on public investment and taking into consideration such factors as regional balance, employment creation and technological requirements. Projects were then rejected, sent back to the OSP for reformulation or granted provisional approval – those passing this hurdle being forwarded to the Ministry of Finance for inclusion in the biennial budget and, if foreign funds were involved, COFIDE for the negotiation of the most advantageous financial terms. Execution and operation of the project was monitored in terms both of capital expenditure and of physical progress by the INP, using a computerized record system and information both from the executing agency and its own regional offices. In administrative terms this system operated with considerable efficiency, partly because of the centralization of executive power in a single institution which had a special division for this purpose, but also because the number of projects of any significance was quite small.[54]

In terms of economic efficiency – that is, in relation to the achievement of the stated objectives of Peruvian economic development – the microplanning system had considerable weaknesses as well as strengths. Its main strength lay in comparatively rapid administration combined with an almost military concentration on the 'output' side of investment projects, and this latter aspect was also the major difficulty. It meant that (as was also the case in macroplanning) the 'resource' side of the accumulation process was not given due attention: finance and employment were both closely related to the choice of technology used in public projects. The system of allocating finance almost automatically meant that, once economic feasibility had been established, capital account deficits – and more seriously, external public debt – were allowed to build up almost unperceived. In order to correct this, a formal system of capital rationing[55] (to allow permissible debt levels for the future to be programmed and then allocated to the most desirable projects) was badly needed. The direct programming of the foreign exchange allocation to projects[56] was introduced in 1975, but more as an emergency measure to save foreign exchange than as part of a rational planning mechanism. The introduction of such a system in 1971 would have been invaluable. The underlying problem was that the technological specification of the projects was such that imports (averaging roughly half the investment cost) seemed unavoidable, leading to the 'need' for foreign finance and a reduction in linkage to domestic industry. Moreover, the capital-intensive nature of such projects was reinforced by the application of engineering criteria alone at the initial design stage, reducing their employment-generating potential at both the construction and operational stages. To overcome this it would have been desirable for the central planners to intervene at the 'pre-feasibility' stage to ensure that wider criteria were introduced from the outset because although a project could be (and often was) rejected by the INP on its arrival there, later modification would have been extremely costly and by that point it would usually have accumulated a considerable 'pressure group' drawn both from within the bureaucracy and from the potential beneficiaries.[57]

Although the regional offices of the INP were very active and prepared extensive '*diagnosticos*' of the local situation, no specific regional plans were produced. The role of planning at a regional level was mainly confined to the administrative coordination of public investment projects and activities such as land reform and agricultural marketing. The large projects in mining or energy were generally administered from Lima on the basis of national criteria and thus overrode local considerations despite their enormous regional impact.

Planning was central to the Peruvian state-capitalist model of accumulation, and betrayed its contradictions. We have already noted the serious weakness in state finance which largely arose from the insufficient control of both domestic funds and foreign exchange. It would be too simple to suggest that this was due to inefficient planning – the weakness was derived from the inconsistency in the Peruvian form of state capitalism, where investment was socialized but not profits. The same inconsistency also prevented the direct determination by the state of final consumption and trade patterns. Finally, the relative neglect of 'social' objectives such as employment or regional balance (and thus by implication income distribution) arose as much from the continued concentration of the model of accumulation on the corporate sector as from errors in the Plans as such. Nonetheless, in view of the influence of civilian planners upon the thinking of the military in other fields,[58] it would be reasonable to suppose that some of these contradictions could have been ameliorated if not resolved by more explicit provision in the development plans.

Table 8.4 shows planned public and private investment. The first feature is the successful shift in public investment away from transport and public buildings (the main component of 'other') towards agriculture, mining and industry as part of the effort to strengthen productive capacity. However, the shortfall in overall state investment due to serious delays in mining projects (such as Cerro Verde) and the establishment of a capital goods industry – both due to financing problems in the early 1970s as well as inefficiency – meant that the target was not reached and the pattern was distorted. Ironically, had the public sector fulfilled its plans without a tax reform the public sector financing requirement would have been far greater and the strain on the balance of payments from foreign borrowing and domestic credit expansion even greater. The second feature we have already noted: the absolute fall in real terms of public investment after 1975 under the stabilization programme, until in 1978 the out-turn was half what it had been planned to be in 1974.

Concluding remarks

When coming to some overall conclusion as to the conduct of economic policy and planning in Peru between 1956 and 1978, we must bear in mind two underlying structural phenomena: the process of import-substitution on the one hand and the declining rate of private investment on the other. The former led to a steadily increasing rigidity in the structure of production and the pattern of trade, because the shift from external to internal sources of supply meant that demand restraint or devaluation would not automatically reduce imports and right the balance of payments; the latter meant that there was a need to support the increasing burden of state investment with complementary macroeconomic measures. These combined to make the traditional stabilization policy an increasingly irrelevant response to the problems of the Peruvian economy, and to make the need for a comprehensive planning system the more apparent – assuming of course that state intervention was to be extended. Above all, if macroeconomic policy was to support an increased rate of accumulation it had to control consumption and increase savings: before 1968 this meant lower wage consumption and higher private investment; after that date lower profit consumption and higher public investment.

The Peruvian system of economic policy-making and planning did not develop in this way. On the contrary, despite the growing importance of central planning, this was confined to the public sector and traditional stabilization policy was still resorted to for the rest of the economy. This latter course was more the result of increasing indebtedness to foreign banks than of political conviction after 1975, an indebtedness that had arisen from the attempt to restore the rate of investment and industrialization without adequate access to the necessary resources, a shortcoming unresolved by either policy or planning. Thus, even though considerable progress had been made in the reduction of dependency on external capital in terms of ownership of fixed assets and control over exports, the reliance on external technology and finance still left Peru in an extremely vulnerable position. An undercurrent running beneath this effort to establish sustained industrialization was the neglect of agriculture, and above all of food production. The Belaunde administration did start to reassign resources towards the rural sector and implement appropriate pricing policies, but apparently the Velasco government believed that in some way the land reform would contribute to food supply as well as to distributive justice. Although it might well still do so in the long run, with the small peasant producers unaffected by reform, unsupported by government funds and only receiving price rises at the last moment, it was hardly likely to do so in the short or medium term.

It is even more difficult to make a general comparison of economic policy in Latin-America than it is to compare the structure of their economies, because the circumstances and objectives vary so much from one country to another. For instance, the existence of a vigorous agricultural sector in Argentina that produces both exports and wage goods means that the depression of internal demand not only restrains imports but also increases exports almost automatically;[59] political resistance may make such a stabilization policy difficult or bloody, but it is clearly a policy option that a small mineral exporter such as Peru does not have. Again, Mexico in the 1960s had a strong financial sector which meant that increased government spending to counterbalance a decline in private investment could be financed by the domestic banks without tax reform, inflationary pressure or excessive foreign borrowing; although it is true that the Mexican money markets could not really accommodate the vast increase in the budget deficit under Echeverria, the access of the Mexican authorities to private savings and the implicit control of capitalist consumption gained thereby was not available to a smaller economy with underdeveloped capital markets such as Peru.[60]

Economies on the periphery of the world market experience demand fluctuations transmitted from the centre, so that restraint of domestic demand is a common reaction to an exogenous deterioration in their trade position as much as a reaction to internal inflationary conditions. In this context, it would seem that 'orthodox' stabilization policies based on devaluation and real wage cuts have become steadily less effective as the process of industrialization in Latin America has integrated the import demand to the production structure. This is essentially because when consumer goods (or producer goods for which there are local substitutes in elastic supply) are imported, then at the margin imports will be highly elastic to fluctuations in domestic demand; in contrast, when only inputs without immediate substitutes are imported (i.e. the technical coefficients are fixed in the short run), as is the case when the later stages of import-substitution have been reached, to achieve a certain reduction in the import bill a *pro rata* fall in manufacturing output must be brought about – a very difficult task. This factor, compounded by the traditional short-run inelasticity of supply for natural resource exports, has made stabilization steadily more difficult in Latin America.[61] This has not, however, stopped the IMF from continuing to make such policies a condition for financial support, and, more importantly, for the 'good housekeeping certificate' which gives access to international private bank credit.[62]

Countries with restrictive import controls can, of course, maintain external stability, but at the cost of internal inflation. This is particularly true of countries with a tradition of strong wage pressure from a unionized labour force such as Chile and Argentina. Peru did not, as we have seen, really suffer from this particular form of instability until the 1970s, when imports came under direct restriction and wage demands became more difficult to restrain. This was the experience of Chile in the 1950s and 1960s.[63] The three post-war stabilization programmes – those of Ibañez (1956–58, usually known as the 'Klein–Saks' programme after the consultants advising the Chilean government at the time), Alessandri (1959–61)

and Frei (1965–69) appear to have been concerned more with the
reduction of internal inflation than with the restoration of balance
of payments equilibrium as such. This came about for two reasons,
both having interesting contrasts with Peru before 1968 but possible
parallels after that date: first, that state intervention in the economy,
particularly in the form of credit and import controls, had been
much more developed since the 1930s; second, that the pressure of
organized labour on wages and thus on both prices and demand was
much greater. Given a steady rate of devaluation, the external account could just about be kept under control and stabilization
policy could be used for price restraint. This was particularly true of
the Ibañez programme, where a combination of wage cuts (by abandoning automatic cost-of-living adjustments), credit restraint and
import liberalization reduced the inflation rate dramatically. Much
the same was tried again in the Alessandri programme, but the increased difficulty of restraining wages and the decline in copper
prices in 1961 meant that the result was a worsening external disequilibrium even though inflation rates were cut again. The improvement in copper prices in the middle of the decade allowed the
Frei administration to use imports again as a means of controlling
prices and also to allow real wages to rise significantly once more.
The failure of the government was not in macroeconomic policy but
in its political strength. Apart from the political implications of, and
reactions to, the attempted transition to socialism under Allende,
the problems of macroeconomic policy were not dissimilar.[64]
Although considerable structural change was anticipated in the
longer term, the economy was to be stabilized in the short run by
direct price controls and the redistribution of existing income rather
than just wage increases. However, the advent of workers' control
involved vast increases in wage demands and the subsidization of
items of popular consumption raised effective demand in the non-
corporate sector too, but apparently without any large reduction in
demand from the upper strata. The consequence, as in previous
periods of Chilean economic history, was a massive balance of
payments disequilibrium. This is not to suggest, of course, that inept
macroeconomic policy was the reason for the downfall of Allende. It
is merely to point out the parallel with Peru: that a major objective
of macroeconomic policy, particularly in a period of reform, must

be to ensure that consumption demand is held down to a level consistent with foreign exchange earnings on the one hand and the desired level of investment on the other. Whether that is feasible in political terms is another matter.

The record of attempts to establish central planning units in Latin America is not an inspiring one.[65] By the early 1960s most countries had established a planning office, generally within the presidency, but these served mainly to produce 'development plans' consisting of little more than macroeconomic forecasts, a list of projects requiring foreign finance and a public sector budget drawn up by the Ministry of Finance; indeed, the role of the INP under Belaunde was a typical case of this. In no other case[66] was a planning system with central control over state capital formation (let alone over private sector production) established, despite the apparent advantages of a more efficient use of public funds – particularly to private enterprise. The explanation of this paradox may well be that while more effective support would be desirable on the economic plane, the powers invested in the planners would not be attractive to the private sector in the political sphere. Furthermore, it can be argued that the Latinamerican political system itself depends considerably upon the personal patronage of the president and ministers (in the awarding of construction contracts and so on) and that efficient planning would remove this essential balancing mechanism.[67] These two points would seem to imply that, to the extent that a strong central planning system was established in Peru after 1968, it reflected the relative autonomy of the Peruvian state in terms of both its independence from different fractions of capital and its internal coherence.

9

Industrialization

Here we shall be examining industry separately because of its central importance to the concept of economic development in general and to the restructuring of capital in particular. However, we cannot analyse this sector in the depth it merits in the space of one chapter; rather we shall concern ourselves with the problems of structure, ownership, accumulation and policy that we have discussed in previous chapters. As all Peruvian exports require some form of processing, a certain degree of 'industrialization' has always been present in the economy, even if confined to mining and sugar enclaves. At the turn of the century,[1] temporary isolation from international markets did enable Peruvian capital to make a start on the more traditional manufacturing lines such as textiles and beer and even foundry products, but the return of adequate foreign exchange availability in the form of a primary export boom that carried the economy through the First World War reduced the pressing need for a local supply of manufactures, and occupied the energies of local and foreign capital. Even during the Great Depression, which forced countries such as Chile to provide a domestic supply of manufactures, Peru managed with a small manufacturing sector; it was only from 1940 onwards that any real start was made on import-substitution, but this did not really constitute an industrialization process as such until the subsequent decade. The 1950s saw the eventual expansion from food and textiles into heavy industry such as cement by local finance capital, but much of the dynamism in manufacturing growth was supplied by the multinationals in their wave of expansion across Latin America, so that even at this late point industrial capitalists did not emerge as an independent class, remaining as a subordinate fraction of the domestic bourgeoisie.

Between 1956 and 1976, manufacturing was finally established in Peru on a substantial scale and almost reached the point of providing a dynamic to replace the export sector as the main 'engine of growth' if size is taken as a measure of importance, because by 1968 manufacturing accounted for almost a quarter of national income and over a half of 'material production' (i.e. GDP other than services) in Peru. But the expansion of the sector had reproduced the features of dependent dualism present elsewhere in the Peruvian economy: relatively little employment, widespread foreign ownership, few links with other sectors and considerable import requirements. Indeed, the impact of this sector on the balance of payments and the extent of foreign involvement within it made manufacturing one of the more vulnerable points of the economy.

At the outset, we might ask a simple question: is it reasonable to classify Peru as an 'industrial' country? Sutcliffe[2] suggests a rough yet pragmatic classification which has the considerable merit, when applied on a world-wide basis, of sorting out most of those cases that would be intuitively so classified. His criterion is composed of three tests: that more than 25 per cent of gross domestic product be in 'industry' (including mining, construction and utilities as well as manufacturing); that more than 60 per cent of 'industry' be in 'manufacturing'; and that more than 10 per cent of the population be in the industrial workforce. This definition avoids the problem of defining industrialization in terms of the output share alone (where construction may have a disproportionate weight) as well as that of implicit association with the level of national income that a criterion based on manufacturing output per head would have. Using the 'Sutcliffe method', Peru scores as follows: the 'industrial' share of GDP was 32 per cent in 1955 and 39 per cent in 1975; the 'manufacturing' share of this was 56 per cent in 1955 and 67 per cent in 1975; and the industrial workforce rose from the equilvalent of 6 per cent of the population in 1955 to 7 per cent in 1975.[3] Therefore, by the first two tests we can classify Peru as 'industrialized', or at least as having become so during the period, although by the third it has not yet reached that status – which in a way illustrates the real problem. The *corporate sector* was clearly industrialized in the sense of using modern technology and capital-intensive plant, both in processing raw materials and in supplying consumers (although it lacked a capital goods branch), but this is very different from claiming that the Peruvian *economy* was industrialized.

The industrial structure

In the 1956–76 period the Peruvian industrial structure reflected the disarticulation and duality of the economy which we identified in Chapter 4. In limiting the subject matter of this chapter to 'factory manufacturing', we can illustrate this point neatly. Manufacturing 'proper' excludes industrial activities such as electric power generation and (more significantly in the Peruvian case) the processing of raw materials for export; the exclusion of these elements gives a sector which was to a great extent isolated from the rest of the production structure[4] as either supplier of inputs or purchaser of outputs. Within manufacturing itself, there was a clear distinction[5] between 'factory' production – defined as establishments with five employees or more – and artisans (the remainder) in terms of production and employment: the factory stratum accounted for 83 per cent of value added but only 35 per cent of the labour force in 1968, with an implicit productivity ten times that of artisan production; in concentrating our attention on manufacturing as defined in this way, therefore, we are talking of about a twentieth of the national workforce and a fifth of national product during the 1960s.

Although the pattern of output experienced considerable change during our period, above all in the first half, its main characteristics can be considered as a whole. Production was dominated by two branches – food and clothing – which accounted for about half of value added in the sector. The dynamic branches were industrial inputs and *metalmecánica*,[6] which generated roughly a third of output, and the remainder was made up of construction materials and miscellaneous branches such as printing. Each branch combined the production of 'traditional' and 'modern' goods – bread and condensed milk, for example, or wine and instant coffee – which related to different technologies and forms of ownership; within a particular commodity line such as bread, moreover, there was a considerable difference between the mass production of steam-baked bread (sliced and polythene-wrapped in an automated factory) on the one hand and the produce of the village baker on the other.

The definition of development in the productive structure of manufacturing must be related to the respective shares of the various branches in total value added in the first place, and their integration both with one another and with the rest of the economy in the second. As a guide to the first, we can take the proportions of total value added generated by the first two rows of Table 9.1 as representing 'light' branches, and that by the third and fifth as representing the 'heavy' branches – even though *metalmecánica* is predominantly concerned with consumer durables it does contain the seeds of a true capital goods sector. We can then argue that, further to Sutcliffe's criterion, industrialization involves not just expansion of the share of manufacturing in output but also an increasing weight[7] of 'heavy' as opposed to 'light' branches. Applying this extension of the 'Sutcliffe test', we find that considerable development took place during the first half of the period: the 'light' share fell from 59 per cent to 42 per cent and the 'heavy' share rose from 27 per cent to 43 per cent between 1958 and 1965; but between 1965 and 1974 the former declined by only two points to 40 per cent and the latter only rose by one point to 44 per cent.

The trends in output volume indicate a more complex picture. Food processing output grew relatively slowly between 1960 and 1968, and continued to do so thereafter, reflecting continued agricultural stagnation. In contrast, the wide and inconsistent fluctuations in the growth of textiles and clothing are very difficult to explain. Nonetheless, consumer goods production as a whole does appear to have grown at a fairly steady pace over the period as a whole, reflecting an income elasticity of demand of approximately 1.3 with respect to real GNP growth. 'Capital goods', which were in fact household durables and vehicles in the main, expanded extremely rapidly indeed during the 1960–68 period, reflecting an import-substitution process which had only started in the late 1950s; but after 1968 market saturation appears to have slowed down the rate of growth in electrical goods production although prohibition on imports of cars stimulated vehicle production considerably. In contrast, output of industrial inputs grew more rapidly in the second half of our period than in the first, although this was far from fast enough to cover the large import bill built up by the input requirements of other branches. As we shall see, little or no new capacity was installed in the private sector after 1968, which doubtless accounts for the low growth rate in producer goods production – in contrast to what would normally be anticipated in

Table 9.1. *The structure of manufacturing output in Peru*

	1958	1965	1970	1974
Per cent of value added at current prices:				
1 Food, drink and tobacco	33	23	24	21
2 Textiles, clothing and shoes	26	19	16	19
3 Industrial inputs	17	23	25	21
4 Construction materials	7	8	7	6
5 *Metalmecánica*	10	20	18	23
6 Other	7	7	10	10
Total	100	100	100	100
Value added at current prices[a]	4.2	17.0	39.6	101.5
Value added at 1963 prices[a]	5.4	14.7	18.1	34.1

	Output index (1968 = 100)					Growth rate (per cent per annum)	
	1960	1965	1970	1973	1976	1960–68	1968–76
Selected branches:							
20 Food processing, etc.	61	81	111	153	159	6.4	6.0
23 Textiles, etc.	81	104	105	171	184	2.7	7.9
24 Clothing, etc.	47	82	116	134	127	9.9	3.0
27 Paper, etc.	49	86	114	115	126	9.3	2.9
31 Chemicals, etc.	35	74	117	182	280	14.0	13.7
33 Non-metallic minerals	50	85	102	138	183	9.1	7.8
34 Basic metals	81	90	98	174	182	2.7	7.8
35 Simple metal products	51	80	125	167	186	10.1	8.1
36 Non-electric machinery	47	75	123	181	314	11.4	15.4
37 Electric machinery	26	41	131	181	257	21.2	12.5
38 Transport equipment	62	98	169	275	298	7.1	14.6
Factory production[b]	54	83	113	164	193	8.0	8.6
Consumer goods[c]	57	83	110	158	173	7.2	7.1
Intermediate goods[d]	54	74	109	162	203	8.0	9.3
Capital goods[e]	30	83	137	203	258	16.2	12.6

Value added definitions: (1) is SITC 20 (less 207), 21, 22; (2) is 23, 24, 29 (3) is 27, 30, 31, 32; (4) is 25, 33; (5) is 34 (less 342), 35, 36, 37, 38; (6) is 26, 28, 39.

Value added sources: 1958 from ONEC *Anuario Estadístico 1960*; 1965 from Ministerio de Fomento y Obras Públicas *Estadística Industrial 1965*; 1970 from ONEC *Anuario Estadístico 1971*; 1974 directly from the Ministerio de Industrias y Turismo (Oficina Sectorial de Planificación). Constant price estimate calculated by applying deflator derived for Table 8.1.
Output index sources: ONEC *Anuario 1966, 1969*; BCR *Memoria 1976*.
Notes: [a] Billion soles; [b] excluding fishmeal processing; [c] SITC 20–25, 28,39; [d] SITC 25,27,28, 30–34; [e] SITC 35–38.

the 'second phase' of import substitution – although a comparison of physical output trends with the changing composition of value in Table 9.1 implies that price restraint imposed on industrial inputs after 1968 explains why their share in value added fell off between 1970 and 1974.

The formation of this manufacturing structure was based upon the process of import-substitution which by the end of the 1960s had reached completion of the 'first' or 'easy' stage of substituting for most imported consumer goods; the first half of the 1970s saw a start on the second stage (industrial inputs) but the creation of a capital goods sector remained a task for the future. Although the concept of import-substitution (the replacement of a pattern of imported commodities by the domestic product) is quite clear, the measurement of its full consequences is necessarily complex because the substitution for one class of imports (e.g. cars) may well involve increase in other categories (e.g. kits for car assembly) and the use of domestic inputs (e.g. plastics) increase the import of foreign inputs (e.g. chemicals). Even 'successful' import substitution need not involve the reduction of the total import bill, as there is no point in accumulating foreign exchange reserves uselessly, but rather may lead to the use of the exchange in such a way as to obtain the maximum domestic supply of commodities. In the shift away from importing consumer goods towards their local production with imported inputs, it is quite possible that the net foreign exchange cost might increase (or at least be reduced disproportionately to the value of the local inputs used) due to the low efficiency of local plant, however.

The evidence[8] for Peru varies according to the production branch, but it can broadly be summarized as follows: the substitution for consumer goods was largely carried out between 1958 and 1968, but in the non-durable lines the net effect was much more 'positive' than for durables, the latter raising imported input requirements much more than the former and in some cases (e.g. paper and glass products) apparently even more than proportionately to the reductions in imports of the final product. Thus, although the proportion of imported commodities in total supply fell, the imported share of industrial inputs supply rose, accounting for the major part of the total import bill by the end of our period. Baulne estimates[9] that the process of import-substitution saved the Peruvian economy some 12 billion soles at 1963 prices between 1958 and 1969 (that is, imports would have been higher by this amount if the same proportion of the domestic market had been supplied from abroad in 1969 as had been in 1958) but that imports of inputs for industry were 4 billion soles higher than otherwise – giving a net effect of 8 billion. This figure is equivalent to only 8 per cent of 1969 GNP, which Baulne

Table 9.2. *Import-substitution in selected manufacturing branches*

| | Import penetration[a] | | | Imported inputs[b] | | ISI/ΔQ[c] |
	1958	1963	1969	1958	1969	1958–69
231 Textiles	0.08	0.07	0.08	0.16	0.31	0.05
243 Clothing	0.10	0.05	0.01	0.15	0.13	0.16
271 Paper	0.42	0.36	0.45	0.42	0.54	—
311 Chemicals	0.82	0.72	0.63	0.55	0.65	0.60
341 Steel, iron	0.65	0.67	0.48	0.59	0.43	0.46
350 Metal products	0.56	0.46	0.27	0.72	0.78	0.51
360 Non-electrical machinery	0.86	0.85	0.71	0.46	0.72	0.93
370 Electrical machinery	0.88	0.85	0.44	0.41	0.62	0.84
383 Automobiles	0.90	0.89	0.33	0.95	0.90	0.90
385 Motorcycles	1.00	0.95	0.48	0.44	0.44	1.00

Source: Baulne (1975) pp. 66, 86, 94, 138.
Notes: [a] imports as a proportion of total supply; [b] imported inputs as a proportion of raw materials [c] the 'Chenery' measure of the reduction of import penetration as a proportion of the increase in domestic branch output – and thus the proportion of output growth (ΔQ) attributable to import-substituting industrialization (*ISI*).

sees as a sign of failure; but in fact imports of goods and services in 1969 were 28 billion 1963 soles, so that these imports were a quarter lower (and manufacturing output possibly a third higher) than they would have been had import-substitution not taken place. A complete evaluation would require a costing in terms of international prices and an estimation of the value of the other resources involved in production; but nonetheless, it would appear that a large part of industrial growth in the 1956–67 period took the form of import-substitution, particularly in the *metalmecánica* branches, as Table 9.2 indicates.

We do not have a similar source of analysis for later years, but what evidence there is on the intensity of imported inputs[10] suggests that after 1969 (when one third of all material inputs to manufactured consumer goods and a half of those to intermediate goods were imported) import-substitution did not make much more progress and the import coefficients remained fairly stable. This is hardly surprising in view of the lack of investment in the sector after 1968. In consequence, the main source of industrial growth must have been domestic market expansion, stimulated by rapidly rising wage and profit consumption.

One of the major roles of manufacturing in economic development is supposed to be the linkage of different production sectors, but the Peruvian economy remained disarticulated despite the expansion of manufacturing, because much of this was based on little more than the processing of imported inputs. These characteristics lent a new rigidity to the economy during the 1960s; industrial expansion placed constant pressure on the balance of payments rather than relieving it, while imports could only be cut back by reducing industrial production – not just by reducing domestic luxury consumption as had been possible when consumer durables were imported directly. Within manufacturing the degree of integration between branches was quite low (as Table 9.3 shows) and within these intersectoral sales there was a high degree of concentration in terms of purchases by one firm from another in the same ownership group.[11] This phenomenon, combined with the monopoly condition of many lines, almost eliminated meaningful competition within Peruvian industry, and thus weakened the pressure for efficiency and innovation unless brought in from outside.

The domestic market for manufactures was also highly concentrated in terms both of income and space. At least three quarters of their market in 1968 appears to have been located in the Lima–Callao area because this proportion of both consumer expenditure and manufacturing capacity was to be found there – the sources of demand for final and intermediate goods. Within this metropolitan area the highest income quartile of households accounted for about half the total market for clothing and consumer durables, and the next quartile for another quarter[12] – so that quite possibly only a tenth of the population provided a half the national market for consumer manufactures. This concentration reinforced

Table 9.3. *Input–output matrix for manufacturing (billion soles in 1969)*

	Consumer goods	Intermediate goods	Metal-mecánica	Total mfg.	Outputs Other sectors	Invest-ment	Exports	Consump-tion	Total output
Inputs									
Consumer goods	—	0.8	0.2	1.0	5.8	—	3.8	37.2	46.8
Intermediate goods	3.1	—	0.8	3.9	10.1	0.5	0.6	15.2	26.4
Metalmecánica	0.3	0.2	—	0.5	2.8	2.5	0.2	5.2	10.7
Total manufacturing	3.4	1.0	1.0	5.4	18.7	3.0	4.6	57.6	83.9
Other sectors	14.5	5.0	1.9	21.4					
Total national inputs	17.9	6.0	2.9	26.8					
Imported inputs	6.3	4.3	2.7	18.3					
Value added	22.6	16.1	5.1	43.8					
Total inputs	46.8	26.4	10.7	83.9					

Source: Calculated from INP (1972), classified as for Table 9.1: with 'consumer goods' including rows 1, 2 and 6 of that table; 'intermediate goods' including rows 3 and 4; 'metalmecánica' is row 5. See also Torres (1975) for further discussion of the INP matrix.

the tendency to purchase 'international' goods, with either international technical standards (such as television) or internationally known brand names (such as Coca-Cola), thus contributing to the ease of penetration by the multinational corporations. On the basis of the 1968 Household Budget Survey, from which the relevant income elasticities can be gleaned, it has been argued[13] that a redistribution of income in Peru would not change the pattern of demand (e.g. the balance between clothes and cars) and thus that the concentration of income was not a determinant factor in market size, but rather the size of total national income. This conclusion may well derive from the failure of budget surveys to reveal the heterogeneity of products within a single commodity category: for example a rich and poor family may spend the same proportion of their incomes on clothing, and thus a redistribution would not change the total amount of money spent on clothes, but the different nature of the commodity purchased (fibres, foreign exchange content and so on) would have an effect on the demand for manufactures and the pattern of production. What is also true, although neither of the authors cited mention this, is that large corporations taking part in the import-substitution process did tend to 'modernize' wage consumption through massive advertising campaigns, thus widening the market for factory as opposed to artisan products and foreign as opposed to local brands. It is difficult to avoid the conclusion that the narrowness of the market for non-essential goods was a significant constraint on industrialization in Peru, imposing limits on scale economies and innovative competition.

As the rapid expansion of manufacturing could be expected to slow down once the import gap was filled,[14] if a major income redistribution was not undertaken in order to widen the domestic market, the logical alternative was to turn to exports. But Peru was never very successful in placing manufactures on overseas markets, either in Latin America or further afield: by 1975 manufactured exports accounted for only five per cent of both total exports and sectoral output. This was due to three factors: the relatively small scale of Peruvian plant and thus lack of scale economies; the lack of enthusiasm in the private sector for new ventures as the traditional model of accumulation collapsed; and the fact that Peru did not feature as an 'export base' in the global strategies of the multinational corporations. The response to the first factor was the enthusiasm of Peru for the Andean Pact, which would have guaranteed wider markets and stimulated local industrialists, thereby helping to overcome the second problem – and in fact an association of exporters (ADEX) was founded in 1970 which started to articulate the voice of independent industrial capital prepared to cooperate with the state. The subsequent collapse of the Andean

Table 9.4. *Structure of industry-related imports ($US millions at 1963 prices)*

	1956	1963	1967	1970	1975
Consumer non-durables[a]	25	25	32	20	15
Consumer durables	43	49	37	10	46
Inputs for industry	113	199	280	283	433
Capital goods[b]	84	130	174	132	361
Transport equipment	36	72	91	53	130
Sub-total	301	475	614	498	985
Other imports[c]	81	77	118	75	293
Total imports	382	552	732	573	1278

Source: 1963–70 from BCR (1975); 1975 from BCR *Memoria 1976*; 1956 from BCR *Cuentas Nacionales* dollar import figures deflated by GDP import deflator adjusted for changes in the exchange rate.

Notes: [a] excluding food products; [b] includes mining equipment and military hardware; [c] mainly food and oil.

Pact as an effective organization meant that these initiatives did not lead to much, and the attraction of foreign capital was obviously hampered by the reform programme, although the rationalization of the automobile sector did result in Peru becoming the potential base for the Toyota export operations to the rest of Latin America. There is also some reason to believe that the overvaluation of the sol in the 1970–75 period hampered the export of traditional lines such as textiles.

The impact of industry on the external trade account was predominantly on the import side, therefore. Imported manufactures and inputs to produce them locally consistently accounted for about three quarters of the total import bill, because the reductions in the relative volume of consumer goods and transport equipment were matched by the rise in industrial inputs and capital equipment.

As the expansion of output was mainly conditioned by the needs of the domestic market and productivity growth determined by technological change induced from abroad, the employment requirements of the sector emerged as a dependent variable. Increases in employment resulted, therefore, from the relative rates of growth of output and productivity – determined by national income growth and industrial accumulation, respectively – but with positive values for both these variables, employment was bound to rise less rapidly than production. It is not surprising, therefore, that while

Table 9.5. *Indices of manufacturing employment, productivity and earnings (1955 = 100)*

	1950	1955	1960	1965	1970	1975
Employment	90	100	115	113	156	181
Production	67	100	139	213	283	404
Productivity	74	100	121	188	181	223
Real salary rates	79	100	109	115	153	155
Real wage rates	85	100	117	125	120	150

Source: First two rows from BCR *Cuentas Nacionales* (*op. cit.*) and 1975 from BCR *Memoria 1975*, all divided through by 1955 values; the third row is the ratio of the first two; the last two ratios direct from BCR national accounts division.

between 1950 and 1975 output rose six-fold, manufacturing employment only doubled; Table 9.5 shows the best estimates available[15] for the period as a whole. The doubling of output per head over two decades undoubtedly indicates increasing capital intensity, but the concept must be treated with caution because productivity also rises when more inputs per worker are used (with the introduction of automobile assembly from imported kits, for example) and with improved capacity utilization. Factory employment ('corporate manufacturing' in Table A.5) in 1968 was no more than five per cent of the national workforce. Taking the 1955–65 and 1965–75 periods separately, the effect of the falling-off of the rate of investment is immediately clear: in the first period output grew at 7.9 per cent per annum, but because productivity rose at 6.5 per cent as rapid investment built up excess manufacturing capacity (see below), employment rose at only 1.2 per cent; in sharp contrast, between 1965 and 1975 production expanded into excess capacity at 6.6 per cent but as private investment was so low, productivity rose at only 1.7 per cent and thus employment could rise at 4.8 per cent.

At a branch level,[16] output per head in the early 1970s appears to have been highest in industrial inputs, as might be expected, but it was actually higher in food than in *metalmecánica* – probably because of the existence of large food processing plant as against the proliferation of small repair workshops. The main point here would seem to be that it is the size and type of the firm (in both ownership and product) that determine technology and labour productivity, rather than the nature of the branch.[17] Moreover, apart from large plant using less labour per unit of output, its establishment may displace many labour-intensive but smaller firms from the market, thus reducing total employment 'net' – or at least its rate of growth.

The labour supply to factory industry was never a problem in Peru, due to the existence of a large 'reserve army' in the form of reasonably skilled workers in artisan shops. This enabled employers to maintain a high turnover (even after the introduction of legislation designed to secure job stability in 1970) often by making use of a 1930 law on 'training periods' which allowed workers to be dismissed after a few months and then taken on again, thus preventing the privileges of continuous employment so as to reduce union militancy and restrain wage rate rises. The share of labour remuneration in value added also appears to have fallen over the period as a whole and wages too have risen more slowly than productivity, which could be taken as an indication of either increasing capital intensity if the return on capital was constant, or of rising profit rates: the data presented elsewhere in this chapter would suggest that the first explanation would have been correct for the 1955–65 period and the second for subsequent years. The bargaining power of trades unions undoubtedly increased over this period, particularly after 1968. Nonetheless this seems to have been confined to negotiation at a plant level, with most success in large firms with monopoly positions which could afford to raise wages but which employed relatively few workers. With an excess of labour at the 'lower end' of the market, this probably did not pull up wage rates in smaller firms, where most of the employment was to be found.

Industrial ownership

The ownership of manufacturing industry in Latin America during our period was not a simple matter of individual industrial entrepreneurs. On the one hand, much of the capital in the sector was either linked to multisectoral financial groups or else controlled by the affiliates of the giant multinational corporations. On the other, ownership did not just involve managing the firm itself on a competitive market or receiving the profits, but was also a matter of control over techniques of production, brand names, preferential access to credit and tied imports. Thus the analysis of ownership should facilitate an explanation of the structural problems we have just identified and place the pattern of accumulation in the proper organizational context.

Peruvian manufacturing was highly concentrated in our period, as Table 9.6, indicates. First, although 'factories' accounted for only a third of employment they produced the bulk of sectoral output, forming the basis of dualism in the sector. Second, within the '*estrato fabril*' the two hundred or so largest establishments (those with more than two hundred employees) accounted for nearly half of output, but only a third of employment; again, the effect of capital-intensity is noticeable. The figures appear to indicate some reduction of concentration between 1963 and 1973, but it should be remembered that firms owned more than one establishment in many cases – a phenomenon that became more pronounced as markets and capacity expanded. At branch level[18] concentration ratios were extremely high: taking the proportion of sales by the top four establishments in each three-digit ISIC grouping in 1969, we find this to be well over two thirds in most cases. The overall effect was to severely reduce effective competition on the domestic market. Further, the concentration of both sales and employment in Lima become more pronounced, reflecting the spatial pattern of duality that we have already noted. This appears to have been due in part to the more rapid growth of demand in the metropolis and the immediate coastal area, and also to the penetration of rural markets by the products of Lima plant as transport facilities improved.

Table 9.6. *Size and location of manufacturing establishments
(per cent of total)*

	1963			1973		
	Estab-lishments	Sales	Employ-ment	Estab-lishments	Sales	Employ-ment
Factories:						
small[a]	65.3	5.9	15.9	68.9	10.4	18.9
medium[b]	31.2	36.2	44.0	28.1	43.0	46.9
large[c]	3.5	57.9	40.1	3.0	46.6	34.2
	100.0	100.0	100.0	100.0	100.0	100.0
Factories:						
Lima–Callao	..	62	70	..	69	74
Rest of Peru	..	38	30	..	31	26
		100	100		100	100
Factories	..	89	36	..	90	35
Artisans	..	11	64	..	10	65
		100	100		100	100

[a] 5–19 employees; [b] 20–199 employees; [c] 200+ employees.
Source: MIT–OSP on the basis of the 1963 and 1973 Censuses.

Table 9.7. *Fixed asset ownership in 1969 (billion soles)*

	Foreign control	Domestic control	Total assets	Foreign share (%)
1 Food etc.	2.2	3.6	5.8	38
2 Clothing etc.	2.2	3.3	5.5	40
3 Industrial inputs	5.5	3.4	8.9	62
4 Construction materials	2.0	2.2	4.2	48
5 *Metalmecánica*	2.2	2.4	4.6	48
6 Other	0.3	1.7	2.0	15
Total	14.4	16.6	31.0	46
Large firms	10.0	6.2	16.2	62
Other firms	4.4	10.4	14.8	30

Source: Data from Anaya (1975) classified as in Table 9.1; 'large' means equity of 25 million soles or more, 'foreign control' means that over 20 per cent of this equity is foreign owned.

But concentration between firms was even greater. According to Espinoza,[19] a group of some 79 firms with assets of over 100 million soles in 1968 made up only 3 per cent of all firms with ten employees or more but accounted for 54 per cent of fixed assets and 49 per cent of sales. Only 27 of these were fully nationally owned, and these held only 18 per cent of fixed assets. Moreover, six large ownership groups linking firms in different sectors accounted for 34 per cent of sales alone. In other words, Peruvian manufacturing was dominated by domestic finance capital and the multinationals – in 1968 nearly half of manufacturing assets were controlled by foreign capital (see Table 9.7), and a further third by the large domestic ownership groups, meaning that at most one quarter of sectoral capital was in the hands of independent industrialists, and largely in the medium and small categories at that. The definition of 'foreign control' used here includes minority ownership (more than a fifth of equity) because effective control was often exercised through the use of technology contracts, brand royalties and tied imports. This position was built up over the previous two decades, representing the addition of new lines to the existing ones within each branch, so that foreign entry was not confined to typically 'dynamic' branches such as vehicle assembly but extended to foods (e.g. Nestlé instant coffee), clothing (e.g. Bata shoes), heavy industry (e.g. Pilkington float glass) and chemicals (e.g. Bayer pharmaceuticals) as well as the inevitable Westinghouse assembly lines. Collaboration with both large finance capital groups and previously independent capital was involved in such penetration, but apparently not a great deal of 'take-overs' of existing firms.

The extent of foreign control was a crucial factor in the determination of a number of structural problems that we have already noted – particularly import intensity and low employment absorption. Technologies developed for use in the metropolitan economies and based on product differentiation, heavy advertising and sophisticated processing plant were used as a means both of preventing domestic competition and of remitting profits abroad. In consequence, the existence of relatively cheap labour, abundant natural resources and a national pattern of tastes did not lead to an adaptation to local conditions but rather attempts to modify the nature of the local market – particularly through advertising. Vaitsos[20] shows that the foreign firms in Peruvian manufacturing were significantly more import-intensive than local firms of equivalent output in the early 1970s, and thus accounted for a disproportionately large share of the import bill for industrial inputs. Similarly, he shows that foreign firms were more capital-intensive and had a lower share of labour costs in value added, despite their somewhat higher wage rates, all of which contributed to a lower employment creation potential. What is more, the presence of foreign firms in an oligopolistic market, where competition was by product differentiation and mass advertising rather than price or even quality, forced local producers to adopt similar technologies, often by acquiring foreign franchises, and thus further extending the dislocatory effects. Finally, he demonstrates the control by the multinationals over potential export lines and their unwillingness to compete with their 'sisters' in other countries;[21] a small economy such as Peru was not considered suitable as a base for low-cost exports to the metropolis using cheap labour, particularly after 1968 when restrictions were imposed on foreign investors.

The direct impact on ownership of state intervention in the sector after 1968 was limited by the strategic decision to protect and stimulate the private industrialist. Under the 1970 Industrial Law the state acquired control over iron, steel, non-ferrous metals, basic chemicals (e.g. oxygen, sulphur, caustic soda, sulphuric acid, urea), fertilizer, cement and paper; much of this plant derived from the bankruptcy of the Prado group, the effect of the land reform on the Grace holdings, and the nationalization of Cerro de Pasco – these were three of the six large ownership groups mentioned above. Moreover, under the same law majority foreign equity holdings had to be reduced to minorities over a number of years – although technological and management control was not necessarily reduced thereby. A few cooperatives were formed from bankrupt textile mills. The establishment of capital goods lines in the public sector steadily extended state participation in manufacturing but did not affect the extent of private (above all, foreign) control over final production. State enterprises accounted for only five per cent of factory output in 1968, as opposed to 45 per cent owned by foreign-controlled firms and 50 per cent by local capital; in 1975 these shares were 20 per cent state, 35 per cent foreign and 45 per cent domestic.[22] Manufacturing remained, nonetheless, dominated by foreign technology and organized on market criteria.

One of the major pieces of reform legislation did, however, affect manufacturing directly – the creation in the 1970 Law of the

Comunidad Industrial.[23] Although the restriction of this reform to factory manufacturing limited the labour force included to about a third of the sectoral total (see Table 9.6) it did cover the greater part of production and provide a direct means of access not only to profits but also to management decisions. As far as ownership was concerned, the original provision for 15 per cent of book profits to be issued to the *Comunidad Industrial* in the form of equity could eventually have brought its share to one half; it was intended that the only way that the owners could 'keep ahead' was for them to maintain a high rate of reinvestment and thus fresh equity issues. In reality, even though true profits were very high as the sector moved towards full capacity, the joint ownership of manufacturing and commercial firms allowed 'transfer pricing' to take place (i.e. the ex-factory price was set low and profits built up in a separate marketing firm with no *Comunidad*) so as to reduce book profits. Plans to overcome this by introducing a *'Comunidad Comercial'* were abandoned in 1976 under pressure from foreign bankers and the equity participation limited to 35 per cent at the same time. As we have already seen, the initial experiments in the establishment of independent state-controlled cooperatives in manufacturing (*Propiedad Social*) were also virtually suspended in 1976, mainly because the high degree of industrial concentration at branch level meant that the assignment of priority to these enterprises would inevitably have meant the takeover of existing private firms (many of them foreign) or at the very least a severe curtailment of their operations. As we have seen in Chapter 5, the main effect of these initiatives was not (as had been intended) to identify the interests of capital and labour within the firm and by reducing industrial conflict raise private investment; rather it strengthened trades union solidarity and by legitimizing worker participation in management alarmed private investors.

Industrial strategy before 1963 had been explicitly based upon government approval of an alliance between domestic finance capital and multinational manufacturing corporations. Under Belaunde, an attempt was made to favour the 'independent industrialist' as against those two groups, with the intention of strengthening the industrialization process itself and indirectly weakening the hold of financial and foreign groups on the economy. The instruments chosen were the provision of subsidized inputs from state corporations, cheap finance from banks, tax concessions and tariff protection from imports. However, the multinational corporations and their local financial partners took full advantage of these facilities too, and continued to consolidate their hold on the sector. After 1968, industrial strategy was still based upon the supposedly dynamic force of the independent industrialists; it was expected that if the impediments of the 'oligarchs' and 'imperialists' were removed and incentives were increased, they would surge forward with new investment, which could then be diverted into the branches required for the restructuring of manufacturing capital – and, in particular, the completion of the 'second phase' of import-substitution so as to assure domestic supply of industrial inputs. This group was, therefore, of central importance to strategy from 1962 onwards. There is considerable evidence to the effect that independent industrialists were growing in political importance in the 1960s;[24] their tendency to stem from families of comparatively recent arrival in Peru strengthened their opposition to traditional ownership groups, and their fear of the encroachments of multinationals strengthened their nationalism. However, despite their number and vociferousness – especially as manifested through the *Sociedad Nacional de Industrias* – their control over production was in fact quite limited. At most, they controlled a quarter of manufacturing production as late as 1968. Oligopoly control from the very start of the Peruvian industrialization process had not left room for the emergence of independent industrial capital on a substantial scale. The attempt to design policy in order to favour the independent industrialist under Belaunde was almost inevitably of most advantage to large domestic or foreign capital, whether intentionally or not; after 1968 the disarticulation of large domestic capital meant that the only force other than the state capable of restarting accumulation, and thus in a position to extract further concessions from the government in the name of 'private enterprise', were the multinationals.

Industrial accumulation

During the 1960s the rate of investment in manufacturing fell from a relatively high level to one barely exceeding the long-run requirements for the replacement of existing plant. This reflected two phenomena that we have already mentioned – the excess capacity built up in the first half of the decade and the lack of confidence among private investors after 1968 – but in a wider sense the decline was an integral part of the breakdown of the traditional model of accumulation in the economy as a whole because the pattern of ownership in manufacturing was such that the bulk of investment was undertaken by domestic finance capital and foreign enterprises: the asset ownership figures would suggest that at least half the capital formation in the sector during the 1960s was undertaken by foreign firms, and possibly another quarter by the large financial groups. Although there is little reliable data[25] available on fixed assets it would be safe to say that capital intensity rose until 1965, and then fell as spare capacity was used up – if we measure capital intensity by either assets per worker or assets per unit of output. The evidence on asset structure by branch is equally unreliable, but in 1973 it would appear that while the production of industrial inputs was naturally the most capital-intensive in terms of assets per worker, the food branch was next, preceding even *metalmecánica* in this ranking – the reason being that while the leading firms in the factory production of food were using large sophisticated plant (e.g. beer production) the assembly of vehicles, for example, required little more than 'a warehouse and a screwdriver'. However, this ratio of capital per head was roughly correlated with output per head, as might be expected, so that the ratio of capital per unit of output is much more consistent for the whole of factory manufacturing: the modernization and concentration process affected every branch.[26] The explanation would seem to lie in the fact that the relatively slow-moving mass consumption lines such as food and clothing went through a process of modernization and concentration that involved the replacement of existing plant so as to change both techniques of production and the product itself, while the expansion of entire dynamic branches such as household durables was based on capital-intensive plant.

The effect of this investment pattern was to shift the structure of production towards heavy industry in the years between 1956 and 1965 but to restrain it in subsequent years. After 1965, private investment suffered a serious decline in both absolute and relative

terms, becoming hardly sufficient to cover replacement requirements, let alone return to the previously high level: the fixed asset
values of 18 billion soles in 1965, 35 in 1969 and 53 in 1974 (Table
9.9) indicate annual depreciation requirements of the order of 3, 7
and 10 billion soles, as compared to private investment in those
years of 2.5, 4.0 and 11.2 billion soles respectively. State investment
did not rise fast enough to cover this gap and was mostly directed
towards heavy industry (steel, fertilizers and chemicals) rather than
final production.

Table 9.8. *Levels of private manufacturing investment*

	1960–64	1965–68	1969–72	1973–75
Annual rate (billion soles at 1963 prices):				
Private	3.5	2.6	2.2	4.3
Public	0.3	0.5	0.6	1.9
Total	3.8	3.1	2.8	6.2
Per cent of GDP at current prices:				
GFCF	5.2	2.2	1.7	2.6
depreciation	1.9	2.1	2.2	2.3

Source: 1960–64 from INP (1966); 1965–73 from MIT (1974); 1974–75 from MIT (1976).
Depreciation calculated by applying the coefficients of depreciation to sales given in Torres
(1978) p. 54 and Table 10.

The structure of manufacturing capital is not made up of fixed
assets alone, but also of working capital on the one hand and equity
plus loans on the other. An examination of trends in this structure
reveals a significant phenomenon – the withdrawal of private capital
from manufacturing. The tentative estimates shown in Table 9.9 imply that the ratio of fixed to variable assets (i.e. working capital)
remained stable at about two to one, but that the proportion of
equity in liabilities fell from four fifths to little over half between
1965 and 1974 – bank credit making up the difference. Fixed assets
were, of course, revalued during this period to allow for inflation,
but this revaluation was balanced mostly by borrowing rather than
by using the owners' own capital, and in fact much of this
borrowing was from state banks: the Banco Industrial and Cofide
accounted for half the total bank credit to industry outstanding in

1974. This shift also affected profitability: the move towards full capacity increased the return on fixed assets, while the higher 'gearing' of the asset structure (ratio of loans to equity) allowed profitability – expressed as the return on equity after capital charges – to rise even higher. Lack of profits cannot have been the reason, therefore, for the poor investment record of the sector after 1968; nor was lack of demand an immediate problem, as full capacity utilization was rapidly being approached.

Table 9.9. *Estimated capital structure and profitability in private manufacturing (billion soles at current prices)*

	1965	1969	1974
Capital structure:			
Assets: Fixed	18	35	53
Variable	7	15	21
Total capital	25	50	74
Liabilities: Equity	20	35	41
Credit	5	15	33
Operating account:			
Operating surplus	10	18	37
Capital charges	4	9	13
Gross profits	6	9	24
Tax and *Comunidad*	1	2	9
Net manufacturing profit	5	7	15
Profitability (net profit/equity)	25%	20%	37%

Source: Data and methodology given in FitzGerald (1975).

Coherent data on the sources of finance for industrial accumulation are not available but we can build up a reasonable picture from various pieces of information we have already examined in other contexts. The capital structure of the sector indicates the growing reliance on bank finance over the decade 1965–75, and given the common ownership pattern in the various branches we may assume that credit was allocated between them in proportion to requirements, except that larger firms are believed to have received a more than proportionate share and (before the 1970 banking legislation

prevented this) foreign affiliates even more so. The low rate of investment, particularly in relation to depreciation allowances, would
imply that, after 1965 at least, net profits were almost all extracted
from the sector – and, given the level of state credit, possibly much
of the depreciation allowances too.[27] In the decade up to 1965, it is
reasonable to suppose that the reverse occurred, and that funds were
brought in from outside the sector, principally through the banking
system, which was allocating a quarter of commercial credit to industry as early as 1955. Industrial accumulation in Peru did not
become a self-sustaining process based on the reinvestment of its
own profits. The provisions under the 1969 Agrarian Reform law for
the cashing of compensation bonds for industrial investment[28] were
hardly used at all: of the 8 billion soles issued, only 233 millions had
been used in this way by the end of 1975 – and in any case if all of
them had been cashed over (say) the years 1973–75, private
manufacturing investment would have been increased by less than a
quarter.

Industrialization policy

Throughout our period the underlying strategic assumption of
Peruvian policy was that private capital should bear the greater part of
the burden of industrialization, so that state intervention could be
limited to the provision of infrastructure and finance on the one hand
and of tariff protection and tax incentives on the other. There was also
an ostensible commitment to the ideal of the independent industrialist
although those in power (particularly the civilian governments with
their close business connexions) must have known this to have been a
chimera at best and an open invitation to foreign capital at worst.
Despite this common assumption, the extent of state control and the
attitude to foreign capital varied widely over time.

Until the Second World War it is not really possible to discern an
industrialization policy as such. Even then, the industrial protection
laws promulgated by the first Prado administration and the complementary measures in trade and exchange controls established under Bustamante were mainly attributable to temporary war-time
shortages.[29] Thus Odría was able to dismantle these in 1947 with

considerable support from foreign capital and little 'industrialist' opposition, returning Peru to 'economic liberalism' for the next decade. In 1956 the second Prado administration initially continued the effective discrimination against a still mainly local manufacturing industry, insofar as there were no special tax concessions (as there had been in the 1950 Mining Code) and very low tariff barriers by Latinamerican standards. Various factors did, however, begin to create the political climate within which a specifically industrial policy could emerge, of which the most important were the evident difficulty of maintaining the balance of payments on the basis of raw materials exports alone, the slow emergence of professional groups with an interest in modernization, and the shift in foreign investment patterns worldwide towards manufacturing.

It was the influx of foreign capital that finally started off the process of import-substitution in consumer durables and 'modern' food products, but the form of the first *Ley General de Industrias* in 1959 seems to have been more a consequence than a cause of this. Although the Law contained some tariff increases, these mainly related to consumer goods (despite the declared intention to promote heavy industry) and thus responded closely to the interest of multinationals. The major instrument of policy was tax incentives of up to a hundred per cent of profits with duty exemption on imported inputs for 'basic' branches – which term included even consumer durables and foods. Further, the benefits were extended to existing firms as well as new ventures, making the Law somewhat ineffectual as far as developing the industrial structure was concerned, although it certainly made the sector very profitable just when domestic finance capital and the multinationals were moving into it. Nonetheless, the degree of protection remained comparatively low[30] and the extent of state support limited, so that both the 1962–63 junta and the Belaunde administration felt it necessary to increase their effect. Tariffs were raised substantially in 1964 but mainly on consumer goods again, and the *fomento* activities of the public sector were extended in finance through the expansion of the Banco Industrial and in infrastructure through the establishment of the steel plant and hydroelectric generation capacity. More significant, perhaps, was the way that the continuation and widening of the scope of the 1959 Law encouraged plant proliferation and spatial concentration on Lima, while the high profitability afforded by low taxes and tariff protection permitted the building up of an enormous amount of excess capacity. No effort was made, despite the existence of investment licences after 1959 and the formal establishment of the planning system in 1962, to channel manufacturing in such a way as to take advantage of scale economies, to generate linkages between sectors, or to protect regional firms – despite a clear awareness within the administration that measures of this type, combined with some restrictions on the activities of the multinationals, were becoming necessary.[31]

Table 9.10. *Nominal tariff structure on manufactures*
(per cent of c.i.f. value)

	1958[a]	1964[a]	1964[b]	1967[b]
Consumer goods	47	57	62	91
Industrial goods	38	42	47	57
Capital equipment	34	34	35	38
Overall average	38	42	44	55

[a] 1963 weights; [b] 1966 weights.
Source: GIECO (1972) p.v–18

In contrast, industrialization as a means of gaining economic autonomy was a central theme of the economic strategy of the *Gobierno Revolucionario*: so as to obtain 'accelerated and self-sustaining economic development, fundamentally of the nation's internal potential, through an articulated and integrated productive structure . . . let permanent and self-sustained industrial development be declared as being of national importance, of primary interest for the socioeconomic progress of the nation and essential as a guarantee of its economic independence'.[32] We have already mentioned the three main conditioning factors in policy after 1968: the reliance on the independent industrialist to revive investment under state protection, the state takeover of basic industry and the foundation of a capital goods branch, and the limitation of foreign ownership and control. In the light of these criteria the 1970 *Ley General de Industrias* was framed, the main provisions of which were as follows: the definition of branches of first priority (heavy industry and capital goods) and second priority (wage goods and industrial inputs) which would receive consistent tariff reductions, tax relief on reinvestment and preference in state credit; the establishment of the *Comunidad Industrial* and the *Instituto de Investigación Tecnológica Industrial y de Normas Técnicas*; the gradual reduction of foreign shareholdings by compulsory sales to local capital and the limitation of expatriated profits to a 'reasonable' rate of return; and the reserving of basic industry (steel, non-ferrous metals, chemical fertilizers, cement and paper) to the state sector. Three complementary policy lines that were also implemented at that time were the

Table 9.11. *Capacity utilization in manufacturing*

	1963	1968	1972	1975
Production index[a] (1963 = 100)	100	140	183	225
Capacity utilization[b]	56%	52%	72%	85%
Implicit capacity index[c]	179	269	254	265

Source: [a] as in Figure 8.1; [b] supplied by the MIT–OSP, based on the 1963 Census, a special study by the Universidad Nacional de Ingeneria for 1968 and 1972, and own estimates for 1975; [c] derived by dividing 'production index' by 'capacity utilization'.

redirection of both state and commercial credit towards industry, the imposition of price controls on a series of essential industrial inputs and wage goods (e.g. cement and bread), and the refusal of import licences on luxury goods (e.g. cars) and commodities in adequate local supply – such as paper. Although the final prohibition on competitive imports did enable the first stage of import-substitution to be completed, this was achieved within the existing (excess) capacity and the required intermediate inputs could still be freely imported. But neither finance capital nor foreign enterprises were willing to invest in the substitution of these inputs, and in consequence the hoped-for restructuring of industry did not take place despite the incentives. Direct foreign investment in the sector virtually stopped, except for a few joint ventures with the state; this appears to have been due more to the 'political' effect of the *Comunidad* and the nationalizations in other sectors than to the ownership and profit repatriation restrictions as such. These, and the disarticulation of the old ownership groups, led to a virtual halt in private sector capacity expansion – investment being only enough to maintain existing plant. Table 9.11 below shows how the low rate of capacity utilization prevented this from forming a 'bottleneck' for some years, but by 1975 the situation had become critical in a number of essential wage goods, ranging from condensed milk to plastics, without any signs of a major revival in private investment. The depression of demand consequent upon the 1976–77 stabilization programme prevented a supply crisis from developing in the short term, but did nothing to increase capacity.

In principle, great weight was placed on the development of a domestic technological base after 1968, but the actual measures were confined to control over the outflow of royalties and to the initiation of research. Intintec was established under the 1970 Law and was financed by a two per cent levy on all manufacturing profits; its main activities were to process all foreign technology contracts signed by firms operating in Peru and to research into domestic technologies for the production of 'popular' consumer goods. In the former task, Intintec appears to have been strikingly successful in reducing permitted technology payments and various restrictive clauses,[33] but in the latter little progress was made, possibly because no clear policy guidelines were ever laid down as to exactly what consumer goods were required. More significantly, it was not made clear what production apparatus these technologies should be fitted into – so that proposals from Intintec ranged from renewals of Inca lifestyles to the imitation of US machines. Further, the problem of how private firms could be persuaded to use the new technologies, or could compete against the multinationals with them if they did, remained unresolved, and this difficulty was not ameliorated by the practice of state corporations of insisting on the most 'advanced' (i.e. foreign) technologies on grounds of efficiency, speed of delivery and access to external finance.

Although manufacturing was included in the 1962 and 1967 Plans, the absence of a coherent strategy for the sector or a substantial public investment programme therein limited the sectoral plans to a series of optimistic output forecasts. After 1968, the creation of the Ministry of Industry (previously the sector had come under the *Ministerio de Fomento y Obras Públicas*) and the establishment of a strong Sectoral Planning Office permitted a more determined planning effort. However, the 1971–75 Plan period was not one of great public investment in the sector (apart from the steel and fertilizer works) and as most of manufacturing remained under private control, integrated production targets and concomitant investment programmes could not be implemented and the indicative forecasts were vitiated by the paralysis in private investment. For the 1975–78 Plan a complete sectoral programme was produced,[34] resting on the expansion of wage goods supply, progressive reduction of imported inputs, the establishment of a capital goods sector, increased public investment and the rapid growth of social property. But the Plan did not face the need to restructure final output as such, nor specify what the ownership pattern was to be, nor fit into any longer-term supply strategy other than that thrown up by foreseeable shortages in the medium term. The modifications in economic strategy imposed in 1976, moreover, meant the tacit abandonment of the Plan even though the administrative capacity to enforce desired changes had actually increased with the growing reliance of private firms on finance from the state banks and the discretion exercised by the Ministry over the allocation of foreign exchange to the sector. Nonetheless, the capital goods programme[35] was continued and should have a substantive impact in the near future.

In sum, industrial policy in the 1969–75 period cannot be judged a great success: not because of inadequate aims but rather because of the underlying assumption that Peruvian industry worked according to an orthodox 'market' model with the dynamic of private accumulation only waiting for import protection, tax incentives, credit and infrastructure in order to rush forward with expansion schemes which could then be channelled towards the required structure – particularly the second stage of import-substitution. On the contrary, by 1975 a severe capacity crisis was emerging in many branches and the practice of overinvoicing on imported inputs, particularly by multinationals, was reaching serious levels.[36] When it was realized that a change of direction was needed, two options were open – to extend state control further or to allow foreign capital to operate freely again, given that Peruvian private capital could not, or would not, undertake the task. A start was made on the former strategy in 1974: *propiedad social* was established as an alternative to the absent industrialist and rationalization of the private sector was started by concentrating vehicle assembly. In 1975, the production of machine tools and tractors by state enterprise finally got under way, and the specifications for *producción concertada* (state contracts for wage goods supply with private firms) were drawn up. By 1976, however, the conflict between the state and foreign capital had come to a head and, as part of the much wider policy reversal the second option had been adopted: price rises and wage controls, relaxation of restrictions on foreign investment and profit remittance, limitations on the *comunidad* in small firms and cutbacks in the budget assignment to social property. How a return to the 'old' model of industrialization could be expected to make more progress than it had before 1968 was not explained.

In terms of industrialization strategy as a whole, the problem lay not only in the issue of ownership and control of the sector as it then stood but in the function that this sector was to perform within the economic development of Peru. This was not just a matter of whether further stages of import-substitution or even relative autarky would contribute to the resolution of the disarticulation of the sector from the rest of the economy, but rather of how these aims could be achieved without such integration. The potential relationship of manufacturing to the state-controlled export branches and the new forms of agrarian enterprise was never properly worked out, and even if full articulation of the corporate sector had been achieved through industry it would presumably have continued to absorb only an insignificant fraction of the national workforce into skilled and well-paid employment.

Concluding remarks

We can identify three broad characteristics of post-war industrialization in Peru: the rapid growth of manufacturing as the import-substitution took hold; lack of structural development after the mid 1960s; and the 'technological distortions' in output patterns and input use related to foreign ownership. State intervention up to 1968 merely served to accentuate these characteristics, and after that date it did little to counteract them. Without either a high rate of private investment which the authorities could channel towards the desired structure of output – particularly capital equipment and cheap wage goods – or direct state control over production, which would have permitted more rapid substitution of imported inputs and the reinvestment of industrial profits, there was little it could do.

Table 9.12 below shows some of the more salient characteristics of industry in the 'big seven' economies of the region. The share of manufacturing in gross domestic product was clearly much higher in Argentina and Brazil than elsewhere, while its internal structure became more 'advanced' in the sense of moving towards the 'third stage' of import-substitution (as defined by the ECLA) where the *metalmecánica* branches are not only in balance with the other two groups but contain a significant proportion of capital goods lines as well as consumer durables. The high shares of intermediate output in Mexico and Chile are indicative of the 'second stage' in this context, although in the case of Venezuela this was largely the result of an un-integrated but substantial petrochemicals branch. Curiously, the share of manufacturing in national output for Colombia is lower than for Peru, although the structure is more advanced by these criteria – possibly because of the linkage with a dynamic agricultural sector. On the employment side, the poor record in labour absorption is evident throughout the continent, and is clearly not confined to Peru, which in this as in the production pattern seems to be fairly typical. As to the less easily quantifiable aspects, Nolff[37] observes the prevalence of duality within Latinamerican manufacturing as a whole, with an extremely low level of productivity even in the factory stratum despite the use of modern technology, and the concentration of production in terms of both space and ownership. These characteristics, combined with the saturation of consumer goods markets based on the concentration of purchasing power in the hands of upper income groups and the difficulty of integrating industry with the rest of the economy, gave rise to a widespread critique of the 'dead end' encountered by various economies at the stage in import-substitution appropriate to their domestic market size.[38]

We have already noted the general Latinamerican experience of both ownership concentration and multinational penetration in manufacturing. Although in the case of the more advanced economies such as Mexico and Argentina this involved the displacement of domestic capitalists who had built up consumer branches in

Table 9.12. Comparative manufacturing structure

	GDP share at 1960 prices (per cent)		Growth rate (% p.a.)	Composition of output						Labour force (% EAP)	
				1960			1971				
	1960	1973	1960–73	A	B	C	A	B	C	1960	1970
Argentina	31	38	5.9	45	27	29	34	32	24	24	22
Brazil	23	27	8.7	42	29	29	30	33	37	12	15
Colombia	17	20	6.8	63	27	9	59	29	12	15	16
Chile	23	27	4.7	61	29	10	58	33	9	18	19
Mexico	19	24	8.5	54	36	11	48	38	14	14	17
Peru	18	24	7.5	63	29	8	60	28	12	13	15
Venezuela	12	18	7.4	64	29	7	50	40	10	12	19
All Latin America	22	26	7.3	57	26	17	51	30	19	15	16

Sources: ECLA (1974) except for last two columns, which are from Nolff (1974, p. 25).
Definitions: 'A' is SITC 20 to 26, 28, 29 and 39; 'B' is SITC 27, 31, 32, 34; 'C' is SITC 35, 36, 37, 38 according to the ECLA definitions. Note that the 'all Latin America' average is overwhelmingly biased towards these seven.

the period between 1930 and 1950, as opposed to the case of Peru or Colombia where much of the initial industrialization was a post-war phenomenon and carried out by the multinationals themselves, the end-result is strikingly similar. The consequences for technological control, transfer pricing and import dependence are experienced all over the continent[39] – as might be expected, given that the same group of multinationals was operating throughout the area with considerably less restriction than that experienced in Peru after 1968.

Starting from a reasonably common point of departure in the mid 1960s, if generalization can indeed be made in the way the ECLA does,[40] the general reaction appears to have been to react against import-substitution in its traditional form in a number of ways. Firstly, there were moves to rationalize tariff systems and reduce the degree of protection to local industry; secondly, legislation designed to increase the taxation on foreign enterprise and exclude it from certain 'strategic' sectors such as energy was introduced; and thirdly, a determined effort was made to expand manufactured exports – both to the metropolitan economies and regionally, to which end organizations such as the Andean Pact were established. The implication is that attempts to achieve autonomous industrialization were to be abandoned in the sense of achieving further stages of import-substitution, while resistance to foreign capital was to be confined to negotiating better terms for an essentially dependent relationship.[41] As a result, it was intended to develop a more 'efficient' industry, while abandoning any hope that manufacturing might resolve the problems of urban unemployment. There are, of course, wide variations on this theme – ranging from the drastic reopening of the economy in Argentina and Chile in recent years to the continued pursuit of capital goods capability in Brazil and Mexico – but the general picture seems to hold true.

Against this background, the Peruvian experience until 1968 was clearly part of the Latinamerican 'mainstream': in common with other late starters such as Colombia, rapid industrial development quickly met the limits of the first stage of import-substitution, and the distortions were all the more severe for this speed and the lavish welcome to foreign enterprise that accompanied it. But after 1968, instead of switching to a more 'open' policy and exports, the opposite course was taken: to block the multinationals and press forward with import-substitution. As we have seen, the success of this strategy depended upon two factors – an independent national industrial group and domestic technology – neither of which Peru really had. To rejoin the mainstream, as Peru appeared to be attempting to do by 1978 implied not only accommodation with the multinationals but more importantly, the assignment of a much less 'developmental' role to industry.

10

Conclusions

We have tried to show in this study that the political economy of Peru between 1956 and 1978 can be fruitfully analysed in terms of successive attempts to restructure capital as a means of achieving economic development through the transition from an economy where the main motor is primary exports – with all the implications this has in terms of dependency and dualism – to one where the dynamic is provided by industry. This restructuring involves a shift of the pattern of production towards manufacturing, the rearrangement of ownership and organizational systems and the reallocation of the surplus; in other words, the establishment of a new model of accumulation. This restructuring was attempted three times in Peru – all during the last quarter-century[1] – on the basis of different economic and political arrangements in each case, but each attempt appears to have failed.

The first attempt, under President Prado between 1956 and 1962, was essentially the project of the 'oligarchy' and involved an alliance between foreign capital and the domestic financial elite, continued labour repression and an open economy; the second attempt, under President Belaunde between 1963 and 1968, was more of a 'middle class' project relying on domestic industrialists, with a protected economy and the co-option of labour through welfare measures; the third, under President Velasco between 1969 and 1975, was the project of a reformist and relatively autonomous military, and involved opposition to foreign penetration, widespread ownership reforms and the incorporation of labour through worker participation at the enterprise level. In a strict sense, the first attempt was the most coherent in economic terms, combining as it did sufficient control over the surplus to balance high investment rates with savings out of profits and access to foreign technology from the multinationals, but Prado could neither mobilize sufficient political support nor rely upon the military to impose it. Had this attempt been successful, the result would presumably have been a political economy similar to that of Colombia. The second attempt was undermined by political weakness and an unbalanced model of accumulation – the effort to counter declining private investment rates by protection and higher public expenditure led to increased foreign penetration and macroeconomic instability. The ownership arrangements were politically unsatisfactory and the surplus had not been reallocated to support the new model of accumulation. In contrast to the two previous attempts the Velasco project did enjoy considerable political strength – or more accurately, relative autonomy and internal cohesion – to carry through ownership reforms but the state capitalist model established created severe economic imbalances from insufficient control over the surplus which, without a wider political base in civil society, it was powerless to resolve. In all three attempts, foreign capital played a crucial role, first by undermining the social basis of the state and then by weakening its economic position.

Despite the fact that the quest for economic development was central to the political agenda – or perhaps because of that fact – the problem of achieving a domestic political base for state intervention on the one hand and for a negotiated reduction in external dependence on the other remained essentially unresolved throughout our period; in consequence a new and coherent model of capital accumulation was not established to replace the traditional one. This is why political as much as economic matters have dominated our discussion. In a wider historical context, however, the political problem can be regarded as an economic one, not just in terms of the constraints of an export-led growth model[2] itself but rather in those of the dualism and dependency of the class structure which resulted from it, creating a social structure upon which it was virtually impossible to establish a hegemonic capitalist state.[3]

Although the failure of successive governments to achieve sustained capitalist expansion have been stressed in these pages, we should not overlook the very real achievements of the period. Despite the failure to overcome external dependency and establish an endogenous growth dynamic, or to overcome internal dualism and improve the relative incomes of the poorer strata, or to sustain industrialization into the final stages of import substitution, considerable progress was made towards economic development in general and the restructuring of capital in particular between 1956 and 1978. First, a process of industrialization did take place; even though manufacturing remained largely unintegrated to the rest of the economy it did become a sector of substantial proportions yielding a value of production greater than that of the primary sector and supplying all the consumption goods and much of the intermediate inputs required by the economy. Second, the grosser aspects of external dependence manifested by foreign ownership of the very basis of production and trade were removed; much of what remained sprang from the continued integration of the economy to the international capitalist system and the immediate problem of external debt. Third, the corporate sector was reorganized so as to link its constituent elements together on the basis of inter-sectoral transactions and an effective system of central planning instituted. The fact that the economy did not literally collapse under the impact of the balance of payments crisis between 1976 and 1978 is testimony to this. Fourth, and perhaps of most moment in the long run if not in the short, the social structure of the rural sector was fundamentally changed by the agrarian reform, a matter of more concern for half the population and the long-run development of the Peruvian economy than any other policy measure. On the one hand, the transfer of corporate agriculture to cooperatives should assure their modernization and higher accumulation in processing activities which will help to integrate the rural economy; on the other the removal of the traditional rural elite should result in a new social dynamic in the countryside, and even a revival in peasant production in the long run, particularly if more state resources are devoted to food production.

Despite the failure to establish a new and stable model of accumulation based on state capitalism and a comprehensive system of worker participation in the profits and management of corporate enterprise, there was progress on these two fronts too. The Peruvian state, which had existed as hardly more than an apparatus for repressing labour and negotiating with foreign powers before the

1950s, became the main provider of welfare services and industrial infrastructure during our period and the major investor and controller of foreign trade by the end of it. In the process, the state was greatly strengthened both as an administrative and planning unit and as a negotiator with foreign capital. The labour movement, after forty years of APRA control, finally attained a degree of class consciousness during our period and the attempts at introducing worker participation, far from breaking up trades union solidarity, strengthened it by demonstrating that the relevant aim was not higher wages but rather control over production. These two 'progressive elements' eventually came together in the industrial conflicts within public enterprises, the general strike of July 1977 which clearly defined the class nature of state capitalism and the electoral gains of the left in June 1978. In this sense, Peruvian politics 'came of age'.

In view of Peru's own somewhat slow economic and social development in the past, particularly in comparison with the experience of her continental neighbours, these achievements are not inconsiderable. In essence they add up to the modernization of Peruvian capitalism – albeit a somewhat lopsided modernization – and more specifically to the construction of a solid foundation for national development based on the productive use of foreign exchange earnings, '*desarrollo hacia adentro*' and coherent domestic control over the evolving structure of production rather than a continued reliance on growth impulses from abroad. For those who would only consider a 'transition to socialism' as equivalent to development (or define 'development' in terms such as to effectively make socialism part of it), then the Peruvian experience over the last twenty years may well seem unpromising, but to employ such a criterion is to logically imply that the economic and political preconditions for such a transition were at least potentially present, which was patently not true for Peru. Apart from the immediate circumstances such as the debilitating effects of APRA control of popular movements for much of the period and the role of the military throughout, there are deeper structural reasons for this absence. In the classical scheme of things, only the full maturity of capitalism will bring the extension of capitalist relations of production to (and thus the proletarianization of) the whole national workforce and the concentration of capital sufficient to bring about a breakdown by internal contradiction.[4] Clearly, such a stage of 'mature' monopoly capitalism has not been reached by Peru, and indeed the internal dualism produced by unbalanced capitalist growth limited the scope of the ownership reforms. Alternatively, the modern experience of revolution on the periphery of the world economy – in underdeveloped nations, that is – would seem to indicate that for countries at very early stages of capitalism, where the overthrow of feudal rural structures permits popular control of both state and economy, a transition to socialism may also be possible, particularly if associated with a struggle for independence. But for a country like Peru at the 'half way stage' so to speak, neither of these necessary conditions – let alone sufficient ones – obtain. The relevant criterion for judgement must be therefore, as we pointed out at the beginning of this study, the extent to which national capitalism develops, and this is the criterion we have attempted to apply.

The parallel to the Peruvian experience between 1968 and 1975 that first comes to the mind of many scholars[5] is that of Mexico under Lázaro Cárdenas between 1934 and 1940. Without going into this in any depth,[6] we can identify a number of points that throw light upon the Peruvian case. In the wake of the Mexican Revolution, despite the destruction of the agrarian oligarchy by the popular agrarian movements of Villa and Zapata, these movements were unable to form a stable government and were themselves suppressed by Carranza and Obregón. In this political vacuum, it took the military–bureaucratic elite a decade to build a national state. This state apparatus, consolidated by Calles between 1925 and 1930, had two main strengths: a political base in the form of a corporativist party (the *Partido Revolucionario Institucional*) and the extensive fiscal and financial reforms which gave the public sector economic independence. The subsequent 'intermediate regime'[7] of Cárdenas managed to reduce substantially the degree of foreign ownership in mining, oil, finance and public utilities as well as complement the land reform by starting a massive programme of irrigation works and transportation networks. The differences between this and the Peruvian experience after 1968 are instructive. In the first place, the Mexican land reform was initially a spontaneous movement arising from the pressure of tenant farmers and landless labour upon the decaying haciendas, as opposed to the Peruvian land reform which although more sweeping (in the sense of eliminating all private capitalist farmers of any significant size) was imposed from above and in which rural mass movements were deliberately suppressed from the outset. In the Mexican case the peasant movement was eventually contained and subjugated to the state, but by channelling it through the PRI (to which were added representatives of small business and urban labour) the relative autonomy of the state from both domestic capital and labour was guaranteed. This the Peruvian military never achieved, SINAMOS being only a half-hearted attempt to capitalize on the reforms and generate the populist support which would have been so useful during the 1976–77 economic crisis. In the second place, the foreign mines, oilwells and power facilities nationalized by Cárdenas did not operate at high levels of technology, so that the natural resource base could be nationalized without the need to return to the multinationals for cooperation to assure further expansion, as occurred in the Peruvian case. Indeed, the expansion of the Mexican economy during this period was based on the extension of irrigated agriculture without foreign investment. Further, in the absence of a major industrial sector, there was little need for foreign technology or imported inputs. In the third place, and as a consequence of the destruction of the agrarian oligarchy, the lack of a strong financial or industrial elite and the sharply reduced presence of foreign capital, the Mexican state enjoyed a far greater autonomy – particularly in the external sphere – than Peru, where by 1968 agriculture was no longer central to the economy,[8] the industrial sector was already quite large and the corporate sector reliant upon foreign technology.

If a parallel is to be found in Peruvian economic (but not political) history to Cárdenas, then the nearest resemblance would be in the Bustamante regime at which point in time had the Aprista plans for the cooperativization of agriculture been carried through in what was still predominantly a rural economy, the effects might have been similar to those of Mexico. However, and this is perhaps the most interesting point to be drawn from the comparison, the rapid industrialization process for which *cardenismo* had laid the foundations served to reconstitute a capitalist class structure based on a new urban bourgeoisie and proletariat, and reintroduced extensive external ownership through foreign investment in manufacturing. The relative autonomy of the Mexican state from domestic and foreign capital was steadily reduced after 1945, so that when towards the end of the 1960s economic growth began to decline and social conditions deteriorate as the result of unbalanced development, the reformist expansion of the public sector under Echeverría (1970–76) met massive resistance from multinationals and banking groups. The blocking of tax reform and currency speculation severely weakened the economic basis of the Mexican state and prevented it from carrying out the restructuring of capital necessary for continued economic development.

What, then, of the future of the Peruvian economy? Such forecasts are hazardous, if not foolhardy, for embarrassing changes – embarrassing to the author, that is – can arise even before the date of publication. Against this, it can be argued that if the analysis of an economy has any merit then its future course is implicit in that analysis. Fluctuations on international markets or events in the metropolitan economies themselves can have random effects on the periphery (indeed this is the essence of 'dependency' in Dos Santos' definition[9]) but the main constraints upon and options open for economic growth in a particular country should be identifiable. Complete withdrawal from the international capitalist system is presumably not a realistic option for Peru, not only because of the political prerequisites but because the maintenance of the existing productive system is crucially dependent upon foreign trade. Nonetheless, there are two major structural phenomena which must influence if not determine the future course of the Peruvian economy. The first is the fact that now that the Cuajone and Cerro Verde projects are 'on stream' there are no foreseen or foreseeable natural resource projects to significantly increase the supply of foreign exchange needed to sustain industrialization or even economic growth itself. There appear to be no immediately feasible major mining projects after these two, fishmeal is exhausted, oil will only be enough for domestic requirements and irrigated land on the coast is needed for domestic food production. In consequence, the economy may well be forced inwards upon itself for continued expansion, for there seems to be little prospect of a successful export drive based on Peruvian manufacturing.[10] The second is the continued neglect of peasant agriculture which, if continued, will give rise to continued internal migration and worsening conditions in the urban slums as manufacturing has already shown itself incapable of providing enough employment. Although the problem of food supply to the towns might conceivably be resolved by capitalizing the cooperatives, the alternative of modernizing peasant agriculture may eventually be forced upon the government in order to stem the migratory flow. This will require a massive diversion of resources away from the corporate sector if average rural incomes are to be raised again to anything like the parity with average urban wages obtaining at the outset of our period, to the detriment of the short- but not necessarily the long-run objective interests of urban groups. These two phenomena – the exhaustion of the natural resource export base and the need to restore the dynamic of food agriculture – may well combine therefore not only to turn the economy away from '*desarrollo hacia afuera*' but also to make a different industrialization model necessary. On the one hand, the lack of foreign exchange will probably force a reduction on the reliance of industry upon imported inputs and the development of the capital goods branches established in recent years; on the other, the new agricultural input requirements and the rising rural demand for wage goods should allow industry to expand both consumer and intermediate branches on the basis of existing technology. If stagnation is to be overcome, this path alone would seem to be the only way of maintaining growth in the Peruvian economy: the positive consequences for employment and independence would not have to be the object of the exercise, but would serve to legitimize such a strategy politically. In addition, such a change of course would presumably be made less difficult by the strength gained by the Peruvian state and the achievement of agrarian reform. In this way, the restructuring of capital that was successively attempted in Peru between 1956 and 1978 might eventually be achieved in the 1980s, and the basis for economic development secured by necessity rather than invention.

This somewhat optimistic outlook notwithstanding, the experience of the Peruvian political economy between 1956 and 1978 would seem to indicate an inescapable conclusion, albeit a trite one: that capitalism has its own logic. On the periphery of the world economy, successful capitalist industrialization – of which Brazil and Mexico are the best (if not the only) examples in Latin America – requires the freedom for domestic capital to work out its own compromise with manufacturing multinationals, supported rather than rivalled by the public sector, and with a labour force contained by a hegemonic state, itself underpinned either by the military or a strong party system. These political conditions are as important as a healthy agricultural sector, low wages, a large domestic market and adequate fiscal resources. Attempts to restructure capital and achieve economic development through capitalist industrialization on the basis of other arrangements – such as a weak state (Prado), reliance on domestic capital alone (Belaunde) or opposition to foreign capital (Velasco) – appear to be inconsistent and probably destined to fail, if the Peruvian experience is at all generalizable. This conclusion is, of course, a gross oversimplification, but seems to lie at the core of the problem and contain the essence of what 'one nation can learn from another' in this case.

Statistical appendix

This appendix contains some of the statistical series upon which the more important tables in the text are based. They include accumulation (savings and investment), public finance and foreign capital flows – all based on the estimates provided by the Central Reserve Bank of Peru for national accounts purposes. The calculations of the estimates of dualism and ownership are also given, set within the national accounts framework. In this way the key quantitative indicators used in this book have been brought within a single framework so that they are not only as correct as possible but also mutually consistent.

Since 1946, the Central Bank (the *Banco Central de Reserva del Perú*) has been responsible for the compilation of national accounts, and the first estimates were produced for the late 1940s and 1950s in the form of *La Renta Nacional* (Lima, various years) but with a somewhat idiosyncratic methodology. The Central Bank embarked upon a new set of national accounts in 1963, working with IMF help from the basis of the 1961 Census. The BCR national accounts department (in which Richard Webb Duarte was to play a prominent part) produced over the next ten years the *Cuentas Nacionales del Perú 1950–65* (Lima, 1966), *Cuentas Nacionales del Perú 1950–67* (Lima, 1967), and the *Cuentas Nacionales del Perú 1960–74* (Lima, 1976). With the valuable *Anexo Estadístico 1960–69* (Lima, 1970) and the *Anuario Estadístico Económico y Financiero 1963–73* (Lima, 1975), these make up the '*cuentas nacionales*' mentioned in the text. The BCR *Memoria* (annual) and the *Boletín* (monthly) give some financial, external trade and national accounts data, but unfortunately with considerable delay. For this study, unpublished data for 1970–78 have been obtained directly from the BCR, being the best estimates available as of late 1978.

These publications represent the successive updating of the estimates of national income aggregates available in Peru (themselves the only consistent reconciliation of the various sectoral statistics) and are noted for their helpful definitional footnotes. Nonetheless, for all their excellence as estimates in 1965, neither the scope nor the methodology of these national accounts has been modified since, which is unfortunate. Although the Instituto Nacional de Planificación did attempt to construct an alternative series in the mid 1960s, this was not continued. The Instituto Nacional de Estadística (which as the Officina Nacional de Estadística y Censos until 1975 produced the valuable and comprehensive *Anuario Estadístico*) took over the national accounting function from the Central Bank in 1976 using the United Nations 'new SNA' methodology and working from the results of the 1973 Census; but the results have yet to be published.

Savings and investment

The series for savings and investment is derived from Tables 5 and 16 of the *Cuentas Nacionales*, divided through by gross domestic product and shown in Table A.1 as a percentage. As is usual in national accounts for developing countries, the set is derived from the estimate for gross fixed capital formation, itself based on the imports and local production of capital goods (machinery and construction materials) with an appropriate 'mark-up' for installation costs. Fixed investment relates, therefore, to the corporate sector in the main – as does our sectoral breakdown in Chapter 6. From this is subtracted the known figure for public sector fixed capital formation to give the private amount, and to this is added an estimate of stock variations derived from a special survey of corporate enterprise carried out annually by the Central Bank to give gross capital formation.

Gross capital formation is, by definition, equivalent to gross national savings. Subtracting 'external savings' (i.e. current account deficit on the balance of payments as defined by the excess of imports over exports of goods and services in the composition of GDP) gives domestic savings. From this is then subtracted government savings (i.e. the surplus of the current income of general government over its current expenditure) to give non-government savings; company savings (i.e. undistributed profits and depreciation allowances derived from the Central Bank survey and including state enterprise) are deducted in turn to give personal savings. This last item is therefore the result of adding up and subtracting a long string of approximate estimates, and has little reliability. We have here divided 'external savings' as given in the national accounts into a 'public' and 'private' figure; we have defined the former as the official capital inflows, net of amortization, as given in the balance of payments (see Table A.3 below); the 'private' figure in the table is then the difference between this and 'external savings', which means that in effect not only are the long-term capital flows to and from the private sector included but also the 'errors and omissions' item in the balance of payments statistics (which is mostly covert capital flight) and any residual changes in the reserve position of the Central Bank, which are by implication required to equilibrate the foreign exchange balance of the private sector because public sector imports are covered automatically by long-term credits.

Table A.1 (per cent of GDP at current prices)

	Domestic savings			Foreign finance		Total saving or investment	GFCF		Stock variation
	Company	Personal	Govt	Public	Private		Public	Private	
1955	9.1	5.7	2.4	3.4	2.0	22.6	3.9	14.7	4.0
1956	9.4	9.6	1.2	0.3	5.5	26.0	2.9	20.4	2.7
1957	8.9	10.4	1.1	0.6	7.1	28.0	2.4	22.3	3.3
1958	7.7	10.2	0.2	0.5	6.7	25.3	2.5	20.3	2.5
1959	8.6	7.3	0.8	−0.4	2.5	18.8	1.7	16.0	1.1
1960	11.2	8.7	2.6	−0.4	−0.5	21.6	2.3	14.4	4.9
1961	10.0	9.4	2.5	−0.3	0.6	22.2	4.4	14.8	3.0
1962	10.9	8.6	1.9	0.7	0.7	22.8	3.8	16.8	2.2
1963	10.8	5.9	1.0	0.2	2.5	20.4	3.9	14.9	1.6
1964	12.8	6.5	−0.2	0.2	−0.6	18.7	4.8	11.1	2.8
1965	13.8	2.4	−0.4	2.9	−0.1	18.6	5.3	11.4	1.9
1966	14.2	2.7	−0.4	2.6	1.0	20.1	5.1	11.4	3.6
1967	12.4	3.2	−1.0	2.0	3.1	19.7	4.0	10.9	4.8
1968	13.7	0.1	−0.4	1.9	−1.4	13.9	3.8	9.2	0.9
1969	10.5	1.4	2.0	2.6	−3.2	13.3	4.2	8.2	0.9
1970	11.9	3.2	1.9	1.8	−5.9	12.9	4.5	7.0	0.5
1971	12.9	2.4	0.5	1.9	−2.7	15.0	4.8	7.8	2.4
1972	12.9	1.5	0.5	1.8	−2.6	14.2	5.0	7.8	1.4
1973	11.3	4.2	−0.3	3.8	−3.8	15.7	5.5	7.2	3.0
1974	11.5	1.4	0.6	6.7	−1.3	18.9	8.3	6.9	3.7
1975	8.7 }		1.2	6.3	3.5	19.7	8.8	8.7	2.2
1976	12.0 }		−0.3	3.6	2.5	17.8	8.0	8.6	1.2
1977	13.2 }		−2.5	4.5	−0.1	15.1	7.2	7.4	0.5
1978*		14.5 }		2.8	−2.7	14.6	5.0	8.1	0.5

* Estimate

Fiscal account

The fiscal account series is based in the first place upon Table 12 of the *Cuentas Nacionales* (income and expenditure of general government) divided through by GDP, the figures for 1973–78 being provided directly by the BCR national accounts department. Central government GFCF is also given in Table 12 of the *Cuentas* and in the *Memoria,* and that for state enterprise taken from INP (1966), the BCR *Anuario Estadístico* (*op. cit.*) and the BCR *Memoria 1976.* The *Anuario* and BCR (direct) are the sources for state enterprise funds (profits plus depreciation). 'Financial investment' is the financial investment of the central government (*Memoria,* various years) plus the increase in long-term credits extended by the state development banks to the private sector in each year, given in the BCR *Boletín;* this then gives us total public sector investment.

The difference between the public sector surplus on current account (which is the 'government savings' item in Table A.1 plus state enterprise funds) and total state investment gives the public sector financing requirement as we have defined it in this study, which is naturally a much more comprehensive concept that the central government deficit, and indicates much more clearly the total amount of resources the state must acquire from outside the fiscal sector in order to balance its books – a definition particularly apposite for the Peruvian case since 1968 where it was the state enterprises rather than central government which expanded so fast. The sources of finance to cover this deficit are internal finance (monetary issue and domestic borrowing) and external (foreign) finance. The latter we have already calculated for Table A.1, and the former is then the difference: in this way we avoid having to disentangle the complex web of suppliers credits, government paper issues and state enterprise overdrafts while sticking as closely as possible to real resource movements. The negative items on the domestic and foreign finance figures represent reductions in public sector liabilities resulting from the excess of amortization over new obligations.

Long-term capital inflows

The capital inflows shown in the table are taken from the *Cuentas* (Table 16) for 1955–74; the *Memoria* for 1975–76 and directly from the BCR for 1976. The data is recorded originally by the Central Bank as part of its exchange control function. As these are long-term capital flows (i.e. with a maturity of a year or more) they do not involve short movements, a restriction which mainly affects the private sector. It should be noted that the gross inflow of funds for the public sector, particularly in 1969–76, contains a considerable amount of 'refinancing', that is, of the postponement of amortization otherwise due ('rolling over'), equivalent to some US $60 millions a year between 1969 and 1971 and US $120 millions a year between 1972 and

Table A.2 (per cent of GDP)

	Current general govt. Income	Current general govt. Expenditure	GFCF Central Govt	GFCF Other	Financial investment	Enterprise surplus	Financing requirement	Finance Internal	Finance External
1955	13.2	10.8	3.4	0.5	0.7	0.0	2.2	-1.2	3.4
1956	13.9	12.7	2.4	0.5	0.9	0.0	2.6	2.3	0.3
1957	13.9	12.8	1.9	0.5	0.8	0.0	2.1	1.5	0.6
1958	12.4	12.2	2.2	0.3	0.7	0.0	3.0	2.5	0.5
1959	13.5	12.9	1.5	0.2	0.6	0.0	1.7	2.1	-0.4
1960	14.9	12.3	1.2	1.1	0.5	0.0	0.2	0.6	-0.4
1961	15.8	13.3	1.9	2.5	0.6	0.0	2.5	2.8	-0.3
1962	15.5	13.6	2.0	1.8	0.4	0.0	2.3	1.5	0.7
1963	17.0	16.0	1.3	2.6	1.1	0.0	4.0	3.8	0.2
1964	17.1	17.3	1.9	2.9	0.7	0.0	5.7	5.5	0.2
1965	17.8	18.2	2.6	2.7	1.1	0.0	7.0	4.1	2.9
1966	17.8	18.2	3.1	2.0	1.7	0.1	7.1	5.5	2.6
1967	17.7	18.7	2.4	1.6	1.7	0.1	6.6	4.6	2.0
1968	18.0	18.4	1.8	2.0	0.9	0.0	5.1	3.2	1.9
1969	18.8	16.8	1.9	2.3	0.6	0.8	2.0	-0.6	2.6
1970	18.9	17.0	2.6	1.9	0.5	0.9	2.2	0.4	1.8
1971	18.5	18.0	3.1	1.8	1.2	1.1	4.4	2.5	1.9
1972	18.8	18.3	3.0	2.0	1.7	0.8	5.4	3.8	1.8
1973	18.3	18.6	2.4	3.1	2.4	0.9	7.3	3.5	3.8
1974	19.1	18.5	2.9	5.4	2.7	0.3	10.1	3.4	6.7
1975	19.5	18.3	2.8	6.0	2.6	-0.6	10.8	4.5	6.3
1976	17.7	18.0	2.8	5.2	3.2	-0.3	13.0	9.4	3.6
1977	17.4	19.8	3.8	3.4	2.0	1.3	11.6	7.1	4.5

Table A.3 (US $ millions)

	Direct investment	Private sector Loan capital Inflow	Private sector Loan capital Amortization	Public sector Official loans Inflow	Public sector Official loans Amortization	Other inflows•	Total long capital	Current account balance
1956	41	10	−1	27	−18	−2	57	−99
1957	51	48	−2	28	−20	1	107	−143
1958	30	62	−2	24	−19	3	98	−123
1959	18	35	−4	16	−20	−3	42	−36
1960	22	17	−12	13	−24	2	18	+8
1961	14	21	−31	25	−29	−4	−4	−8
1962	16	27	−25	51	−31	2	40	−36
1963	−5	33	−24	77	−30	0	51	−81
1964	11	24	−24	89	−30	13	83	+16
1965	32	44	−27	98	−22	48	177	−138
1966	23	6	−12	204	−67	−2	152	−228
1967	−18	55	−18	184	−54	−3	96	−282
1968	−23	41	−31	218	−131	−6	68	−41
1969	19	25	−24	221	−89	−9	143	0
1970	−79	28	−26	190	−121	31	30	+185
1971	−50	66	−59	183	−56	−13	−29	−34
1972	24	25	−54	286	−164	−1	115	−32
1973	49	63	−43	672	−352	−6	383	−192
1974	144	111	−53	1035	−338	−4	895	−807
1975	316	27 }		1077	−284	−1	1135	−1538
1976	171	25 }		846	−299	−68	675	−1192
1977	54	15 }		993	−391	−6	665	−811
1978†	52	10 }		1016	−642	−4	432	−421

• Includes 'variations in overseas assets' of the public sector.
† Estimates.

1975. The deficit on the current account of the balance of payments is included for illustrative purposes; the difference between this and the net capital inflow being short-term funds and monetary adjustments. 'Other' public sector inflows include state bank borrowing not registered with the Dirección General de Crédito Público, nationalization compensation payments and revaluation of overseas assets.

Economic indicators

These indicators are compiled from the *Cuentas Nacionales* updated by INE/BCR, and most are self-explanatory. The internal terms of trade have been calculated as the ratio of the implicit deflators for agriculture and industry in the national accounts, themselves the result of dividing the sectoral contribution to national income by the constant price series for the sectoral contribution to GNP for 1955–68 and the ratio of current to constant price sectoral contributions to GDP for 1969–76. This is a defective index at best, but probably indicates the trends adequately enough in the absence of direct price series for manufactures and farm prices. Similarly, there is no official estimate of dollar price indices for imports and exports on a continuing basis: here we have calculated the external terms of trade as the ratio of the GDP deflators (1963 = 100 for 1955–70, 1970 = 100 for 1970–76) for exports and imports of goods and services – this does not involve the parity problem, of course.

Estimation of dualism

As a central element in the argument presented in this book is the existence of dualism in the Peruvian economy – a dichotomy represented by capitalist 'corporate' and household 'non-corporate' forms of organization of production but not by a functional separation – it is clearly necessary to assess the extent of this phenomenon in quantitative terms, which requires considerable over-simplification of reality. The problems of theoretical and practical definition have been discussed at some length in Chapters 2 and 4; here the basis for estimation is that enterprises of five employees or more are to be counted as 'corporate'. Below this size one cannot really argue that an enterprise is a corporate one in the sense of a formal distinction between management and workers, wages and profits, or even a proper accounting framework – and in any case the law would probably not recognize it as such. (Indeed the legal minimum for trades union recognition at the plant level in Peru is twenty employees.) Further, and very importantly from our point of view, this is the borderline used in the Census material and thus data are available for it. In practice, moreover, given that a borderline is to be drawn, raising it to (say) ten employees would not overly affect our figures and still less the overall argument.

Here we take each sector in turn and calculate the shares of employment and output accruing to the corporate sector, the remainder being attributed to the non-corporate sector. This fraction is then applied to the share of employment and output in GDP for that production sector in the *Cuentas Nacionales* for that year, which form the row totals in Table A.5 below.

(i) It is assumed that *mining, utilities, government* and *banking* all take place in the corporate sector only, as these are all large-scale activities.

(ii) *Agricultural* output is allocated on the assumption that all 'industrial' crops (e.g. sugar, cotton, etc.) and livestock are produced on corporate farms, and all foodcrops by peasants, the value added share being allocated *pro rata* to the proportion of sales shown in the agricultural production statistics in the BCR *Anuario*. This would tend to somewhat underestimate the corporate share as foodcrops are produced on large estates, but this is slightly offset by the fact that the sales proportion does not allow for inputs, which would reduce the corporate value added share. Employment shares have been calculated on the basis of the employment figures in the *Cuentas*, 'employees' being allocated to the corporate sector and 'agricultural independents' not.

(iii) *Fishing* output is divided between industrial and human-consumption output, attributing only the former to the corporate sector, which is an underestimate, and employment in industrial fishing at the two dates from Roemer (1970) and Malpica (1976) respectively.

(iv) *Manufacturing* estimates are much easier, as the *Estadística Industrial* gives a breakdown between 'factory' and 'artisan' production and employment on the same basis as ours. See Table 9.6.

(v) *Construction* output has been roughly divided up on the basis of the share of total sectoral sales (from the 1969 input–output table) recorded by members of the *Cámera Peruana de Constructores* being allocated to the corporate sector; the employment share has been arbitrarily allocated one half to each sector.

(vi) The shares of employment and sales in the *commercial* sector, attributable to firms of five employees or more, is given in the 1963 Economic Census (Appendix IV); this assumed constant over the period.

(vii) In the absence of any other information, we have assumed that the corporate sector accounted for twenty per cent of employment and thirty per cent of output in *transport* and *services*. These are both very conservative estimates, and thus probably understate the extent of duality in these two sectors.

For the Lima–Callao proportions of the total workforce (see Table 4.12) we have INP (1973a). Output has been allocated as follows:

Table A.4

	A	B	C	D	E	F	G	H	I	J	K	L	M	N
1955	5.0	281	295	23	18	4.9	103	118	2.4	9.1	52	19.0	14.1	9.8
1956	4.6	320	342	26	22	7.0	104	114	-4.5	2.6	67	19.0	14.5	9.8
1957	1.0	332	402	28	25	8.6	104	106	0.4	8.8	34	19.0	14.2	10.0
1958	3.4	292	345	25	22	7.7	89	105	7.3	-3.1	31	24.5	13.5	10.4
1959	3.5	322	281	19	17	12.9	86	96	5.2	8.1	59	27.7	14.3	10.5
1960	9.1	444	341	22	19	10.1	92	93	6.8	13.8	50	26.8	14.5	10.8
1961	8.1	510	429	22	18	3.7	90	98	3.7	10.4	84	26.8	15.6	11.4
1962	9.2	556	478	23	19	5.4	94	93	5.0	10.3	108	26.8	13.8	12.0
1963	3.8	555	510	20	16	5.8	100	100	-2.1	7.0	126	26.8	14.1	12.4
1964	6.9	647	518	19	14	13.0	114	100	4.2	9.4	151	26.8	13.6	12.7
1965	4.8	685	660	19	13	13.4	111	107	0.0	7.9	166	26.8	12.6	13.0
1966	5.8	789	811	20	15	12.3	126	120	1.3	9.8	156	26.8	12.3	13.2
1967	1.6	742	810	20	15	12.2	127	114	2.0	5.0	149	39.7	12.5	13.7
1968	0.7	840	673	14	10	17.9	130	113	-6.5	2.7	140	43.4	12.4	12.7
1969	4.4	880	659	13	9	7.8	143	105	5.6	1.6	191	43.6	12.5	12.7
1970	9.0	1034	700	13	8	6.6	159	100	7.9	10.7	372	43.4	13.7	13.2
1971	5.1	889	730	15	10	3.8	146	102	2.4	8.8	349	43.4	13.8	14.1
1972	5.8	944	812	14	9	4.9	133	117	0.8	7.4	522	43.4	14.9	14.9
1973	6.2	1112	1033	16	9	14.7	163	116	2.4	7.3	535	43.4	14.8	16.1
1974	6.9	1052	1908	19	10	16.6	178	119	2.3	7.5	810	43.4	15.1	16.5
1975	3.3	1291	2390	20	10	20.0	155	132	1.0	4.7	431	43.9	14.4	16.4
1976	3.0	1359	2100	18	10	34.5	155	136	3.3	4.2	307	57.5	12.6	15.2
1977	-1.2	1768	2095	15	8	38.0	147	..	-0.2	-6.4	282	87.5	10.9	12.2
1978*	-1.8	2082	1974	15	8	55.2	128	..	0.4	-4.6	..	..	..	10.5

A GDP growth at 1970 prices, per cent per annum; 1955–59 at 1963 prices.
B Exports f.o.b. (US $ millions).
C Imports f.o.b. (US $ millions); the Peruvian authorities estimate the c.i.f. value by adding 20 per cent to the f.o.b. value.
D Total capital formation as a percentage of GDP.
E Private capital formation as a percentage of GDP.
F Prices: change in GDP deflator; 1963 =100.
G External terms of trade; 1963 =100.
H Internal terms of trade; 1963 = 100.
I Agricultural output growth; per cent per annum.
J Manufacturing output growth; per cent per annum.
K Reserves: US $ million in gold and foreign currency at year-end.
L Exchange rate: trading parity in soles per US dollar, average for year.
M Money supply: *'medios de pago en moneda nacional'* (equivalent to 'M_1'), as per cent of GDP.
N Total earnings per head of *obreros* (see Table 6.10) in thousand soles at 1963 prices.
   The 1963 level is equivalent to US $ 463 at that date.

• Preliminary estimate

agriculture, fishing and mining outside Lima, government within; industry from Table 9.6; banking in proportion to the regional allocation of credit (BCR *Memoria*); all other sectors *pro rata* to these. Employment was then allocated for the corporate sector in proportion to the division of corporate output in each production sector between Lima–Callao and the rest of the country.

Table A.5 (per mille of GDP)

	1968 Corporate	1968 Non-corp.	1968 Total	1975 Corporate	1975 Non-corp.	1975 Total
Output:						
Agriculture	58	88	146	58	69	127
Fishing	23	3	26	6	1	7
Mining	88	—	88	60	—	60
Manufacturing	211	25	236	235	27	262
Construction	15	23	38	25	36	61
Utilities	11	—	11	11	—	11
Banking	28	—	28	35	—	35
Government	85	—	85	77	—	77
Transport	15	37	52	17	38	55
Commerce	85	46	131	100	50	150
Services	48	111	159	47	108	155
Total	667	333	1000	671	329	1000
Absolute total (billion soles at 1970 prices)	143	71	214	211	104	313
Employment:						
Agriculture	103	367	470	95	335	430
Fishing	13	2	15	10	2	12
Mining	22	—	22	23	—	23
Manufacturing	48	90	138	50	92	142
Construction	19	20	39	22	22	44
Utilities	3	—	3	4	—	4
Banking	7	—	7	7	—	7
Government	67	—	67	76	—	76
Transport	7	26	33	7	28	35
Commerce	40	60	100	46	69	115
Services	21	85	106	22	90	112
Total	347	653	1000	359	641	1000
Absolute total (millions)	1.36	2.57	3.93	1.69	3.02	4.71

The pattern of ownership

Having derived the share of output and employment to be attributed to the corporate sector, we can now move on to the ownership pattern, which changed dramatically between 1968 and 1975. The sources for the shares have already been discussed in Chapter 5, and are as follows:

(i) Corporate *agriculture* had foreign ownership (in the sense of ownership by foreign companies, as opposed to foreigners resident in Peru, whom we count as domestic capital) only by Grace (sugar) and the highland estates of the Cerro de Pasco corporation, and these cannot have generated more than two per cent of GDP in 1968; all corporate ownership is in the cooperative sector by 1975;

(ii) Corporate *fishing* was approximately a third foreign in 1968 (Malpica, 1976), and all state by 1975;

(iii) *Mining* is allocated according to the shares of the various companies in total sectoral sales, '*pequeña minería*' is taken to be all domestic capital – sources in Chapter 5;

(iv) *Manufacturing* ownership in 1968 is assumed proportional to asset ownership (Table 9.7) – the 1975 figure assumes complete state ownership of heavy industrial branches and a token entry for cooperatives (such as textiles from the bankrupt Prado group) and *propiedad social*;

(v) *Utilities* were a third foreign owned (Espinoza, 1972) in 1968 but all taken over by the state for the 1975 figure;

(vi) *Banking* allocated *pro rata* to the shares of various banks in market credit, see Chapter 6;

(vii) *Government* is no problem!

(viii) *Construction, transport* and *commerce* and *services* are conservative estimates by the author.

The employment shares are shown in Table 5.4, and are calculated by allocating the workforce for the corporate sector of that production branch *pro rata* to the proportion of production controlled by that ownership form. The figure for 1950 is a rough estimate derived by applying the same ownership pattern as in 1968 except for lower foreign penetration of mining, manufacturing and banking, and no state involvement except in banking and government; the private sector is the residual.

Table A.6 (per mille of GDP)

	1968				1975				
	State Sector	Foreign capital	Domestic capital	Corporate sector	State sector	Foreign capital	Domestic capital	Cooperatives	Corporate sector
Agriculture	—	2	56	58	—	—	—	58	58
Fishing	—	8	15	23	5	—	1	—	6
Mining	—	74	14	88	26	22	12	—	60
Manufacturing	10	92	109	211	45	80	104	6	235
Construction	—	2	13	15	—	3	22	—	25
Utilities	3	4	4	11	11	—	—	—	11
Banking	7	14	7	28	23	1	11	—	35
Government	85	—	—	85	77	—	—	—	77
Transport	1	1	13	15	3	—	10	4	17
Commerce	—	15	70	85	10	5	80	5	100
Services	5	5	38	48	10	—	32	5	46
Total	111	217	339	667	210	111	272	78	671

Notes

1 It is difficult to define precisely what is meant by the 'mainstream' although, like the elephant, most observers can recognize it when they see it. The articles in, say, the *Journal of Development Studies* are a good measure of the current, while two standard textbooks, Kindleberger (1958) and Todaro (1977) are representative tidemarks. The former concentrates on GDP growth per head as the object in view and aggregate capital formation, trade and foreign investment as the means of achieving it, while the latter stresses income distribution and intersectoral integration as aims and the choice of appropriate technology, employment of surplus labour and reduction of external dependency as means.

2 Schumpeter, writing as early as 1911, makes this point: 'By "development", therefore, we shall understand only such changes in [the] economic life [of a nation] as are not forced upon it from without but arise by its own initiative, from within . . . Nor will mere growth of the economy, as shown by the growth of population and wealth, be designated here as a process of development' (1961, p. 63).

3 See Chapter 2.

4 This is the 'motto' of the well-known proposal for the future of development economics in Seers (1963).

5 'Most of the theorizing on economic development has been done by economists who live and were trained in the industrial west. Almost all . . . are ignorant of much of the economic history of the countries about which they are theorizing' (Griffin, 1969, p. 19).

6 See the introductory chapters to, respectively: Roemer (1970), Pike (1967) and Lowenthal (1975).

7 In any case, there already exist excellent monographs on most of the main Peruvian production sectors, as we shall see, and the first major study of Peruvian economic history over the past century has recently been published as Thorp & Bertram (1978).

8 See Chapter 2.

9 See Chapter 3.

10 See Chapter 4.

11 See Chapter 5.

12 See Chapter 6.

13 See Chapter 7.

14 See Chapter 8.

15 See Chapter 9.

16 That is, those that impede its normal expansion, as opposed to its 'fundamental' long-run contradiction. As for this latter, Napoleoni (1975, p. 5) points out that: 'simple state intervention is quite unable to resolve the fundamental disequilibrium of the system – that of the alienation of the worker from his product – for this disequilibrium is rooted in the nature of material production associated with the capitalistic relationship'.

Notes to Chapter 2

1 Here we are using the term in the broad sense in which it is now commonly employed; we shall discuss its particular role in Latinamerican thought later on.

2 Baran (1957)

3 Frank (1967).

4 Broadly defined as the difference between the material output of the economy and the basic consumption requirements of the workforce.

5 Literally 'third world-ist'.

6 O'Brien (1975) p. 12.

7 The key work here is Emmanuel (1972).

8 Barret-Brown (1974) Chapter 10. The point here is that although the working class at the centre cannot *directly* extract a surplus from the periphery by acting in the commodity markets – which is self-evident – it certainly can benefit indirectly from its extraction by the metropolitan bourgeoisie and also from the speedier growth of productive forces which this extraction makes possible.

9 The best critique is probably Palloix (1971) – the publication dates for Emmanuel and Palloix in English are in reverse order to their French originals.

10 See particularly Amin (1974), of which this is the title, but also Kay (1975) who examines the way in which merchant capital drew out surplus without modernizing the mode of production, and argues that the subsequent strategy of industrialization only reinforced the conditions of underdevelopment so created.

11 Although indeed some variant of the dependency model is now incorporated in orthodox interpretations of underdevelopment – including those of the United Nations.

12 And perhaps Russia too, under some interpretations.

13 Kay (1975) p. x; Warren (1973) makes much the same point.

14 The insufficient explanation of what was meant by this concept, along with a certain weakness in the political analysis of the state, bore the main brunt of criticism in reviews of my *The State and Economic Development: Peru since 1968*

15 In the *Critique of the Gotha Programme*, for instance.

16 See Braverman (1974), especially Chapter 19.

17 *Op. cit.* p. 412.

18 Lewis (1954).

19 By authors such as Fei & Ranis (1964) and Barber (1970).

20 Such as Laclau (1971).

21 Perhaps the best – as well as the most succinct – analysis of the effect of dualism on accumulation in a developing economy is given in Kalecki (1972a). His central point is that if income distribution is not to deteriorate, national income cannot be allowed to grow faster than food (i.e. wage goods) supply; he regards land reform as essential if this constraint is to be lifted.

22 This point is formally developed in FitzGerald (1976b).

23 Barret-Brown (1974) pp. 276–7.

24 *Loc. cit.*

25 As Kay (1975) does, for example.

26 Sutcliffe, in Owen & Sutcliffe (1972) p. 190.

27 Vaitsos (1974) p. 59.

28 Usually known by its acronym 'ECLA', 'CEPAL' in Spanish – from whence the generic adjective *'cepalino'*.

29 At the time of writing, this task is being undertaken by Octavio Rodriguez of the ILPES; but for a representative collection of papers see ECLA (1969), and for a good discussion of ECLA ideas, Cardoso (1977a).

30 The leading member is, of course, Prebisch. Other prominent ones are Cardoso, Dos Santos, Furtado, Paz, Pinto, Sunkel and Braun.

31 Gerschenkron (1952) argues that in backward countries the adoption of certain institutional innovations and the acceptance of specific ideologies in favour of industrialization are necessary in order to bridge the gap between the obstacles to industrialization and the promises inherent in such development. But, as O'Brien (1975, p. 9) points out: 'Unlike, for example, Adam Smith's *Wealth of Nations* which reflected the ideology of the powerful industrial bourgeoisie of England, ECLA espoused an ideology for a class too weak to implement it – the Latin-American industrial bourgeoisie aided by an educated middle class running the state machine.'

32 That is, before the recent renaissance of non-dogmatic Marxist thought in Europe.

33 In its pathbreaking *Economic Survey of Latin America: 1949* (Santiago de Chile, 1951), although these ideas had been propounded by its director,

Raul Prebisch, at the University of Buenos Aires in the 1930s.

34 A constant stream of reports on trade patterns, production structure, inflation and so on came from the ECLA of a quality exceeding that of any other UN agency and of most third-world research institutions.

35 The best presentation is Sunkel & Paz (1970).

36 The key author here is Furtado (1964, 1968, 1970), but the annual *Economic Surveys* contain a sustained exposition of this view – and still do.

37 Furtado (1964) pp. 141–3.

38 An interesting discussion of this comparative neglect of ECLA ideas outside Latin-America is to be found in Cardoso (1977a).

39 Furtado (1968) p. 187 – author's translation.

40 See Chapter 8.

41 Levinson & Onis (1970).

42 See Chapter 9.

43 Although even this took some years to come to the notice of anglophone development economists: see, for example, the introduction to Leys (1975). It is unfortunate, perhaps, that Frank – whose work in any case is better classed with that of Baran and the 'Monthly Review' school – should have been so popular and his loose arguments and inaccurate historiography taken as representative of dependency theory.

44 For an excellent survey, see Cardoso (1974).

45 Sunkel (1969).

46 Dos Santos (1970).

47 Dos Santos (1973).

48 Pinto (1971).

49 Sunkel & Paz (1970) pp. 363–4.

50 O'Brien (1975).

51 Braun (1973); see also the papers in FitzGerald *et al.* (1977).

52 Chilcote (1974).

53 This is Baran's term, apparently culled from the Orient. The only Spanish equivalent is '*intermediaria*'.

54 Kaplan (1969).

55 Cardoso & Faletto (1969).

56 Giddens (1971).

57 Mandel (1975).

58 Poulantzas (1973) works not from the confusing slogan of the *Communist Manifesto* ('a committee for managing the common affairs of the whole bourgeoisie') but from the *Eighteenth Brumaire*. See particularly *op. cit.* pp. 255–321.

59 On the 'fiscal crisis of the state' see FitzGerald (1978a) and Chapter 7.

60 Cardoso (1977b).

61 Petras (1977) makes this point persuasively, giving a number of examples from the developing world.

62 Such as Bettelheim (1975), for example.

63 Szentes (1973) makes this point quite convincingly.

64 The distinction drawn by Cutler *et al.* (1977) between 'agents of' and 'owners of' capital is crucial here: state enterprise managers clearly cannot be 'capitalists' in the sense that a nineteenth-century mill-owner was, nor do bureaucrats have a direct part to play in the process of production but both are clearly controlling the state capitalist system, in much the same way as the directors of a joint-stock bank.

Notes to Chapter 3

1 We cannot attempt to complete political history, of course, but excellent surveys of the period are to be found in Pike (1967), Astiz (1969) and Lowenthal (1975), while for the historical background Basadre (1961–64) is indispensable and Yepes (1971) useful on the formation of the modern class structure.

2 Nominally in 1821, but the Battle of Ayacucho (1824) saw the final defeat of Spanish forces.

3 As Owens (1963 p. 37) points out: 'It was only natural, therefore, that the military should occupy the power vacuum left by the Spaniards' departure, and that the early history of republican Peru is concerned with a super-party, the army, rather than political parties.'

4 Bonilla (1974).

5 See Astiz (1969, Chapter 6) and Villanueva (1975) on the history of APRA, which was founded by Victor Raul Haya de la Torre in 1928. At the time of writing he is still leader of the party, and indeed president of the constitutional assembly.

6 Carey (1964). We will not discuss US–Peruvian relations in this chapter, but there are excellent surveys in Sharp (1972) and Pratt (1977).

7 For an excellent account of this brief attempt to restructure capital with protectionist policies and improved labour conditions, see Thorp and Bertram (1978) Chapter 10.

8 See Payne (1968) on this coup.

9 On this period see Astiz (1969) pp. 149–55; the oligarchy apparently had enough influence within the military to stop this reformist initiative.

10 Jaquette (1971) probably provides the best survey of this period, but see also the excellent 'insider' account in Kuczinski (1977).

11 Jaquette (*op. cit.* p. 141) argues, in fact, that 'Belaunde's program was not redistributive, it put most of its confidence in the ability to create new wealth rather than redistribute the old'.

12 On the military conspirators, see Philip (1976), and on ideological divisions within the senior ranks of the armed forces after 1968, see North (1978).

13 See the *Manifesto del Gobierno Revolucionario de la Fuerza Armada* (2 Oc-

tober 1968) and the *Estatuto del GRAF* (Decree-Law 17063 of 3 October 1968).

14 Listing the reforms that did in fact take place between 1968 and 1974, upon which see Chapter 5. Lowenthal (1975) supports the commonly-held view that it was drawn up much later.

15 This had been foreshadowed by Belaunde's *'Cooperación Popular'* programme. The acronym, incidentally, also means 'without bosses'.

16 This is best expressed in the book by the chief civilian ideologue of the Velasco regime and director of SINAMOS – Delgado (1972).

17 See, for example, the *Plan Tupac Amaru*, released in 1976, which maintains the verbal commitment to 'revolutionary' goals but stresses the importance of private enterprise and stated that the 'first phase' of the Peruvian Revolution was now complete, and that the second, 'consolidation', phase would be embarked upon with the emphasis on production rather than on ownership changes.

18 The phrase was used first by Hobsbawm in the *New York Review of Books* (16 December 1971).

19 See Rochabrun (1977) and the author's earlier attempt at this topic – FitzGerald (1976a).

20 Here we are basing ourselves on the taxonomy fruitfully employed by Tezanos (1975) in the case of Spain, which he derives from the classical typology used in *Capital* and the *Eighteenth Brumaire*.

21 Commonly held to be composed of forty-four families in the early 1960s – see Astiz (1969) Chapter 4. Webb (1976) calculates that in 1961 corporate stock ownership was confined to the top percentile of the income distribution, going to 'some one or two hundred wealth-holders earning over one million soles' (p. 17). For a good description of this group, and support for its consideration as an oligarchy, see Bourricaud (1970) and Spaey (1972). For a detailed account of three leading families (the Aspillagas, the Prados and the Miro-Quesadas) see Gilbert (1977).

22 See Chapter 4.

23 See Chapter 5.

24 See Chapter 5, and also Malpica (1968).

25 Such as Bravo Bresani (1969).

26 Wils (1975), Ferner (1977), Quijano (1971), Petras & La Porte (1971) and Bourricaud (1969).

27 They controlled about two fifths and a third of assets in manufacturing, respectively, as late as 1968 – see Chapter 9 – leaving at most a quarter for independent capitalists whose interests were based mainly on manufacturing industry, which must be the definition of 'industrialists'.

28 Nonetheless, there is very little written upon the 'middle classes' in Peru; but see Astiz (1969, Chapter 4), and Bourricaud (1970). The latter points out the important cultural definition: 'the middle class can very

well be defined by its exclusion from the elite, either because it has been excluded against its will or because it refuses to enter. Since, on the other hand, the country has a high percentage of illiterate Indians, the middle class will perceive everything that distinguishes it from them, particularly when the hierarchical distinction between the high and the low is symbolically reinforced by the qualitative, racial and cultural distinction between Indians and non-Indians,' (p. 54). The quotation should serve as a reminder that the Indian problem transcends class in Peru, and although we cannot discuss it here, the efforts to overcome this by the designation of Quechua as an official language in 1975 and the use of the word '*campesino*' instead of '*indio*' after 1968 should be noted – as should bourgeois resentment at the racial origins of President Velasco.

29 About 10 and 15 per cent of the economically active population respectively – see Chapter 4.

30 Webb (1975) ONEC *Anuario Estadístico de Perú 1971*.

31 The main source on the Peruvian military is Villanueva (1972, 1973), but see also Astiz (1969, Chapter 7), Castro (1975) and Stepan (1978).

32 See Mercado-Jarrin (1975): prime minister, minister of war and army commander under Velasco.

33 Villanueva (1973) and Castro (1975).

34 See Chapter 4.

35 Bayer (1975).

36 See Chapter 4. The point here is that only in enterprises of some minimum size do the division of labour and labour discipline obtain and is capital equipment used to any significant extent.

37 By far the best source in the labour movement in Peru is Sulmont (1972, 1975, 1976).

38 Founded in 1928 by Carlos Mariategui – whose writing has profoundly influenced Peruvian radicals ever since; see Mariategui (1928).

39 See Chapter 4, where this process is discussed more fully.

40 The author is indebted for this point to Alison Scott.

41 See Thorp and Bertram (1978), Chapter 6.

42 Bamat (1977)

43 It was this intervention, rather than that of 1968, therefore, which most closely corresponds to the 'middle-class military coup' paradigm discussed by Nun (1968).

44 Jaguaribe (1973) pp. 514–15.

45 Lowenthal (1975) pp. 31–2.

46 Cotler (1975) pp. 44–5.

47 And not by them alone: this had originally been APRA policy too in the 1930s – see Villanueva (1975).

48 This was conventional ECLA wisdom too – see Furtado (1970).

49 Stepan (1978).

50 The only known survey of popular reaction to the Velasco regime, covering some eight hundred shop employees in 1972, encountered quite widespread support, although 'the pattern that emerges from the data is surprisingly consistent: men support the government more than women; lower classes more than higher ones; immigrants to Lima more than those born there; and by those that seek better positions rather than those in a stable or declining situation' (Scurrah and Montalvo, 1975, p. 11, author's translation).

51 Booth (1978), who also has an excellent critique of the position held by the authors in note 54.

52 ILO *International Labour Statistics* (various years).

53 See Chapter 9.

54 Good examples are Quijano (1971), Dore and Weeks (1976) and Bollinger (1977).

55 Quijano (1975); Zaldivar (1974) makes much the same error.

56 Views which were continuously expressed in the publications and congresses of the *Sociedad de Industrias* – see Ferner (1977).

57 Put forward by Petras and LaPorte (1971).

58 Dore and Weeks (1976).

59 North (1978), Stepan (1978) chapter 4.

60 Stepan (1978) chapter 8.

61 See Chapter 8 below.

Notes to Chapter 4

1 See Chapter 2.

2 See Yepes (1971) for the 1820–1920 period, and Thorp and Bertram (1978) for 1890–1955 in particular, although there is tendency in the former to exaggerate the importance of politics relative to economics, and perhaps the reverse in the latter.

3 Indeed, one of the only explanatory equations that Thorbecke and Condos (1966) could convincingly fit to the macroeconomic data in their econometric study of Peru was that linking GDP growth directly with that of exports.

4 Further on in this chapter, the extent of this is estimated in quantitative terms.

5 See the work of Webb and Figueroa in this field, discussed in Chapter 5. In round figures about half of all consumption demand was generated in the upper decile of the income distribution in the late 1960s, while three quarters was generated in Lima. In combination, this would attribute about half the domestic consumer market (and possibly two thirds of that for manufactured goods – see FitzGerald (1975)) to the upper quartile of households in the capital.

6 As we have already seen in Chapter 2, this is a crucial element in the

analysis of the ECLA school, and it is unfortunate that in the case of Peru that we do not have the data (particularly household budgets) to test it.

7 That is, primary (agriculture, fishing, mining), secondary (manufacturing, construction, utilities) and tertiary – the rest.

8 See Figure 1 for details of output growth on an annual basis over the period and within the three cycles.

9 The masterly treatment of the main export sectors (mining, cotton, sugar and fishmeal) in Thorp and Bertram (1978) makes an extended discussion of the primary sectors here somewhat otiose. Industry, moreover, is the exclusive subject of Chapter 9.

10 For example, the enormous Majes, Chira-Puira and Tinajones projects to bring water down to the coast from the Andes had an estimated cost in 1971 of $300 millions in order to irrigate 150 000 hectares, according to INP (1971); an outlay equivalent to $2000 per hectare. IBRD (1973) points out that at least one million hectares of arable land could be theoretically opened up in the Huallaga Central area of the Atlantic slopes of the Andes – but at a cost of over $2000 per hectare; the same report recommends, in fact, that priority be given to the recovery of 0.2 million hectares of already irrigated but saline land on the coast.

11 For a good general description of the production aspects of the sector, see Coutu & King (1969) and IBRD (1973).

12 Assuming an income elasticity of demand for food of approximately one half, then, without relative price changes or a change in the income distribution, a population growing at about 3 per cent per annum and receiving annual increases in income per head of the order of 3 per cent will generate a demand of this magnitude.

13 See USDA (1976). The estimates for foodcrop output per head in the FAO *Yearbooks*, incidentally, are more pessimistic than Table 4.3. It is also worth noting that the greater importance of livestock in national food supply would tend to favour the upper income strata who can afford animal protein.

14 Roemer (1970) has a good description of the evolution of the sector up to 1968, and Malpica (1976) describes the reorganization.

15 There is no known study of the construction sector as a whole in Peru for our period. The only source of statistical information on the private sector is the files of the *Cámera Peruana de Constructores*, which were used for the estimates of gross fixed capital formation in housing given in Chapter 6.

16 More detailed indices of integration between these sectors are given in FitzGerald (1976a), where the inversion of the 1969 input–output matrix is discussed. The main aggregate values (p. 112) are as follows:

	Export sectors	Food agriculture	Industry: Consumer goods	Producer goods	Service sector and other
Intersectoral/total sales	17%	16%	12%	46%	14%
Export/total sales	73%	2%	7%	2%	—
Imports/total inputs	32%	16%	31%	55%	13%

It should also be noted that if inputs are divided between 'traded' and 'non-traded' (e.g. electricity and transport that could not be imported anyway) then the imported content of traded inputs is much higher.

17 For further discussion along these lines, see Chapters 7 and 9.

18 See Morawetz (1974) for an account of the foundation and main provisions of the 'Acuerdo de Cartegena'.

19 See Chapter 8.

20 Between 1973 and 1976, Peruvian import prices rose by 98 per cent while the world price index given in the IMF *International Financial Statistics* rose by only 57 per cent. There is considerable evidence of over-invoicing by multinational companies in Peruvian manufacturing as a means of capital flight after 1968, upon which see Chapter 9; and some more debatable indications of under-invoicing by foreign mining companies, upon which see Chapter 8.

21 This is a central point in Braun (1973), who likens this effect to a backward-sloping supply curve for marketed foodstuffs in a peasant economy; see also Chapter 2.

22 See the analysis of foreign investment and overseas borrowing in Chapter 6 and the discussion of balance of payments policy in Chapter 8.

23 These are the estimates given in the *Cuentas Nacionales*, and, although they are rightly considered to be approximate, they do give a valid idea of the relevant orders of magnitude.

24 Roberts (1974) contains a perceptive analysis of the migration process; Deler (1975) details the historical expansion of Lima.

25 See Twomey (1973), and also the theoretical discussion in Griffin (1974).

26 Bertram (1974).

27 Lewis (1973) has an excellent quantitative analysis of these patterns for Lima barriadas.

28 The data is collected on a sample basis by the *Servicio de Recursos Humanos* of the Ministry of Labour, and published annually. The source used here is ILO (1976).

29 There is a good discussion of the difficulty of defining underemployment except in income terms, and then distinguishing it from poverty as such, in Weeks (1973).

30 Webb (1977) gives evidence of this.

31 See Lewis (1973) for a confirmation of this in practice, and FitzGerald (1976b) for a model incorporating the theoretical implications of such an equilibrium. The central result is simply summarized thus: assume that of a given wage (w) received by the urban corporate workforce (L_1) a certain proportion (z) is spent on petty services; the income so generated is 'shared' by the urban non-corporate workforce (L_2), who will be joined by peasants so long as the income per head exceeds that obtainable in non-corporate agriculture (a); thus, at any one time the equilibrium condition $zwL_1/L_2 = a$ will be approached, dividing through by the total workforce, the equilibrium proportion of the urban lumpenproletariat (L_2) will then be $l_2 = zl_1w/a$. In other words, despite the fact that the corporate share in the workforce (l_1) is not increasing, the widening gap between corporate wages and peasant income (w/a) forces internal migration. FitzGerald *op. cit.* gives an illustration of this model using Peruvian data.

32 See Appendix for a full discussion of the estimation methods used.

33 BCR *Cuentas Nacionales 1968–73* (Table 10).

34 Which would seem to contradict the somewhat simplistic analysis in Lipton (1977), where dualism is based on 'urban bias'.

35 Webb (1977). Unfortunately his discussion of dualism is lacking in any explanation of the evident productivity differentials and has a tendency to make corporate wages the sole independent variable.

36 Sciari (1976), makes explicit reference to the estimates in Webb (*op. cit.*) and FitzGerald (1976a).

37 ILO (1970) p. 172.

38 Roberts (1974).

39 According to ECLA (1973) between 1960 and 1970 these seven economies accounted for 88 per cent of GDP in Latin America and 81 per cent of population. In this section, and in similar sections of other chapters, the figures for Peru in the comparative tables may not correspond exactly to those given in the main body of the text, due to minor differences in definition but the comparability of the original source seems to be worth preserving.

40 Reported in Pinto and Di Filippo (1976) p. 95.

41 Berry (1972).

42 ILO (1970). An excellent critique of this is given in Franco (1977); this source (p. 201) also estimates that the 'high productivity' sector of the Colombian economy employed 33 per cent of the workforce and accounted for 78 per cent of output in 1963 – an even greater degree of dispersion than we have encountered for Peru.

43 Moran (1974).

44 Behrman (1977).

45 See Furtado (1970, Chapter 13) for a discussion of this phenomenon.

46 Pinto (1971).
47 Furtado (1970, pp. 113–14).

Notes to Chapter 5

1 Barraclough (1973).
2 For good surveys of land ownership in previous years, see Keith (1977) on the establishment of the *hacienda* system in Peru, Torres (1974) on the first two decades of the century and Bertram (1974) on the period leading up to our own.
3 Petras & La Porte (1971) have a good account of the attempts at land reform before 1968.
4 *Decreto Ley 17716* of 1969. See Harding (1975) on the initial modifications of the Law, and Caballero (1977) on its final results and Valderrama (1976) for a survey of the process itself.
5 This could be used as collateral against industrial investment loans from the government, although (see Chapter 9) this facility was hardly used at all.
6 Caballero (1977), from whom the figures in the following two paragraphs are taken.
7 Goodsell (1974) pp. 153–4.
8 See Hunt (1974) on Marcona's manipulation of freight rates and the discussion by Bossio (1976) of the absence of quality premia on copper exports by SPC; both of these resulted in a reduction in the declared export price and thus the export of profits from the local affiliate to the (buying) mother company.
9 Brundenius (1972).
10 See Bossio (1976) and also Chapter 7, where the problems of state enterprises are discussed; overall Peruvian strategy with respect to foreign capital is examined in Chapter 8.
11 Sees Philip (1976) and Kuczinski (1977).
12 Philip (1976) and Chapter 8.
13 See Roemer (1970) and Caravedo (1977) as well as the details of the final expropriation in Malpica (1976). Torres (1975) shows how extensive foreign control over export marketing was before 1968.
14 As this sector is discussed in some detail in Chapter 9, we shall only give a brief summary of ownership developments here, in order to complete the overall picture.
15 See Chapter 3.
16 For an interesting discussion of this process, see Thorp (1972). The figures are given in Superintendencia de Banca y Seguros *Memoria* (various years).
17 See Consiglieri (1975), Malpica (1968) and Deler (1975). On the *Pueblos Jóvenes* see Collier (1975).

18 Both Espinoza (1972) and Malpica (1968) give details of these groups.

19 See Chapter 2.

20 On both these see the excellent article by Anaya, E. 'El Poder Ejecutive y los Gobiernos Invisibles en el Perú: 1956–68' in *Marka* (Lima, 15 January 1976).

21 This was more extreme than, but not untypical of, Latinamerican standards – as we shall see in the concluding section of this chapter.

22 Specifically, Casa Grande estate accounted for a third of sugar output in 1968, and was owned by German nationals; however, the Gildemeister family conducted its affairs from Peru, and thus should be considered as 'national' capital.

23 'Plan Inca' Article 6b, Presidencia (1974).

24 Knight (1975) has a good account of this ideological development.

25 Articles 29 and 45 of the 1933 Constitution.

26 See Caballero (1977) and Horton (1974) on these problems. The original plans for the creation of 'PIARs' – which would unite production cooperatives with surrounding communities in large area enterprises to distribute the profits – were abandoned in 1977 in favour of the scheme to convert the CAPs and SAIS to EPS.

27 Of which more in Chapter 9.

28 See Chapter 6.

29 'After five years of Enterprise Reform, the cases of conflict between private enterprises and the CIs have changed from being predominantly about ownership and profits, towards a demand for an active participation in the administration of the firm and sometimes even in the reorganisation of production. In this way, conflicts over decisions on topics such as supply, technology, finance and marketing have arisen' (Ministry of Industry *Evaluación del Proceso de Industrialización: Situación Actual y Perspectivas*, Lima, March 1976, pp. 24–5, author's translation).

30 The official interpretation placed upon the word 'predominant' varied considerably with the political complexion of the spokesman. In quantitative terms, the drafts of the 'Plan Tupac Amaru' foresaw 25 per cent of output (over a third of corporate sector production, therefore) as coming from EPS by 1982, while the 1977–78 Plan (INP, 1975a) contains a target of 12 per cent by the latter year – but both estimates depend upon rural cooperatives (about 8 per cent of production) being converted to EPS, and the published version of the Plan Tupac Amaru (Presidencia, 1977) contains no quantitative estimate.

31 'The priority and preponderance of the Social Property Sector are essential to the very idea of the Peruvian Revolution, because if they are not so, the EPS will eventually end up as no more than a group of modernised cooperatives. Without Social Property, there is no authentic Peruvian Revolution ... The Social Property Sector will be hegemonic when it covers the economic activities that are central

[*motrices*] to the growth and development of the economy' (Lecaros (1975) pp. 115–16, author's translation).

32 These were: Moto Andina (motorcycles), Normetal (electrical equipment), Transportes de Lima (bus lines), Incolana (alpaca sales), Mineropuno (silver mining) and Confecciones Populares (clothing). On the firms in gestation, see GIECO (1975a).

33 Vaneck (1970) is the key text for this sort of theorizing.

34. An error mercilessly exposed in Frank (1967).

35 Malpica (1975, pp. 20–5) quotes the outflows of profits generated by US firms as published by the US Department of Commerce – some $81 millions a year on average between 1961 and 1971, which sums to $890 millions on an average book value of investment of $560 millions over the same period. This is may not be a large sum in absolute terms, but in relation to the firms' capital represents an average return of 14 per cent per annum.

36 See Anaya (1975) for an examination of the Peruvian case, and Vaitsos (1974) for a discussion on a wider scale.

37 Espinoza (1971) contains some partial data for the pharmaceutical industry in Peru, and Vaitsos (1974) does the same for the Andean Pact countries. See also note 8 above.

38 Based on the national accounts data for declared export of profits, Anaya (1975) and Ministry of Industry data for royalties, and a guess (based on Bossio (1976) and Ministry of Industry estimates) of 10 per cent underpricing on copper exports and 10 per cent overpricing on industrial imports.

39 See Webb (1977) for a published summary of the results.

40 Webb (1977), pp. 39, 78; the notorious difficulty of estimating the income of the poorest strata in developing countries means that too much reliance should not be placed on these trends, although Webb does include estimates of non-monetary income.

41 Thorp (1969); Table 5.7 also indicates that within the lower 40 per cent (roughly equivalent to Webb's 'rural traditional group') there was a sharp difference between the two quintiles.

42 Jain (1975) is an IBRD publication which cites Webb for the 1961 estimate and bases the 1971 estimate on statistics supplied by the Peruvian Ministry of Labour.

43 See Figueroa (1976) p. 43.

44 Webb (1977, pp. 80, 81).

45 Assuming the top 5 per cent to receive 35 per cent of personal income in 1971 and the next 25 per cent about 38 per cent (see Table 5.7), then the result of the transfer would be to raise the latter and lower the former by about one fifth. The ratio between income per head in the two groups would then fall from about five to three times.

46 Giddens (1971) p. 22.

47 Webb (1977, pp. 94–5). In all fairness, it should be pointed out that Webb does agree (*op. cit.*) that dualism is at the root of the problem, but fails to integrate this with the issues of asset ownership and external dependency – which are not discussed at all in his book.

48 That carried out by the *Comité Interamericano de Desarrollo Agricola* (CIDA) in the late 1960s and synthesized in Barraclough (1973).

49 Feder (1976).

50 Ceceña (1975), Fajnzylber & Martinez (1976).

51 US Senate (1975).

52 Chudnovsky (1974).

53 Wionczek (1976).

54 Moran (1974).

55 See De Vylder (1976), especially Chapters 6 and 7.

56 ECLA (1968) makes the general point about dualism in the economy being the underlying structural determinant of income distribution in Latin America; Graciarena (1974) stresses the power structure as determining distribution within the corporate sector: 'The point of structural convergence between income and social power is to be found in the organization of productive forces' (*op.cit.*p. 261, author's translation). See also the *Introduction* to Foxley (1976).

Notes to Chapter 6

1 Peru is not an imperialist power with access to surplus generated in other economies. Even the surplus available as loans or investment at any one point in time from foreign capital must be repaid, in amortization or profits, in the future – from surplus generated in Peru. Aid donations were insignificant in our period.

2 This point is well made, albeit from a neo-classical point of view, in Little & Mirrlees (1974).

3 Although this underlies the history of Peru in the long run, of course. The point being made here is that organized labour did not play a large part in the balance of political forces at a national level – but see Chapter 3.

4 See Hymer (1972) on the contribution of the multinationals to unbalanced growth on a world scale.

5 See Tables 6.9 and 6.10.

6 See Chapter 2, and also Griffin (1969).

7 As Thorp & Bertram (1978) argue, particularly in relation to the period between 1910 and 1930.

8 These were derived by the author from the data on investment rates given in the appendix, which are reasonably consistent within each phase but differ sharply between them; the changes in regime and macroeconomic conjuncture then fell into place. See Figure 1.

9 See appendix and Table 6.1; the reason for the long-run tendency for the rate of stockbuilding to fall is not readily apparent, but it may be due to improvements in the transport system, which permitted a lower level of inventories to be held; the rise at the end of the period is believed to be mainly speculative.

10 See Chapter 7.

11 It would obviously be of interest to know what proportion of investment was carried out by foreign firms, as an indication of their direct control over accumulation, but no reliable estimates are available. However, a rough guess based on the sectoral estimates in Table 6.1 and the ownership patterns from Chapter 5 would indicate that we can take all private mining investment, a third of that in fishing and a half of that in manufacturing as a conservative estimate of foreign firms' investment. This gives us a figure of 2.4 per cent of GDP in 1960–68 and 2.1 per cent in 1969–76. See also Table 6.8.

12 See Harberger (1972), which is also the methodological source used by the INP.

13 Again, we have little information to work from. The book value of US investments in 1965 was the equivalent of only 20 billion soles (Malpica, 1975), a mere 5 per cent of stock for that year (Table 6.2). However, if we allow for a third each of the stock for housing and public works, respectively, and for the US to have half the total of foreign book value, then the ratio comes to about 30 per cent (= 40/132). Moreover, the practice of local borrowing gave an even greater control over assets, especially in manufacturing (see Chapter 9) so that the proportion of the productive capital stock (i.e. assets) controlled by foreign enterprise by the late 1960s could well have been as much as a half of the total.

14 J. Torres, in 'Input-Output Models and Structural Analysis of the Peruvian Economy' (PhD dissertation, University of California, Berkeley, 1973) shows in Table 3.8 a capital–output coefficient for agriculture of 1.69, although the derivation is not clearly explained. With agriculture accounting for 15 per cent of GDP in 1965–70, investment of the order of 1.5 per cent of GDP per annum would be required to maintain a growth rate of 5 per cent in the output of that sector, therefore.

15 See appendix and Table 6.4.

16 Webb (1977, p. 198) indicates that in 1961 – and there is no reason to believe that this changed over the subsequent decade – the top percentile of the Peruvian population (the bulk of whose income came from property) accounted for four fifths of all private savings.

17 See Chapter 7.

18 An average rate of private saving amounting to 15 per cent of GDP over the period may seem large, but with declared property income at around 25 per cent, plus 6 per cent for depreciation funds and (say) another 10 per cent for owners 'salaries', the rate of capitalist savings

works out at little over a third.

19 Considering that foreign firms were also undertaking new investment in oil and mining at a rate of about 1 per cent of GDP in this period, the net outflow (mainly in the form of depreciation of fixed assets and amortization of private loans, rather than capital flight) from other sectors, principally industry, must have been of the order of 3 per cent of GDP: See Table 6.8.

20 Footnote 5 to Table 3 of the 1960–74 *Cuentas* states that the series includes: '*Las utilidades de las empresas no encuestadas estimadas para cada sector mutiplicando sus remuneraciones por el coeficiente de utilidades a remuneraciones de empresas de tamaño semejante si registradas por la encuesta; y una provisión, calculada en parte por los resultados de auditorías fiscales, para la sub-estimación que por lo comun se produce en las declaraciones de utilidades.*'

21 The Peruvian economy exhibited an extremely high degree of 'financial intermediation': according to Reynolds (1973, p. 38) the mean ratio of total financial assets to GNP between 1965 and 1969 was 171 per cent, which 'is far higher than (say) Colombia or Brazil but also outdistances all but a handful of the developed countries' ratios for the past few decades'.

22 A cross between a merchant bank and a holding company, a form of financial intermediary already developed in Mexico. On the evolution of Peruvian financial institutions in the 1950s and 1960s, see CEMLA (1968).

23 See, however, Chapter 9, where it is argued that this trend also reflects the withdrawal of equity capital from the sector and its replacement by loan capital, especially from state banks.

24 See IBRD (1973) on the plight of small farmers, and Vega (1974) on that of small manufacturers.

25 See Chapter 7.

26 IMF (1977); see also the IMF and BCR negotiating documents cited in Cabieses and Otero (1978). The argument can be formally expressed in terms of monetary supply and demand (the fiscal deficit being the total supply of 'money' – claims on government – and the surplus of private savings over private investment the demand) where excess creation of money forces it 'across the exchanges' for foreign currency. In terms of asset balances, the same point can be made in relation to the fact that the creation of liabilities by the public sector must be balanced by changes in private domestic and foreign demand for them as assets.

27 See note 18 and Chapter 5, as well as the discussion below.

28 See Chapter 2.

29 See Chapters 7 and 8.

30 CNSEV (1973) does contain an analysis of the flow of funds in the Peruvian economy between 1965 and 1970, but as this is confined to a

narrow definition of financial assets and is unintegrated to the national accounts, it is not of great use to us here. Nonetheless, the data do support our argument: of all financial assets in private hands in 1970, 77 per cent were held by financial institutions and the other 23 per cent by households; of the institutional holdings, 78 per cent were held by commercial banks, the rest by '*mutuales*' (10 per cent), insurance companies (6 per cent), '*financieras*' (3 per cent) and savings cooperatives (3 per cent); of the household assets, 43 per cent were in '*mutuales*', 25 per cent in insurance and 17 per cent in savings cooperatives.

31 The significance of this coincidence is not entirely clear, but it does make comparison easier.

32 See Chapter 7.

33 A point supported by the analysis in Webb (1977, Chapter 5).

34 See also Chapter 8.

35 ECLA (1970).

36 ECLA (1971), author's translation.

37 See FitzGerald (1974).

38 De Vylder (1976), Chapter 1. It should be remembered, however, that the natural resource endowment in Chile (which was developed not by Chilean but by foreign capital, unlike much of Peru's exports) was such as to give mineral exports equivalent to some US $100 per head of population in 1970, compared to $33 per head in Peru. This meant that, leaving aside differences in efficiency of exchange use, Chilean industrial output could rise to much higher levels than in Peru before meeting the foreign exchange constraint on inputs.

39 Fortin (1978).

40 Levinson and Onis (1970).

41 Foxley and Muñoz (1976).

42 Fortin (1978) p. 15; see also Chapter 8 below.

43 Sideri and Evers (1979).

Notes to Chapter 7

1 Chapters 5 and 6, respectively.

2 See FitzGerald (1974).

3 Jaquette (1971), Kuczinski (1977).

4 See Chapter 3.

5 Frankman (1974).

6 Dating from 1922, the year of the first *Ley Orgánica del Presupuesto*, before which there had only existed fragmentary '*Estados*'. On the economic role of government in the first half of the century, see Hunt (1971).

7 Literally 'ink-sucker', although better translated as 'pen-pusher'.

8 *Ley Orgánica del Sistema Nacional de Control de la Actividad Pública* (*Decreto-Ley* 19039).

9 See Chapter 8.

10 See, for example BCR (1961).

11 Jaquette (1971), chapter 4.

12 INP (1967).

13 INP (1971) pp. 76, 77 – author's translation.

14 INP (1971) p. 31 – author's translation.

15 Decree-Law 20736 – author's translation.

16 Chapter 5, Table 5.4.

17 Stockholm International Peace Research Institute (1975), Stepan (1978), see also Table 7.12 below.

18 This is discussed more fully in Chapter 8.

19 See Chapter 9.

20 See Chapter 8.

21 Hunt (1971).

22 ECLA (1973).

23 D.L. 19326 of 1972, the 'General Law of Education', upon which see the interesting discussion in Drysdale & Myers (1975).

24 Including the notorious one at Tarma, Odría's home town, which to this day remains oversized and understaffed.

25 For example, according to Malpica (1975, p. 102) the number of hospital beds per thousand population declined from 2.08 in 1958 to 1.75 in 1968, and rose to only 2.10 by 1974; moreover, even in this last year, the ratio was 5.7 in Lima and 1.7 elsewhere in Peru.

26 ECLA (1973) p. 48.

27 Collier (1975) has an interesting discussion of urbanization policy and the 'feedback' from the interested parties in our period.

28 ECLA (1973).

29 Consiglieri (1975). A decree-law was in fact passed in March 1976 to make the state housing agency (Emadi) the sole agent for urban land development sales but business opposition was so strong that it had to be repealed by the end of that year.

30 See Chapter 6.

31 See Chapters 2 and 10, where our discussion of this problem is opened and closed, respectively.

32 An interesting early example of the state negotiating with foreign capital in behalf of the national bourgeoisie as a whole. There had also existed a system of state railways before the War of the Pacific, but this was ceded to British interests as a result of the infamous Grace Contract of 1889. On both of these topics, see Yepes (1971).

33 With substantial private-sector participation.

34 See Table 7.7 below.

35 See Chapter 6.

36 The *Caja de Depositos y Consignaciones*, itself the successor to the eponymous *Compañía Recaudadora de Impuestos,* which had taken over tax and customs collection along with the administration of the *estancos* in 1922, the year that the *Presupuesto General de la República* was reformed.

37 CDES (1965), INP (1966).

38 See Chapter 5.

39 Presidencia de la República Peruana, *Linamientos de Plan Nacional de Desarrollo para 1975–78*, Lima (1974) – author's translation. There are similar statements in the 1971–75 plan, the Plan Inca and the Plan Tupac Amaru.

40 There is a scarcity of published data on these enterprises, and much of the following has been gathered directly. The rapid proliferation of and acronyms for public enterprises gave rise to the following *limeño* joke: the Archangel Gabriel rang up St Peter after President Velasco died and went to heaven ('*cielo*') to be greeted by the response 'Cieloperu speaking'.

41 See Chapter 5.

42 See Chapter 4.

43 Capacity rose from 250 000 tons of liquid steel in 1969 to 500 00 in 1975 and 750 000 in 1978; plant under construction should raise this to one million tons by 1980.

44. Chapter 5 and appendix.

45 As defined by value added and investment at constant prices – see Table 7.1.

46 See Chapter 8.

47 FitzGerald (1976a) p. 48.

48 See Chapter 9.

49 This is discussed in the context of the fiscal structure as a whole and over a longer period below.

50 Hunt (1975).

51 The activities of three crucial enterprises (Petroperu, Mineroperu and EPSA) are discussed in FitzGerald (1976a) pp. 50–4.

52 See Chapter 8.

53 There were official regulations designed to counter this, but any competent purchasing manager can specify his requirements in such a way as to preclude all but one (foreign) supplier.

54 See Webb (1977, Chapter 4) on the tax structure in general, and Calonge (1973) on corporation tax in particular. Taylor (1969) is an official survey, recommending mainly administrative reform.

55 Most income-tax payers were in the top decile (Tables 5.7) which received roughly half of national income in the 1960s.

56 Kuczinski (1977, pp. 204–5). The tax reforms were derived from the study by the Organization of American States (Taylor, 1969).

57 This had the status of law, being Decreto Supremo No. 015–71–PM,

author's translation.

58 For example, the 'grassroots' public works projects carried out by the Ministerio de Fomento ('economic') until 1968 were subsequently transferred to SINAMOS ('general') – see FitzGerald (1976a, pp. 45–6) for a discussion of this problem.

59 Although in 1968 only one third of the nation's workforce, mostly white-collar workers, was covered by the social security system.

60 See Chapter 8.

61 In Chapters 8 and 6 respectively.

62 Until 1963, the *Juntas de Obras Públicas* were classified as part of the *Sub-sector Público Independiente,* and were almost outside budgetary control.

63 See IMF (1977) and the negotiating documents between the IMF and the Peruvian authorities reproduced in Cabieses and Otero (1978).

64 See appendix, and also Chapter 8.

65 Webb (1977, Chapter 4).

66 Hunt (1971) p. 389.

67 Webb (1977).

68 See, for example Malpica (1975).

69 See Bird & de Wulf (1973) for an excellent discussion of this problem in the context of fiscal incidence for developing countries generally. They conclude that, data limitations apart, such an exercise has little meaning in any case, due to its depending upon arbitrary (or at least non-economic) criteria for expenditure allocation.

70 Webb (1977).

71 Although we have criticized his definitions of the 'modern' and 'traditional' sectors in Chapter 5, they are satisfactory for this part of the argument.

72 Chelliah (1971).

73 These paragraphs are based on FitzGerald (1978a), where the case for a structural fiscal crisis of the Latinamerican state is presented in more detail.

74 See O'Connor (1973) and the discussion in Chapter 2.

Notes to Chapter 8

1 Chapter 6.

2 The apparent chronological regularity of these crises, which seem to occur in the second half of each decade, is related to cycles on international commodity markets and therefore outside the scope of this study; see Chapter 3.

3 This is considered separately in Chapter 9.

4 Kalecki (1972a); the Peruvian food problem is quantified in Chapter 4, while tax pressure and aggregate consumption are discussed in Chapters 7 and 6, respectively.

5 Cabieses and Otero (1978) pp. 188–91.

6 See Chapter 9.

7 Dragsic (1971) points out the similarity of these two crises to the stabilization programme of 1947–49, and later on in this chapter we shall see the parallels in the policy reaction to the crises of 1977–78.

8 Thorp (1967) p. 185.

9 See Chapter 4.

10 This is the main theme of the discussion in Jaquette (1971).

11 Jaquette (1971, p. 151) quotes Belaunde as stating at end-1968 that the US aid agencies 'always said "may be" and asked for more feasibility studies. By the time we had finished these, I was flying to Argentina.'

12 This point is demonstrated by Hunt (1975).

13 This case is discussed by Payer (1975), and argued to be typical of IMF operations in the Third World.

14 BCR (1974).

15 See Chapter 7.

16 Because of rising world prices and increased over-invoicing – see Chapter 9. On the terms of trade, see Chapter 4; in constant price terms the balance of payments deficit on current account in 1976 (at 5 per cent of GDP) was not much greater than in 1970 (4 per cent), but in current dollar terms, it was a sevenfold increase.

17 See the excellent analysis of the 1976–77 stabilization attempts in Thorp (1979).

18 See Cabieses and Otero (1978) pp. 142–6.

19 Thorp (1979).

20 See Chapter 9, Table 4.7.

21 See Chapter 4.

22 Between 1971 and 1975, the GDP deflator rose by 80 per cent and the Lima cost of living by slightly more; import prices just about tripled, but as they were only one sixth of total supply, they would have added only about 20 per cent to domestic prices directly, the difficulty being that these external increases tended to be 'passed on' through the industrial pricing structure, only public enterprise prices being held back, at the expense of large subsidies.

23 See Chapter 6.

24 And which corresponded not only to the view of the foreign creditors – see IMF (1977) – but also that of the Central Reserve Bank and increasingly the Ministry of Finance itself.

25 Conventionally expressed as a ratio of debt service to export income of no more than twenty per cent.

26 Which coincided with that of the 'progressive bureaucrats' in general and *Instituto Nacional de Planificación* in particular.

27 One of the main goals of the 1971–75 Plan (INP, 1971) is stated to be: 'The elimination . . . of the subordination of the Peruvian economy to

foreign centres of decision where actions originate which fundamentally affect the economic life of the nation and prevent an autonomous
development process geared to the achievement of national objectives'
(p. 15 – author's translation). The expropriation programme is
specified in the *Plan Inca*.

28 Philip (1975) argues that the approach can be best characterized as an
ad hoc one response to changing circumstances, while Portocarrero
(1976) suggests that the eventual form of reaccommodation with
foreign capital was also originally intended; both of these views seem to
be exaggerations.

29 That is, their power to make decisions on political as opposed to commercial criteria, although the two may well coincide in the long run.

30 In the Peruvian case this was normally negative, given the prevailing
average interest rates and levels of international inflation; this is not to
suggest – needless to say – that such banks lose money, for they are
themselves paying still lower interest rates to their depositors.

31 There are several surveys of this period, of which the best are Ballentyne
(1974), Hunt (1975) and Stallings (1979). On the oil contracts in particular, see Philip (1975).

32 Bossio (1976). See also Gonzalez & Parodi (1975).

33 $76 millions in cash payments and $74 millions in the form of permis-
sion to remit accumulated profits.

34 At this point in time the US strategy for Latin America as a whole formulated by Kissinger was bearing fruit, leaving Peru in an increasingly
isolated position.

35 On the role of the IMF and the US banks in these negotiations, see
Thorp (1979).

36 *Institutional Investor* (New York, October 1976).

37 Some sort of planning, in the sense of setting objectives and coordinating action in order to achieve them, is presumably implicit in all
budgeting and thus might be said to have existed previously – albeit in
an embryonic form. For a description of Peruvian planning before
1968, see Kilty (1967) and Roel (1968): the former is the more detailed
but lacks the critical judgement of the latter.

38 BCR (1961).

39 Roel (1968), p. 55, author's translation.

40 Planning had become a central element in the new military
ideology – see Chapter 3.

41 INP (1967).

42 Indeed, the second item in the 'Plan Inca' was the reform of the planning system, preceded only by the expropriation of IPC.

43 INP (1971).

44 FitzGerald (1976a) Chapter 6.

45 INP (1975a).

46 INP (1975a) p. 7; author's translation.

47 INP (1977) p. 17; author's translation.

48 See Thorp (1979) in which this IBRD report is cited. Stallings (1979) gives a convincing *ex-post* defence of the INP decision, in view of the information available at the time, to take a 'calculated risk'.

49 Thorp (1979).

50 In addition, the INP also acted as the secretariat for COAP (see Chapter 3) after 1968, and since its foundation had been influential in forming opinion within the progressive wing of the military – see Lowenthal (1975). The planners formed a certain elite in the public administration, being young well-trained technocrats, mainly engineers and social scientists. Interestingly, a marked shift in their economic formation from North American neo-classical schools of thought to a classical European one could be observed after 1968.

51 INP (1973b) gives details of a mathematical model used; for a critique of this model, see FitzGerald (1976a, Chapter 6).

52 For an example of an operating manual for this process, see OSPA (1972).

53 The methodology was based on UN (1958) but in addition the cash flows at market prices were adjusted for taxes and subsidies, a shadow exchange rate (some twenty per cent above the nominal rate in 1975) applied to foreign exchange items, and the whole discounted by a ten per cent discount rate at constant prices. No shadow wage rate was applied, which is indicative of the lack of concern for the employment potential of public investment.

54 In 1973, the public sector had about three thousand investment projects under way, but only a hundred and fifty had a programmed capital cost of more than a million dollars, and these accounted for nearly three quarters of fixed investment by the state sector in that year.

55 The ranking of projects according to the ratio of net present value to the capital cost, known as the 'cost–benefit ratio', as an alternative to the system of including projects on a 'first come first served' basis. On the optimality of such a procedure, see Millward (1971).

56 A system of direct foreign exchange rationing was also introduced to the private sector in 1976; it differed radically from ordinary import controls, which are widespread in Latin America, in that a total foreign exchange allocation was divided up between sectors in advance according to priorities rather than requests being evaluated on an individual basis. See INP (1977, p. 124) for an example.

57 Repeated attempts were in fact made by the INP from 1974 onwards to introduce legislation to permit this (entitled *Proyecto-Ley de Estudios de Prefactibilidad para la Inversión Publica*), but opposition from the 'line' ministries was too great to overcome.

58 See note 50.

59 See Eshag & Thorp (1965) for a discussion of the Argentinian case, which comes to similar conclusions.

60 FitzGerald (1978b).

61 This argument is well expressed in the introductory chapter to Thorp and Whitehead (1979).

62 Serrano (1977) analyses a number of recent cases in Latin America.

63 See Ffrench-Davis (1973) and Behrman (1977); we have excluded the 1974–77 'stabilization programme' as being more of a political than an economic exercise.

64 De Vylder (1976).

65 FitzGerald (1974), Griffin & Enos (1972).

66 The exception is the establishment of the *Secretaría de Programación y Presupuesto* in Mexico in 1977 – see FitzGerald (1978b) – which was endowed with control over all public sector expenditure.

67 Wynia (1972) makes this point in relation to Central America.

Notes to Chapter 9

1 Thorp and Bertram (1974) make an extremely strong case for this historical pattern, which seems at first sight to contradict the traditional ECLA chronology for industrialization – but presumably the point is the effect of the foreign exchange constraint rather than the dates.

2 Sutcliffe (1971), Chapter 2.

3 Drawn from Chapter 4. We have not included either sugar or fishing but if these were added in, as 'industrial' in the spirit if not the letter of Sutcliffe's definition, then Peru would just pass all three tests.

4 See Table 4.5.

5 This is that used in the 1963 and 1973 Economic Censuses, and by the Ministry of Industry.

6 There is no exact translation in English, it being a composite category of 'metal products' and 'engineering' – ISIC numbers 34 to 38.

7 This measure is complicated by relative price movements, of course, but no deflators at a branch level are available. Nolff (1974) suggests that the application of international prices would reduce the weight of heavy industry in Latin America as a whole, due to its relatively high level of protection, but the reverse would appear to be the case for Peru.

8 The most thorough statistical study of import-substitution in Peru is definitely that by Baulne (1975), but GIECO (1972) contains more detail on the economic background, while Saberbein (1973) has the most convincing conceptual framework. All three coincide with the view presented here.

9 Baulne (1975, p. 60).

10 Appendix to FitzGerald (1976a). Recent work by Jorge Torres at the

Department of Applied Economics, Cambridge, on the 1973 input–output matrix indicates that the technical coefficients did not change greatly after 1969; the overall proportion of imports in total inputs to manufacturing was 32 per cent in 1973 as opposed to 33 per cent in 1969. FitzGerald (1975, p. 20) estimates the ratios to be 31 per cent in 1965 and 37 per cent in 1973 on the basis of *Estadística Industrial*.

11 Torres (1975).

12 Figueroa (1974). For comparison it is worth noting that the ECLA (1973, p. 26) states that 'in the seven largest cities in Colombia in 1970, the top 5 per cent [of the income distribution] accounted for 74 per cent of expenditure on private car purchase and maintenance, while the next 15 per cent accounted for another 21 per cent. In Mexico in 1963 the equivalent proportions were 72 and 19 per cent. In Santiago in 1969 they were 51 per cent and 37 per cent'.

13 Both Figueroa (1974) and Tokman (1975) take this view.

14 Thorp (1977) gives an excellent survey of the problems of Peruvian industrialization in the 'post import-substitution era'.

15 The only constant-price output estimate is that used in the Central Reserve Bank's *Cuentas Nacionales* (*op. cit.*) which include export processing and artisan production. These have been used to construct the index in the table, but the trend should be fairly reliable as the artisan element was calculated by the Central Bank by grossing up factory production by a constant factor in the first place.

16 For the 1973 figures, see FitzGerald (1975).

17 See Tokman (1975).

18 INP (1975b) indicates that of the 54 three-digit ISIC groups used in Peru, the four largest firms in each accounted for over three quarters of sales in nineteen cases, for over a half in twenty cases, and over a fifth in all the others. Weeks (1977, p. 133) shows that between 1954 and 1963 the degree of concentration in the 18 two-digit branches of manufacturing, as measured by the 'Herfindahl Index' (the sum of the squares of the share of employment in a branch of industry employed by each firm) decreased by an average of 30 per cent, rising in only 3 out of 18, as foreign firms entered and competed with existing enterprises; during 1963–67 the trend was reversed, with concentration rising by an average of 3 per cent across branches. Weeks (*op. cit.*) also estimates that about 30 per cent of fixed investment in manufacturing was carried out by foreign firms in the 1950s and 50 per cent in the 1960s.

19 Espinoza (1972). The six large groups in 1968 were Cerro, Grace (both foreign), Prado-Wiese, Copsa-Pacocha, Ferreyros-Rizo Patron, and Lercari-Aspillaga.

20 Vaitsos (1976), working with 1973 data made available to the Andean Pact secretariat, shows that foreign firms in the food branch import 46 per cent of total inputs as opposed to 37 per cent by local firms; for

chemicals the ratios are 72 per cent and 55 per cent; and for *metalmecánica* they are 60 per cent and 38 per cent, respectively.

21 Also, contracts for technology with domestic firms usually include specific prohibitions on exports in the licensing agreement – see Anaya (1975) for some Peruvian examples.

22 See Appendix Table A.6.

23 See Chapter 5. According to MIT–OSP, by the end of 1975 the CIs still owned only 7 per cent of equity in the eligible firms, but this share rises to 12 per cent if the non-capitalized funds of the CIs are included. On the theoretical rate of acquisition of shares, see Llarena (1972). Bankrupt companies could also pass to cooperatives based on the CI: by the end of 1975, some twenty enterprises had come under DL 20023 with an equity of some 79 million soles.

24 Wils (1975), on the basis of a questionnaire survey, does identify the 'industrialists' as a vocal and independent group, but qualifies his position on their political strength in his discussion of the results. Ferner (1977) has a more radical approach, but still tends to exaggerate his subject's social and political importance by ignoring their limited economic role, despite his Marxian framework.

25 Net fixed assets estimates have been published in the *Estadística Industrial* since 1965, but these are book value and, due to the restrictions on revaluation, are grossly undervalued: the ratio of fixed assets to value added fell from 1.06 in 1965 to 0.73 in 1974.

26 FitzGerald (1975, p. 17) indicates that assets per head in 1973 were as follows: food, US $11 100; clothing $5800; industrial inputs $12 700; construction materials $5300 and *metalmecánica* $5700.

27 Net fixed assets, undervalued as they were, totalled 32 billion soles in 1969 (see Table 9.7), so that depreciation requirements must have been of the order of 3–5 billions. According to MIT (1976), a sample covering about half of private manufacturing investment in 1973 indicated that financial sources were made up of depreciation funds (46 %), profits (5%) and borrowing (49%), the uses being fixed assets (52%), working capital (30%) and purchase of financial assets (18%).

28 Both Quijano (1971) and Zaldivar (1974) argue that this provision was included in order to permit the landowners to convert themselves into an industrial bourgeoisie!

29 For example, the Law 9140 ('*Protección Económica e Industrial*') of 1940 allowed government to celebrate *convenios* with private manufacturers but was concerned with assuring supplies of essential commodities in wartime rather than industrial promotion as such.

30 ECLA (1965) calculates, on the basis of a 125-commodity sample, that the nominal rates in Latin America around 1960 were such that the average for Peru (34%) was very low compared to Argentina (131%), Brazil (168%), Colombia (112%), Chile (138%) and Mexico (61%).

31 INP (1966) makes this quite clear.

32 The two quotations are from the second of the 'National Objectives' (see Chapter 3, note 13), and the preamble to the 1970 Law (DL 18350) itself.

34 MIT (1974). The programmes for investment over the period 1975–78 were: state, 35%; private, 50%; social property and cooperatives, 15%. The state budget was composed as follows: iron and steel (40%), heavy industry (32%), *metalmecánica* (19%), chemicals (6%) and various (3%). A return to a high output growth rate for the sector was foreseen as a consequence of the relaxation of capacity constraints.

35 A large range of heavy industrial projects were under way in the public sector in 1976, which could not easily be cancelled. By 1978, Cemento Andino (with plant at Tarma, Pacasmayo and Yura) had increased its production from 1.9 to 2.9 million tons of cement, tractor production capacity was up from 700 to 2000 units a year, and newsprint output had reached 120 000 tons. Before the end of the decade, the Trujillo Complex will be producing 15 000 diesel motors, 250 lathes, 600 drills and 3500 air compressors a year, as well as automobile castings and gearboxes. Early in the 1980s plant already being installed should expand steel production to 2.25 million tons a year and petrochemicals output to 150 000 barrels a day.

36 MIT (1976).

37 Nolff (1974, p. 14) estimates that, on average, in the early 1970s the artisan sector in Latin America accounted for about seven per cent of manufacturing output but forty per cent of employment in the sector, while output per worker at the factory level was only a quarter of that in the USA.

38 The classic statement of this is to be found in ECLA (1965).

39 Garcia (1974).

40 In fact, the very generalizations made by the ECLA as an authority on the matter themselves affect the changes in policy in individual countries as this institution not only produces the best comparative data but also consultants and valuable training.

41 ECLA (1974, p. 93) calls this an '*eficientista*' policy. It points out somewhat mordantly that 'the predominant participation of multinational firms in the greater part of the trade generated by expanded markets forces us to question the degree to which the respective countries really gain any benefit'. The same document also suggests that the 'open' policy is eliminating small and medium domestic firms and thus promoting monopoly positions.

Notes to Chapter 10

1 Excepting the short-lived Bustamante regime (1943–48), which was an

inconsequential – albeit significant – attempt, as we have seen.

2 Thorp and Bertram (1978) are essentially arguing this, although they do stress the organizational (as opposed to the political) role of the domestic entrepreneur – whether private or public.

3 Cotler (1978).

4 'The self-consciousness of the proletariat expands progressively along with the undermining of the position of the entrepreneurial capitalist by the centralisation and concentration of capital. The conjunction of these circumstances makes possible the achievement of a socialist society' (Giddens, 1971 p. 60).

5 Stepan (1978), for example.

6 The following paragraphs are based upon Hansen (1971), Cordova (1974), Leal (1975) and FitzGerald (1978b).

7 A concept sketched in Kalecki (1972b) but unfortunately not developed further: it is a term used by him to denote populist regimes which, in the vacuum caused by the removal of a traditional elite as the result of decolonization or revolution assume a reformist course between capitalism and socialism. State capitalism is characteristic of such regimes, examples of which are Turkey under Ataturk, Egypt under Nasser and post-independence India. Kalecki suggests, however, that intermediate regimes are inherently unstable and tend to revert to dependent capitalism if they do not progress to socialism. See FitzGerald (1977) for a somewhat unsuccessful attempt to apply this concept to Latin America.

8 In 1968 only a sixth of output and exports in Peru were from agriculture; in 1948 these proportions were about a third and a half.

9 See page 31.

10 On the basis of an exhaustive linear-programming study of alternative resource allocations in Peruvian manufacturing, carried out at Cambridge and the headquarters of the Andean Pact in Lima, Torres (1978) finds that, with or without protection, the scope for Peruvian industry to resolve either the immediate problem of exports or the longer-term ones of employment and basic needs is extremely limited. He suggests that what is required is '*profundos cambios estructurales en las relaciones sociales de producción en la economía peruana*'. Zuñiga (1979), in contrast, suggests that the problems of the state-capitalist model were essentially ones of *transition*; now that it has been established, the model can form the basis of a coherent system of capital accumulation and economic development, once the immediate balance of payments difficulties have been overcome by the eventual recovery of world trade.

Bibliography

Amin S. *Accumulation on a World Scale: a Critique of the Theory of Underdevelopment* New York: Monthly Review Press (1974).

Anaya E. *Imperialismo, Industrialización y Transferencia de Tecnología en el Perú* Lima: Horizonte (1975).

Astiz C. A. *Pressure Groups and Power Elites in Peruvian Politics* Ithaca: Cornell University Press (1969).

Ballentyne J. 'The Political Economy of Peruvian Gran Minería' *Latin American Dissertation Series No 60* Ithaca: Cornell University (1974).

Bamat T. 'Relative State Autonomy and Capitalism in Brazil and Peru' *The Insurgent Sociologist* Vol. 7 (1977).

Baran P. *The Political Economy of Growth* New York: Monthly Review Press (1957).

Barber W. 'Dualism Revisited: Economic Structures and the Framework of Economic Policy in a Post-colonial Setting' in Streeten P. (ed.) *Unfashionable Economics* London: Weidenfeld and Nicolson (1970).

Barraclough S. *Agrarian Structure in Latin America* Lexington, Mass: Heath (1973).

Barret-Brown M. *The Economics of Imperialism* Middlesex: Penguin (1974).

Basadre J. *Historia de la República del Perú* (10 vols.) Lima: Ediciones Historia (1961–64).

Baulne M. *Industrialización por Sustitución de Importaciones: Perú 1958–69* Lima: Campodónico (1975).

Bayer D. L. *Descapitalización del Minifundio y Formación de la Burguesía Rural* Lima: Universidad Agraria (1975).

BCR *Plan Nacional de Desarrollo Económico y Social del Perú: 1962–71* Lima: Banco Central de Reserva (1961).

El Desarrollo Económico y Financiero del Perú Lima: Banco Central de Reserva (1974).

Behrman J. R. *Macroeconomic Policy in a Developing Country: the Chilean Experience* Amsterdam: North-Holland (1977).

Berry A. R. 'Farm Size, Income Distribution and the Efficiency of Agricultural Production: Colombia' *American Economic Review* Vol. 62 (1972).

Bertram I. G. 'Development Problems in an Export Economy: Domestic Capitalists, Foreign Firms and Government in Peru 1919–30' (unpublished DPhil dissertation) Oxford University (1974a).

'Recent Thinking on the Peruvian Highland Peasantry' *Pacific Viewpoint* November (1974b).

Bettelheim C. *Les Luttes des Classes en URSS: première periode 1917–1923* Paris: Maspero (1974).

Economic Calculations and Forms of Property New York: Monthly Review Press (1975).

Bird R. M. and De Wulf L. H. 'Taxation and Income Distribution in Latin America: A Critical Review of Empirical Studies' *IMF Staff Papers* Vol. 20 (1973).

Bollinger W. 'The Bourgeois Revolution in Peru: a Conception of Peruvian History' *Latin American Perspectives* Vol. 4 (1977).

Bonilla H. *Guano y Burguesía en el Perú* Lima: Instituto de Estudios Peruanos (1974).

Booth D. 'Newspapers, Relative Autonomy and Dependence: Peru 1968–78' (mimeo) paper given to the National Development Conference, Glasgow (1978).

Bossio J. C. 'Cambios en la Política Minero-metalúrgica' in Kerbusch E. (ed.) *Cambios Estructurales en el Peru 1968–75* Lima: ILDES (1976).

Bourricaud F. *Power and Society in Contemporary Peru* New York: Praeger (1970).

Braun O. *Comercio Internacional e Imperialismo* Mexico: Siglo XXI (1973).

Braverman H. *Labor and Monopoly Capital* New York: Monthly Review Press (1974).

Bravo-Bresani J. *Mito y Realidad de la Oligarquía Peruana* Lima: Instituto de Estudios Peruanos (1969).

Brundenius C. 'The Anatomy of Imperialism: The Case of the Multinational Mining Corporations in Peru' *Journal of Peace Research* No. 3 (1972).

Caballero J. M. *Agrarian Reform and the Transformation of the Peruvian Countryside* Working Papers Series No. 29. Cambridge: Centre of Latin American Studies (1977).

Cabieses H. and Otero C. *Economía Peruana; un Ensayo de Interpretación* Lima: DESCO (1978).

Calonge O. 'Propuesta Metodologica para la Sectorización de los Impuestos Directos de las Empresas 1967–70' (unpublished thesis) Lima: Universidad Católica (1973).

Caravedo B. 'The State and the Bourgeoisie in the Peruvian Fishmeal Industry' *Latin American Perspectives* Vol. 4 (1977).

Cardoso F. H. 'Notas Sobre el Estado Actual de los Estudios sobre Dependencia' in Serra J. (ed.) *Desarrollo Latinoamericano: Ensayos Críticos* Mexico: Fondo de Cultura Economica (1974).

The Originality of the Copy: ECLA and the Idea of Development Working Papers Series No. 27. Cambridge: Centre of Latin American Studies (1977a).

'Capitalist Development and the State: Bases and Alternatives' in FitzGerald E. V. K., Floto E. and Lehmann A. D. (eds.) *The State and Economic Development in Latin America* Occasional Paper No. 1. Cambridge: Centre of Latin American Studies (1977b).

Cardoso F. H. and Faletto E. *Dependencia y Desarrollo en América Latina* Mexico: Siglo XXI (1969).

Carey J. C. *Peru and the United States 1900–1962* Indiana: University of Notre Dame Press (1964).

Carlson J. *Peru's and Colombia's Policies on Private Foreign Investment and Foreign Technology* Copenhagen: IDR (1974).

Castro J. 'La Doctrina del CAEM del Perú' *Interrogations* Paris (December 1975).

CDES *Las Empresas Estatales* Lima: Centro de Documentación Económico – Social (1965).

Ceceña J. L. *México en la Orbita Imperial* Mexico: Ediciones 'El Caballito' (1975).

CEMLA *El Mercado de Capitales en el Perú* Mexico: Centro de Estudios Monetarios Latino-Americanos (1968).

CEPAL (Comisión Económica para América Latina) *El Pensamiento de la CEPAL* Santiago de Chile: Editorial Universitaria (1969).

Chelliah R. J. 'Trends in Taxation in Developing Countries' *IMF Staff Papers* Vol. 18 (1971).

Chenery H. B. (ed.) *Redistribution with Growth* London: Oxford University Press for IBRD (1974).

Chilcote R. H. 'Dependency: a Critical Synthesis of the Literature' *Latin American Perspectives* Vol. 1 (1974).

Chudnovsky D. *Empresas Multinacionales y Ganancias Monopólicas en una Economía Latinoamericana* Mexico: Siglo XXI (1974).

CNSEV *Flujo de Fondos Financieros en el Peru: 1965–70* Lima: Comisión Nacional Supervisora de Empresas y Valores (1973).

Collier D. 'Squatter Settlements and Policy Innovation in Peru' in Lowenthal (1975).

Consiglieri J. *La Propiedad Inmobilaria en Lima, Perú* Buenos Aires: Instituto di Tella (1975).

Córdova A. *La Política de Masas del Cardenismo* Mexico: Ediciones Era (1974).

Cotler J. 'The New Mode of Political Domination in Peru' in Lowenthal (1975).

'The Peruvian Experiment Reconsidered: A Political Overview' (mimeo) paper given to the Wilson Center Workshop on 'The Peruvian Experiment Reconsidered', Washington DC (1978).

Coutu A. J. and King R. A. *The Agricultural Development of Peru* New York:

Praeger (1969).

Cutler A., Hindess B., Hirst P. and Hussain A. *Marx's Capital and Capitalism Today* (two vols.) London: Routledge and Kegan Paul (1977–78).

De Vylder S. *Allende's Chile: The Political Economy of the Rise and Fall of the Unidad Popular* Cambridge: Cambridge University Press (1976).

Deler J. P. *Lima 1940–70: Aspectos del Crecimiento de la Capital Peruana* Lima: Centro de Investigaciones Geográficas (1975).

Delgado C. *El Proceso Revolucionario Peruano* Mexico: Siglo XXI (1972).

Dore E. and Weeks J. 'The Intensification of the Assault against the Working Class in "Revolutionary" Peru' *Latin American Perspectives* Vol. 3 (1976).

Dos Santos T. 'The Structure of Dependence' *American Economic Review* (1970).

'The Crisis of Development Theory and the Problems of Dependence in Latin America' in Bernstein H. (ed.) *Underdevelopment and Development* Middlesex: Penguin (1973).

Dragsic J. 'Peruvian Stabilization Policies: 1939–68' (unpublished PhD dissertation) University of Wisconsin (1971).

Drysdale R. S. and Myers R. G. 'Continuity and Change: Peruvian Education' in Lowenthal (1975).

ECLA *El Proceso de Industrialización en América Latina* Santiago de Chile: Economic Commission for Latin America (1965).

El Desarrollo Económico y la Distribución del Ingreso en la América Latina Santiago: Economic Commission for Latin America (1968).

Development Problems in Latin America Austin: Texas University Press (1969).

'La Movilización de Recursos Internos' *Boletin Económico de América Latina* Vol. 16 (1970).

'El Desarrollo Reciente del Sistema Financiero de América Latina' *Boletín Económico de América Latina* Vol. 16 (1971).

Evaluación Regional de la Estratégia Internacional de Desarrollo Santiago: Economic Commission for Latin America (1973).

El Proceso de Industrialización en América Latina en los Primeros Años del Segundo Decenio para el Desarrollo Santiago: Economic Commission for Latin America (1974).

Economic Survey of Latin America 1973 Santiago: Economic Commission for Latin America (1975).

Emmanuel A. *Unequal Exchange* London: New Left Books (1972).

Eshag E. and Thorp R. 'The Economic and Social Consequences of Orthodox Economic Policies in Argentina in the Postwar Years' *Bulletin of the Oxford University Institute of Economics and Statistics* Vol. 27 (1965).

Espinoza H. (ed.) *Dependencia Económica y Tecnológica* Lima: Villarreal University Press (1971).

El Poder Economica en la Industria Lima: Villarreal University Press (1972).

Fajnzylber F. and Martinez T. *Las Empresas Transnacionales: Expansión a Nivel Mundial y Proyecciones en la Industria Mexicana* Mexico: Fondo de Cultura Económica (1976).

Feder E. 'How Agribusiness Operates in Underdeveloped Agricultures' *Development and Change* Vol. 7 (1976).

Fei J. C. and Ranis G. *Development of the Labour Surplus Economy: Theory and Policy* New Haven: Yale University Press (1964).

Ferner A. M. 'The Role of the Industrial Bourgeoisie in the Peruvian Development Model' (unpublished DPhil dissertation) Sussex University (1977).

Ffrench-Davis R. *Políticas Económicas en Chile 1952–1970* Santiago: Ediciones Nueva Universidad (1973).

Figueroa A. 'The Impact of Current Reforms on Income Distribution in Peru' in Foxley (1976).

Figueroa A. (ed.) *Estructura del Consumo y Distribución de Ingresos en Lima Metropolitana 1968–69* Lima: Catholic University Press (1974).

FitzGerald E. V. K. *The Public Sector in Latin America* Working Papers Series No. 18 Cambridge: Centre of Latin American Studies (1974).

Aspects of Industrialization in Peru: 1965–75 Working Papers Series No. 22 Cambridge: Centre of Latin American Studies (1975).

The State and Economic Development: Peru since 1968 Department of Applied Economics Occasional Paper No. 49 Cambridge: Cambridge University Press (1976a).

'The Urban Service Sector, the Supply of Wagegoods and the Shadow Wage Rate' *Oxford Economic Papers* Vol. 28 (1976b).

'On State Accumulation in Latin America' in FitzGerald E. V. K., Floto E. and Lehmann A. D. (eds.) *The State and Economic Development in Latin America* Occasional Paper No. 1, Cambridge: Centre of Latin American Studies (1977).

'The Fiscal Crisis of the Latinamerican State' in Toye J. F. J. (ed.) *Taxation and Economic Development* London: Cass (1978a).

'The State and Capital Accumulation in Mexico' *Journal of Latin American Studies* Vol. 10 (1978b).

'Stabilisation Policy in Mexico: the Fiscal Deficit and Macroeconomic Equilibrium, 1960–77' in Thorp and Whitehead (1979).

Fortin C. 'The State and Capital Accumulation in Chile' (mimeo), paper presented to the CEDLA Workshop on Industrialization and the State in Latin America, Amsterdam (1978).

Foxley A. *Income Distribution in Latin America* London: Cambridge University Press (1976).

Foxley A. and Muñoz O. 'Income Redistribution, Economic Growth and Social Structure: the case of Chile' in Foxley (1976).

Franco G. 'Towards Understanding Full Employment in Colombia: a

Critical View of the ILO Employment Mission Report' (unpublished MSc dissertation) The Hague: Institute of Social Studies (1977).

Frank A. G. 'The Development of Underdevelopment' *Monthly Review* Vol. 18 (1966).

Capitalism and Underdevelopment in Latin America New York: Monthly Review Press (1967).

Frankman M. J. 'Sectoral Policy Preferences of the Peruvian Government 1946–68' *Journal of Latin American Studies* Vol. 6 (1974).

Furtado C. *Development and Underdevelopment* Berkeley: University of California Press (1964).

Teoría y Política del Desarrollo Economico Mexico: Siglo XXI (1968).

The Economic Development of Latin America London: Cambridge University Press (1970).

Garcia A. 'Industrialización y Dependencia en la América Latina' in Nolff (1974).

Gerschenkron A. 'Economic Backwardness in Historical Perspective' in Hoselitz B. (ed.) *The Progress of Underdeveloped Areas* Chicago: Chicago University Press (1952).

Giddens A. *Capitalism and Modern Social Theory: An Analysis of the Writings of Marx, Durkheim and Weber* Cambridge: Cambridge University Press (1971).

GIECO *Industrialización y Políticas de Industrialización en el Perú* Lima: National Engineering University (1972).

Evaluación Socioeconomica del Conjunto de Proyectos de Propiedad Social Lima: National Engineering University (1975a).

La Capacidad Ociosa y la Política de Inversiones en la Industria Manufacturera Lima: National Engineering University (1975b).

Gilbert D. L. 'The Oligarchy and the Old Regime in Peru' *Latin American Dissertation Series No. 69* Ithaca: Cornell University (1977).

González F. and Parodi C. *Los Grupos Financieros Internacionales y el Sistema Financiera Internacional* Lima: Universidad del Pacifico (1975).

González H. 'US Arms Policy in Latin America' *Inter-American Economic Affairs* Vol. 32 (1978).

Goodsell C. T. *American Corporations and Peruvian Politics* Cambridge, Mass.: Harvard University Press (1974).

Graciarena J. 'Estructura de Poder y Distribución del Ingreso en América Latina' in Foxley A. (ed.) *Distribución del Ingreso* Mexico: Fondo de Cultura Económica (1974).

Griffin K. B. *Underdevelopment in Spanish America* London: Allen & Unwin (1969).

(ed.) *Financing Development in Latin America* London: Macmillan (1971).

The Political Economy of Agrarian Change London: Macmillan (1974).

Griffin K. B. and Enos J. *Planning Development* London: Addison (1972).

Hansen R. D. *The Politics of Mexican Development* Baltimore: Johns Hopkins

(1971).

Harberger A. C. *Project Evaluation* London: Macmillan (1972).

Harding C. *Land Reform and Social Conflicts in Peru* in Lowenthal (1975).

Horton D. 'Haciendas and Cooperatives: a Study of Land Reform and New Reform Enterprises in Peru' *Latin American Dissertation Series No. 67* Ithaca: Cornell University (1974).

Hunt S. 'Distribution, Growth and Government Economic Behaviour in Peru' in Ranis G. (ed.) *Government and Economic Development* New Haven: Yale University Press (1971).

'Direct Foreign Investment in Peru under the Ancien Regime' (mimeo) Cambridge: Centre of Latin American Studies (1974).

'Direct Foreign Investment in Peru: New Rules for an Old Game' in Lowenthal (1975).

Hymer S. 'The Multinational Corporation and the Law of Uneven Development' in Bhagwati J. (ed.) *Economics and the World Order from the 1970's to the 1990's* London: Macmillan (1972).

IBRD *The Current Economic Position and Prospects of Peru* Washington DC: International Bank for Reconstruction and Development (1973).

ILO *Towards Full Employment* Geneva: International Labour Office (1970).

Situación y Perspectivas del Empleo en el Perú: 1975 Lima: International Labour Office (1976).

IMF 'Peru – Recent Economic Developments' *Executive Board Papers* (SM/77/43) Washington DC: International Monetary Fund (1977).

INP *La Evolución de la Economía en el Periodo 1950–64* Lima: Instituto Nacional de Planificación (1966).

Plan Nacional de Desarrollo Económico y Social: 1967–70 Lima: Instituto Nacional de Planificación (1967).

Plan del Perú 1971–75 Lima: Instituto Nacional de Planificación (1971).

Proyecciones a Largo Plazo de la Población y la Economía del Perú Lima: Instituto Nacional de Planificación (1973a).

Modelo de Simulación INP-1 Lima: Instituto Nacional de Planificación (1973b).

Plan Nacional de Desarrollo 1975–78 Lima: Instituto Nacional de Planificación (1975a).

La Concentración de la Producción Manufacturera en el Perú, 1969 Lima: Instituto Nacional de Planificación (1975b).

Plan Nacional de Desarrollo para 1977–78 Lima: Instituto Nacional de Planificación (1977).

Jaguaribe H. *Political Development: a General Theory and a Latin American Case Study* New York: Harper and Row (1973)

Jain S. *Size Distribution of Income: Compilation of Data* Washington DC: IBRD (1975).

Jaquette J. 'The Politics of Development in Peru' *Latin American Dissertation Series No 33* Ithaca: Cornell University (1971).

Kalecki M. 'Problems of Financing Economic Development in a Mixed Economy' in *Essays on the Economic Growth of the Socialist and Mixed Economy* Cambridge: Cambridge University Press (1972a).

'Social and Economic Aspects of Intermediate Regimes' in *Essays on the Economic Growth of the Socialist and Mixed Economy* Cambridge: Cambridge University Press (1972b).

Kay G. *Development and Underdevelopment* London: Macmillan (1975).

Kaplan M. *Formación del Estado Nacional en América Latina* Santiago: Editorial Universitaria (1969).

Keith R. G. *Conquest and Agrarian Change: the Emergence of the Hacienda System on the Peruvian Coast* New Haven: Harvard University Press (1977).

Kilty J. *Planning in Peru* New York: Praeger (1967).

Kindleberger C. P. *Economic Development* New York: McGraw-Hill (1958).

Knight P. T. 'New Forms of Economic Organization in Peru: Toward Workers' Self-management' in Lowenthal (1975).

Kruijt D. and Vellinga M. 'The Political Economy of Mining Enclaves in Peru' *Boletín de Estudios Latinoamericanos y del Caribe* No. 23 (1977).

Kuczinski P. P. *Peruvian Democracy under Economic Stress* New Haven: Princeton University Press (1977).

Kuznets S. *Modern Economic Growth* New Haven: Yale University Press (1969).

Laclau E. 'Feudalism and Capitalism in Latin America' *New Left Review* No. 67 (1971).

Leal J. F. *La Burguesía y el Estado Mexicano* Mexico: Ediciones 'El Caballito' (1974).

Lecaros F. *Propiedad Social: Teoría y Realidad* Lima: Ediciones Rikchay (1975).

Levinson J. and Onis J. *The Alliance that Lost its Way* Chicago: Twentieth Century Fund (1970).

Lewis A. 'Economic Development with Unlimited Supplies of Labour' *Manchester School* Vol. 22 (1954).

Lewis R. A. 'Employment, Income and the Growth of the Barriadas in Lima' *Latin American Dissertation Series No. 36* Ithaca: Cornell University (1973).

Leys C. *Underdevelopment in Kenya* London: Heinemann (1975).

Lipton M. *Why the Poor Stay Poor* London: Temple Smith (1977).

Little I.M.D and Mirrlees J. A. *Project Appraisal and Planning for Developing Countries* London: Heinemann (1974).

Llarena A. *La Comunidad Industrial* Lima: Villarreal University Press (1972).

Lowenthal A. F. *The Peruvian Experiment: Continuity and Change under Military Rule* Princeton: Princeton University Press (1975).

Malpica C. *Los Dueños del Perú* Lima: Editorial Ensayos Sociales (1968).

El Desarrollismo en el Perú: una Década de Esperanzas y Fracasos 1961–1971 Lima: Horizonte (1975).

Anchovetas y Tiburones Lima: Runamarka (1976).

Mandel E. *Late Capitalism* London: New Left Books (1975).

Mariategui J. C. *Siete Ensayos de Interpretación de la Realidad Peruana* Lima: Amauta (1928).

Mercado-Jarrín E. *Ensayos* Lima: Ministerio de Guerra (1975).

Millward R. *Public Expenditure Economics* London: McGraw-Hill (1971).

MIT *Plan Sectorial de Desarrollo 1975–78* Lima: Ministerio de Industria y Turismo (1974).

Evaluación del Proceso de Industrialización: Situación Actual y Tendencias Lima: Ministerio de Industria y Turismo (1976).

Moran T. H. *Multinational Corporations and the Politics of Dependence: Copper in Chile* Princeton: Princeton University Press (1974).

Morawetz D. *The Andean Group: a Case Study in Economic Integration among Developing Countries* Cambridge, Mass.: MIT Press (1974).

Napoleoni C. *Smith, Ricardo, Marx* London: Oxford University Press (1975).

Nolff M. (ed.) *Desarrollo Industrial Latinoamericano* Mexico: Fondo de Cultura Economica (1974).

North L. 'Perspectives on Development Policy and Mass Participation in the Peruvian Armed Forces' (mimeo) paper presented to the Wilson Center Workshop on 'The Peruvian Experiment Reconsidered' Washington DC (1978).

Nun J. 'A Latin American Political Phenomenon: The Middle Class Military Coup' in Petras J. and Zeitlin M. (eds.) *Latin America: Reform or Revolution?* New York: Fawcett (1968).

O'Brien P. J. 'A Critique of Latin American Theories of Dependency' in Oxaal I., Barnett T. and Booth D. (eds.) *Beyond the Sociology of Development* London: Routledge (1975).

O'Connor J. *The Fiscal Crisis of the State* New York: St Martin's Press (1973).

OSPA *Metodología para Dar Prioridad Sectorial a los Proyectos de Inversión* Lima: Ministerio de Agricultura, Oficina Sectorial de Planificación (1972).

Owen R. and Sutcliffe R. B. (eds.) *Studies in the Theory of Imperialism* London: Longman (1972).

Owens R. J. *Peru* London: Oxford University Press (1963).

Palloix C. *The World Capitalist Economy* Paris: Maspero (1971).

Payer C. *The Debt Trap* London: Penguin (1975).

Payne A. *The Peruvian Coup d'Etat of 1962: The Overthrow of Manuel Prado* Washington DC: Institute for the Comparative Study of Political Systems (1968).

Petras J. 'State Capitalism and the Third World' *Development and Change* Vol. 8 (1977).

Petras J. and La Porte R. *Peru: Transformación Revolucionaria o Modernización?* Buenos Aires: Amorrortu Editores (1971).

Philip G. D. E. 'Policy-making in the Peruvian Oil Industry with Special Reference to the Period since 1968' (unpublished DPhil dissertation)

Oxford University (1975).

'The Soldier as Radical: the Peruvian Military Government 1968–75' *Journal of Latin American Studies* Vol. 8 (1976).

Pike F. B. *The Modern History of Peru* New York: Praeger (1967).

Pillado A. *Acumulación, Crisis, Estado y Socialismo* Lima: DESCO (1978).

Pinto A. 'El Modelo de Desarrollo Reciente de America Latina' *El Trimestre Economico* No. 150 (1971).

Pinto A. and Di Filippo A. 'Notes on Income Distribution and Redistribution Strategy in Latin America' in Foxley (1976).

Portocarrero F. *El Gobierno Militar y el Capital Imperialista* Lima: Perugraph Editores (1976).

Poulantzas N. *Political Power and Social Classes* London: New Left Books (1973).

Pratt B. S. 'The External Relations of Peru since 1959, with Special Reference to the United States' (unpublished doctoral dissertation) Cambridge University (1977).

Presidencia *Plan del Gobierno Revolucionario de la Fuerza Armada* ('Plan Inca') Lima: Presidencia de la República (published in 1974, but officially stated to have been written in 1968).

Plan de Gobierno Periodo 1977–82 ('Plan Tupac Amaru') Lima: Presidencia de la República (1977).

Quijano A. *Nationalism and Capitalism in Peru* New York: Monthly Review Press (1971).

'La Reforma Agraria en el Perú' in Feder E. *La Lucha de Clases en el Campo* Mexico: Fondo de Cultura Económica (1975).

Reynolds C. W. *The Use of Flow of Funds Analysis in the Study of Latin American Capital Market Development* Washington DC: Organization of American States (1973).

Roberts B. R. 'The Inter-relationships of City and Provinces in Peru and Guatemala' in Cornelius W. and Trueblood F. (eds.) *Latin American Urban Research IV* Beverly Hills: Sage Publications (1974).

Rochabrún G. 'Apuntes para la Comprensión del Capitalismo en el Perú *Análisis* Lima January–March (1977).

Roel V. *La Planificación Económica en el Perú* Lima: Editorial Grafica (1968).

Roemer M. *Fishing for Growth: Export-led Development in Peru, 1950–1967* Cambridge, Mass.: Harvard University Press (1970).

Saberbein G. 'Industrie et Sous-developpement au Peròu' (unpublished doctoral dissertation) Grenoble University (1973).

Sagasti F. 'The INTINTEC System for Industrial Technology Policy in Peru' *World Development* Vol. 3 (1975).

Schumpeter J. A. *The Theory of Economic Development* Cambridge, Mass.: Harvard University Press (1961).

Sciari A. J. *Política Económica y Empleo en el Perú* Lima: International Labour Organization (1976).

Scurrah M. and Montalvo A. *Gobierno Revolucionario del Perú: Bases Sociales que lo Apoyan* Lima: ESAN (1975).

Seers D. 'The Limitations of the Special Case' *Bulletin of the Oxford University Institute of Economics and Statistics* Vol. 25 (1963).

Serrano P. 'Algunas Intervenciones del FMI en América Latina' *Comercio Exterior* Vol. 27 (1977).

Sharp D. A. (ed.) *U.S. Foreign Policy and Peru* Austin: University of Texas Press (1972).

Sideri S. and Evers B. (eds.) *Structural Change in a Dependent Economy: Critical Studies of Allende's Economic Policies* The Hague: Nijhoff (1979).

Spaey P. *L'elite Politique Peruvienne* Paris: Editions Universitaires (1972).

Stallings B. 'Peru and the US Banks: the Privatization of Financial Relations' in Fagen R. F. (ed.) *Latin America and United States Foreign Policy* Stanford: Stanford University Press (1979).

Stepan A. *The State and Society: Peru in Comparative Perspective* Princeton: Princeton University Press (1978).

Stockholm International Peace Research Institute *The Arms Trade with the Third World* London: Penguin (1975).

Sulmont D. 'Dinámica Actual del Movimiento Obrero Peruano' (mimeo) Faculty of Social Science, Catholic University, Lima (1972).

  El Movimiento Obrero en el Peru 1900–56 Lima: Universidad Catolica (1975).

  'El Movimiento Sindical en el Contexto de Reformas: Peru 1968–76' *Nueva Sociedad* No. 26, Caracas (1976).

Sunkel O. 'National Development Policy and External Dependence in Latin America' *Journal of Development Studies* Vol. 6 (1969).

Sunkel O. and Paz P. *El Subdesarrollo Latinoamericano y la Teoría del Desarrollo* Mexico: Siglo XXI (1970).

Sutcliffe R. *Industry and Underdevelopment* London: Addison (1971).

Szentes T. *The Political Economy of Underdevelopment* Budapest: Akademai Kiado (1973).

Taylor M. C. *Estudio Fiscal del Perú* Washington DC: Organization of American States (1969).

Tezanos J. F. *Estructura de Clases en la España Actual* Madrid: Edicusa (1975).

Thorbecke E. and Condos A. 'Macroeconomic Growth and Development Models of the Peruvian Economy' in Adelman I. and Thorbecke E. (eds.) *The Theory and Design of Economic Development* Baltimore: Johns Hopkins (1966).

Thorp R. 'Inflation and Orthodox Economic Policy in Peru' *Bulletin of the Oxford University Institute of Economics and Statistics* Vol. 29 (1967).

  'A Note on Food Supplies, the Distribution of Income and National Income Accounting in Peru' *Bulletin of the Oxford University Institute of Economics and Statistics* Vol. 31 (1969).

  'Inflation and the Financing of Economic Development' in Griffin

(1971).

La Funcion Desempeñada por las Instituciones Financieras en el Proceso del Ahorro Peruano: 1960–69 Lima: Comisión Nacional de Valores (1972).

'The Post-Substitution Era: the Case of Peru' *World Development* Vol. 5 (1977).

'Stabilization Policies in Peru, 1959–1977' in Thorp and Whitehead (1979).

Thorp R. and Bertram I. G. 'Industrialization in an Open Economy: a Case Study, 1890–1940' (mimeo) Oxford: Institute of Economics and Statistics (1974).

Peru 1890–1977: Growth and Policy in an Open Economy London: Macmillan (1978).

Thorp R. and Whitehead L. *Inflation and Stabilisation in Latin America* London: Macmillan (1979).

Todaro M. P. *Economics for a Developing World* London: Longman (1977).

Tokman V. *Distribución de Ingreso, Tecnología y Empleo: Análisis del Sector Industrial en Ecuador, Perú y Venezuela* Santiago de Chile: Cuadernos de ILPES No. 23 (1975).

Torres R. J. *Estructura de Poder Económico y Sistema Político en el Perú de 1900 a 1925* Lima: UNMSM (1974).

Torres J. A. *Estructura Económica de la Industria en el Peru* Lima: Horizonte (1975).

'Políticas Alternativas para el Perú en la Década 1980' *Trabajos de Investigación No. 8* Lima: Universidad del Pacifico (1978).

Twomey M. 'Ensayos Sobre la Agricultura Peruana' (mimeo) Lima: CISEPA (1973).

UN *Manual on Economic Development Projects* New York: United Nations (1958).

United States Senate *Multinational Corporations in Brazil and Mexico: Structural Sources of Economic and Non-economic Power* Washington DC: Committee on Foreign Relations (1975).

Urrutia M. and Villalba C. E. 'El Sector Artesanal en el Desarrollo Colombiano' *Revista de Planeación y Desarrollo* Vol. 1 (1969).

USDA *Agriculture in the Americas: Statistical Data* Washington DC: US Department of Agriculture (1976).

Vaitsos C. V. *Intercountry Income Distribution and Transnational Enterprises* Oxford: Oxford University Press (1974).

Employment Problems and Transnational Enterprises in Developing Countries: Distortion and Inequality Mexico: Centro de Investigación y Docencia Económicas (1976).

Valderrama M. *Siete Años de Reforma Agraria Peruana* Lima: Catholic University Press (1976).

Vaneck J. *The General Theory of Labour-managed Market Economies* Ithaca: Cornell University Press (1970).

Vega M. 'El Financiamiento de la Pequeña Industria' (mimeo) Lima: CISEPA (1974).

Villanueva V. *Cien Años del Ejército Peruano: Frustraciones y Cambios* Lima: Editorial Juan Mejia Boca (1972).

El CAEM y la Revolución de la Fuerza Armada Lima: Instituto de Estudios Peruanos (1973).

El APRA en Busca del Poder Lima: Editorial Horizonte (1975).

Warren B. 'Imperialism and Capitalist Industrialization' *New Left Review* No. 81 (1973).

Webb R. C. *Government Policy and the Distribution of Income in Peru, 1963–73* Cambridge, Mass.: Harvard University Press (1977).

Weeks J. 'Does Employment Matter?' in Jolly R. (ed.) *Third World Employment* London: Penguin (1973).

'Backwardness, Foreign Capital and Accumulation in the Manufacturing Sector of Peru' *Latin American Perspectives* Vol. 4 (1977).

Wils F. *Industrialists, Industrialisation and the Nation State* The Hague: Institute of Social Studies (1975).

Wionczek M. 'Notes on Technology Transfer through Multinational Enterprises in Latin America' *Development and Change* Vol. 7 (1976).

Wynia G. *Politics and Planning: Policy in Central America* Madison: Wisconsin University Press (1972).

Yepes E. *Peru 1820–1920: Un Siglo de Desarrollo Capitalista* Lima: Campodónico (1971).

Zaldivar R. 'Agrarian Reform and Military Reformism in Peru' in Lehmann D. (ed.) *Agrarian Reform and Agrarian Reformism* London: Faber (1974).

Zimmerman A. *El Plan Inca – Objetivo: Revolución Peruana* Lima: El Peruano (1974).

Zuñiga E. 'The Process of Capital Formation in Peru, 1968–78' (unpublished MPhil dissertation) Cambridge University (1979).

Index

accumulation of capital, 61, 65, 87, **142–79**, 199, 295
  in industry, 278–82
Acción Popular, **43,** 44, 55, 56, 123
agrarian reform, *see under* land reform
agriculture, 68, **70–2,** 138, 200, 295
  employment in, 88
  investment in, 150–2, 160
  ownership of, 106–10, 137
  policy towards, 233, 244–55 *passim*
  see also under food supply, land reform, landlords, peasantry
Alianza Popular Revolucionaria Americana (APRA) **41,** 42, 43, 44, 47, 50–8 *passim,* 65, 107, 123, 201–2, 296
Alliance for Progress, 30, 244
Andean Pact, 82, 130, 238, 291
Argentina, 11, 77, 100–4 *passim,* 136–41 *passim,* 173–8 *passim,* 214–16 *passim,* 231, 256, 257, 289–92 *passim*
Asamblea Constituyente, x, 47, 65

balance of payments, **85–7,** 147, 167, 222–43 *passim, see also under* exports, external debt, foreign finance, imports
Banco Central de Reserva (BCR), ix, 46, 190, 216–55 *passim*
Banco de Crédito Agrícola, 190
Banco de la Nación, 191, 194
Banco Hipotecario, 190
banks,
  domestic, 48, 76, 94, 118, 154–61 *passim,* 167, 234
  foreign, 64, 214, 222–43 *passim, see also under* foreign capital
Belaunde, president,
  administration of, 8, 44, 57, 62, 70, 107, 123, 161, 176, 181, 200–1, 209, 226, 293, 301
  as capitalist, 118
  as presidential candidate, 43
Bolivia, 82, 238
bourgeoisie, 49–51, 57, 58, 79, 114, 119, 136,

144, 160 *see also under* industrialists, oligarchy
Brazil, 11, 51, 54, 100–4 *passim,* 136–41 *passim,* 173–8 *passim,* 185, 189, 214–16 *passim,* 289–92 *passim*
Bustamante, president, 42, 282, 298–9

capital,
  accumulation of, *see under* accumulation of capital
  finance of, 154–61
  foreign, *see under* foreign capital
  ownership of, *see under* ownership of capital
  restructuring of, **4–5,** 10, 38, 55, 148, **153–4,** 217, 295
  stock of, 152–3
  see also under bourgeoisie, profits, state capitalism
capital goods, 75, 145, 255, 262, 287, 291
Centro de Altos Estudios Militares (CAEM), 51, 56
CENTROMIN (*Compañía Minera del Centro*), 111, 192, 198, *see also under* Cerro de Pasco
Cerro de Pasco, 110, 192, 240, *see also under* Centromin
Chile, 11, 65, 82, 100–4 *passim,* 136–41 *passim,* 173–8 *passim,* 185, 214–16 *passim,* 238, 257–9 *passim,* 260, 289–92 *passim*
class structure, **47–54,** 119, 144
  and income distribution 129–30, 170–1
COFIDE (*Corporación Financiera del Desarrollo*), 192, 252
Colombia, 11, 82, 98, 100–4 *passim,* 136–41 *passim,* 173–8 *passim,* 289–92 *passim,* 294
comunidad industrial (CI), 10, 60, 124–5, 134, 246, 277, 285
construction, 67, 70, 75, 94
Comisión Nacional de Comunidades Industriales (CONACI), 125
Comisión Nacional de Propiedad Social (CONAPS), 126
cooperatives, rural, 59, **108–10, 123–4**

copper, 66, 73, 77, 79, 80, 84, 139, 167, 225, 239
cotton, 72

dependency, 30–3, 38–9, 67, 99, 105, 141, 145, 167, 236, 293, *see also under* foreign capital
dualism, 11, 38–9, 52, 67, 145, 251
  and accumulation, 170–1
  in Colombia, 100–1
  definition of, 19–24
  and income distribution, 132–3, 141
  and industrialization, 262, 289
  measurement of in Peru, 91–9

Economic Commission for Latin America (ECLA), 2, 13, **26–33**, 85, 91, 96, 173, 289, 291
economic planning, 244–55, 286–8, *see also under Instituto Nacional de Planificación*
economic policy, 70, 79, **217–36**
  on industry, 282–8
  see also under stabilization programmes *and individual sectors*
economy,
  cycles in, **68–70**, 85, 155
  development of, defined on, **4–5**, 68, **77**
  structure of Peruvian, **66–104**, 85
Ecuador, 51, 82, 113, 185
education, 187, 212–13
employment, **87–91**, 198
  dual structure of, 91–9 *passim*
  in industry, 271, 272–3
empresa de propiedad social (EPS), *see under propiedad social*
ENAFER (*Empresa Nacional de Ferrocarriles*), 192
ENTELPERU (*Empresa Nacional de Telecomunicaciones del Perú*), 192
EPCHAP (*Empresa Peruana de Comercialización de Harina y Aciete de Pescado*) 114, 193
EPSA (*Empresa Pública de Servicios Agropecuarios*), 193, 198, 233
exports, 76, 77, **79–80**, 86, 91, 144, 216–59 *passim,* 261
  crisis in, 79
  of manufactures, 80, 269–70, 291–2
  markets for, 81–2
  prices of, 82–5
  volume of, 82–5
external debt, 61, 86, 156–61 *passim,* 208–9, 235, **236–43**

fiscal system,
  deficits in, **206–9**, 234
  incidence of, 209–12
  reform of, 60, 156, **201–3**, 230
  structure of, 199–209

fishing,
  employment in, 89
  exports from, 84
  investment in, 150–2
  planning of, 244–55 *passim*
  production from, 67, **74–5**, 79, 97, 225
  ownership of, 113–15
  taxation of, 200
flow of funds, 163–5, *see also under* investment, savings
Fondo Nacional de Propiedad Social (FONAPS), 126
food supply, 61, 67, **70–2**, 79, 92, 97, 110, 143, 171, 186, 218, **232–4**, 263, 295
foreign capital, 15, 17–18, 46, 58, 62, 105–22 *passim,* 144
  in agriculture, 107
  in banking, 116
  in fishing, 113–14
  government negotiations with, 236–43
  in industry 68, 82, 91, 115, 274, 287
  in mining, 110
  in oil, 112–13
  in other Latinamerican countries, 138–9
  profitability of, 130–1
  in services, 117
  as source of finance, 155–61 *passim*
foreign investment, 142–79 *passim,* 236–43 *passim,* 285

Gobierno Revolucionario de la Fuerza Armada (GRAF) ix, 45, 58, 123, 125, 171, 238, 242, 282
government, 180–9,
  centralization of, 180–1
  contribution to national income by, 76, 94
  in employment, 88, 94
  expenditure by, 204–9
  investment by, 148
  see also under public investment, state

health, 188–9, 212–13
HIERROPERU (*Empresa Minera de Hierro del Perú*), 111, 192, 240
housing, 92, 148, 189
  investment in, 150–2, 160

imports, **80**, 86, 91, 144, 216–59 *passim,* 265
  controls on, 79, 253
  prices of, 84
  substitution of, *see under* industrialization
  sources of, 80–2
  tariffs on, 79, 82, 201, 209, 222, 284
  volume of, 84
income distribution, 91, 109, **128–36**, 252
  and capital accumulation, 170
  in different countries compared, 140–1, 145
  and industrialization, 268–9

and taxation, 210–12
see also under dualism, profits, wages
industrial community, *see under comunidad industrial*
Industrial Law of 1970, *see under Ley General de Industrias*
Industrialists, 49, 60, 62, 63, 115, 125, 260–92 *passim*, 273–8, *see also under* bourgeoisie
industrialization, 260–92
    Andean Pact and, 82
    ECLA on, 28
    and the model of accumulation, 144
    of the Peruvian economy, 75–6, 85
    planning of, 244–55 *passim*
    policy towards, 222
    political implications of, 57
input–output matrix,
    for economy as a whole, 76–8
    for industry, 268
Instituto Nacional de Planificación (INP), 43, 182, 185, 216–44 *passim*, **244–55**
International Bank for Reconstruction and Development (IBRD), 236–43 *passim*, 248
International Monetary Fund (IMF), 46, 64, 165, 204, 207, 227–43 *passim*, 249, 257
International Petroleum Company (IPC), 44, 45, 58, 74, 110, 112, 192, 226, 238
investment,
    foreign, *see under* foreign investment
    private, *see under* private investment
    public, *see under* public investment
iron ore, 75, 79, 240–1

land reform, 56, 59, 62, 63, 107–10, 228, 295
    in Chile, 139–40
    income effect of, 130, 134–5, 171, 173
    and industry 282
landlords, 48, **51–2**, 63, **106–7**, 108, 124
Latin American Free Trade Area (LAFTA), 82
Ley General de Industrias (1970), 125, 187, 283

manufacturing,
    in the economic structure, 67, 70, **75–6**, 94, 97
    employment in, 88, 271
    investment in, 150–52, 278–82
    ownership of, 115, 273–8
    taxation of, 200
    see also under industrialization
Marcona, 111, 192, 241, *see also under* Hierroperu
Mars, 144
Marx, vi, 15, 19, 135, 301
Mexico, 11, 54, 77, 100–4 *passim*, 136–41 *passim*, 173–8 *passim*, 189, 256, 289–92 *passim*

as an intermediate regime, 297–8
migration, 76, 88–9, 92
military,
    expenditure on, 185–6, 216
    as an institution, 50–1, 56, 58, 65, 242
MINEROPERU (*Empresa Minera del Peru*), 111, 193, 199
mining,
    employment in, 88, 94
    exports from, 79–80
    investment in, 150–2, 159, 161
    ownership of, 110–12
    policy on, 180, 244–55 *passim*
    production from, 67, **72–4**, 75, 79, 102–3
    taxation of, 200
Morales, president, 44, 45, 63, 230, *see also under Gobierno Revolucionario de la Fuerza Armada*
multinationals, *see under* foreign capital

National Planning Institute, *see under Instituto Nacional de Planificación*

Odría, president, 42, 111, 224, 282
oil, 73, 79, 199, 239, 248
    investment in, 150–2, 167
    ownership of, 150–2, 167
    trans-Andean pipeline for, 185–6, 240
    see also under IPC, Petroperu
'oligarchy' (*oligarquía*), 48, 55, 56, 58, 62, 65, 107, 115, 143, 278
ownership of capital, 105–28
    in different countries compared, 137–41
    in industry, 273–8
    in the model of accumulation, 145–6
    see also under individual production sectors, comunidad industrial, propiedad social

peasantry, **51–2**, 61, 63, 70–2, 88, 92, 106–10 *passim*, 124
    income of, 128–36 *passim*, **170–73**
PESCAPERU (*Empresa Pesquera del Peru*), 114, 193
PETROPERU (*Petroleos del Peru*), 112–13, 190, 192, 240
Plan Inca, 45, 203
Plan Tupac Amaru, 47, 65
planning, 37, **244–55**, 259, *see also under Instituto Nacional de Planificación*
Prado, president,
    administration of, 8, 42, 55, 56, 62, 65, 114, 181, 187, 283, 293, 301
    as capitalist, 114, 118
private investment, 142–79 *passim*, 222–36 *passim*
    in manufacturing, 271–2
    see also accumulation of capital

profits, 59, 61, 86, 125, **128–36**, 141, 143, 147, **158**, 170
  as finance for capital accumulation, 154–61
  in industry, 281
  remittance of, 82, 130–1
  taxation of, 200, 210, 215–16
propiedad social, 11, 59, 125–7, 194, 246, 287
public enterprise, *see under* state enterprise
public investment, 76, 84, 142–79 *passim,* 206, 244–55 *passim, see also under* government, state enterprise

real estate, 76, 108, 116–17

savings, 154–61
  of government, 205–6
  of state enterprises, 195
SIDERPERU (*Empresa Siderurgica del Peru*), 193
Sistema Nacional de Apoyo a la Movilización Social (SINAMOS), **45,** 54, 59, 60, 61, 64, 125
social property, *see under propiedad social*
socialism, 123, 127, 140
socialist bloc, 82, 231
Southern Peru Copper Corporation (SPCC), 110–12, 113, 234, 239
spatial pattern of the economy, **94–5,** 99
stabilization programmes, 84, **168–9,** 217–36 *passim*
state,
  definition of the role of, 182–3
  fiscal crisis in, 200
  relative autonomy of, 5, 35–7, 55, 63, 259
  size of, 183–4
  and underdevelopment, 33–8
state capitalism, 11, **37–8,** 58, **59,** 135, 294, 296

contradictions of, 61, 64, 145, 147, 161, 167, 198
establishment of, 120, 127–8, 182–3, 190
as a model of accumulation, 143, 254
state enterprise, 76, 77, 105–28 *passim,* 148, 159, 187, **190–9,** 246, 276, 288
  see also under individual enterprises
sugar, 72, 75, 94, 107

tariffs, *see under* imports (tariffs on)
taxation, *see under* fiscal system
technology, **24–6,** 91, 139, 144, 145, 148, 198–9, 275, 286
  and negotiations with foreign capital, 236–43

underdevelopment, **14–26,** 33–8, 54, 76–7, 99, 104, 134
USA, 119
  as arms supplier, 185, 215–16
  as financier and negotiator, 222–43 *passim*
  as trading partner, 81–2, 281
USSR, 185, 215–16

Velasco, president, 45, 46, 54, 62, 176, 180, 202, 209, 227, 293, 301
Venezuela, 82, 100–4 *passim,* 136–41 *passim,* 173–8 *passim,* 289–92 *passim*
Venus, 144

wages, 61, 64, 68, 92, 128–36 *passim,* 141, 143, 147, **167–73,** 227–36 *passim*
  and capital accumulation, 154–61
  in industry, 271, 272–3
  taxation of, 210–11
working class, 52–3, 59, 61, 65, 99, 296
  employment, pattern of, 87–91
  participation in enterprises, 123–8, *see also under comunidad industrial,* cooperatives, *propiedad social*

DATE DUE			
NO 12'85			
MR 21'89			
MY 18'94			
OC 26 '94			

Fitzgerald   170685